Participation in Sport

Although there is growing interest from governments in participation levels in sport, the extent to which governments actively promote 'sport for all' and their motives for doing so vary greatly. This is the first book to examine the sport participation policies of national governments around the world and to offer a comparative analysis of the motives for, and successes and failures of, those policies.

Organized around a series of sixteen national case studies, including the UK, the US, Australia, China and India, the book enables students and practitioners to compare and contrast the development, implementation and impact of sport participation policies throughout the world. An introductory chapter provides a framework for understanding and interpreting those case studies and each chapter then addresses the following key themes:

- national structures for sport
- national sporting cultures
- participation levels in organized sport
- the nature and extent of government intervention
- implementation of government policy
- the impact of government policy.

With contributions from many of the world's leading experts on sport policy and sport development, this book is essential reading for anybody with an interest in the role of governments in relation to supporting and regulating their citizens' involvement in sport.

Matthew Nicholson is Associate Professor of Sport Management in the Centre for Sport and Social Impact at La Trobe University, Australia.

Russell Hoye is Professor of Sport Management and Director of the Centre for Sport and Social Impact at La Trobe University, Australia.

Barrie Houlihan is Professor of Sport Policy in the Institute of Sport and Leisure Policy in the School of Sport, Health and Exercise Sciences at Loughborough University, UK.

Participation in Sport

International policy perspectives

Edited by
Matthew Nicholson,
Russell Hoye and
Barrie Houlihan

 Routledge
Taylor & Francis Group

LONDON AND NEW YORK

First published 2011
by Routledge
2 Park Square, Milton Park, Abingdon, Oxon, OX14 4RN

Simultaneously published in the USA and Canada
by Routledge
270 Madison Avenue, New York, NY 10016

Routledge is an imprint of the Taylor & Francis Group, an informa business

Typeset in Baskerville by Swales & Willis Ltd, Exeter, Devon
Printed and bound in Great Britain by CPI Antony Rowe,
Chippenham, Wiltshire

British Library Cataloguing in Publication Data
A catalogue record for this book is available from the British Library

Library of Congress Cataloging in Publication Data
Participation in sport : international policy perspectives /
   edited by Matthew Nicholson, Russell Hoye, and Barrie Houlihan.
   p. cm.
   1. Sports and state. 2. Sports. I. Nicholson, Matthew.
   II. Hoye, Russell, 1966– III. Houlihan, Barrie.
   GV706.35.P37 2010
   306.483—dc22

ISBN13: 978–0–415–55477–0 (hbk)
ISBN13: 978–0–415–55478–7 (pbk)
ISBN13: 978–0–203–87049–5 (ebk)

Contents

vi *Contents*

Figures

Tables

Notes on contributors

Nils Asle Bergsgard is a Senior Researcher at the International Research Institute of Stavanger, Norway. Nils's research interests are sport sociology and sport policy, especially the relationship between government and sport organizations, and elite sport development. He holds a doctoral degree in sport policy from 2006 for a thesis titled 'Dissolving or Stability? Relationships and Power Struggle within the National Policy of Sport' (in Norwegian). Other recent publications (in English) include the chapter on Norway in *Comparative Elite Sport Development* with P. Augestad (2008), *Sport Policy: A Comparative Analyses of Stability of Change* with B. Houlihan, P. Mangset, S.I. Nødland and H. Rommetvedt (2007), *The Institutionalization of an Elite Sport Organization in Norway: The Case of 'Olympiatoppen'* with P. Augestad and A.Ø. Hansen (2006) and *Sport and Politics: The Case of Norway* with H. Rommetvedt (2006).

Matthew T. Bowers is a PhD candidate in Sport Management in the Department of Kinesiology and Health Education at the University of Texas at Austin, USA. His research focuses on youth sport development, the socio-cultural antecedents and consequences of sport policy, and context-specific variations in the sport experience.

Cora Burnett is Professor in the Sociology of Sport in the Department of Sport and Movement Studies at the University of Johannesburg, South Africa. She holds two doctorates, one in Human Movement Studies (ethnic dance) and one in Social Anthropology (violence and poverty). She is also lecturing in Research Methodology and is currently involved in Sport for Development postgraduate supervision. Cora has developed a tool for impact assessments and is currently involved in several national and international research projects in this regard. She has published extensively on topics such as gender and the media, politics and sport, social impact of sports programs, sport-related violence and indigenous knowledge systems. Currently she is busy with a national research project to determine the impact of higher education institutions on the different sectors of sport and recreation in South Africa.

Laurence Chalip is Professor and Coordinator of the Sport Management Program at the University of Texas at Austin, USA. His research focuses on policy and marketing. He has published three books, four research monographs, and over 80 articles and book chapters. He is a Research Fellow of the North

American Society for Sport Management, and has served as Editor of *Sport Management Review* and *Journal of Sport Management*. He is a consultant for sport organizations throughout the world, and was awarded the Earle F. Zeigler Award from the North American Society for Sport Management, and named to the International Chair of Olympism by the International Olympic Committee and the Centre for Olympic Studies.

Packianathan Chelladurai is Professor in the College of Education and Human Ecology of the Ohio State University, Columbus, Ohio, USA. He specializes in organizational theory and organizational behaviour in the context of sport. Dr Chelladurai has authored three books (*Sport Management: Macro Perspectives*; *Human Resource Management in Sport and Recreation*; and *Managing Organizations for Sport and Physical Activity*), two monographs (*Leadership in Sports* and *Cohesion in Sports*), and contributed over 90 articles and over 25 chapters to sport management literature.

Shane Collins is Lecturer in Sport in the School of Applied Social Sciences at Durham University, UK. Shane's research interests are broadly focused upon the development and examination of sport policy through the analysis and review of meso-level approaches to the policy making process. In particular, Shane is interested in comparative policy relating to increasing levels of participation in sport, sport development and the theorizing of the policy process. Shane also has a keen interest in the role of the Olympic movement with regard to the development of sport policy. She is particularly interested in the role of the Olympic movement in influencing the direction and focus of national sport policies, principally as they relate to elite and mass sport development. Shane's recent publications include 'Do Policies Determine Politics? Sport Development in Australia and Finland' (2008), 'The Australian Institute of Sport' (2007) and 'New Zealand' in *Elite Sport* (2007).

Gyöngyi Szabó Földesi is Professor in Sociology in the School of Physical Education and Sport Sciences (TF) at Semmelweis University, Budapest, Hungary, where she is the head of PhD studies in social sciences. Her teaching and research work cover special social and political issues in sport. She serves a number of national and international scientific bodies, editorial boards and sport organizations. She is the first woman in her discipline in Hungary to receive the title of Doctor of the Hungarian Academy of Sciences (2006). Her recent awards include: Order of Merit of the Hungarian Republic (2007), Pro universitate (2009) and Life Work Award for serving university sport (2009). She has published five books, around one hundred papers, and edited six books.

Vassil Girginov is Reader in Sport Management/Development in the School of Sport and Education at Brunel University, UK where he is a leader of the Management of Sport Development program. His research interests are in the field of the Olympic movement, sports development and policy analysis. Vassil's most recent publications include: *Olympism: A Critical Reader* (2010), *Management of Sports Development* (2008), 'The Political Process of Constructing a Sustainable London Olympics Sports Development Legacy' (2009), 'Canadian National Sport Organisations' Use of the Web for Relationship Marketing' (2009),

'A Sustainable Sports Legacy: Creating a Link between the London Olympics and Sports Participation' (2008) and 'Understanding the Changing Nature of Sports Organisations in Transforming Societies' (2008). Vassil is an Executive Academic Editor of the Routledge 2012 Olympics Special Issue.

B. Christine Green is Associate Professor in Sport Management in the Department of Kinesiology and Health Education at the University of Texas at Austin, USA, where she directs the Sport Development Lab. She has authored or co-authored a book and more than 50 articles and book chapters. She is a Research Fellow of the North American Society for Sport Management, the former Editor of *Sport Management Review*, and an Associate Editor of *Journal of Sport & Tourism*. Her research examines the factors that facilitate or inhibit the development of sport at each level, and seeks to determine the separate, cumulative, and interactive effects of those factors within and across levels.

Fan Hong is Professor in Chinese Studies and Head of the School of Asian Studies at National University of Ireland-Cork, Republic of Ireland. Fan Hong's main research interests are in the areas of culture, politics, gender and sport. Her most recent publications include *China Gold: China's Quest for Global Power and Olympic Glory* (2008) with Duncan Mackey and Karen Christensen, *On the Right to Sport* (2008) with Lu Zhouxiang, *Doping in Sport: Global Ethical Issue* (2007) with Angela Schneider, *Sport, Nationalism and Orientalism: The Asian Games* (2006), *Modern Sport: the Global Obsession: Politics, Class, Religion, Gender* (2005), *Sport in Asian Society: Past and Present* (2003), *Women, Soccer, Sexual Liberation: Kicking Off A New Era* (2003) and *Freeing the Female Body: Inspirational Icons* (2001) with J.A. Mangan.

Barrie Houlihan is Professor of Sport Policy in the School of Sport, Exercise and Health Sciences, Loughborough University, UK. His research interests include the domestic and international policy processes for sport. He has a particular interest in sports development, the diplomatic use of sport, and drug abuse by athletes. His recent books include *Elite Sport Development: Policy Learning and Political Priorities* with Mick Green (Routledge 2005), *Sport Policy: A Comparative Analysis of Stability and Change* with N.A. Bergsgard, P. Mangset, S.I. Nødland and H. Rommetvedt (Butterworth-Heinemann 2007), and *Sport and Policy: Issues and Analysis* with Russell Hoye and Matthew Nicholson (Butterworth-Heinemann 2010). In addition to his work as a teacher and researcher, Barrie Houlihan has undertaken consultancy projects for various UK government departments, UK Sport, Sport England, the Council of Europe, UNESCO and the European Union. He is currently chair of the UK Sport Social Research Committee on Doping in Sport and has chaired, and been a member of, various working groups in the sports councils. He is Editor in Chief of the *International Journal of Sport Policy*.

Russell Hoye is Professor in Sport Management in the School of Management and Director of the Centre for Sport and Social Impact at La Trobe University, Melbourne, Australia. His research interests focus on the governance of sport organizations, the impacts of public policy on sport and the engagement of volunteers in sport. He is the author of *Sport and Policy: Issues and Analysis* (2010),

Sport Management: Principles and Applications (2nd edn) (2009), *Sport and Social Capital* (2008) and *Sport Governance* (2007), all published with Elsevier, UK, and *Working with Volunteers in Sport: Theory and Practice* (2006) with Routledge, UK. Russell is a member of the editorial board and Case Study Editor for *Sport Management Review*, editorial board member for the *International Journal of Sport Policy* and the *Australian Journal on Volunteering*, President of the Sport Management Association of Australia and New Zealand (SMAANZ), and a graduate of the Australian Institute of Company Directors.

Lisa M. Kikulis is Associate Professor in the Department of Sport Management in the Faculty of Applied Health Sciences at Brock University in St Catharines, Ontario, Canada. Lisa teaches and researches in the area of qualitative inquiry and sport policy. She has published articles on strategic and institutional change in national sport organizations. Her current research includes projects on collaborative policy implementation and the role of intergovernment relations, partnerships and citizenship engagement, and a community development approach to sport participation.

Matthew Nicholson is Associate Professor in Sport Management in the Centre for Sport and Social Impact and the School of Management at La Trobe University, Melbourne, Australia. Matthew's research and teaching interests focus on policy development and practice, the relationship between sport and the media, and the contribution of sport and volunteering to social capital. His most recent publications include *Sport and Policy: Issues and Analysis* (2010), *Sport Management: Principles and Applications* (2nd edn) (2009), *Sport and Social Capital* (2008) and *Sport and the Media: Managing the Nexus* (2007), all published with Elsevier, UK, *A National Game* (2008) published by Viking-Penguin and *Australian Sport: Better by Design? The Evolution of Australian Sport Policy* (2004) with Routledge.

Karen Petry is a researcher at the Institute of European Sport Development and Leisure Studies at the German Sport University Cologne and General Secretary of the European Network of Sport Science, Education and Employment (ENSSEE). The main areas of Karen's research and teaching are: European sport policy, leisure studies, sport and social development, gender studies. Her most recent publications include *A Perfect Match? Sport and the European Union* (2009), *Higher Education in Sport in Europe: From Labour Market Demand to Training Supply* (2008), *European Education Policy and the Implementation of the Bologna Process in Sport* (2008), *Elite Sport Development in Germany: Systems, Structures and Public Policy* (2007).

Mike Sam is Senior Lecturer with the School of Physical Education at the University of Otago, New Zealand. His research and teaching broadly encompass areas of policy, politics and governance as they relate to the public administration and management of sport. He has published widely in journals such as *Public Management Review, Policy Sciences*, the *Sociology of Sport Journal* and the *Journal of Sport Management*. Mike's forthcoming co-edited book (with Professor John Hughson) entitled *Sport in the City: Cultural Connections* (Routledge) is due for publication in 2010.

Ivan Sandanski is Principal Lecturer in Sport Management at the National Sports Academy, Sofia, Bulgaria. His main research interests are in the field of sport sponsorship (doctoral thesis), sports events management, marketing, and management of youth football development. Ivan's most recent publications include: *Marketing and Sponsorship of School Sport Clubs* (2009, 2nd edition), *Management of Sports Events* (2009), *Understanding the Changing Nature of Sports Organisations in Transforming Societies* (2008). He has been collaborating with several national sports governing bodies such as the Bulgarian Hockey Federation, the Bulgarian Football Union and the Bulgarian Volleyball Federation as expert on youth development and member of two committees. Currently he has been delivering lecturers on training of sport administrators at various conferences and seminars organized by public, municipal and voluntary sport governing bodies in Bulgaria.

Bernd Schulze received his PhD and habilitation at the University of Münster, Germany in Sport Sociology. Bernd's research and teaching interests focus on European sport structures, intercultural comparative studies, sport organizations, system theory of sport, sociology of school sport and sociology of sport activities. His most recent publications include *Sport als Teilsystem der Gesellschaft: Konsens und Kontroversen* [*Sport as a Subsystem of Society: Consensus and Controversies*] (2007) and *Sportarten als soziale Systeme* [*Sporting Disciplines as Social Systems*] (2005).

D. Shunmuganathan is Professor and Head of the Department of Physical Education and Sports of Manonmaniam Sundaranar University, Tirunelveli, India. Shunmuganathan's research and teaching interests focus on sports management, fitness management, performance analysis, social health, and event management. He has organized and conducted 21 national level tournaments and five international conferences on sports management. His most recent publications include *Dynamic Facets of Physical Education and Sports* (2009), *Ideal Profile for Women Volleyball Players* (2007), *Hand Book on Indigenous Activities* (2006), *Proceedings of Asia-Specific International Conference for Sports Administrators* (Editor 2003), and a chapter titled 'Sports in Modern India: Policies, Practices and Problems' in *Sport In Asian Society* with Routledge.

Sheila Stephen PhD, is Principal of the YMCA College of Physical Education, a prestigious institution of the National Council of YMCAs of India. Sheila's teaching interest focuses on physical education in general and sports management in particular, and her current research is focused on leadership styles. She also develops and organizes adapted physical education programs for special populations. She is a recipient of the 'Jewel of India' award for her contribution and services towards rural sports. She serves on a number of editorial boards, governing bodies of sports and academic councils.

Jan Ove Tangen is Professor in Sport Sociology at Telemark University College, Norway. He received his PhD in sociology at the Institute for Sociology, University of Oslo. Jan Ove's main research interests are sport as a social system, sport participation and sport facilities, inclusion and exclusion processes in sport, and drugs in sport. His most recent publications include *Kampen om* *idrettsanleggene* (2009) [*The Struggle for the Sport Facilities*] (editor together with K. Rafoss), 'Kroppspresentasjon og andre prestasjoner: en omfangsundersøkelse om bruk av doping' (2009) ['Presentation of the Body and Other Performances: A National Study on the Use of Drugs Among Youths'] (co-authored with B. Barland), 'Making Space: A Sociological Interpretation of Sport and its Facilities' in *Sport and Society* (2004), 'Embedded Expectations, Embodied Knowledge and the Movements that Connect: A System Theoretical Attempt to Explain the Use and Non-Use of Sport Facilities' in *International Review for the Sociology of Sport*, vol. 39, no 1. Sage, London, and *Hvordan er idrett mulig? Skisse til en idrettssosiologi* [*How Is Sport Possible?*], Høyskoleforlaget, Kristiansand, 2004.

Lionel Teo is Lecturer in the Sport & Wellness Studies Section of the School of Business Management at Nanyang Polytechnic, Singapore, where he is the Course Administrator of the Diploma in Sport & Wellness Management program. He completed an MSc in Sport & Leisure Management at Loughborough University and received his B PhyEd degree from the University of Calgary. Prior to lecturing, he spent 10 years in the Polytechnic's Sports & Recreation Department where he was involved in sport administration, leadership training, student development and the management of the sports facilities in the institution. He recently contributed a chapter on Singapore's elite sport development in the book *Comparative Elite Sport Development: Systems, Structures & Public Policy* (2008).

Lucie Thibault is Professor at Brock University, Ontario, Canada and was a former editor of the *Journal of Sport Management*. In 2008, she received the Dr Earle F. Zeigler Award from the North American Society for Sport Management for her contributions to scholarship, research, and leadership in sport management. Lucie teaches sport policy, globalization of sport, and organizational theory. Her research has appeared in such publications as the *Journal of Sport Management*, the *European Sport Management Quarterly*, the *Journal of Sport and Social Issues*, the *International Review for the Sociology of Sport*, *Human Relations*, *Leisure Studies*, and *Nonprofit and Voluntary Sector Quarterly*. Dr Thibault is co-editor of *Contemporary Sport Management* and she has published book chapters in various edited books.

Kazuo Uchiumi is Emeritus Professor in the Graduate School of Social Sciences at Hitotsubashi University, Tokyo, Japan. Kazuo's research focuses mainly on three areas: the comparative sport policies between Japan and Britain, Olympics and peace, and sport sociology. His most recent publications are: *Sport for All in Britain: A Sport Policy in a Welfare State* (2004), *Sport for All in Japan: A Sport Policy in an Immature Welfare State* (2006), *Olympics and Peace* (2011, forthcoming) with Fumaido, *Professional Sport: A Pioneer of Sport Culture* (2003), *On Amateurism: For a New Sport Thought without Discrimination* (2008) and *On Sport Research* (2009), with Soubun Kikaku *et al*. All were published in Japanese.

Maarten Van Bottenburg is Professor of Sport Development at the Utrecht School of Governance of Utrecht University, the Netherlands. Prior to being appointed as Professor at Utrecht University, Maarten had been engaged in both academic research and consultancy in the field of sports since 1988. In his academic work he has focused on various themes such as the globalization and commercialization of sport, elite sport policy, sports participation trends, the societal meaning of sport, and sport management. Among many other books, Maarten was author or co-author of *Jacht op Goud* (*The Hunt for Gold*, 2009), *The Global Sporting Arms Race* (2008), *Sport Participation in the European Union* (2005) and *Global Games* (2001). He has also published in journals such as *American Behavioral Scientist*, *Actes de la Recherche en Sciences Sociales*, *Sport Management Review*, *International Review for the Sociology of Sport* and *European Sport Management Quarterly*.

Lu Zhouxiang is a PhD candidate in the School of Asian Studies at National University of Ireland-Cork, Republic of Ireland. Lu Zhouxiang's research interests focus on sports management; comparative studies between the West and China in the field of sport; nationalism and globalism. His most recent publications include *From Celestial Empire to Nation State: Sport and the Origins of Chinese Nationalism between 1840 and 1927* (2010) with Fan Hong, *An Emerging Consumer Market: China's Sport and Leisure Industry* (2009), *Olympic Education in China* (2008) with Fan Hong and Ian Henry, and *On the Right to Sport* (2008) with Fan Hong.

Acknowledgements

A book of this scope, size and breadth would not have been possible without the contributions and support of our authors. We would like to thank them and acknowledge their outstanding work, which was achieved within tight timelines and via communication with editors who were often on the other side of the world. We would particularly like to thank Simon Whitmore and his team at Routledge for their enthusiasm for this book; as editors and authors it is fantastic to have such a supportive commissioning editor (except during the Ashes). Finally, we are again indebted to our respective families, who have been patient and understanding as we have worked to complete this project – thank you for your enduring support.

Matthew Nicholson
Russell Hoye
Barrie Houlihan

1 Introduction

Matthew Nicholson, Russell Hoye
and Barrie Houlihan

Over the last thirty years the governments of most developed nations have implemented sport policies focused on two key pillars – supporting elite sport performance and increasing rates of participation in organized competitive sport. The elite performance policy area has been well researched, as exemplified by Green and Houlihan (2005) and Houlihan and Green (2008). The participation area, however, has not received nearly as much attention. There have been a range of texts that have intersected with the broad area of sport development (Coalter 2007; Houlihan and White 2002; Hylton *et al.* 2001; Hylton and Bramham 2008) or sport for all (DaCosta and Miragaya 2002), but none have specifically focused on participation policies. This is surprising given that most national governments have policies that emphasize increasing sport participation. This book attempts to fill a significant gap in the research literature by examining national sport participation policies via an international comparative framework. In the process it is hoped that the sport policy research agenda will be broadened, a starting point being the collection in this book of chapters that explore the efficacy of government involvement in sport participation within diverse settings and contexts.

The importance of sport, participation and policy

Sport has long been an important feature of developed and developing nations. Sport has become a cultural, social and economic clarion call, providing opportunities for global recognition; sporting success within these nations is often inextricably bound to perceptions of national worth. In many respects Australia is a perfect example of this phenomenon, whereby sport has been provided with substantial political and financial support, and the achievements of its elite athletes are met with almost universal acclaim. The public profile of sport, gained in particular through events such as the Olympic Games or the FIFA World Cup, has both facilitated and exaggerated this phenomenon. For other nations, elite sport has been represented as an opportunity for engagement with the rest of the world. This is invariably delivered through major events, which give the host nation or city a global profile that might not otherwise have been achieved, the 2006 Asian Games in Doha, Qatar being an exemplar. It is clear that elite sport, and the success and opportunity it confers, is considered in most countries to be an increasingly significant political resource.

By contrast, sport participation or the sport activities of a nation's non-elite athletes has remained less obviously politicized and as a result has received less public attention. While it is acknowledged that the growth in publicly funded opportunities for sport participation is a feature of the last fifty years or so and is common to most economically developed countries, there has been relatively little academic interest in explaining this phenomenon. One possible explanation is that the expansion of provision is a consequence of the maturing welfare state found in most economically developed countries. For example, Maslow's (1943, 1954) hierarchy of needs implies that a maturing pattern of welfare provision would seek to meet personal (self-actualization) needs higher in the hierarchy, resulting in public sector support and/or provision in the arts, sport and other cultural services. Although the association between public provision of sport opportunities and improved quality of community life is often acknowledged, more plausible motives, particularly in recent years, tend to be more narrowly instrumental, with governments at many levels becoming increasingly interested in the benefits that sport participation can generate in relation to nation-building, social and health objectives.

The association between nation-building, the pursuit of national prestige and sport for all relates to the heavy investment by many governments in elite performance infrastructure and success, with governments often concerned to maximize their investment by ensuring that there is a large talent pool from which to identify, select and develop elite athletes. In many respects the motivation to remain globally competitive is the most instrumental rationale for national governments encouraging participation in sport. This is particularly true for nations that are internationally competitive but have a relatively small population. In other words, the imperative to increase participation as a means of increasing the talent pool from which elite athletes are drawn is not as strong for the United States of America and China as it is for nations with medium-sized populations such as the United Kingdom, or small nations such as Australia and New Zealand. It is likely that increasing sport participation as part of a strategy of improving elite sport performance will remain important in the future, as the competitive advantages gleaned through infrastructure, systems, resources and technology begin to diminish – at least until such time as talent identification systems become more reliable.

There is a recent but increasingly firmly established belief that sport is a vehicle for the creation of social capital and the associated benefits of social inclusion, social connectedness, community strengthening, community wellbeing, improved local governance and greater civic participation and volunteerism. For example, the European Union declared that sport 'makes an important contribution to economic and social cohesion and more integrated societies', 'facilitate[s] the integration into society of migrants and persons of foreign origin as well as support[ing] inter-cultural dialogue' and 'promotes a shared sense of belonging and participation and may therefore also be an important tool for the integration of immigrants' (Commission on the European Communities 2007: 7). In general these outcomes are only possible through participation in community-based sport organizations. The merits and motives of this particular belief are beyond the scope of this book, yet it seems reasonable to conclude that many national and pan-national governments believe that greater levels of sport participation will lead to improved social outcomes. In many respects this belief is based on a somewhat unsophisticated set of assumptions, such as that people in sporting organizations engage in social interaction by necessity and the nature of their activities require teamwork and cooperation. As noted by Nicholson and Hoye (2008), however, social capital is not always positive and sport organizations might be incubators for bonding or intra-group social capital exclusively. Governments rarely recognize or refer to this phenomenon in their policies or practices.

The final and increasingly important explanation for an increase in government interest in sport participation is the contribution sport can make to ameliorating the myriad health problems faced by contemporary societies. Most pressing, particularly for many Western developed nations, is the concern with overweight and obesity. As noted by Hoye, Nicholson and Houlihan (2010), in the UK in 2001 one in five adults were obese, a figure that had increased almost three-fold since 1980, two-thirds of adult men and more than half of adult women were either overweight or obese, and obesity was the cause of 30,000 deaths per year (National Audit Office 2001). In the USA, 65.1 per cent of all adults aged 20 years and over were overweight or obese during the period 1999–2002 (Hedley *et al.* 2004), while the direct medical costs (preventative, diagnostic and treatment services) associated with people being overweight or obese were estimated to be as high as US$78.5 billion in 1998 (Finkelstein *et al.* 2003). Participating in sport is viewed by many national and state governments as one of the ways that people can become more physically active, thereby reducing the overweight and obesity problem, which in turn will reduce government health costs.

While it is true that there are many other ways people can increase their levels of physical activity, sport participation is often considered by government as a good investment because it delivers multiple benefits. Sport organizations can contribute to the physical and mental health of a community, as well as its social health via increased social capital or psychic income gained through improved elite sport performances.

As editors of this book, we are also interested in the intersection of sport, participation and policy, though for different reasons. This book does not attempt to determine what the benefits of sport participation are, nor does it attempt to establish the relative merits or the interconnections between each of the benefits. Rather, we have taken the approach that sport participation, on balance, is likely to have a range of positive physical and social outcomes. We are concerned with establishing which structural arrangements are more successful at improving a nation's sport participation and why; whether a nation's culture and sport structures have a significant influence on the level of sport participation and, if so, what role they play in thwarting or facilitating government policy and programs; what role political ideology has in fostering sport participation; and whether there are patterns that might allow us to conclude how nations with high sport participation levels have achieved them and what nations with low levels can do to improve.

This book is also a response to what we believe to be a paucity of knowledge about what works in a range of national and regional contexts for increasing participation rates in sport. Government policy mechanisms and their efficacy in the area of sport participation are manifestly under-researched. Once again, this is surprising given the degree of policy learning that has occurred and continues to occur between nations in terms of elite sport. Facility provision, sport science, talent identification and coaching are just some of the areas in which nations have learned from each other in the area of elite sport development. This knowledge is continually used to improve systems and training and influences the allocation of financial and human resources. The same is not true in the area of sport participation and we believe it is appropriate to begin to redress this imbalance. We believe it is important to focus on government policy because of its central place in establishing a direction within and across nations. Government policy is an articulation of government priorities, as well as an allocation of resources, particularly financial. This is particularly important for sport, which in many nations is dominated by the non-profit sector and either relies on or collaborates with national, state/regional and local governments in the provision of facilities and services.

As editors, we believed that the most effective and interesting way to establish a research base in this area would be to gather a collection of national case studies, with common organizing principles, which would enable students, scholars and practitioners within the field to compare and contrast the development, implementation and impact of sport participation policies. This book enables a wide-ranging international comparison to be made, which we hope in turn not only leads to future research, but also provides policy makers and sport administrators with new and valuable knowledge. Importantly, we hold firm to the belief that this could not be achieved through single-country studies; an international comparative approach is essential to the success of this enterprise.

Selecting countries

Comparative studies of this scope and type are necessarily selective. However, it is worth providing some contextual comments to clarify the way in which countries were selected. We adopted an approach that was in part driven by a conceptual understanding of sport, participation and policy across the world and in part by pragmatism.

First, we secured authors from countries that represented a diversity of sport delivery systems: club-focused (e.g. New Zealand); education-focused (e.g. United States of America); and state-focused (e.g. Bulgaria). Based on previous work (cf. Bergsgard *et al.* 2008), we concluded that sport delivery systems are likely to facilitate as well as respond to sport participation policies in diverse ways, and that it was important for the purposes of an international comparison to have this diversity represented. In broad terms we recognized that in state-focused sport systems, sport organizations are more likely to be highly integrated with national and state political systems, which will have a significant impact on the ways in which policies are developed, deployed and implemented. On the other hand, in club-based sport systems sport organizations are likely to be more autonomous, which will have an impact on the process of policy development and implementation, as well as its efficacy. We also recognized that some systems cannot be easily categorized, particularly if state-focused and club-focused are considered to be binary. Some of the countries chosen are a hybrid, while others are different again, such as the education institution-orientated US system.

Second, we attempted to secure authors from a range of countries across the world that represented the diversity of regions and continents. We were successful in securing authors from North America, Europe, Africa, Asia and Oceania. The only continent with a substantial human population missing from the collection is South America; we were unsuccessful in this regard, despite our best efforts to attract an author from this region. While large groupings such as continents are not likely to be useful units of analysis, the selection of nations from different parts of the world allowed us to account for a range of other differences, such as political stability, culture and weather, which may influence participation rates and the content of policies focused on sport participation.

Third, we were concerned to select a range of countries that represented the diversity of the world's welfare systems, which we concluded might have a significant impact on the development, implementation and efficacy of government policies that seek to increase or improve sport participation. Esping-Andersen (1990, 1996) provided one of the most influential typologies of European welfare systems and stimulated considerable academic debate concerned not only to test the underlying assumptions, but also to determine whether the typology could be applied in its original form beyond Europe or whether it needed to be modified or augmented to take account of the distinctive cultural and economic-political contexts of welfare provision found outside Europe. Esping-Andersen's original concept of the welfare regime was defined as 'the institutional arrangements, rules and understandings that guide and shape concurrent social policy decisions, expenditure developments, problem definitions and even the respond-and-demand structure of citizens and welfare consumers' (1990: 80). For Esping-Andersen, short-term policy decisions are significantly shaped, if not quite determined, by the accumulated history of past decisions – a process of historical institutionalization. Accordingly, given that in most, if not all, countries the government rationale for spending public money on mass or community sport provision is informed by a range of welfare objectives, it is reasonable to expect that the accumulated history of past welfare decisions will substantially influence the extent and nature of provision for sport participation.

Esping-Andersen identified three welfare regimes – liberal, conservative-corporatist and social democratic – distinguished by examining the balance between public and private provision of welfare, the protection of the individual against market forces (what he refers to as decommodification) and the type of social stratification produced by welfare policies. The liberal welfare regime is characterized by modest universal benefits, the prevalence of means-testing as a mode of benefit allocation and modest social insurance schemes. The conservative-corporatist regime is characterized by modest levels of decommodification, state income maintenance schemes linked to occupational status, limited support for women's participation in the labour market and, generally, a family (rather than individual) orientation to welfare policy. The final type, the social democratic, is characterized by a high level of decommodification and generous and universal benefits. The extensive testing of Esping-Andersen's typology generally strongly endorsed his analysis although a number of researchers identified additional regimes, especially when they extended the analysis beyond western and northern Europe. For example, in relation to the post-communist countries of central and eastern Europe, Deacon (1993, 2000) argued that rather than these countries being seen as comprising a distinct type they should be viewed as welfare regimes in transition – particularly those countries that had successfully applied for membership of the European Union. However, in a more recent assessment Fenger argued that while it was not possible to 'show a distinct, specific type of post-communist welfare state' (2007: 27), these countries did not fit the Esping-Andersen typology. Fenger identified three sub-groups of post-communist welfare regimes differentiated by factors including levels of inter-personal trust, level of egalitarianism, and levels of infant mortality and life-expectancy. A similar case for distinctiveness was made by those examining East Asian welfare systems. Both Jones (1993) and Kwon (1997) argue for an 'East Asian' or 'Confucian' type which, for Jones (1993: 199), is characterized by 'Conservative corporatism without (Western-style) worker participation; subsidiarity without the church; laissez-faire without libertarianism: an alternative expression for all this might be "household economy" welfare states – run in the style of a would be traditional, Confucian, extended family'.

Not all the countries can be located within either Esping-Andersen's typology or the subsequent additions, but the countries in this study represent examples not only of Esping-Andersen's three welfare regimes but also of the two major variants/ additional types – East Asian/Confucian and post-communist. Germany and Norway are respectively archetypes of Esping-Andersen's conservative-corporatist and social democratic welfare regimes while the liberal variant is represented by England, Australia, New Zealand and Canada. The post-communist subset is represented by Bulgaria and Hungary while China, Japan and Singapore are examples of the East Asian/Confucian type.

Fourth, we attempted to select a range of countries based on size of population. The final collection includes the three most populous countries in the world (China, India and the USA), which represent approximately 40 per cent of the world's population, several mid-sized countries such as Japan, Germany and South Africa, and a number of relatively small countries, such as Norway and Singapore. There are no countries represented in the collection with a population of less than four million, although this was primarily because of the paucity of authors able to write on these countries, rather than a conscious omission.

Finally, the pragmatic aspect of the selection process involved inviting authors to contribute to the volume who had previous experience or a significant publication record in areas relevant to sport participation and policy. The result is an assembly of authors with substantial individual and collective expertise and knowledge, which we believe is one of the strengths of the book.

Framework for analysis

As editors, we were concerned to establish consistency as well as comparability across each of the chapters. We requested authors to utilize the following framework for analysis that covered five key questions within each of their chapters.

First, we asked authors to provide information about the structure of sport within the nation they were examining, such as the relative significance of the public, not-for-profit and commercial sectors in the delivery of sport. This establishes a context in which the reader is able to understand the mechanisms by which government is able to influence sport participation, as well as the constraints. In general, we hope that this information will also provide readers with a sense of how mature or well-developed respective national sport systems are in order to contextualize participation rates and the efficacy of government policy.

Second, we asked authors to outline a sense of the culture of sport within their respective nation. Although in many respects this is linked to the structure of sport, we believed that there were other elements of a nation's sporting culture that might influence levels of sport participation: where government might seek to direct its resources, and whether the people of a nation are more or less predisposed to watching or actively participating in organized sport activities or informal physical activity. For example, a sporting culture might develop within a nation as a result of its weather or physical resources, such as an abundance or lack of open urban space for playing fields. The sporting culture might also be particularly distinct because of a historical predilection for particular types of sport, because of the nation's political ideology or because of the relative financial wealth of its citizens. Finally, the sport culture might have been influenced by key moments or events, such as the hosting of an Olympic Games or FIFA World Cup. We believed that it was important to explore these issues, albeit briefly in each chapter, in order to mitigate the notion that the issue of participation in sport is homogenous, and that national peculiarities and differences have no bearing on the articulation, implementation or outcomes of policies aimed at increasing sport participation rates.

Third, we asked authors to provide the most recent and comprehensive sport participation statistics available for their country. This was essential for comparing the efficacy of government policies within a nation, as well as across nations where possible. The issue of participation statistics is vexed for a number of reasons. Definitions of sport and participation vary, and as editors we decided not to apply a strict definition of either, in large part because it would have made the authors' task almost impossible. Readers will discover that in each of the nations a different interpretation of sport and participation has been applied, not necessarily by the authors, but invariably by a government statistical agency, peak sport agency or market research organization. In some nations sport is interpreted as a competitive, formal and rule-bound activity, whereas in others it is interpreted as physical activity, with little distinction placed on the type or setting of the activity. These differences pose problems for both author and reader; however, where possible we have encouraged authors to focus on sport that takes place in an organized setting. In other words, our focus is not on informal, unstructured physical activity, such as taking a walk. The quality of data also varies markedly in many of the nations that feature in this book where there is no national statistical agency. This also occurs, albeit to a lesser extent, even in those nations where there is a national statistical agency responsible for collecting participation data. Where data has been collected, the definitions of sport and participation often change, or the age of an adult or child (i.e. 16 or 18 years of age) varies from survey to survey, meaning that it is often difficult to directly compare data sets. Also, where data has been collected it has either been in a sporadic fashion, or conducted by independent researchers. This means that it is also difficult to directly compare data sets, and even more difficult to assess the efficacy of particular government policies and programs. Lastly, survey sample sizes differ, meaning that validity and reliability are often difficult to ascertain.

Fourth, we asked authors to examine the nature and extent of government intervention in the area of sport participation at national and sub-national levels. By necessity this meant that the authors employed an analysis that included both historical and contemporary aspects. Readers will note that the emphasis shifts between the two depending on the preferences of the authors. For example, the chapter on China in the collection adopts a more historical approach in order to more fully explore the evolution of sport participation in Chinese society, which is entirely appropriate given the relative political and cultural stability in that nation. We also asked authors to examine, and explain where possible, government motives or rationales for government intervention in the area of sport participation.

Finally, we asked authors to review government intervention in the area of sport participation, and using the context of participation rates assess the efficacy of government policies and programs. One of the key difficulties faced by the authors in this collection was that they were charged with examining an area of sport that is often not clearly or obviously articulated in a discrete policy. In many of the nations examined within this book, the process for authors was not as easy as identifying the participation policy, examining the participation rates, exploring government intervention and then making an informed assessment of the efficacy of the policy. Rather, it was often a complex distillation of a range of sometimes disconnected government policies, programs and activities, and assessment based on less than perfect statistical data. It is a credit to the authors that the sections in which they assess the efficacy of government policies in the area of sport participation are particularly useful in highlighting where nations have been successful, or where nations have been deficient. These sections provide a guide to future developments and are often a call to action for the governments of the world.

References

Bergsgard, N. A., Houlihan, B., Mangset, P., Nødland, S. I. and Rommetvedt, H. (2007) *Sport Policy: A Comparative Analysis of Stability and Change*, Oxford: Butterworth-Heinemann.

Coalter, F. (2007) *A Wider Social Role for Sport: Who's Keeping Score?*, London: Routledge.

Commission on the European Communities (2007) *White Paper on Sport*, Brussels: Author.

DaCosta, L. and Miragaya, A. (eds) (2002) *Worldwide Experiences and Trends in Sport For All*, Oxford: Meyer & Meyer Sport.

Deacon, B. (1993) 'Developments in East European social policy'. In C. Jones (ed.), *New Perspectives on the Welfare State in Europe*, London: Routledge.

—— (2000) 'Eastern European welfare states: the impact of politics of globalization', *Journal of European Social Policy*, 10(2): 146–161.

Esping-Andersen, G. (1990) *The Three Worlds of Welfare Capitalism*, Cambridge: Polity Press.

—— (1996) 'After the golden age? Welfare state dilemmas in a global economy'. In G. Esping-Andersen (ed.), *Welfare States in Transition: National Adaptations in Global Economies*, London: Sage.

Fenger, H. J. M. (2007) 'Welfare regimes in central and eastern Europe: incorporating post-communist countries in a welfare regime typology', *Contemporary Issues and Ideas in Social Sciences*, 3(2) http://journal.ciiss.net/index.php/ciiss/article/view/45/37

Finkelstein, E., Fiebelkorn, I. and Wang, G. (2003) 'National medical spending attributable to overweight and obesity: how much, and who's paying?', *Health Affairs*, W3: 219–226.

Green, M. and Houlihan, B. (2005) *Elite Sport Development: Policy Learning and Political Priorities*, London: Routledge.

Hedley, A., Ogden, C., Johnson, C., Carroll, M., Curtin, L. and Flegal, K. (2004) 'Prevalence of overweight and obesity among US children, adolescents, and adults, 1999–2002', *Journal of the American Medical Association*, 291(23): 2847–2850.

Houlihan, B. and Green, M. (eds) (2008) *Comparative Elite Sport Development: Systems, Structures and Public Policy*, Oxford: Butterworth-Heinemann.

Houlihan, B. and White, A. (2002) *The Politics of Sports Development: Development of Sport or Development through Sport?*, London: Routledge.

Hoye, R., Nicholson, M. and Houlihan, B. (2010) *Sport and Policy: Issues and Analysis*, Oxford: Butterworth-Heinemann.

Hylton, K. and Bramham, P. (eds) (2008) *Sports Development: Policy, Process and Practice*, 2nd edn, London: Routledge.

Hylton, K., Bramham, P., Jackson, D. and Nesti, M. (eds) (2001) *Sports Development: Policy, Process and Practice*, London: Routledge.

Jones, C. (1993) 'The Pacific challenge: Confucian welfare states'. In C. Jones (ed.), *New Perspectives on the Welfare State in Europe*, London: Routledge.

Kwon, H.-J. (1997) 'Beyond European welfare regimes: comparative perspectives on East Asian welfare systems', *Journal of Social Policy*, 26(4): 467–484.

Maslow, A. (1943) 'A theory of human motivation', *Psychological Review* 50(4): 370–396.

—— (1954) *Motivation and Personality*, New York: Harper.

National Audit Office (2001) *Tackling Obesity in England*, London: National Audit Office.

Nicholson, M. and Hoye, R. (2008) 'Sport and social capital: an introduction'. In M. Nicholson and R. Hoye (eds), *Sport and Social Capital*, London: Elsevier, Butterworth Heinemann (pp. 1–18).

2 England

Barrie Houlihan

Since sport first emerged as a recognized responsibility of government in the late 1960s, the British government has maintained an interest in community sport participation and has occasionally expressed concern in relation to participation levels but has rarely adopted community sport as a priority. In contrast, elite sport, over a period of ten years or so, has been established as the central priority of sport policy and benefited accordingly; there has been substantial investment in specialist training facilities, extensive support staff and generous personal grants to athletes. Since the mid 1990s, school/youth sport has also attracted substantial additional lottery and Exchequer investment in both staff and facilities. Policy making in relation to community sport has tended to be confined to the symbolic level, indicated by repeated alarmed expressions of disquiet at the low levels of participation, repeated expressions of determination to address the issue and a plethora of short-lived initiatives, but little evidence of a sustained and well-resourced program designed to attract more people to take part in sport on a regular basis. Explaining the relative neglect of community sport by government is a central concern of this chapter and will be considered more directly below. However, an initial step in the analysis is to locate community sport within the broader landscape of sport and sport policy in England.

The structure of sport

The total value of sport to the English economy was estimated at £13,531 million in 2003, an increase of 107 per cent since 1985 compared to an increase of 59 per cent in the value of the English economy generally (SIRC 2007). The contribution of the sport sector to the English economy rose from 1.2 per cent in 1985 to 1.7 per cent in 2003. A breakdown of this total figure gives some indication of the scale and rate of increase in two important aspects of sport – participation and spectating. Over the period 1985–2003 expenditure on 'participation subscriptions and fees' increased by 116 per cent and on 'sport equipment' by 117 per cent, but expenditure on admission to events increased much more rapidly by 169 per cent (SIRC 2007). Just under £4,000 million (28 per cent of total sports expenditure) was spent on participation-related products and services (subscriptions, fees and equipment) in 2003. How that expenditure is divided across the three main sectors (public, commercial and not-for-profit) and the size of market that it represents are difficult to determine with confidence.

According to Mintel, a market research company, local authority sport centres were the most frequently mentioned locations for participation in sport, followed by 'home' and 'private clubs' (see Table 2.1). Home is the only location where women's participation is greater than that of men.

The increasing prominence of the private sector in providing opportunities for participation is evident from a recent Audit Commission report which noted that while local authorities have spent approximately £350m per year on capital investment (and a further £650m per year on revenue costs), the private sector spent, on average, £750m per year between 1990 and 2005 on capital projects (Audit Commission 2006: 10). Much of the private sector investment has, in recent years, been in the development of fitness centres. The United Kingdom (UK) has five of the eight largest fitness businesses in Europe and the UK market is the largest by value (€2,722m). In 2008 it was estimated that slightly less than 12 per cent of the UK adult population were members of a fitness club (7.2m people). The private sector is by far the most significant provider of fitness facilities, with 5,755 gyms. By comparison, the public sector total is 2,622, which includes just over 1,000 facilities that are on educational sites and have limited public access (BISL 2008).

While it is always difficult to gather reliable investment and membership data from the commercial sector, it is also increasingly difficult to provide precise data regarding the public and voluntary/not-for-profit sectors as there has been a gradual blurring of the boundary between the two sectors over the last ten years or so. The problem lies, in large part, in the diversity of management patterns for local authority facilities and services that have developed since the introduction of privatization by the Conservative government in the late 1980s. Local authorities' sport facilities and services are currently managed in one of five main ways: by the local authority itself (which accounts for 1,650 facilities; 47 per cent of the total); through a contract with a private contractor (348 facilities; 10 per cent); through an independent charitable trust (519 facilities; 15 per cent); by schools (559 facilities; 16 per cent); and by community organizations/clubs (153 facilities; 5 per cent). The first three types of management arrangement (62 per cent in total) give local authorities either direct or indirect (as the client of the private contractor or as providers of subsidy to trusts) control over the strategic objectives of the facility. Over the period between 2002 and 2006 the proportion of facilities managed in-house fell while the proportion managed by trusts almost doubled.

Table 2.1 Location of sport participation in the last 12 months (by those aged 16+ who had participated in sport or exercise in the last 12 months)

Location	%
Local authority sport centre	47
Home	45
Private club, e.g. health and fitness club	39
Local park	38
School/college/university	16
Local authority sports ground	15
Place of employment	10
Elsewhere, e.g. hotel/spa	21

Source: Mintel 2007

However, the most recent trend, supported by funding from the national lottery, is for the development of public facilities on school sites and under the control of schools. For example, in 2003, 73 per cent of all new public sector sport facilities were on school sites and in 2004 the proportion was 78 per cent. The trend to develop public facilities on school sites is set to continue as the government has recently embarked on a major schools rebuilding program. The management arrangements for public sport facilities appear to have little impact on levels of participation, with similar participation rates recorded across in-house, trust, private contractor and mixed economy arrangements (Audit Commission 2006).

The culture of sport

England has a long history of promoting participation in sport. In the nineteenth century participation was encouraged as it was considered to develop the leadership qualities of public (fee-paying) school boys necessary for the management of the British Empire, and seen as an effective form of social control for young urban males. The strong culture of sport participation that developed in the country's public schools and universities in the nineteenth century resulted in the establishment of some of the first national sport organizations in the world. Currently, Britain has national governing bodies for over 120 sports. Specifying the number of sport clubs in England is more difficult, but the CCPR reports that its member organizations are responsible for over 150,000 clubs across Britain. Sport England's estimate is more modest at 110,000 community sport clubs, probably due to the adoption of a narrower definition of sport (Sport England 2003). The four major participation sports in England (cricket, football, lawn tennis and rugby union) account for 9.4m participants and 49,000 clubs; rugby union claims over 600,000 participants in over 4,800 affiliated clubs and football 7m participants in 37,500 clubs (House of Commons 2005).

Table 2.2 Sport participation across seven European countries (by percentage, adults 16+)

Type of participation	Finland	Ireland	Italy	Netherlands	Spain	Sweden	UK
Competitive, organized and intensive	6	7	2	8	2	12	5
Intensive	33	11	3	8	7	24	13
Regular, competitive and/or organized	5	7	2	10	2	5	4
Regular, recreational	28	3	3	6	4	17	6
Regular participation	72	28	10	32	15	58	28
Irregular	6	15	8	25	10	11	19
Occasional	2	21	5	6	6	–	20
Irregular/occasional	8	36	13	31	16	11	39
Non-participant (but participant in other physical activities)	16	10	37	38	43	8	15
Non-participant (no physical activities)	3	26	40		26	22	19
Non-participation	19	36	77	38	69	30	34

Source: Compass 1999, p. 65

While the culture of participation in sport in England is long established, it is modest by comparison to that found in other European countries, particularly those in Northern Europe (see Table 2.2). Although published in 1999, there is little reason to expect the findings of the Compass report, which are presented in Table 2.2, to have altered significantly.

Although participation is an important aspect of a country's sporting culture, spectating is also of importance and is particularly significant in England. In football, for example, not only is the Premier League the best supported league in Europe (though Germany has the highest attendance per match) but the Championship (the division below the Premier League) is the fourth best supported league in Europe. Globally, six of the top fifty highest average attendances for outdoor sports leagues are English: Premier League, Championship, and Division One (all football); Guinness Premiership (rugby union); Super League (rugby league); and Twenty-20 Cup (cricket).

Participation in sport

Trend data relating to participation in England are weak. Although national data have been collected since the mid 1980s, changes in the methods of data collection and the questions asked make reliable time series data difficult to compile. From 1987 to 2002 data were collected through the General Household Survey (GHS). Since 2002 there has been a radical change to the collection of participation data with two surveys asking questions about participation in sport – the Active People survey and the Taking Part survey.

In commenting on the GHS trends between 1987 and 2002, Sport England expressed a 'concern that after a number of years when participation rates have remained static there is now an indication that they have started to decline' (Sport England 2004a: 6), a comment clearly illustrated in Figure 2.1.

The GHS provides a familiar profile of participation by gender, age and income, with women participating less than men and participation declining with age and income (Figures 2.2, 2.3 and 2.4). The narrowing of the gap between men's and women's participation is largely due to the growth in private sector fitness clubs.

In 2005 the Active People survey was introduced and replaced a reliance on GHS data. While the Active People survey was far more extensive (363,724 adults

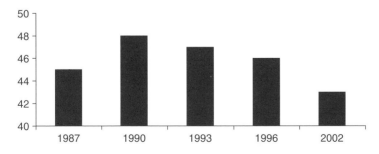

Figure 2.1 Trends in participation in sport (per cent, walking excluded) 1987 to 2002

Source: General Household Survey, various years

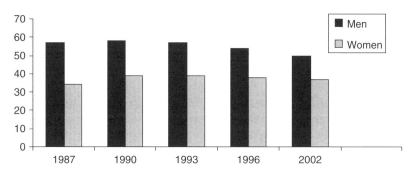

Figure 2.2 Participation in sport for men and women (per cent, excluding walking) 1987 to 2002

Source: General Household Survey, various years

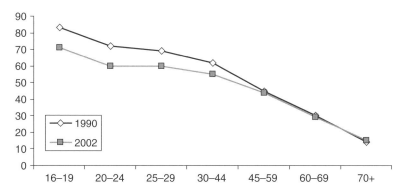

Figure 2.3 Trends in participation in sport (per cent, excluding walking) by age, comparing 1990 to 2002

Source: General Household Survey, various years

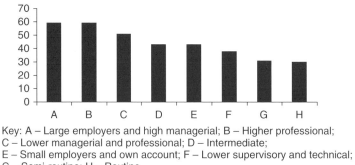

Key: A – Large employers and high managerial; B – Higher professional;
C – Lower managerial and professional; D – Intermediate;
E – Small employers and own account; F – Lower supervisory and technical;
G – Semi-routine; H – Routine

Figure 2.4 Participation in sport, 2002, by socio-economic classification (per cent)

Source: General Household Survey, various years

interviewed between October 2005 and October 2006), its results are not comparable to those of the GHS and cannot be added to the time series. In 2005–6 the parent department of Sport England commissioned a separate survey, Taking Part, which also gathered data relating to sport participation which, while of interest, was also not compatible with the GHS. Nonetheless, these two new surveys do provide a more comprehensive and more robust profile of participation and form a more secure foundation for tracking change.

According to the Taking Part survey, 69 per cent of all adults (*c.* 27.5m) had participated in an active sport at least once in the last twelve months. As Table 2.3 indicates, the most popular sport activities were individual activities with only one team sport, football, making the top ten.

If a more restrictive definition of participation (once in the previous week) is adopted, the 2006/07 Taking Part Annual Report indicated that 40 per cent of all adults had participated in moderate intensity sport for at least 30 minutes and 22 per cent had participated for at least 30 minutes on at least three separate days in the past week. These levels of participation were confirmed by the much more extensive Active People survey which found that 21 per cent of adults over the age of 16 participated in at least three, moderate-intensity 30 minute sessions of sport and physical activity in the previous week (Sport England 2007). In terms of emerging trends in sport participation, one of the most striking is the move away from team sports to individual sports and sport-related physical activity such as jogging, keeping fit and working out in gymnasiums. A second is the clear preference among the young and early adult groups (aged 15 to 34) for 'extreme sports' such as mountain biking, roller blading and bungee jumping, with the number of regular and occasional participants increasing from 11.6 per cent to 13.4 per cent between 2001 and 2003 (Tomlinson *et al.* 2005).

The involvement of government in sport participation

A review of the involvement of government in sport in most countries will produce a broadly similar list of objectives – to protect sectional interests, to strengthen military preparedness, to exercise social control over sections of society, to control/ outlaw particular sports, to engineer social integration at the community and/or national level, to improve health, to contribute to economic development, to boost national morale and to send diplomatic signals (Houlihan 2000). In England governments have, at different times, used sport in pursuit of all of these objectives. However, until the early 1970s government involvement was sporadic, tentative

Table 2.3 Types of activities

Sport/activity	%
Swimming or diving (indoors)	31
Health, fitness, gym or conditioning activities	20
Cycling (not utility)	14
Swimming or diving (outdoors)	14
Snooker, pool, billiards (excluding bar billiards)	14
Tenpin bowling	12
Keepfit, aerobics, dance exercise	11
Golf, pitch and putt, putting	11
Football (including five-a-side) (outdoors)	10
Jogging, cross country, road running	9

Source: Taking Part, Annual Report 2005/2006

and generally reluctant. In the 1960s sport had low salience for the major political parties, and even in the early 1980s there was a lack of enthusiasm for any expansion of the role of government beyond the provision of support for the work of national governing bodies and local authorities.

Although there was some concern with sport prior to 1960, it was the report of the Wolfenden Committee, established by the Central Council of Physical Recreation, that placed sport, both community participation and elite performance, on the government's agenda. As Coghlan noted, the establishment of the Committee 'aroused no particular concern other than general broad interest and yet the results . . . were to alter the face of British sport within the decade' (1990: 8). Two aspects of the Committee's report are worth noting: first, the attempt to balance the interests of the general participant with those of the elite performer, and second, the reluctance to endorse state intervention in preference for 'arm's-length' support for the existing not-for-profit network of clubs and national governing bodies. Consequently, the government's initial involvement in issues of participation was modest and limited to the establishment of an Advisory Sports Council in 1965. As Coalter *et al.* observed, the report of the Wolfenden Committee was firmly located with the 'classic Beveridge tradition [where] state activity was only defensible as a framework for voluntarism' (1986: 46).

The replacement of the Advisory Sports Council with an executive Sports Council in 1972 marked the start of the first phase of government's active involvement in sport and mainly involved the distribution of public funds for the expansion of facility infrastructure. The new Sports Council used its modest public resources to provide grant aid to local authorities and to sport clubs to build new facilities and to transform the opportunity structure for participation. Between 1971 and 1981 the number of swimming pools increased by over 500 and the number of indoor sport facilities by over 450, many of which benefited from the award of Sports Council grants. The role of the Council was endorsed by a report from the House of Lords Select Committee on Sport and Leisure, which couched its support in terms of the regulatory benefits of sport, noting that 'if the welfare state . . . by ignoring a shortage of recreational facilities, allows frustration to build up in non-working hours, then it has failed to provide adequately for national welfare' (House of Lords 1973: ii). A White Paper from the Department of the Environment (the then parent department for the Sports Council) provided a slightly different rationale for government involvement, stressing a distributional motive justified by a concern with the lack of participation opportunities in areas of social deprivation. While the White Paper noted the contribution of the voluntary sector, it concluded that 'voluntary bodies cannot achieve all that is needed' (DoE 1975: 4), thus marking the first cautious steps towards a less deferential attitude to national governing bodies of sport and clubs. During this early phase of the development of the government's policy towards participation, the features that were to define the more mature policy were clearly evident: first, a preference for working with NGBs rather than local authorities; second, a broad interpretation of 'sport for all' that included many aspects of elite sport development; and third, a strongly instrumental attitude towards the value of participation.

The 1980s and the early 1990s saw government interest in sport wane except on those occasions when crises (football hooliganism or urban disorder) prompted government intervention. In general, this period was one of policy drift with the Sports Council generally ignored by the Thatcher governments and sport treated with a mix of disdain and bewilderment. However, some important developments in participation policy and practice did take place during this period. Of particular importance was the realization that while the facility-building program had been successful in meeting latent demand, a more interventionist strategy would be needed if participation levels were to rise further. This realization had encouraged a number of local authorities to begin to employ sport development officers (SDOs) whose role was to intervene in their local communities to stimulate higher levels of participation. However, in those towns and cities where SDOs were employed, SDO employment was often short term and heavily dependent on grants from the Sports Council. The Sports Council's strategy was to offer pump-priming funding in the expectation that financial support for SDO activities would be incorporated into mainstream local authority budgets. However, limiting funding to three years was often too short a time for the program to demonstrate its impact to local authority decision-makers. This problem was exacerbated by the instability of Sports Council objectives, such as shifting from targeting particular under-participating groups (women and the elderly, for example), to focusing on particular issues such as community safety. As Green observed, 'the shift away from spending on targeted groups . . . which was rationalized on the basis of alleviating recreational disadvantage and the fostering of community development, and towards the use of sport and leisure as a form of "benign policing", realigned political priorities for sport . . . policy' (2006: 225).

An additional barrier to incorporation of SDO funding into mainstream local authority budgets was the lack of statutory status for sport and recreation services. Thus local authorities were reluctant to accept further financial commitments when the budgets of their statutory services, such as education and personal welfare, were under increased pressure. A final problem was a perception among many local authorities that the enthusiasm for sport development would wane and that local authorities should make the most of Sports Council-funded programs but avoid long-term commitments. However, these barriers notwithstanding, the 1980s did see an increase in the number of local authorities establishing specialist departments or units for leisure services and developing some capacity for sport development whether Sports Council or internally funded.

The period from the early 1990s up to the election of the Labour government in 1997 marked a turning point in government's attitude towards sport, but also marked the beginning of a long period of relative neglect of community participation. The appointment of John Major as Prime Minister in 1990 brought to the head of government an enthusiast for sport who introduced two changes which consolidated the place of sport on the government agenda: first, the establishment of a new government department with explicit responsibility for sport (the Department of National Heritage) and second, the introduction of a national lottery of which sport would be a substantial beneficiary. In terms of the impact on sport participation policy, the focus on narrow target groups or social issues gave way to a broader emphasis on school sport and young people and on supporting elite-level performance. The Conservative government policy document, *Sport: Raising the Game*, was notable on two accounts. First, the strong twin emphasis on school sport and elite success, and second, the almost complete absence of any mention of local authorities and community sport. The clear implication was that participation in sport by the general population was a responsibility of local government and not a concern for the centre.

Prior to Labour's 1997 victory it had been made clear that, if elected, a Labour government would return to a sport policy which emphasized participation. In its pre-election policy statement, *Labour's Sporting Nation*, there was a commitment to develop a strategy which would give 'sport back to the nation [by increasing] the availability of sporting opportunities' and acknowledge the 'importance of participating in sport for the sake of enjoyment' (1996: 11, 6). However, it was far from clear what substance lay behind this commitment. While the statement indicated that progress towards sport for all would 'begin by taking three important steps to ensure access', two of the 'steps' (broadcasting major events free-to-air and tackling ticket touting) were concerned with spectating rather than participating. Moreover, the references to participation notwithstanding, the general tone of the document gave priority to elite success with the consequence that participation was valued only insofar as it enhanced medal chances in major sports. The statement did make reference to community needs and to the role of local authority SDOs, but the reference to the latter was primarily in terms of their potential to contribute to high-performance sport rather than sport for the average participant.

Following the 1997 election, the Labour government retained and indeed expanded many of the school/youth and elite programs introduced by the previous Conservative government, but it did make some progress in reinvigorating community sport. According to the Minister responsible for sports, 'We believe that the concept of sport for all should be wide-ranging, ensuring sporting enjoyment and opportunity for the public at large' (Parliamentary Debates 1997: col. 1059). He argued that sport for all and elite achievement were complementary and, significantly, was at pains to stress the value of sport in achieving broader personal and community welfare goals. Indeed, the contribution that community sport participation could make to non-sport social policy objectives was to be the defining characteristic of Labour's initial approach to participation. One immediate consequence of the increased concern with participation and its potential to generate welfare benefits was changes to the regulations concerning the use of lottery funds. Under Labour these were to be used more strategically to channel funds to the poorer areas of the country and to the less affluent sports. Further support for community sport was given by the outcome of the 'comprehensive spending review' of public expenditure in which the Minister noted that 'The [English Sports Council] has already adopted progressive policies which seek to engage the widest cross section of the community in sport and physical recreation and for the most part we are satisfied that their work is well directed and deserves continued support' (DCMS 1998: para. 5).

The instrumental rationale for fostering community sport participation was reflected in some of the early English Sports Council (the successor agency to the Sports Council, later to be rebranded as Sport England) programs. The Active Communities program, for example, comprised a series of projects aimed at establishing links with non-traditional partners and with an explicit concern to address pressing social issues. One project that grew out of the Active Communities approach was 'Positive Futures', which had the aim of reducing anti-social behaviour, particularly drug use, among the young and was part funded by the ESC and part by the Exchequer and the Youth Justice Board. The Positive Futures project demonstrated not only the willingness of the ESC to adapt to government priorities but also the extent to which policy towards participation had moved from a concern with 'development of sport' to 'personal and community development through sport'. The welfare objectives underpinning Positive Futures and the Active Communities program were reinforced by the report of Policy Action Team 10 (DCMS 1999), which was established by the government to report to the Social Exclusion Unit on how sport (and the arts) could contribute to achieving greater social inclusion, especially among the disaffected young and ethnic minorities, and address issues relating to crime, health, unemployment and education.

The redirection of sport policy evident in the early years of the Labour government was confirmed and clarified in two major policy documents: *A Sporting Future for All* (DCMS 2000) and *Game Plan* (DCMS/Strategy Unit 2002). *A Sporting Future for All* was clear in linking sport to Labour's social policy objectives at both personal and community level, although the focus was not purely instrumental as the Prime Minister, in his Foreword, noted that 'sport isn't just about being healthy: sport is fun – one of the good things in life' (DCMS 2000: 2). Specifically in relation to participation, it was stated that it was the government's ambition to see 'more people of all ages and all social groups taking part in sport' and consequently set a target 'to reduce over the next ten years, the unfairness in access to sport' (DCMS 2000: 5, 11). In many ways *A Sporting Future for All* was an aspirational document, establishing a vision for the future rather than setting targets. However, unlike the Conservative government strategy document, *Sport: Raising the Game*, the Labour document did pay closer attention to implementation. In particular, the Labour strategy gave a central role to local authorities, but also was more specific regarding the contribution of other partners including voluntary sport clubs and national governing bodies of sport.

However, while it is accurate that the Labour government brought local authorities back into the policy process, it – or rather, Sport England – was reluctant to delegate responsibility to the sub-national tier. The relative autonomy of local authorities could at times prove problematic for a government (or government agency such as Sport England) which had a clear agenda for sport and did not want to negotiate with other partners. Thus while local authorities and particularly their sport development officers were identified as playing a key role, most Sport England initiatives operated through newly established implementation frameworks or through more malleable (and more resource-dependent) partners such as NGBs and clubs.

A program consistent with the new social policy emphasis and typical of the reluctance to rely too heavily on local authorities was Sports Action Zones (SAZs), which targeted areas of low participation where the emphasis was less on capital investment than on providing revenue funding for interventions by sport development officers. The early SAZs were located in areas of rural or urban deprivation or areas where there had been severe de-industrialization (coalfield areas). They were funded for between five and seven years with a clear brief to address social problems, along with low participation, by engineering partnerships between local authorities, local clubs and other community organizations such as youth clubs. In addition, Sport England was acutely aware of the inherent tension in the work of SAZs, which on the one hand were intended to address some severe social problems, while on the other were intended to increase participation in sport. In a press release at the time, Sport England seemed to be reminding itself as well as the government that 'Sport England is a sport development agency and, as such, we will expect over time all projects funded within a Zone to make a contribution to increasing participation' (Sport England, New Sports Action Zones announced, press release, 17 January 2000). The awkward partnership with local government and the tension between achieving participation and welfare goals remain part of the operating environment of Sport England to the present day.

Two years after the publication of *A Sporting Future for All*, the government published a further policy document, *Game Plan*, which reinforced the welfare rationale for sport participation but was clearer in specifying the expectations that the government had of the major partners, such as NGBs, clubs, higher education institutions and local authorities, and in setting specific targets by which progress could be measured. In terms of the expectations held about sport the Minister, in her Foreword, referred to the 'extraordinary results' of sport projects and claimed that sport has the capacity to 'improve all round educational performance, to build confidence, leadership and teamwork in our young people, to combat social exclusion, reduce crime and build stronger communities' (DCMS/SU 2002: 7). The almost miraculous properties of sport identified so confidently by the Minister were sharply at odds with the scepticism of the report's research team, who argued that robust data only existed for the link between sport participation and improved health. *Game Plan* set targets for participation. For example, it specified an increase of 40 percentage points by 2020 in the proportion of the population being 'reasonably active' (i.e. taking part in 30 minutes of moderate exercise five times a week). Commitments were also made to streamline the delivery of participation programs and their funding. What is particularly notable is the inclusion of the term 'exercise', which added further complexity to the work of Sport England and made the organization's earlier reminder that it was a 'sport development agency' appear rather plaintive.

By the middle of the first decade of the new century there was understandable confusion within Sport England about its precise role in many ways reflecting the general mess that government had created around sport participation policy. There were four sources of confusion, the first of which was the uncertainty regarding the emphasis that should be given to the narrow objective of getting more people to play more sport. *Game Plan* appeared to endorse the priority of community participation, but was ambiguous regarding the balance of emphasis between sport and physical exercise. Second, there was a similar level of ambiguity regarding the relative priority to be given to a wide range of social welfare benefits and the narrower objective of increasing sport participation. Third, there was also uncertainty about the contribution that Sport England's participation strategy should make to the identification and development of elite athletes. This policy confusion was exacerbated by the award in July 2005 of the 2012 Olympic Games to London. Finally, despite the rhetoric in *Game Plan* about the important role of partners, it was unclear whether local authorities, which controlled approximately

80 per cent of all public facilities, were Sports England's primary delivery partner or fulfilling some secondary role.

The underlying tensions between the government's (and consequently Sport England's) concern with the promotion of physical activity/exercise for health reasons, the use of sport to generate social welfare benefits and social capital, the utilization of participation as a necessary prerequisite for talent development and the promotion of participation for intrinsic reasons came to a head, though were not resolved, between 2005 and 2009. Early in the new century evidence was accumulating and gaining the attention of politicians regarding the rapid increase in overweight and obesity in the UK. In 2001 a longitudinal study of a sample of UK children found that while there had been little change in the level of over-weight or obesity among children between 1974 and 1984 there had been an increase in overweight from 5.4 per cent in 1984 to 9 per cent in 1994 (Chinn and Rona 2001). Later data indicated that the upward movement had continued and reached 15–16 per cent by 2007 while for adults the rate had increased from 15 per cent in 1993 to 24 per cent in 2007 (NHS 2009). Perhaps not surprisingly, the promotion of physical activity became an important aspect of Sport England's work. Following the lead given in *Game Plan* and reinforced by the increasing gov-ernmental concern with obesity, Sport England stated that 'sport embraces more than traditional team sports' and referred to the nebulous Council of Europe defi-nition of sport as 'all forms of physical activity which, through casual or organized participation, aim at expressing or improving physical fitness and mental wellbe-ing, forming social relationships or obtaining results in competition at all levels' (quoted in Sport England 2004: 4). Such a vague definition is of little or no value in guiding policy as it would seem to justify any activity that raises the heart rate – cleaning the car, gardening and energetic dusting. The dilution of the agen-cy's concern with sport is evident from its action plan, part of which involved developing an 'activity-based marketing strategy' which acknowledged the con-tribution not only of participation in sport but also of 'countryside-based exercise and healthy lifestyles through activity which connects with everyday life' (Sport England 2004b: 20).

Unfortunately, just as Sport England had reconciled itself to being an agency that would promote almost anything as long as the participant broke sweat the policy compass moved yet again. The immediate catalyst was the appointment of a new minister who was concerned to establish a sharper focus for the agency while a broader factor in the reorientation of Sport England was the inter-departmental dispute between the DCMS and the Department of Health about which department had primary responsibility for preventative public health initia-tives. The new Culture Secretary was of the view that the Department of Health should use more of its vast budget to invest in health promotion initiatives includ-ing those aimed at encouraging people to undertake more exercise and physical activity. One immediate consequence was the departure of the chairman of Sport England who accused the government of sending mixed messages and reported that the Minister had told him that participation was now secondary to the pursuit of sporting excellence albeit through the development of community sport.

As a result of this policy change the target of two million more participants in sport by 2012 (set as recently as 2006) was abandoned in favour of a target to 'grow sport participation by at least one million more regular participants by 2012–2013' (DCMS 2008: 8).

The title of the most recent sport policy statement from the DCMS is 'Playing to win: A new era for sport' and was clearly composed by someone with an acute sense of irony as 'eras' tend to last about two years in the DCMS. The policy redefinition announced in 2008 is a dramatic change not only from the policy that it replaced with its focus on the promotion of exercise and physical activity, but also from the policy of the early years of the Labour government which emphasized sport's capacity to contribute to the achievement of a broad range of personal and community welfare objectives. In many ways the current policy is a return to the long-established rationale for investment in community sport, namely that it aids talent identification and development. This 'percolation' rationale was encapsulated in the pyramid model of the 'sport development continuum' used in the late 1980s according to which high levels of participation at the 'foundation' and 'participation' levels were necessary in order to produce the athletes who could move on through the 'performance level' to 'excellence'. Sport England's current strategy document refers to the 'shared goal – maximizing English sporting success' and notes that 'Sport England's role will be to focus exclusively on sport' (Sport England 2008: 1). However, the agency's primary partners are the NGBs and higher education institutions, but not local authorities which Sport England will not work with but merely 'work alongside' (Sport England 2008: 1).

Conclusion

The recent history of sport participation policy in England is one of feverish activity but relatively little action. The core problem is the level of uncertainty, or at least inconsistency, within government about the reason for supporting increased participation. In the last ten years the primary rationale has shifted from contributing to tackling the complex social problems associated with community fragmentation, educational under-achievement and anti-social behaviour, to improving the nation's health and in particular tackling the problem of overweight and obesity, and most recently to providing support for the pursuit of Olympic medals. One consequence of this instability at the centre is that partners, whether NGBs, clubs, local authorities or educational institutions, grow frustrated, disillusioned and cynical.

Apart from lamenting the failure of government to provide policy clarity and stability, it is important to explore why this situation has developed. Part of the problem is the inherent vagueness of the objective of participation. At a time when, in the words of a former chief executive of Sport England, 'if you can't measure it, it doesn't count', the definitional problems with 'participation' are a distinct handicap when trying to demonstrate progress (and are in marked contrast to the use of medal totals at the Olympic Games as a measure of success at the elite level). Conflicts over the definition of key terms and concepts such as sport, participation, duration, regularity and frequency all make data collection and interpretation problematic and controversial. A second aspect of the problem is the absence of a strong voice for community sport in the sport policy arena. Sport England has demonstrated its inability to fulfil this advocacy role as its bends all too easily with the prevailing political wind (or ministerial whim). Whereas elite sport has a cluster of vocal and skilful advocacy groups (including the British Olympic Association, UK Sport, the major Olympic NGBs, and the media) it is hard to identify an equivalent organization that attempts to promote and defend community sport. A third aspect of the problem is Sport England's inability or at least unwillingness to work with local authorities. It is content to work with NGBs and clubs which have, at best, a selective view of their community, but not with those organizations that have the most extensive range of facilities, are the biggest public sector investors in sport and employ specialist sport development staff. Over the last fifteen to twenty years participation rates have stagnated in England and there are few grounds for confidence that this will alter in the medium term. Furthermore, as we move closer to the London Olympic Games it is likely that the government will become ever more preoccupied with delivering a successful event and will have even less capacity and interest in turning its attention and energy to the 20 million adults who do no sport at all or the 11.5 million who participate only occasionally.

References

Audit Commission (2006) *Public sports and recreation services: Making them fit for the future*, London: Audit Commission.

Business in Sport and Leisure (BISL) (2008) *Active Annual: BISL 2009 handbook*, London: BISL.

Chinn, S. and Rona, R.J. (2001) Prevalence and trends in overweight and obesity in three cross sectional studies of British children, 1974–94, *British Medical Journal*, 322: 24–26.

Coalter, F., Long. J and Duffield, B. (eds.) (1986) *Rationale for public service investment in leisure*, London: ESRC.

Coghlan, J.F. (with Webb, I.) (1990) *Sport and British politics since 1960*, Brighton: Falmer Press.

Department of Culture, Media and Sport (DCMS) (1998) *The DCMS comprehensive spending review: A new approach to investment in culture*, London: DCMS.

—— (1999) *Policy Action Team 10: A report to the Social Exclusion Unit*, London: DCMS.

—— (2008) *Playing to win: A new era for sport*, London: DCMS.

Department of the Environment (1975) *Sport and recreation*, White Paper Cmnd. 6200, London: HMSO.

Green, M. (2006) From 'Sport for All' to not about sport at all? Interrogating sport policy interventions in the United Kingdom, *European Sport Management Quarterly*, 6(3): 217–238.

Houlihan, B. (2000) Politics and sport. In Coakley, J. and Dunning, E. (eds.), *Handbook of sports studies*, London: Sage.

House of Commons (2005) *Community sport* (Oral and written evidence to the Culture, Media and Sport Select Committee, 5th April, HC 507-i), London: The Stationery Office.

House of Lords (1973) *First report from the select committee of the House of Lords on sport and leisure* (chairman Lord Cobham), London: HMSO.

Mintel (2007) *Sports participation: UK*, London: Mintel.

National Health Service (NHS) (2009) *Statistics on obesity, physical activity and diet: England*, London: NHS Information Centre.

Sport England (2003) *The value of the sports economy in England in 2000*, London: Sport England.

—— (2004a) *Participation in sport: Results from the General Household Survey 2002* (Research Briefing Note), London: Sport England.

—— (2004b) *The framework for sport in England: Making England an active and successful sporting nation, a vision for 2020*, London: Sport England

—— (2007) *Active People survey: Headline results*, http://www.sportengland.org/research/active_people_survey/active_people_survey_1.aspx (accessed 1 August 2009).

—— (2008) *Sport England strategy 2008–11*, London: Sport England.

Tomlinson, A., Ravenscroft, N., Wheaton, B. and Gilchrist, P. (2005) *Lifestyle sports and national policy: An agenda for research*, London: Sport England.

3   The Netherlands

Maarten van Bottenburg

Sport in the Netherlands has never been a hierarchically governed sector with national authorities acting as an overpowering agency. Rather, sport developed from the late nineteenth century from below through private initiatives of citizens who organized their sport in voluntary organizations (in Dutch: *sportverenigingen*), with local governments facilitating and stimulating this activity. National sport organizations were founded to coordinate the regulation and organization of sport competitions, and for decades they did so without government interference at a national level. It was only after the Second World War that the central government developed ambitions for and through sport.

In the last decades, the national as well as the provincial and local governments have become more strongly involved in sport policy, with increased budgets, aspirations and instruments. Compared to other sectors, however, self-organizing and relatively autonomous networks of civil-society organizations still play a central role in the coordination of sport and sport policies. Together with government and semi-government organizations, and to a lesser extent commercial organizations, these voluntary sport organizations form a policy network which determines the sport governance structure in the Netherlands. In this network, each actor can only achieve goals by building alliances and coalitions with other actors.

To get a more complete understanding of the interdependencies that exist between the actors in the Dutch sport policy network, the following sections discuss the development of the sporting culture and structure in the Netherlands; this is followed by an analysis of the development of government concern for and interference in sport, as well as the rationales, objectives and strategies of the actors involved in the sport policy network. The chapter concludes with comments about the intended and unintended consequences of government policies and initiatives in the area of organized sport participation.

Dutch sporting culture

With over 16 million people living on 3.4 million hectares land area, the Netherlands is a densely populated and highly urbanized country. The country is prosperous and has an open economy, which depends heavily on foreign trade. Dutch society strongly emphasizes equality, with few visible signs of status differentiation, quite informal manners, and a relatively tolerant attitude towards religious, ethnic and cultural diversity. This finds expression in a decentralized administrative power and a policy making process based on consensus decision-making at central, provincial and local government levels, including continuous consultations with industrial associations, labour unions, non-governmental organizations and other political lobby groups (the so-called 'polder model').

These are only a few main characteristics of Dutch society that have impacted the sporting culture in the Netherlands. Characteristic of the densely populated Dutch country is its culture of planning and ordering, based on blueprints and decision-making according to the polder model. Since the Second World War, sport facilities have been part of these planning and ordering procedures. This has resulted in a remarkable infrastructure of sport facilities, with 60 per cent of the population living within only five kilometres of their favourite sport facility, and a unique, extensive network of local, regional and national bicycle paths and lanes (Tiessen-Raaphorst and Breedveld 2009).

This infrastructure – with 32,000 hectares of sport grounds (0.8 per cent of the total surface area) – and the high income and educational levels in the Netherlands are reflected in a high percentage of the population taking part in sport. According to the Social and Cultural Planning Office, which has collected longitudinal data on sport participation every four years since 1979, the percentage of the Dutch population participating at least once a year in sport (excluding walking and cycling) rose from 53 per cent in 1979 to 71 per cent in 2007, out of a current population of 16.4 million (Kamphuis and Van den Dool 2008).[1] At present, 65 per cent participate in sport at least once a month; 37 per cent do so at least once a week (Tiessen-Raaphorst and Breedveld 2009). Older data suggest that this level of sport participation is quite high compared with other European countries. The Eurobarometer surveys of 2003 and 2004, commissioned by the European Commission and offering comparable survey data on sport behaviour in the member states of the European Union, signified that only the Scandinavian countries and Ireland showed higher levels (cf. Van Bottenburg *et al.* 2005).

The emphasis on equality is echoed in limited and decreasing differences in sport participation within Dutch society. Today, more women (72 per cent) than men (69 per cent) take part in sport, which figures were 50 and 56 per cent respectively in 1979. As people get older, participation tends to decline significantly, but these differences have strongly diminished over the last decades. In 2007, more than 90 per cent of young people below 20 years of age participated in sport (outside of school),[2] whereas 55 per cent of people between 50 and 64 years of age and 41 per cent of the 65 to 79 year age group participated. In 1979, these figures were 80 (<20 years of age), 20 (50–64) and 8 per cent (65–79) respectively. The sport participation level among members of non-Western ethnic minorities has also substantially increased over the last ten years, lagging behind only slightly (2 percentage points) as compared to the native Dutch population. The greatest differences in sport participation can still be found with respect to the education and income level of the population, as illustrated in Table 3.1 (NOC*NSF 2009; Kamphuis and Van den Dool 2008).

The relatively high percentage of sport participants is one of the reasons that the Dutch perform quite well in several sports on the international podium: especially in speed skating, swimming, cycling, athletics, equestrian sports, rowing, field hockey and judo (eight sports that account for 94 per cent of all 78 gold

Table 3.1 Sport participation, more than once a year, excluding cycling and walking and sport at school, Dutch population, 6–79 years, by gender, age groups, education and income level, 1979–2007 (%)

		1979	1987	1995	2003	2007
Total		53	59	64	69	71
Gender	Men	56	60	63	68	69
	Women	60	57	64	69	72
Age groups	6–11 years	79	85	89	93	95
	12–19 years	81	82	85	90	92
	20–34 years	66	72	74	77	81
	35–49 years	46	58	64	70	72
	50–64 years	20	31	45	54	55
	65–79 years	8	19	26	33	41
Education level	Lower	35	42	45	51	53
	Middle	62	66	70	72	73
	Higher	65	70	76	79	79
Income level	Lower	41	54	51	56	63
	Middle	54	54	66	70	70
	Higher	62	68	74	79	78

Source: Kamphuis and Van den Dool 2008

medals that Dutch athletes have won at the Olympic Summer and Winter Games between 1948 and 2010); and football (with the adventurous, creative and attacking but sometimes rather naïve and self-destructive playing style of the Dutch national team). World-famous athletes like Fanny Blankers Koen ('The Flying Dutchmam', winning four gold medals in athletics, London 1948), Anton Geesink (the first non-Japanese Olympic champion in judo, Tokyo 1964), and the famous Dutch 'total football' team (reaching two consecutive World Cup finals in 1974 and 1978 and winning the European Championship in 1988) showed the world in the first post-war decades that the sporting climate in the Netherlands not only stimulates a lot of people to participate in sport, but also creates good conditions for top-level sport. The introduction of a deliberate, systematic and planned elite sport policy in the 1990s, with the nationally embraced ambition to rank among the top ten countries in the sport world, has given a further impetus to achieving international sporting success. In the last decade, the Dutch have won almost half of all their gold medals since 1948, ranking tenth in Sydney, seventeenth in Athens and twelfth in Beijing (Van Bottenburg 2009).

Dutch sporting structure

Voluntary sport clubs are the most important framework for organized sport activities – more than schools, municipal organizations or commercial providers. At present, almost a third of the total population, and half of the sporting population, are members of sport clubs in the Netherlands (Tiessen-Raaphorst and Breedveld 2009). Although the percentage of the Dutch population who participate in sport in the context of a sport club has not increased as strongly as the percentage of Dutch people who take part in sport generally, the total number of club members has risen without interruption since the earliest years of collecting membership figures for all national sport associations, as illustrated in Figure 3.1. In 2007, there were 4.7 million officially registered club members in the Netherlands, affiliated to 27,000 sport clubs (NOC*NSF 2008b). As a percentage of the total population, this is probably one of the highest levels of club-related sport participation in the world (Van Bottenburg *et al.* 2005).

These sport clubs are autonomous bodies founded and run by members. In 2008, approximately 1.5 million volunteers (mainly club members, parents of youth club members, and former club members) and 13,000 paid employees (3,600 full-time equivalents) were involved in running these clubs (Goossens *et al.* 2008). Financially, the sport clubs depend mainly on their own members and to a lesser extent on external relations and support: on average membership fees cover 58 per cent and canteen income 13 per cent of the overall budget of sport clubs, whereas sponsorship counts for 9 per cent and local governmental subsidies for 4 per cent (Kalmthout *et al.* 2009).

Sport clubs are generally affiliated to a national sport association. The Royal Netherlands Football Association has always been the biggest sport association by far, with 1.1 million club members in 2007 (which is 23 per cent of the overall number of club members), followed by the national associations of tennis, golf, gymnastics, field hockey, pedestrian sports and skating. The club membership figures of the national associations of pedestrian sports, hockey and especially golf – which multiplied by twelve in the last twenty years – have risen quite rapidly

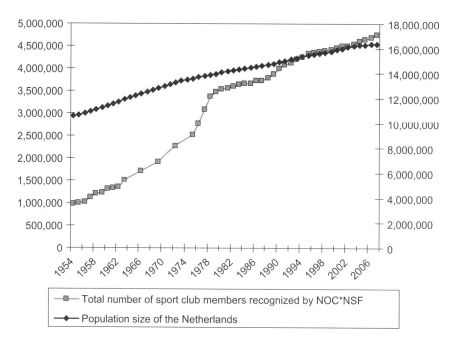

Figure 3.1 Membership figures for Dutch national sport associations relative to the national population, 1954–2007

over the last twenty years, while membership of the national associations of gymnastics, volleyball, badminton and handball declined (Hover 2002; Maanen and Venekamp 1991; NOC*NSF 1993–2007). With respect to non-organized and mainly non-competitive forms of participation, completely different sports come to the fore, with swimming, cycling, fitness/aerobics, running and walking the most practised sports (Kamphuis and Van den Dool, 2008).

Like sport clubs, the national sport associations are private not-for-profit institutions. The bigger ones are managed by a director and a professional staff, under the supervision of a board of volunteers, which is responsible to the General Assembly, the highest decision-making body. The General Assembly is composed of all members of the association, which are typically representatives of the affiliated sport clubs. Overall, these national sport associations spend over €200 million per year on sport for all and elite sport. This is derived from subsidies from the central government, grants from lottery money, sponsorship and, above all, membership subscriptions (from the affiliated sport clubs).

Most national sport associations, which number 72 in total, are united in NOC*NSF. This umbrella organization was created in 1993 after a merger of the Netherlands Olympic Committee (founded in 1912) and the Netherlands Sports Federation (founded in 1959). NOC*NSF is an independent legal entity that pursues its own policy, with responsibilities in both elite sport and sport for all. However, its member organizations convene twice a year for the General Assembly, which is the highest decision-making authority of NOC*NSF, for the approval of policy and budget plans. NOC*NSF also acts as the political interlocutor of the Ministry of Health, Welfare and Sport and has the task of distributing money from the national games of chance (Lotto) to its member associations by mutual arrangement. A part of this lottery money goes to the umbrella organization itself. Besides this, the umbrella organization is mainly financed by subsidies from the central government, sponsorship, and to a lesser extent membership fees and other benefits (NOC*NSF 2008a).

While the system of voluntary organizations still dominates the Dutch world of sport, the popularity of commercial sport providers is increasing. Compared to the 27,000 sport clubs with 4.7 million club members, there are over 3,200 commercial providers in the Netherlands, such as fitness and health clubs, sailing and surfing schools, and riding stables. Of these commercial providers, 1,700 are commercial fitness clubs, which welcome over two million visitors a year. The number of fitness clubs has more than doubled since 1990, while the number of sport clubs declined over 20 per cent during the same period (although their average membership rose from 115 to 177). In 2008, the average commercial fitness club had five times as many members as the average sport club and their average turnover was ten times the average budget of a sport club. As profit organizations, these fitness clubs receive very little or no government subsidies or privileges (Goossens *et al.* 2008; Lucassen *et al.* 2008; NOC*NSF 2009).

The sport clubs and their national associations, on the other hand, are more strongly interwoven with, and – at least partly – dependent on the local and central government. First, most local sport clubs make use of facilities which do not belong or only partly belong to the club. Most of these facilities are owned by the local governments, and rented to the sport clubs at a discounted (subsidized) rate. Second, most local sport clubs and national sport associations receive subsidies from the local and central governments respectively: the clubs most often based on the number of youth members; the associations related to their contribution to governmental projects designed to achieve non-sport policy goals such as enhancing social inclusion, promoting public health and furthering national pride.

The 443 municipalities are by far the most important government actor in the Dutch sporting structure: they account for 87 per cent of public spending on sport, mainly for the construction and financial management of sport facilities and venues (Goossens 2008). The twelve Dutch provinces are responsible for regional planning and environmental matters and fund so-called provincial sport councils, which provide assistance to sport clubs and other sport providers at the local level. The role of the central government is primarily one of coordination and encouragement, although – as will be shown in the next sections – it has gained in significance in sport policy over the last decades.

The emergence of Dutch sport policy

German occupiers first initiated a national sport policy in the Netherlands. In 1941, they made physical education compulsory in all primary schools and commanded that all sport clubs should be affiliated with a national sport federation under the auspices of the Departement van Opvoeding, Wetenschap en Kultuurbescherming (Department of Education, Science and Cultural Protection). The department created a physical education and sport division to implement this decree (Swijtink 1992).[3]

In the context of Dutch society, this was a radical measure that turned the sport sector upside down during the war years. Before 1940, physical education was an optional subject in primary education, while the organization and development of sport were left in the hands of voluntary clubs and associations. These local voluntary sport clubs, founded and run by and for sport-loving citizens, had dominated the sport scene since the adoption of English sports in the second half of the nineteenth century. The sport clubs were relatively stable organizations specializing in one branch of sport, such as football clubs, tennis clubs, rowing clubs, cycling clubs and skating clubs. They operated in a highly autonomous fashion. State influence in the field of sport remained ad hoc and limited until the Second World War broke out. For example, the Dutch parliament had only once debated a sport issue prior to 1939: a proposal by the Minister of Education for the government to act as guarantor up to one million Dutch guilders for the National Olympic Committee to organize the Olympic Games of Amsterdam in 1928 was rejected (Arnoldussen 1994).[4] This rejection did not express an 'initial government antipathy towards sport', as Bloyce and Smith (2010) comment with respect to the United Kingdom, but rather was indicative of disinterest.

This is not to suggest that government involvement in sport started only with the German occupation. It is a myth that sport could have grown from its early beginnings in the second half of the nineteenth century into a relatively popular activity in the late 1930s (in 1938 there were about 400,000 sport club members, while 6,000,000 spectators attended sport matches) without any government involvement and support (Van Bottenburg 1999). From the beginning, private initiatives to practise sport and form clubs to organize sport activities were given space and support by local authorities. In the nineteenth century, several local governments exploited swimming pools and gymnasiums and gave permission to sport clubs to make use of municipal land. After 1900, the bigger cities also started creating and maintaining sport facilities, and somewhat reluctantly subsidized sport clubs to give lessons to the working class in sports such as swimming and gymnastics, mainly to improve their health and hygiene (Stokvis 1979; Van Bottenburg 1999).

However, it makes sense to speak of an active sport policy by the Dutch government only after 1940, at both national and local level. At the national level, the Dutch government stopped intervening in the internal affairs of the sport associations as the German occupiers did, but the government involvement in sport continued at a higher level than before the war. The central government started to stimulate sport as an extra-curricular activity organized by sport clubs (Swijtink 1992). Local authorities increased their investments in sport as well (Stokvis 1979).

With a total budget of less than one million guilders, equivalent to the contemporary purchasing power of €3 million, the scale of central government incentives remained small until the 1960s (Van Bottenburg 2002a). In an indirect way, though, the central government gave far stronger support to the development of sport between 1945 and 1954. During this period, subsidies were provided to local governments to reconstruct houses and infrastructure destroyed during wartime and, in doing so, to promote employment. Out of this money, local governments invested 24 million guilders to create about 750 sport fields and grounds, but as preference was given to house-building, indoor sport centres could not be built with this money (De Heer 2000).

By investing in local sport infrastructure, the local authorities aimed to contribute to the reconstruction of destroyed sport fields and the creation of a favourable living environment. The national authorities stressed the contribution of sport to the 'renewal of man and society' in general and the moral uplifting of the post-war youth generations in particular. In their view, sport offered a meaningful way of spending leisure time – especially for the youth, who outnumbered other age groups by far among sport club participants – and could thus act as a tool to combat what was widely regarded in the first post-war decennium as 'the youth problem'. The central government tried to tackle this problem by supporting the coaches and supervisors of youth members in sport clubs. Thus, the first subsidy provided by the central government in the field of sport in 1946 concerned the training of sport instructors (Stokvis 1979).

The governmentalization of sport

The popularization of sport accelerated from the 1950s onwards. The general economic growth and the accompanying increases in standard of living, leisure time and education opportunities contributed to an unprecedented rise in the number of sport participants and sport club members in the Netherlands. The total number of sport club members increased from one million in 1955 to two million in 1970 and 3.5 million in 1980 (see Figure 3.1). In the 1980s, the percentage of sport participants continued to grow only slowly, while the percentage of club members relative to the total number of sport participants stagnated and started to decline in the 1990s (Breedveld *et al.* 2008).

The extraordinary growth in sport participation in the post war decades was complemented by an increasing willingness by government to invest in sport. At the local level, net public spending on sport increased from 12 million Dutch guilders in 1959 to 385 million in 1971 and 1,094 million in 1981 (Van Bottenburg 1999). At the national level, the government's sport budget rose from 3 million Dutch guilders in 1964 to 11 million in 1972 and 43 million in 1982 (Van Bottenburg 2002a). This sharp increase in spending was made possible by a long-lasting period of economic growth, during which the gross national income of the Netherlands multiplied and tax revenues increased. The tenfold increase of tax revenues between 1960 and 1980 provided the government with the financial means to provide a net of social provisions and services that would constitute the so-called welfare state (Stokvis 1979).

In addition to government subsidies, sport organizations received funding from lottery money, which became important with the legalization of the football pool in 1960 and the introduction of a televised lottery in 1975. Since the introduction of these lotteries, their net profits have been divided among sport organizations (receiving almost three-quarters) and the nation's leading charity in the field of health and culture (one-quarter). These lottery revenues have never been seen as government money in the Netherlands, but are perceived as money from private sources (De Heer 2000). The significance of the lottery money lies in the fact that it is received directly by the sport organizations without interference of the central government, thus making them more independent. This was particularly important after 1994 (see the next section), when the pressure on sport organizations to contribute explicitly to public sport policy goals in return for receiving governmental subsidies increased.

At the local level, the increasing government sport budgets were mainly allocated to the construction and improvement of sport facilities. Between 1959 and 1975, the number of sports fields tripled and the number of sports centres and swimming pools doubled. Moreover, many sports fields were provided with expensive drainage systems which allowed for greater use. In 1975, local municipalities paid, on average, 75 per cent of the construction and operating costs of the sport facilities, while the sport clubs contributed only 25 per cent. This allowed sport clubs to reduce subscription rates significantly and thus contribute further to the rise of the number of sport participants. An unintended consequence of this development, however, was that the sport clubs became more dependent on the financial support of the local government (Stokvis 1979).

At the national level, the same was true for the national sport associations. Government subsidies and lottery money enabled these associations to professionalize and develop their services. Backed by this funding, the sport associations appointed a number of professionals to promote sport participation, develop membership recruitment policies, and support volunteers at the club level, such as trainers, coaches, supervisors, referees and board members, with courses and information services. They also founded the Netherlands Sport Federation (NSF) as their umbrella organization, which acted to lobby and negotiate with the central government on behalf of the organized sport sector, and to distribute government subsidies and lottery money to its member organizations. This subsidization not only contributed to their organizational power, but also created new forms of (inter)dependencies between organized sport and the central government. From the 1960s, the salaries of paid professionals within the sport associations, as well as organizational costs, were financed for the most part by government subsidies and lottery money. In order to justify these government subsidies, the national sport associations had to professionalize their accounting and personnel management, as well as keep and submit membership records of both their association and affiliated local clubs (Stokvis 1979).

The growing interdependencies between municipalities and sport clubs at the local level, and the central government and sport organizations at the national level, changed the balance of power between government and organized sport and created room for the development of government ambitions. Sport was increasingly considered as a merit good which needed and justified public funding. Especially between the 1950s and 1980s, public service positions for sports affairs were created and filled, building up an identifiable new professional group with its own expertise, training, conferences, journals and consultative bodies. With the development of this staff, the government at both local and national level became less dependent on sport organizations in the development and implementation of sport policy.

The development of a new professional workforce in the sport sector became significant after 1965. In that year a new department was established (the Ministry of Culture, Recreation and Social Work). The ideological meaning of this new department was expressed by a leading politician at that time as a 'conscious attempt to break new ground leading from the welfare state to the state of well-being' (De Haan and Duyvendak 2002). Sport became part of this new department instead of the Ministry of Education, Arts and Science, and was thus transferred from an educational to a recreational frame of reference. This transfer was a logical step in the central government's ambition to offer its citizens space and facilities for recreation and sport as compensation for work, with the aim to offer opportunities for self-realization and to prevent heart and vascular diseases.

Working from this frame of reference, the social democratic Minister of Culture, Recreation and Social Work officially announced the promotion and organization of recreational forms of sport outside sport clubs[5]; this would be implemented by (semi-)government bodies at the local level. In doing so, the central government tried to meet the perceived societal need for freedom of expression and informal, casual, non-structured forms of self-development, as well as respond to the resistance against competitive, hierarchical and institutional rules of behaviour, which could also be witnessed in, for example, dance and pop music. As this policy line threatened their monopoly position, it met with stern opposition from the NSF and the sport associations (Stokvis 1979; Van Bottenburg 1999; Van Bottenburg 2002a). Nonetheless, both the NSF and the local and central government came to terms to support two national promotion campaigns to promote 'sportive recreation': Trim je Fit! (which means 'jog yourself fit') between 1968 and 1972, initiated by NSF, and Sportreal ('sportive recreation for all') in 1976, a joint project of

NSF and the central government (De Heer 2000). Interestingly, it was mainly the number of organized sport participants that rose during the 1970s; and this increase had already started before these campaigns were launched (Stokvis 1989).

The politicization of sport

At the end of the 1970s, the government ambitions with respect to sport and recreation in the welfare state were significantly tempered by the worldwide economic crisis. Between 1979 and 1982, the Netherlands witnessed an economic decline accompanied by a sharply rising unemployment rate, heading towards 12 per cent in 1983, and a national debt that jumped in the 1980s from 44 to 71 per cent of the national income. Interest payments on this debt tripled, taking away funds from other areas of investment and burdening future budgets with higher interest payments. To reduce the level of government expenditure, successive centre-right and centre-left Cabinets restructured the government finances, agreed on wage restraint with employers' organizations and trade unions, and reformed the social welfare system. Moreover, they pursued a policy of liberalization and privatization of public utilities and services (Andeweg and Irwin 2002).

In this economic and political atmosphere, public sport policy was given a lower profile in the 1980s and early 1990s than previously. The new political credo was that people had to become less dependent on the government in their sport and leisure activities. 'The minister of leisure is no Santa Claus,' Joop van der Reijden, the state secretary of sport, declared in 1984 (quoted in Van Bottenburg 2002b: 322). Sport promotion by the central government was confined to target groups facing specific barriers in sport participation, instead of the population as a whole. Sport clubs were confronted with frozen subsidies. And sport facilities like swimming pools and sports halls were privatized or run in a more business-like way, with lower subsidies and thus higher tariffs than before (Goossens *et al.* 2008).

It was notable during this period of economic crisis and withdrawing government support that the growth in sport participation stagnated for the first time in the Netherlands. The total number of voluntary sport clubs also started to decline. Their overall membership still grew, albeit at a far slower pace than before (see Figure 3.1). Insofar as there was growth in the 1980s, it came from the commercial sport and leisure industry. The number of commercial fitness clubs rose – without any government subsidies – from a mere 300 in 1980 to around 800 in 1990. This industry continued to grow substantially in the following decades. Moreover, other commercial providers of sport expanded in the 1990s, such as yachting marinas, riding stables and climbing halls (Goossens *et al.* 2008; Lucassen *et al.* 2008). As such, the commercial leisure industry in the Netherlands rapidly moved into a mass participation market that increasingly overlapped and competed with public and voluntary providers, as was the case in the UK, for example (Houlihan and White 2002).

The sport sector was not hit as hard by the public sector reforms during the 1980s as the field of welfare. While the welfare system was operated by professional social workers who were increasingly under attack for being ineffective and creating a 'culture of dependency' among their client groups (Illich *et al.* 2010), the sport sector was not dominated by professionalized bureaucracies but for the most part was still run and administrated by volunteers. The government sport budget was still relatively small compared to other parts of the social welfare policy system. Substantial savings could not be achieved in this area. Nevertheless, the government's detached attitude towards the national sport organizations, and its motion to withdraw its concern for the sport sector, cooled off their mutual relationship during the 1980s (Van Bottenburg 2002b).

To improve the relationship with the government and put sport back on the political agenda, the Dutch sport organizations started a powerful lobby in the 1990s, backed by prominent businessmen and politicians, stressing the societal meaning of sport participation and elite sport. This lobby was reinforced by the merger of the Netherlands Sports Federation with the Netherlands Olympic Committee in 1993, creating NOC*NSF as the overall umbrella organization for both sport for all and elite sport. In several publications, conferences and debates, sport – and elite sport as its flagship – was presented and discussed as a source of inspiration, offering unique opportunities to improve the quality of life in Dutch society (ATKearney 1992; Stam 1996; Van Bottenburg and Schuyt 1996). As has been found in other European countries, this 'sport lobby' received strong support from Members of Parliament and civil servants in ministerial sport departments. These groups articulated a common belief regarding the importance of sport and sport policy, even though they represented different institutions (cf. Bergsgard *et al.* 2007).

This support extended to the new Cabinet that took office in 1994. The new Cabinet was a political novelty, because it was formed by social democrats and right- and left-wing liberals, but without the Christian Democrats who had been in power since 1918. It promised a fresh approach, with a combination of economic reforms, such as tax decreases and flexibility of the labour market, and a progressive outlook on ethical issues, such as same-sex marriage and euthanasia. Erica Terpstra, a former Olympic medallist and president of NOC*NSF between 2003 and 2010, was appointed state secretary of sport. Under this Cabinet, the Ministry of Welfare, Health and Culture was changed into the Ministry of Health, Welfare and Sport. This change symbolized, first, the predominance of health over welfare and, second, the promotion of sport. For the first time in history, the term 'sport' appeared in the name of a Dutch ministry.

Also new was a motion proposed by three Members of Parliament in 1995, to ask the new Cabinet for an 'integral interdepartmental sport policy document, acknowledging the unique chances that sport offers for a well-balanced development of society at large'.[6] This policy document, published in 1996 (Ministerie van VWS 1996), reflected not only a Dutch but also an international tendency in this period to stress the growing social and cultural significance of sport and its multidimensional and malleable character to help achieve non-sport policy goals (Bergsgard *et al.* 2007; Bloyce and Smith 2010). The document strongly emphasized the alleged educational, social, health and economic functions of sport, and the assumed utility of sport as a means for social development, social integration, public health and job creation.

In time, the sport lobby resulted in a substantial increase in the central government's sport budget. Immediately after the Cabinet took power, Terpstra allocated 35 million guilders to the Fund for the Elite Athlete, to cover expenses of officially recognized elite athletes from the fund's interest, and later to also pay stipends to them.[7] Three years later, the leaders of most parliamentary parties promised to double the central government's sport budget after the elections of 1998. Assisted by the strong economic growth rates in the Netherlands, which remained at a relatively high level until 2000, this was indeed effected (Breedveld 2003; Van Bottenburg 2002b). Between 1998 and 2008, the sport budget multiplied by four, as illustrated in Table 3.2.

However, the sport budget of the central government did not rise without significant changes in the distribution and destination of allocated funds. To a large extent, the additional money did not go directly to NOC*NSF and the national sport associations. About 80 per cent went to local government sport projects designed to increase the quality of the local sport infrastructure and to further the utilization of sport for wider societal goals, on the condition that the local authorities themselves contributed an additional 50 per cent of the project costs (Van der Poel 2003). This was partly a way to stimulate local governments to raise their spending, and thus to create a multiplier effect. Indeed, the net local public spending increased from €611 million in 1998 to €895 million in 2006 (see Table 3.2). It was also partly a means of pushing responsibilities down in order to bridge the 'implementation gap' (Kjaer 2004) in sport policy, comparable to what happened in the same period in Canada, Germany, Norway and the UK (Bergsgard *et al.* 2007).

Moreover, in 2003 the Ministry of Health, Welfare and Sport discontinued the institutional subsidies for national sport associations on the basis of their membership figures. The underlying idea of this change was that the government should not financially support societal institutions just because they exist, but because of their contribution to society. The institutional subsidies were therefore converted into subsidies for projects that contributed to explicit goals of the central governmental sport policy (Van der Poel 2006). This switch in policy implied a move to a more contractual-based relationship between national sport organizations and governing bodies. It clearly increased the pressure on the national sport organizations to demonstrate that they deliver (public) value for (public) money (Houlihan and White 2002).

Another change in the distribution and destination of the rising public sport budget was that substantially more money was allocated to elite sport. Until the 1980s, the central government did not develop a separate elite sport policy. An

Table 3.2 Net spending on sport by local, provincial and central government and from the lotteries coordinated by the Stichting Nationale Sporttotalisator, 1971–2006 (in millions)

	1971	1981	1991	1994	1998	2000	2003	2006
Local authorities	175	496	483	496	611	660	813	895
Provincial authorities	NA	NA	7	7	5	5	10	10
Central government	5	19	18	36	28	60	72	118
Total public spending	NA	NA	508	539	644	725	895	1023
Lottery	10	25	21	36	33	33	43	44

Sources: De Heer 2000; Goossens 2008; Van Bottenburg 1999

Note: the amounts before 2000 have been converted from Dutch guilders into euros

illustrative example of this is that elite sport was only first included as a separate entry in the national sport budget in 1987, in the sum of approximately €2 million (Pouw 1999). From the 1990s onwards, however, the Dutch government endorsed elite sport as a policy tool. The elite sport budget gradually rose to €10 million in 1999, followed by a sharp rise to €30 million in 2008.

This policy change started with the establishment of a Fund for the Elite Athlete in 1994 and was followed by a systematic and coherent elite sport policy process directed towards improving the 'elite sport climate' (Van Bottenburg 2000).[8] Initially, the main goal of this policy was to utilize the social value of elite sport, by giving support to national sport organizations, improving the social conditions of elite athletes, and counteracting negative side-effects of elite sport (Ministerie van VWS 1998). Although this policy goal reflected a paradigm shift compared to the government's attitude towards elite sport in the 1980s and before, the government was criticized for its vagueness and lack of ambition. In response to these critics and the public enthusiasm for the historically unparalleled successes of Dutch athletes at the Olympics of 2000 and 2004, the government aligned its elite sport policy goals with the sport organizations. In a new sport policy document, published in 2005, the government declared that it 'supports the aim of the sports sector to ensure the Netherlands ranks among the top ten countries in the international sports world'. As a rationale for this policy goal, the government referred to the importance of elite sport 'as a symbol for ambition, as a source of relaxation and for the benefit of our national image at home as well as abroad' (Ministerie van VWS 2005).

Although the money spent on elite sport increased significantly, its share in the overall sport budget of the central government declined from 36 per cent in 1999 to 28 per cent in 2008 because the net spending on sport for all increased even more (Van Bottenburg 2009). The advocacy coalition for high performance achievement in Olympic sports has undoubtedly become stronger in both sport organizations and government sport policy departments, but other advocacy coalitions have gained influence as well (cf. Houlihan and White 2002). This is particularly true for a cluster of interest groups that urge for higher rates of physical activity among Dutch citizens in the battle against obesity, heart and vascular diseases, and diabetes that are directly related to a lack of exercise. In 1995, a national mass media action plan promoting health-extending physical activities, entitled *The Netherlands on the Move!*, was launched by NOC*NSF, the Dutch Heart Foundation and the Dutch Cancer Foundation. Ten years later, this was followed by a *National Action Plan for Sport & Exercise*. This action plan was initiated by the Ministry of Health, Welfare and Sport and directed towards the adult population that does not meet what is called the 'Dutch Healthy Exercise Standard' (thirty minutes exercise a day).

In general terms, the current central government's sport policy 'focuses primarily on the use of sport for social purposes' (Ministerie van VWS 2005). Improving health (exercise), increasing social cohesion (participate) and stimulating top-class sport (perform) are the three anchor points for this policy. These anchor points should lead to 'the development of a sports society', because 'sport stands for values that the government considers vital', such as leading a healthy lifestyle, participating and delivering top performances, and living in a society where people interact with one another (Ministerie van VWS 2005).

The governmental ambitions to use sport as a means to achieve non-sporting objectives have led to both a politicization of sport (Bergsgard *et al.* 2007) and a widening implementation gap. In the field of sport, this steering problem of the central government exists not only because the ability of central government to give direction to society has been weakened generally (Kjaer 2004), but also because the non-profit and voluntary sport organizations are not established and equipped to meet the governmental demands, and the national authorities themselves only recently stimulated and financed the development of an implementation structure. In that respect, the establishment of the Netherlands Institute for Sport and Physical Activity (NISB) is important. It was founded in 1999 as a merger of several sports development organizations, and has – with substantial subsidies from the central government – rapidly grown into a key institute in the implementation and assessment of sport policy projects, which are mainly directed to the promotion of health-enhancing physical activity outside sport clubs.[9]

The implementation of government sport policy is currently the responsibility of the provinces, municipalities, sport organizations and a range of semi-government and intermediary sport policy and sport service organizations (like NISB) that together form the sport policy network. However, more than implementing the central government sport policy, these 'partners' in the sport policy networks also strive for their own ambitions and strategies (Van der Poel 2003), often leading to extensive consultations to build a consensus on the policy goals and the implementation strategy.

Conclusion

In the second half of the twentieth century, being active in sports has become an increasingly popular pastime in the Netherlands. This increase has been connected more closely to a general growth in the level of prosperity and education than to national promotion campaigns by the central government and national sport organizations. The large-scale construction of sport facilities and venues by local authorities and the expanding infrastructure of non-profit sport clubs and growth of commercial sport providers have been highly important to meet these growing sport and recreational needs of the Dutch population.

Until the 1990s, the main contribution of the central government consisted of the subsidization of sport organizations. This enabled national sport associations to professionalize their organization in ways that would have been unthinkable had they remained solely reliant on their members' subscription fees. An unintended consequence of these subsidies, however, was that the sports associations became more dependent on the financial support of the central government.

This became especially important after 1996, when the central government increasingly came to see sport as a means to achieve non-sport policy goals, in particular to enhance health, social inclusion, national pride and international prestige. This ambition resulted in a sharp growth in the central government's sport budget, but also increased pressure on national sport organizations to contribute explicitly to public sport policy goals in return for receiving governmental subsidies. A similar change occurred at the local level in the relationship between municipalities and sport clubs. However, this instrumental approach to sport by the government poorly matched the raison d'être, principal goals and organizational capacities of the local sport clubs and national sport associations, which were primarily focused on – and framed to – the organization of sport participation and competition for their affiliated members. Their limited capacity to meet the government's ambitions to use sport for non-sport goals generated criticism of the local voluntary sport clubs and their national associations, leading to changes in the distribution and destination of government subsidies and the foundation of a new, powerful organization for sport policy implementation. Interestingly, this instrumentalization of sport was initially advocated by the sport organizations themselves to put sport on the political agenda again in the early 1990s.

A change in the destination of the rising central government's sport budget that did not conflict with the rationale of the governing sport bodies was the increased importance that the Dutch government has attached to elite sport since the mid 1990s. This change reflected a paradigm shift in the attitude of the government towards elite sport compared to the 1980s and before. In 2005, the government even sharpened its elite sport ambition by declaring that it supported the aim of the sport organizations to belong to the top ten countries of the world. Unlike in many other countries, however, achieving this ambition has not been at the expense of sport for all. The ratio between the government expenses for elite sport and sport for all has been quite stable since the mid 1990s at about 25 per cent for elite sport and 75 per cent for sport for all. Thanks to a significant growth of the overall sport budget, the advocates of elite sport and sport for all found themselves playing a positive sum game, in which both lobby groups could win. A fundamental discussion about this ratio has been put off indefinitely; in the hope of an ever increasing sport budget.

Notes

1 Based on a four-yearly household survey (Aanvullend Voorzieningen Onderzoek [Facilities Usage Survey]). From 1979 to 2009, the response groups varied between 13,000 and 17,000 persons of 15 to 79 years of age. A five-yearly Time Use Study, making use of one-week diaries of 1,300 to 3,400 persons, showed that the Dutch spent an average of 2.6 hours per week on sport and physical exercise in their leisure time in 2005, compared to just 1.5 hours in 1975. Recently other, sport-specific research instruments have been added to these longitudinal data; in particular, the Richtlijn Sport Onderzoek (Guideline Sport Survey). According to this sport-specific survey, with a response group of 4,200 persons between 5 and 80 years of age, 68 per cent of the Dutch population practised sport at least once a month (including recreational cycling and walking) in 2008.

2 Apart from sport participation in sport clubs, primary school children (aged 4–11 years) receive two 45-minute PE lessons per week at school. At 40 per cent of the schools, these lessons are given by a gym teacher. At the other schools a regular teacher gives PE. Children in secondary schools (12 years and older) receive PE lessons on average for more than two hours per week, usually taught by a gym teacher (SCP 2007).

3 The same was true for Germany: here too the federal sports associations lost their independence and were incorporated into the German National Socialist Reichsbund of Physical Activities. Bergsgard, N. A., Houlihan, B., Mangset, P., Nodland, S. I. and Rommetvedt, H. (2007) *Sport policy. A comparative analysis of stability and change*, Amsterdam: Elsevier.

4 This would have the same 'purchasing power' as €6.8 million today (http://www.iisg.nl/hpw/calculate.php).

5 This was stated in the first official national sport policy document, published in 1974: Ministerie van CRM (1974). *Nota sportbeleid. Nota van de minister van CRM aan de Tweede Kamer der Staten-Generaal*, Den Haag: CRM.
6 Motion Essers-Middel-Fermida, Tweede Kamer, vergaderjaar 1995–1996, 24400 XVI, nr. 50.
7 35 million guilders had the same purchasing power as €21 million today (http://www.iisg.nl/hpw/calculate.php).
8 The social and organizational environment that provides the circumstances in which athletes can develop into elite sports athletes and can continue at the highest levels in their branch of sport. Bottenburg, M. v. (2000) *Het topsportklimaat in Nederland*. 's-Hertogenbosch: Diopter.
9 In 2008, NISB had 88 employees (73 fte), compared to 41 (27 fte) in 2002.

References

Andeweg, R. B. and Irwin, G. A. (2002) *Governance and politics of the Netherlands*, New York: Palgrave MacMillan.
Arnoldussen, P. (1994) *Amsterdam 1928: Het verhaal van de IX Olympiade*, Amsterdam: Thomas Rap.
ATKearney (1992) *Sport als bron van inspiratie voor onze samenleving*. Amsterdam: ATKearney.
Bergsgard, N. A., Houlihan, B., Mangset, P., Nodland, S. I. and Rommetvedt, H. (2007) *Sport policy: A comparative analysis of stability and change*, Amsterdam: Elsevier.
Bloyce, D. and Smith, A. (2010) *Sport policy and development: An introduction*, London/New York: Routledge.
Breedveld, K. (ed.) (2003) *Rapportage sport 2003*, Den Haag: Sociaal en Cultureel Planbureau.
Breedveld, K., Kamphuis, C. and Tiessen-Raaphorst, A. (2008) *Rapportage sport 2008*, Den Haag: SCP/Mulier Instituut.
De Haan, I. and Duyvendak, J. W. (2002) *In het hart van de verzorgingsstaat: Het ministerie van Maatschappelijk Werk en zijn opvolgers (CRM, WVC, VWS), 1952–2002*, Zutphen: Walburg Pers.
De Heer, W. (2000) *Sportbeleidsontwikkeling 1945–2000*, Haarlem: De Vriescheborg.
Goossens, R. (2008) Economie van de sport. In Breedveld, K. and Tiessen-Raaphorst, A. (eds.), *Rapportage sport 2008*. Den Haag: Sociaal en Cultureel Planbureau.
Goossens, R., Kamphuis, C. and Van Veldhoven, N. (2008) Sportinfrastructuur: organisaties, accommodaties en vrijwilligers. In Breedveld, K. and Tiessen-Raaphorst, A. (eds.), *Rapportage sport 2008*. Den Haag: Sociaal en Cultureel Planbureau.
Houlihan, B. (1997) *Sport, policy and politics: A comparative analysis*, London/New York: Routledge.
Houlihan, B. and White, A. (2002) *The politics of sports development: Development of sport or development through sport?*, London/New York: Routledge.
Hover, P. (2002) *Sporters in cijfers: Ontwikkeling ledentallen NOC*NSF 1978–2000*, Arnhem: NOC*NSF.
Illich, I., Zola, I.K., McKnight, J., Caplan, J. and Shaiken, H. (2010, orig. 1977) *Disabling professionals*, London: Marion Boyars Publishers.
Kalmthout, J., De Jong, M. and Lucassen, J. (2009) *Verenigingsmonitor 2008: De stand van zaken bij sportverenigingen*, 's-Hertogenbosch/Nieuwegein: W.J.H. Mulier Instituut/ARKO Sports Media.
Kamphuis, C. and Dool, R. v. d. (2008) Sportdeelname. In Breedveld, K. and Tiessen-Raaphorst, A. (eds.), *Rapportage sport 2008*. Den Haag: Sociaal en Cultureel Planbureau.
Kjaer, A. M. (2004) *Governance*, Cambridge: Polity Press.

Lucassen, J., Stokvis, R. and Van Hilvoorde, I. (2008) Fitness als industrie: de ontwikkeling van een snel groeiende bedrijfstak. In Breedveld, K. and Tiessen-Raaphorst, A. (eds.), *Rapportage sport 2008*. Den Haag: Sociaal en cultureel planbureau.

Maanen, P. v. and Venekamp, G. J. (1991) *Sporters in cijfers: Ledentalontwikkeling van NSF-organisaties, 1963–1989*, Den Haag: NSF.

Ministerie van VWS (1996) *Wat sport beweegt: Contouren en speerpunten van het sportbeleid van de rijksoverheid*, Den Haag: Ministerie van VWS.

—— (1999). *Kansen voor topsport: Het topsportbeleid van de rijksoverheid*, Den Haag: Ministerie van VWS.

—— (2005) *Time for sport: Exercise, participate, perform*, The Hague: The Ministry of Health, Welfare and Sport.

NOC*NSF (1993–2007) *Ledental NOC*NSF en haar lidorganisaties*, Arnhem: NOC*NSF.

—— (2008a) *Jaarverslag 2008*, Arnhem: NOC*NSF.

—— (2008b) *Ledental NOC*NSF over 2007*, Arnhem, NOC*NSF.

—— (2009) *Expertrapport Nederlandse sport naar Olympisch niveau: Een nadere uitwerking van het sportgedeelte van het Olympisch Plan 2028*, Arnhem: NOC*NSF.

Pouw, D. (1999) *50 Jaar nationaal sportbeleid: Van vorming buiten schoolverband tot breedtesport*, Tilburg: Tilburg University Press.

Stam, P. J. A. (1996) *Sportief bewegen en gezondheidsaspecten*, Amsterdam: SEO.

Stokvis, R. (1979) *Strijd over sport: Organisatorische en ideologische ontwikkelingen*, Deventer: Van Loghum Slaterus.

—— (1989) *De sportwereld: Een sociologische inleiding*, Alphen aan de Rijn/Brussel: Samsom.

Swijtink, A. (1992) *In de pas: Sport en lichamelijke opvoeding in Nederland tijdens de Tweede Wereldoorlog*, Haarlem: De Vrieseborch.

Tiessen-Raaphorst, A. and Breedveld, K. (2009) *Sport in the Netherlands: A short introduction*, The Hague: Social and Cultural Planning Office/WJH Mulier Instituut.

Van Bottenburg, M. (1999) *Van pro tot prof: 50 jaar lokaal sport- en recreatiebeleid*, Dordrecht: Landelijke Contactraad.

—— (2000) *Het topsportklimaat in Nederland*, 's-Hertogenbosch: Diopter.

—— (2002a) Op de drempel van een vrijetijdsmaatschappij: Recreatie- en sportbeleid, 1965–1982. In De Haan, I. and Duyvendak, J. W. (eds.), *In het hart van de verzorgingsstaat: Het ministerie van Maatschappelijk Werk en zijn opvolgers (CRM, WVC, VWS) 1952–2002*, Zutphen: Walburg Pers.

—— (2002b) Ruim baan voor de sport: Rijkssportbeleid, 1982–2002. In De Haan, I. and Duyvendak, J. W. (eds.), *In het hart van de verzorgingsstaat: Het ministerie van Maatschappelijk Werk en zijn opvolgers (CRM, WVC, VWS), 1952–2002*, Zutphen: Walburg Pers.

—— (2009) *Op jacht naar goud: Het topsportklimaat in Nederland, 1998–2008*, Nieuwegein: Arko Sports Media.

Van Bottenburg, M. and Schuyt, K. (1996) *De maatschappelijke betekenis van sport*, Arnhem: NOC*NSF.

Van Bottenburg, M., Rijnen, B. and Van Sterkenburg, J. (2005) *Sport participation in the European Union: Trends and differences*, Nieuwegein: Arko Sports Media.

Van der Poel, H. (2003) Ontwikkelingen in het sportbeleid. In Breedveld, K. and Tiessen-Raaphorst, A. (eds.), *Rapportage sport 2003*, Den Haag: Sociaal en Cultureel Planbureau.

—— (2006) Ontwikkelingen in het sportbeleid. In Breedveld, K. and Tiessen-Raaphorst, A. (eds.), *Rapportage sport 2006*. Den Haag: Sociaal en Cultureel Planbureau.

4 Germany

Karen Petry and Bernd Schulze

Since its establishment, the German Olympic Sports Confederation (DOSB) has published a range of program-related documents on sport participation in Germany: for example, the *Resolution on the Second Way* (1959), the *German Sports Charter* (1976) and the *Leisure Concept* (1976). The increasing social importance of sport was further reflected in 2006 when the DOSB launched an initiative that aimed to incorporate sport into the German Basic Law as a government objective. The Basic Law defines a number of so-called national objectives, such as the principle of a social state, equal rights for men and women, and achieving a united Europe. 'The national objective of sport should be incorporated into a new paragraph 2 of Article 20a of the Basic Law together with the national objective of culture. The wording could be as follows: "the state shall protect and promote culture and sport"' (DOSB 2006: 2). However, whether sport does actually become a national objective depends primarily on the position of the German Bundestag and the 16 federal states that are involved in the decision-making process under the principle of Germany's federal structure.

The first objective of this chapter is to explain the German sport system, in particular the German system of sport clubs and federations, focusing on describing the membership structure. Second, it will examine various academic studies that explore the participation of the population in sport. Third, the role the government plays in terms of support services in sport will be described. Fourth, the Federal Government's main target groups for sport funding will be outlined, focusing particularly on health-related activities. Finally, conclusions will be drawn that assess the extent to which these sport-related interventions can be considered successful.

The structure of sport in Germany

The organization of sport in Germany is based on the principles of the autonomy of sport, subsidiarity (a larger organizational unit provides support to a smaller unit in which there is a lack of sufficient resources, while the smaller unit does what it is able to support the larger unit) and cooperation based on the spirit of partnership. These principles, like the federal structure of the state and administration, are the result of historical processes that extend beyond sport. They are firmly embedded in the political thinking of the German people and are therefore extremely resistant to all types of reform endeavours. The organizational structure of the sport system is also shaped, to a large extent, by the federal structure that is characteristic of the Federal Republic and is a feature of both public sport administration and the structures of autonomous civic or self-administration of sport.

The organization of sport at the federal level has two distinct pillars: one of public administration and a two-tier pillar of autonomous or self-administration of sport. In the public administration of sport, both the Federal Government (through the Federal Ministry of the Interior) and the 16 federal states (for instance, via their Ministries of Culture or the Interior) have joint responsibility for sport in their area. There are consequently no independent specialist ministries of sport. However, sport issues at local government level are the responsibility of specialist sport offices. As a result of the country's federal structure, these public structures do not constitute a hierarchically integrated, top-to-bottom system, as in other countries. Rather, the individual ministries operate largely independently although they do, at regional level, coordinate their activities as part of the Conference of Ministers of Sports of the regions. The situation is different with regard to the self-administered autonomous sport sector where approximately 90,000 sport clubs form the basis of an integrated sport system, as shown in Figure 4.1. The clubs are organized both at the level of specific disciplines (into governing bodies) and at the level of multiple sports (into sport confederations). Integration at all levels is via voluntary membership, in other words from the bottom up. Since the merger of the German Sport Confederation (DSB) and the National Olympic Committee (NOC) in May 2006, the German Olympic Sports Confederation (DOSB) has represented the interests of its member organizations as the sole umbrella organization (cf. Petry *et al.* 2007).

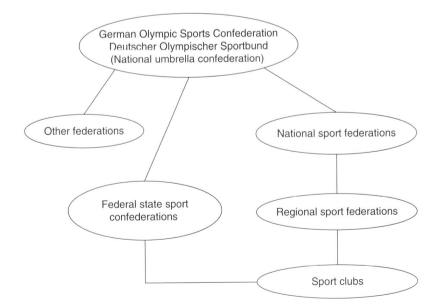

Figure 4.1 Sports federations in the Federal Republic of Germany

According to Jütting (1994), sport providers in Germany can be divided into four main sectors: the government, the market, the non-profit sector and the informal sector. In the Federal Republic, the government is involved in particular in the organization of Physical Education and as a rule acts in many ways as a promoter and supporter of sport. Physical Education comes under general compulsory education (for pupils up to the age of 16 and up to the tenth grade), which means that nearly all children and adolescents in the relevant age groups can participate (cf. Balz and Neumann 2005; Richter 2006). Within the framework of government promotion of top-level sport, there is, for instance, support of top-level athletes in the Federal Armed Forces and the police force by special working conditions. Commercial sport providers, which have gained respectability since the 1980s, are primarily gyms that cater for the needs of various target groups, but also include a range of sport academies (ballet, riding, etc.) and sport tourism providers. However, non-profit sport clubs continue to be the most important formal organizational structure for the population as a whole. Typically, these clubs constitute a community of like-minded people that help their members to develop an identity, and are multifunctional yet non-political (cf. Heinemann 1999). Owing to their special importance, sport clubs are described in greater detail below. In addition, a large number of formally organized sport programs are provided within the framework of companies, adult education centres, the ecclesiastical sport movement and social institutions.

As discussed in a later section, the majority of people who participate in sport do so in an unorganized fashion, although it is not clear to what extent this involves traditional sporting activity or merely recreational activities involving physical exercise. This is where the sport disciplines of swimming, running and cycling are relevant, as they are disciplines in which people can engage alone, with friends or with family members. Unorganized, informal groups are also gaining momentum, particularly as far as new types of exercise such as Street Ball, Skateboard, Parkour, etc. are concerned (cf. Bindel 2008; Schmidt 2002).

The non-profit sport movement in Germany

The system of sport clubs and the non-profit sport movement in Germany as a whole has its historical roots in the German gymnastics movement of the early nineteenth century. Contrary to English sports, German gymnastics was traditionally not oriented to comparing performance, to competition or to breaking records, but was used for keeping the body in shape, for physical fitness, and for the military training of young men. Even though there were major divides between the supporters of sport and gymnastics, a more or less uniform gymnastics and sport movement emerged, particularly after World War II, which helped 'to turn gymnastics into a sport' and 'inject sport into gymnastics' (Heinemann and Schubert 1999: 146–151).

Social features of sport clubs

Unlike companies and government authorities, the majority of sport clubs in Germany are registered and they belong to the voluntary associations that are characterized by certain features (Heinemann and Schubert 1994: 15): membership is voluntary; members can join or leave a sport club without any external constraints; the decision to become a member of a club can hence be swayed by the sport programs offered by the club; if clubs cease serving the interest of their members, they risk losing members; and if the program clubs offer is very attractive, they stand to gain new members.

Sport clubs are not dependent on third parties as they provide their services by and large through the financial contributions and voluntary involvement of their members. The fact that they are dependent on their members ensures that they are not dependent on third parties. Sport clubs represent the interests of their members, who are only willing to contribute resources (e.g. money or time) if this facilitates activities that align with their interests. The decision-making structure of German sport clubs is also democratic. The objectives and services provided by the club are jointly determined by the members and this ensures that the club's financial resources are allocated in accordance with the members' interests. Members exert their influence via their voting rights and not via personal ownership of the club.

The most important resource within sport clubs is the voluntary involvement of their members, who work free of charge and without directly receiving anything in return. The involvement of members in this way facilitates cooperation, based on the spirit of solidarity in the pursuit of their interests. Voluntary involvement enables the clubs to be organized in accordance with the interests of their members. The extent to which sport clubs are being transformed from communities of like-minded people into service organizations has been a subject of debate and, in some cases, a source of controversy, especially in large multi-branch clubs that offer a comprehensive range of sport opportunities for all.

Sport programs offered by sport clubs

The sport programs offered by sport clubs have diverged since the 1960s, with new types of exercise and programs that are not oriented first and foremost to performance-based competition joining traditional competitive sports. In 1970, sport clubs were only offering around 30 sport disciplines. By contrast, by 1996 sport clubs were offering 605 different types of sport. These include fitness and health programs that are part of sport for all (Step Aerobics, Pilates), beach sport disciplines (Volleyball, Football), East Asian sport disciplines (Jujutsu) and sport disciplines that are currently in vogue (Inline skating, Snowboarding). In contrast to traditional membership, for which a fee is payable, sport clubs frequently offer non-members these new types of exercise possibilities in the form of a course, subject to a fee, without requiring them to join the club. In doing so, the sport clubs cater for new and changing sport needs which are less performance-oriented and focus more on aspects such as keeping the body in shape, experiencing fun and enjoyment from physical exercise, fitness, health, relaxation, recreation, experience, adventure, socializing, developing a sense of community and enabling people to experience nature. Sport clubs traditionally provide a range of additional services as a part of the social life of the association. About 87 per cent of sport clubs offer non-sporting activities such as travel, excursions, holidays and other activities (Nagel 2006: 47–48).

Membership structure of sport clubs

The over 90,000 clubs that were registered with the German Olympic Sports Confederation in 2008 had only slightly fewer than 27.5 million registered members, with the majority a member of more than one club (DOSB 2009). About 26 per cent of all women and 34 per cent of all men are members of a sport club. All in all, the differences in terms of age, gender, school leaving certificate and socio-economic status are diminishing. Nonetheless, women, older people and those from lower socio-economic groups are under-represented (Nagel 2003: 165–199). In 1994 (in West Germany only), 35.2 per cent of clubs had fewer than 100 members, 34.9 per cent had between 101 and 300 members, 25.3 per cent had between 301 and 1,000 members and 5.5 per cent of all sport clubs had over 1,000 members (Heinemann and Schubert 1994: 49). Sport clubs with up to 100 members are used by 5.9 per cent of sport club members. Around one-fifth (20.5 per cent) have joined a club that has between 101 and 300 members. Clubs that have between 301 and 1,000 members represent the largest group, accounting for 44 per cent of sport clubs. Of all members of sport clubs, 20.6 per cent are organized in large clubs that have up to 1,000 members (Heinemann and Schubert 1994: 49).

Federations in German sport

In the aftermath of World War II, new umbrella sport organizations emerged in the Federal Republic which replaced the state-dominated sport movement of the National Socialists. In 1949, the National Olympic Committee for Germany (NOK) was set up and in 1950 the German Sports Association (DSB) was established. The NOK was designed to represent the Olympic ideal in Germany and the DSB was set up as the national umbrella organization representing all sport federations. In 2005, these organizations merged into the German Olympic Sports Confederation (DOSB), which means that the Olympic and non-Olympic sport disciplines now have a common umbrella organization. In terms of statutes, the DOSB distinguishes its fields of tasks into general goals, performance-oriented goals and goals that relate to sport for all. Generally speaking, sport is intended to promote personal development, the aim being to achieve equal participation of children, young people, men and women, people with disabilities and senior citizens. It strives to pursue the basic Olympic principles and to support sport science. In terms of sport policy, the DOSB is keen to preserve the independence of its member organizations and to facilitate cooperation with government agencies and international sport federations. It aims to develop adequate sporting facilities and to procure the necessary funds to promote and consolidate public awareness of sport.

In sport for all, the DOSB provides impetus for the changes that seem to be necessary. The member organizations receive advice about club development, international cooperation and promoting sport scientific research. The DOSB presents and evolves the German sport badge, which is a certificate that is handed out after passing a determined combination of physical exercises. In the area of the promotion of sport for all, the DOSB is keen to strengthen and highlight the social integration that participants might receive from sport, as well as the health benefits and enhanced quality of life that can be achieved through sport. To this end, all concepts, programs, models and activities involving all sport disciplines, such as the campaign 'Sport is the most fun in a club', are launched by the DOSB in cooperation with its member organizations.

In accordance with the federal structure in Germany, on the level of the federal states the state sport confederations and federations play a similar role to the DOSB at federal level. The central fields of action of the sport confederations at the level of the federal states involve top-level sport and sport for all, as well as sporting facilities. They are funded mainly by direct government grants or government sources of income (sport stamps, lottery money). The services they render for sport clubs primarily involve running basic and advanced training courses, providing advice, running sport academies, insuring athletes, providing information and forwarding public funds, such as grants for coaches, to the sport clubs (Regional Sport Federation of North Rhine-Westphalia 1997).

Membership structure of the German Olympic Sport Confederation (DOSB)

The DOSB has 95 member organizations comprising more than 27 million members (including people who are members of two or more sport clubs). The member organizations of the DOSB unite 16 federal state sport confederations/federations, 60 national federations of the various sport disciplines and 19 sport federations with special tasks (e.g. German Olympic Society, German Association for Sport Science, German Association of Physical Education Teachers, Makkabi in Germany). The DOSB Board comprises one IOC member and 15 other members. The German Youth Sport is the umbrella federation of youth organizations belonging to the German Sports Confederation and it focuses, in particular, on working with children and young people (DOSB 2009). Table 4.1 lists the 15 sport federations within the DOSB that have the highest number of members: the

Table 4.1 German sport federations with the largest number of members (15)

Federation	Members
Football Federation	6,563,977
Gymnastics Federation	5,006,039
Tennis Federation	1,586,663
Shooting Confederation	1,463,290
Track and Field Association	891,006
Handball Association	842,070
German Alpine Association	782,753
Equestrian Federation	752,964
Federation of Sportsfishermen	653,300
Table Tennis Federation	616,796
Skiing Federation	605,633
Swimming Federation	574,825
German Lifeguard Association	559,987
Golf Federation	552,388
Volleyball Federation	485,815

Source: DOSB 2009: 11

German Football Federation has the largest number of members, with 6 million in total; four federations have over 1 million members; and another ten federations have more than 500,000 members.

Participation rates in organized sport

It took a very long time to conduct nationwide scientific surveys on sporting activity in Germany, which might perhaps have been due to the structure of the Federal Republic. The special importance of local authorities in building sporting facilities led to a large number of population surveys being conducted at the local level on sporting activity, the utilization of sporting facilities and the sport-related needs of the resident population in the late 1980s (Hübner 2004: 17). These surveys were conducted within the framework of local sport development plans, in which a large number of academics and university institutes were involved. This led to a number of different approaches being adopted (telephone interviews, questionnaires sent out by mail, interviews conducted with experts) and questions being formulated (Schwark 1994). A standard survey has not been used, and the formulation of questions still varies considerably. Five currently active teams of researchers in Germany at the Universities of Stuttgart, Wuppertal, Osnabrück and the German Sport University Cologne need to agree on uniform standards (Hübner and Wulf 2008: 144–149), otherwise the results of these local surveys will only be able to be compared to a limited extent.

   The social determinants of sporting activity have been a particularly pressing issue in national level (West Germany) research. Hake's (1959) study found that there was a significant correlation between sporting activity and the profession and status of fathers. Lüschen (1963) reanalysed the material and was able to ascertain that social class and social mobility also had a significant impact. Specht (1960) also identified correlations between social class and profession, most of which were significant. Artus (1974) conducted a representative survey with young people aged 14 to 21 years on behalf of the federal state of Hesse, and determined that social class and social mobility do indeed have a significant impact on sport participation. Similarly, Schlagenhauf (1977) published a representative study of people aged 16 to 65 in West Germany, in which the correlation with social class was for the most part significant. Voigt (1978) found that social class, social mobility, education, profession and income tend to have major impacts on sport participation, while Opaschowski (1987) also identified a significant correlation between the level of education, profession and income. Hoffmeister *et al.* (1992) reported that social class, school education, professional status and income impact on sporting activity. In a study that was conducted on young people aged 8 to 19 years and is representative of the federal state of North Rhine-Westphalia, Kurz *et al.* (1996) documented the impact of social class and school education. In a secondary analysis, Winkler (1998) evaluated the data collected in the German Cardiovascular Prevention Study (representative of people aged 25 to 69 years) and also established correlations between social class and sport participation. Other non-representative studies were published by Opper (1998) and Tofahrn (1991) and also Wieland and Rütten (1991). Unfortunately, no survey on sporting activity has been conducted at regular intervals, nor has a longitudinal study been conducted. Furthermore, a standard or common definition of sporting activity was not used in these studies.

If sporting activity is distinguished according to the various non-school organizational structures, it becomes apparent that one-third of people who engage in sporting activity use sport clubs, making sport clubs the most important provider of organized sport programs. As illustrated in Table 4.2, people who engage in sporting activity through commercial providers comprise 17.8 per cent, while 14.1 per cent use other facilities. Companies (7.6 per cent) and adult education centres (5.3 per cent) play a lesser role. The most frequent type of sporting activity is informal, in which people engage either alone (45.4 per cent) or with others (20.3 per cent). Individuals were able to select more than one type of activity and therefore the total percentage exceeds 100.

A study (Nagel 2003) conducted in 2001 provides the most recent data collected within the framework of a representative population survey. It concluded that sporting activity was influenced by trends in society as a whole and by individual features (life circumstances, lifestyle, age, gender, educational background). German people over the age of 18 were interviewed for the study, which was representative of the population as a whole in the relevant age groups. The feature 'sporting activity' was surveyed based on the alternative question: 'Do you engage in sport regularly, i.e. at least once a week?' By choosing this question Nagel focuses on the widespread broad understanding of sport containing a lot of physical activities like gymnastics, games, dance and play, not only traditional sports. On the other hand, unlike some of the local studies (Nagel 2003: 115), this question does not extend the term 'sport' to all kinds of movement-oriented recreation (walking, cycling). For the entire Federal Republic, it was established that 55 per cent of respondents engaged in sporting activity and 45 per cent were not engaged in sport. In West Germany, the quota of respondents who engaged in sporting activity was around 58 per cent, whereas it was 10 percentage points lower in East Germany. There are three aspects that may explain why this is the case: Most importantly, the quality and quantity of sport infrastructure still varies greatly and conditions in East Germany are not yet equivalent to conditions in West Germany, despite the fact that comprehensive government development programs have been implemented. In particular, the facilities for informal leisure sport and the necessary transport infrastructure to enable people to reach sporting facilities are not yet available to the same extent in East Germany. Other reasons

Table 4.2 Sporting activity (expressed as a percentage of all sporting activities broken down into types of organization)

Category	Percentage
Informal, alone	45.4
Sport clubs	33.8
Informal, with others	20.3
Commercial organizations	17.8
Other organizations	14.1
Companies	7.6
Adult education centres	5.3

Source: Nagel 2003: 155

for the disparity in participation rates include the lower population density, the lower financial resources of private households and the greater orientation to competition in East Germany.

As presented in Table 4.3, the percentage of women who engage in sporting activity (55.2 per cent) has reached almost the same level as men (55.3 per cent). In East Germany, the proportion of women who engage in sporting activity is 49 per cent, compared to 46.2 per cent of men. It is also evident from the Nagel (2003) study that as people grow older they tend to engage less in sporting activity. Young adults tend to engage in sport more frequently than middle- or older-aged people. Overall, women tend to engage slightly less in sport than men as they grow older. However, there are differences within various age groups: women participate slightly less than men between the age of 18 and 29; slightly more than men between the age of 60 and 69; and a lot more than men from the age of 80 (Nagel 2003: 126–132).

Results in the school leaving certificate appears to have only a minimal impact on sport participation: 51.4 per cent of people with poor results in their school leaving certificate engage in sport, compared to 56.1 per cent of people with medium results and 56.9 per cent of people with good results in their school leaving certificate. The differences between East and West Germany and between men and women are minimal in this respect (Nagel 2003: 139–143).

Socio-economic status has a particularly high impact on sporting activity in West Germany, particularly among men. The correlation for Germany as a whole is best described as a U curve, with people in the middle classes engaging the least in sport (46.8 per cent), whereas both people in the lower classes (54.6 per cent) and those in the higher classes (high status: 57.4 per cent; very high status: 67.8 per cent) engage more frequently in sport. All things considered, it is true to say that people with a higher socio-economic status engage more frequently in sport although the trend does not follow a linear pattern (Nagel 2003: 143–147). An explanation could be that especially in the middle classes non-sporting activities (e.g. cultural activities, music, languages) are regarded as more important for individual development and career than sporting activities.

The analysis of people who engage in sport by organizational structure reveals interesting results, as illustrated in Table 4.4. There are almost no gender-typical differences among the users of sport clubs, of commercial providers and other organizations. However, women tend to participate less in informal sporting activity and company sports than men. By contrast, women are more highly represented

Table 4.3 Participation rates of the population (in per cent) by age

Age	Women	Men	Total
18–29	62.2	67.6	64.6
30–39	54.2	54.2	54.2
40–49	51.4	52.7	51.9
50–59	55.5	56.5	55.5
60–69	57.7	51.4	54.7
70–79	51.0	50.0	51.0
80–87	45.9	13.0	34.4

Source: Nagel 2003: 126, 131

Table 4.4 Sporting activities by type of organization (in per cent)

	Informal individual	Informal with others	Sport clubs	Commercial organization	Other organization	Company	Adult education centres
Total	45.4	20.3	33.8	17.8	14.1	7.6	5.3
Gender							
Male	47.4	24.7	35.6	16.6	12.3	10.0	3.3
Female	43.8	16.6	32.2	18.8	15.6	5.5	7.0
Age							
18–29	44.1	19.9	38.3	23.0	18.4	10.7	7.3
30–39	42.6	24.9	31.6	29.2	8.5	9.3	4.3
40–49	44.7	19.5	36.6	19.5	8.9	7.2	6.0
50–59	39.0	18.5	35.5	15.6	13.7	8.5	7.1
60–69	51.5	18.0	33.5	7.8	20.4	6.8	2.9
Over 70	51.9	19.9	26.1	5.6	18.3	1.7	3.9
Status							
Low	48.7	19.3	30.3	23.5	7.6	10.9	4.2
Medium	48.8	19.5	41.5	26.8	8.1	12.2	7.3
High	41.8	23.9	36.9	24.3	13.4	7.5	4.6

Source: Nagel 2003: 157

at adult education centres doing activities like yoga, pilates and health-oriented kinds of gymnastics.

Commercial providers seem to attract fewer people in the older age groups and younger people seem to prefer to engage in company sport. As people grow older, they tend to engage less in company sports and less in sport opportunities offered by commercial sport providers, but tend to engage more in solitary, informal sporting activity. People in the lower and middle classes tend to engage more in solitary, informal activity while people in the upper classes tend to engage in sport in informal groups. There is a strong demand for sport clubs in the middle classes of society. This strong demand in the middle classes also applies to adult education centres and company sports and to a lesser extent to commercial providers (Nagel 2003: 156–159).

Government intervention in sport development

Historically speaking, three phases of government intervention can be identified since World War II, each of which has made a significant contribution to sport in Germany in its own particular way. First, the complete reorganization of the sport system after World War II; second, the ideological battle between sport systems during the division of Germany; and third, the integration of the sport system developed by the German Democratic Republic (GDR) into the sport system of the Federal Republic of Germany following reunification.

New courses of action were needed after sport had been subjected to totalitarian political exploitation and used as a tool for indoctrination under the National Socialists between 1933 and 1945. When Directive 23 of the Allied Control Council entered into force on 17 December 1945, all fascist organizations and all branches of the Nazi sport system right down to club level were disbanded, and any activities by sport organizations were banned. The German sport system was subsequently reorganized from scratch between 1945 and 1950 (cf. Grupe 1990: 18; Nitsch 1990: 21ff.). In the course of this reorganization, against the backdrop of the previous experience of the misuse of sport by a totalitarian state, the key principles governing support for sport, including top-level sport, were developed and remain deeply enshrined in the federal German sport system to the present day. These are, specifically, the autonomy of sport, the principle of subsidiarity, and the principle of cooperation between sports and the state based on the spirit of partnership.

State responsibility and competency in respect of participation in sport

Under Article 30 of the Basic Law, the 16 states are generally responsible for sub-sidizing sport in the Federal Republic of Germany. The main focus in this regard is on the area of subsidies for sports, university sport, sport for all and leisure sports within and outside the federations, and on the construction of sport facilities. Responsibility for top-level sport, however, lies with the Federal Government, with the Federal Ministry of the Interior operating as the specialized department. The latter plays the leading role in the area of state support for top-level sport.

Adhering to the principle of the autonomy of sport, the state interprets its role as that of a sponsor who merely creates the framework that facilitates autonomous sport. For this reason, the government does not become involved in dealing with issues through its own programs or initiatives, but rather by participating in the different bodies involved in the self-administration of sport.

The sport policy of the Federal Government, the states and local authorities in the history of Germany is based, by and large, on the provision of financial support. Lösche (2010) established the following:

> In addition to direct financial support, the government provides indirect maintenance grants that benefit organized sport. These include:
>
> - tax exemption owing to the non-profit making status of sport clubs and sport federations
> - free or cost-effective use of local sporting facilities by sport clubs
> - employment of conscientious objectors and people with low-income jobs in sport
> - the regulation that lotteries are required to spend 25 per cent of their revenue for charitable purposes, 50 per cent of which goes to sport organizations.

The Federal Government continually emphasizes the importance of sport, especially the promotion of sport for all. This is why the Federal Government supports the autonomous sport movement in the certain fields, which will be examined in more detail in the following sub-sections (cf. 11th Sport Report of the Federal Government 2006: 74 ff).

Support for the German Gymnastics Federation

The German Gymnastics Federation plays a special role in the landscape of sport federations, because it is the second largest sport federation (with approximately 5 million members) and combines a large number of sport for all programs under its umbrella. The Federal Government promotes projects involving sport for all in the areas of sport for children and young people and sport for older people (including fitness and nutrition). The Federal Government also helps to fund the German Gymnastics Festival and the Gymnaestrada (the largest international general gymnastics festival).

Youth sports and the Federal Youth Sport Games

A substantial amount of Federal Government funding is allocated to sport for children and young people; the measures are coordinated and financed by the Federal Ministry of Family Affairs, Senior Citizens, Women and Youth. The Federal Government's plan for children and young people envisages supporting the so-called free and public youth welfare organizations. It provides funds mainly for the German Youth Sport, although it also supports other youth associations of the various sport federations, two bilateral youth offices – the Franco-German Youth Office and the German-Polish Youth Office – and the implementation of the Federal Youth Sport Games. The Federal Youth Sport Games has been implemented in schools and sport clubs since 1951, and is the biggest sporting event in Germany (approximately 5 million children and young people take part). The German Youth Sport receives financial support from the Federal Government, in particular for international youth exchange measures (including bilateral programs and youth-related measures). The Federal Government shows special interest in the following projects/organizations:

- fan projects (target group: young football fans of the first and second German Football League)
- model project 'Street football promoting Tolerance' and 'Streetfootball-world'
- module on motor function aimed at establishing the health and sport behaviour of young people.

Women and girls in sport

Women and girls are equally represented in organized sport in Germany although they are clearly under-represented in the management bodies of organized sport (federations, DOSB and sport clubs). The Federal Government has promoted a number of campaigns and projects, including:

- model project 'Women at the Top'
- campaign 'Sport is good for women – women are good for sport'
- project 'Girl's football in the spotlight'.

Sport for seniors and sport for families

Together with the Federal Ministry of Family Affairs, Senior Citizens, Women and Youth (BMFSFJ), a number of projects were implemented in 2008 aimed at including older people and families into organized sport. The Federal Government also used the tool of campaigns and model projects in this respect and supported the following activities, among others:

- model project 'Staying fit at 50 +'
- development of working materials for practical use
- project 'Families and Sport' aimed at developing a range of sport programs with a view to identifying joint activities for families in their leisure time.

Other important areas in which the Federal Government emphasizes the socio-political importance of sport are: (a) Sport and integration; (b) Sport and the prevention of violence; (c) Sport and voluntary involvement; (d) Sport and health; and (e) Sport and the environment. The areas 'Sport and voluntary involvement' and 'Sport and health' are important for the inclusion and participation of citizens.

Sport and voluntary involvement

In the 90,000 sport clubs in Germany, approximately 2.2 million people work in a voluntary capacity (i.e. they work for little or no money; cf. 11th Sport Report of the Federal Government 2006: 93). A committee of the German Bundestag issued further recommendations in 2002 on how to strengthen voluntary involvement (inter alia comprehensive tax and social insurance improvements).

Sport and health

The promotion of health-related activities is perceived as a task that needs to be tackled by society as a whole, in which the Federal Government, the states, sport federations and clubs as well as government and non-government organizations are involved. As such, the following aspects are important:

- The statutory health insurance funds are supported under the leitmotif principle of 'Helping people to help themselves', i.e. financing of permanent measures is not the objective.
- The public promotion of fitness and exercise is based on the principle of subsidiarity, i.e. support is only provided for activities that cannot be financed fully by an organization's own funds.

(cf. Fischer 2010)

Sport federations and sport clubs play a very important role in implementing sport-related health measures and have developed a lot of activities in the past few years. The Federal Ministry of Health launched a wide range of measures in cooperation with the DOSB, all of which were aimed at enhancing and strengthening health behaviour. Prevention measures involving physical exercise and sport were also developed (inter alia, the implementation of health campaigns). Together with the German Gymnastics Federation, activities were developed with the objective of offering high-quality sport programs in sport clubs, in order to help people stay fit and healthy across the country: 'The DOSB has been able to award the quality label "Sport promotes Health" to approximately 14,000 programs and the German Gymnastics Federation has been able to award the quality label "Health Benefit. German Gymnastics Federation" to more than 40,000 programmes' (cf. Fischer 2010).These quality labels are a prerequisite for the costs being borne in part or in full by the health insurance funds.

The national action plan 'IN FORM – Germany's initiative for a healthy diet and more exercise' envisages achieving closer integration among the players in the health sector (urban development, environment and education) in order to reach the sections of the population that do not engage in sport. It is intended to lead to higher participation rates in all sectors: targeting specific groups and providing high-quality programs are also intended to encourage sections of the population that do not engage in sport to adopt a more active lifestyle that involves sport. At present, children and young people are being specifically identified as the relevant target groups for sport programs aimed at health and fitness. Deficits in sport motor ability, poor diet and excessive weight are just a few aspects that are evidenced in today's young generation. Empirical studies show that 'more and more children with motor deficits and health problems (particularly children with obesity) are emanating from families with a low socio-economic status' (Burrmann 2008: 373).

Conclusion

The German sport system is characterized by the strong autonomy of sport and by the self-organization which is a feature of the political system in Germany as a whole. As a result of these two factors, it is only possible to gain a uniform picture of national sport participation policies to a very limited extent. Expressed in positive terms, the system allows individual solutions to problems and issues within different disciplines and regions.

Nonetheless, sport has been incorporated into the 15 states and into their constitutions, while local authorities are fundamental to promoting sport for all. Against the backdrop of the diversity, it is very difficult to manage the development of sport in political terms. The use of public funds is always a subject of controversial discussion in the German sport system, particularly within local authorities. The question of the extent to which government needs to get involved in order for sport programs to be effective (and hence to enhance participation rates) is discussed primarily in the towns and local authorities. The basis for a demand-based range of sport programs presupposes not only a good sport infrastructure but also an integrated approach by local sport clubs, commercial providers and political players.

To what extent can the efficiency of this government support policy in the field of health be assessed? In this respect, it needs to be noted first and foremost that only a very few studies have been conducted on this, which means that the question can only be answered indirectly: Breuer and Wicker (2009) reached a positive conclusion from the results of the report on the development of sport in Germany:

'30 percent of sport clubs in Germany (27,000 sport clubs) [are offering] programs that are aimed explicitly at health promotion, prevention and rehabilitation, thereby making an essential contribution towards delivering health care to the population' (Breuer 2010).

Measurement and evaluation of the efficacy of government intervention in the area of sport participation is difficult. In large part this is because there is no national approach to sport participation surveys, and the academic community cannot agree on the use of common definitions or research tools. This must change if the role of organized sport participation is to be assessed in meeting other social needs.

The political structure in Germany makes it very difficult to talk about a national approach to organized sport participation. This seems to be because of two main features. First, the German states are both powerful and have the responsibility for fostering sport participation. This is allied to the important role that local authorities have. Second, the autonomous nature of German sporting clubs and the federations means that specialized programs are more prevelant than nationwide programs. In this context, the Federal Government has been 'reduced' to a provider of funds. The government has a direction and a set of priorities, but it is not prepared to use a financial impetus to gain greater control over the sport system and direct the activities of a diverse set of organizations, as has happened in other countries.

References

11th Sport Report of the Federal Government (2006) Deutscher Bundestag. 16. Wahlperiode, Drucksache 16/3750.

Artus, H.-G. (1974) *Jugend und Freizeitsport: Ergebnisse einer Befragung: Daten – Fakten – Analysen*, Gießen: Achenbach.

Balz, E. and Neumann (2005) Physical Education in Germany. In U. Pühse and M. Gerber (Hrsg.), *International Comparison of Physical Education: Concepts – Problems – Prospects*, Aachen: Meyer & Meyer (pp. 292–309).

Bindel, T. (2008) *Soziale Regulierung in informellen Sportgruppen: Eine Ethnographie*, Hamburg: Feldhaus.

Brandmaier, P. and Schimany, P. (1998) *Die Kommerzialisierung des Sports: Vermarktungsprozesse im Fussball-Profisport*, Münster: Lit.

Breuer, Ch. (2010) Der Beitrag des Sports zur Kommunal- und Regionalentwicklung. In W. Tokarski and K. Petry (Hrsg.), *Handbuch Sportpolitik*, Schorndorf: Hofmann.

Burrmann, U. (2008) Soziologie des Gesundheitssport. In K. Weis and R. Gugutzer (Hrsg.), *Handbuch Sportsoziologie*, Schorndorf: Hofmann (pp. 368–378).

Cachay, K., Dierkes, E. and Krüger, M. (1989) Menschen im Sport 2000: Inhaltsanalytische Auswertung des DSB-Kongresses Berlin 1987, Tübingen: Institut für Sportwissenschaft.

DOSB (2006) Staatsziel Sport. Positionspapier des Deutschen Olympischen Sportbundes.

—— (2009) Bestandserhebung 2008.

Fischer, B. (2010) Möglichkeiten und Grenzen öffentlicher Förderung von bewegungsbezogenen Gesundheitsprogrammen. In W. Tokarski and K. Petry (Hrsg.), *Handbuch Sportpolitik*, Schorndorf: Hofmann.

Gebauer, G., Braun, P., Suaud, C. and Faure, J.-M. (1999) *Die soziale Umwelt von Spitzensportlern: Ein Vergleich des Spitzensports in Deutschland und Frankreich*, Schorndorf: Hofmann.

Hake, C. (1959) Die soziale Schichtung der westdeutschen Sportjugend und ihre Stellung zur Familie: Ergebnisse einer empirisch-soziologischen Untersuchung unter der west-deutschen Sportjugend im Alter von 15 bis 25 Jahren im Sommer 1958. Unveröffentlichte Dissertation, Karl-Franzens-Universität Graz.

Heinemann, K. and Schubert, M. (1994) *Der Sportverein: Ergebnisse einer repräsentativen Studie*, Schorndorf: Hofmann.

—— (1999) Sports Clubs in Germany. In K. Heinemann (Hrsg.), *Sports Clubs in Various European Countries*, Schorndorf: Hofmann (pp. 143–167).

Hofmeister, H., Hüttner, H., Stolzenbert, H., Lopez, H. and Winkler, J. (1992) *Sozialer Status und Gesundheit. Nationaler Gesundheits-Survey 1984–1986*, München: MMV.

Hübner, H. and Wulf, O. (2004) *Grundlagen der Sportentwicklung in Bremen: Sportverhalten – Sportstättenatlas – Sportstättenbedarf*, Münster: LIT.

—— (2008) Strategien und Erfahrungen mit kommunalen Sportstättenentwicklungsplanu ngen in Deutschland. In E. Balz and D. Kuhlmann (Hrsg.), *Sportentwicklung, Grundlagen und Facetten*, Aachen: Meyer & Meyer (pp. 141–157).

Jütting, D. H. (1994) Management und Organisationsstruktur. In D. H. Jütting (Hrsg.), *Sportvereine in Münster*, Münster: LIT (pp. 136–162).

Kurz, D., Sack, H.-G. and Brinkhoff, K.-P. (1996) *Kindheit, Jugend und Sport in Nordrhein-Westfalen: Der Sportverein und seine Leistungen: Eine repräsentative Befragung der nordrhein-westfälischen Jugend*, Düsseldorf: Moll.

Landessportbund Nordrhein-Westfalen (Hrsg.) (1997) *Sport in Nordrhein-Westfalen*, Duisburg.

Lösche, P. (2010) Sportpolity, Sportpolitics und Sportpolicy als theoretische Annäherung an eine Sportpolitikwissenschaft. In W. Tokarski and K. Petry (Hrsg.), *Handbuch Sportpolitik*, Schorndorf: Hofmann.

Lüschen, G. R. F. (1963) Soziale Schichtung und soziale Mobilität bei jungen Sportlern, *Kölner Zeitschrift für Soziologie und Sozialpsychologie*, 15: 74–93.

Nagel, M. (2003) *Soziale Ungleichheiten im Sport*, Aachen: Meyer & Meyer.

Nagel, P. (2006) *Sportvereine im Wandel: Akteurstheoretische Analysen zur Entwicklung von Sportvereinen*, Schorndorf: Hofmann.

Opaschowski, H. W. (1987) *Sport in der Freizeit: Mehr Lust als Leistung: Auf dem Weg zu einem neuen Sportverständnis*, Hamburg: BAT.

Opper, E. (1998) *Sport: ein Instrument zur Gesundheitsförderung für alle? Eine empirische Untersuchung zum Zusammenhang von sportlicher Aktivität, sozialer Lage und Gesundheit*, Aachen: Meyer & Meyer.

Petry, K., Steinbach, D. and Burk, V. (2007) Comparative Elite Sport Development in Germany: Systems, Structures and Public Policy. In B. Houlihan and M. Green, *Comparative Elite Sports Development*, London: Butterworth-Heinemann.

Richter, C. (2006) *Konzepte für den Schulsport in Europa: Bewegung, Sport und Gesundheit*, Aachen: Meyer & Meyer.

Schlagenhauf, K. (1977) *Sportvereine in der Bundesrepublik Deutschland: Teil 1: Strukturelemente und Verhaltensdeterminanten im organisierten Freizeitbereich*, Schorndorf: Hofmann.

Schmidt, R. (2002) *Pop – Sport – Kultur: Praxisformen körperlicher Aufführung*, Konstanz: UVK.

Schulze, B. (2002) *Sportverbände ohne Markt und Staat*, Münster: Waxmann.

—— (2005) *Sportarten als soziale Systeme*, Münster: Waxmann.

—— (2009) Die Organisation des Sports. In V. Scheid and R. Prohl (Hrsg.), *Sport und Gesellschaft*. 4. Auflage. Wiesbaden: Limpert (pp. 101–122).

Schwark, J. (1994) Kritische Anmerkungen zur Ermittlung von Sportaktivenquoten. In D. H. Jütting and P. Lichtenauer (Hrsg.), *Bewegungskultur in der modernen Stadt: Bericht über die 1: Münsteraner Sommeruniversität*, Münster: LIT (pp. 279–287).

Tofahrn, K. W. (1991) *Arbeit und Betriebssport: Eine empirische Untersuchung bei bundesdeutschen Großunternehmen im Jahre 1989*, Berlin: Duncker und Humblodt.

Voigt, D. (1978) *Soziale Schichtung im Sport: Theorie und empirische Untersuchungen in Deutschland*, Berlin: Bartels & Wernitz.

Wieland, H. and Rütten, A. (1991) *Sport und Freizeit in Stuttgart: Sozialempirische Ergebung zur Sportnachfrage in einer Großstadt*, Stuttgart: Nagelschmid.

Wopp, C. (2002) Selbstorganisiertes Sporttreiben. In J. Dieckert and C. Wopp (Hrsg.), *Handbuch Freizeitsport*, Schorndorf: Hofmann (pp. 175–184).

5   Norway

Nils Asle Bergsgard and Jan Ove Tangen

There is a general opinion in Norway that participation in sport is good both for the individual and for society. For more than 100 years the Norwegian government has taken responsibility for making sport available to both adults and children who are interested. In this chapter we will explain how government intervention has influenced sport participation in general and organized sport participation specifically, particularly since 1990. We will also comment on a range of other societal and political processes that influence the population's participation in sport.

For some sport philosophers and sport sociologists, sport and sport participation are social phenomena which require description and definition (Morgan and Meier 1988; Tangen 2000; Tangen 2010). Other social scientists use only ad hoc definitions to achieve some sort of classification and categorization (Tangen 2004b). For the purposes of this chapter, however, our analysis will be grounded in concepts close to what politicians, sport administrators and sport leaders consider as sport and sport participation. As such, we will base this chapter partly on the classifications and categorizations that are used in different research reports, in order to sort and identify different forms of participation in the field of Norwegian sport policy. A stricter and more theoretical approach to sport participation (cf. Tangen 2010) will not be applied. We will, however, conclude by discussing how a more academic approach to the terms could lead to the realization of political goals.

Before we dig deeper into the details of organized sport participation, the structure of sport participation will be related to the culture of sport and recreation. We will then examine the political motives and rationales for governmental intervention in sport and the implementation of sport policy in Norwegian society; we will claim that sport policies have had only limited success. In the last section of the chapter we will discuss the possibility of changing sport policy so that the government's goal of 'sport for all' could better be realized.

The structure of sport and sport participation

Owing to historical, sociological and political circumstances, sport and sport participation in Norway is rather heterogeneous, multifaceted, and difficult to subsume within a single definition. The term 'sport' is often applied to different forms of leisure-time activities that involve physical exercise. We find it appropriate to characterize the structural properties of sport participation according to four distinctive features: 'what is going on?', 'how is it organized?', 'where is it taking place?' and 'why is it taking place?' This will give some indication as to what forms of sport and sport participation are taking place in Norwegian society.

The term 'physical activity' is often used when researchers wish to say something general and quantitative about the population's more physically demanding leisure activities. When asked 'How often would you say that you are physically active in the form of training or exercise?', about three-quarters of Norwegians over 15 years of age answered 'once a week' or more (in 2007), according to the study *Norsk Monitor*.[1] The level of activity has increased in the last 25 years, as Figure 5.1 illustrates.

With the exception of the mid 1990s, when the rate of participation dropped a little (and the number of people who never participated in sport increased), there has been a steady growth in activity, especially among the most physically active group (those who participate in sport at least three times a week). Females are slightly more active than males: in 2007, 78 per cent of women and 70 per cent of men were active at least once a week. As expected, the youngest age group (15–24 years of age) is most active (82 per cent), while the differences between the other age groups are minimal (surprisingly, though, people over 60 are as active as the younger groups). In a survey of children and youth (ages 8–24) in 2007, the same figures are apparent: 78 per cent were active once a week or more; however, the figure dropped a little in 2009 (to 72 per cent) (Synovate 2009).[2] The activity level is lower among youth aged 16–19 years (62 per cent) than for children aged 8–12 years (88 per cent).[3]

In *Norsk Monitor* the most popular activities for the adult population (15 years of age or older) were 'hiking in fields and forests', 'cross-country skiing' and 'cycling'. Ordinary sport activities like football, athletics, gymnastics, wrestling and boxing

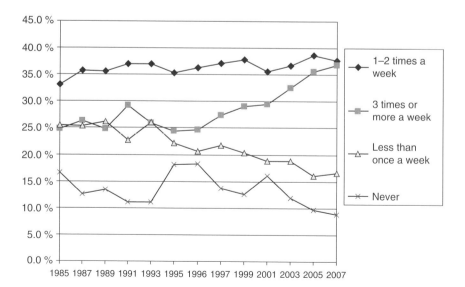

Figure 5.1 Physical activity and exercise in the Norwegian population, 15 years and older (N = 45100)

are less popular. A somewhat contradictory picture is given when the most popular activities for children and youth (8–15 years) are examined, as illustrated in Table 5.1 (Synovate 2009: 28–32).

From the data it is possible to conclude that the vast majority of people in Norway practise traditional outdoor-life activities and exercise, while ordinary sport activities are less popular. The exception is weight training. In addition, when children and youth engage in sports and outdoor activities on their own, they rank traditional outdoor activities and exercise highest, apart from football. Football is also the most popular activity among children and youth in the context of sport club participation, where, naturally, other ordinary sport activities take place. Football is by far the most popular *main* activity for children and youth.

These patterns of activity are also reflected in the organizational frames in which these activities are undertaken (see Figure 5.2). Most people engage in sport and physical activity on their own: 37 per cent regularly practise their physical activity and sport mostly 'alone' (and nearly three-quarters engaged in physical activity and sport on their own at least once in the last year). The second and third most popular contexts are 'with family' and 'with friends, neighbours and colleagues'. These 'self-organized' forms of participation have consistently been the most common way of engaging in physical activity and sport (however, more people are exercising alone today than in the mid 1990s).

The most substantial changes in the structure of the organizational frame during the last 20 years are that the number of people that engage in physical activity

Table 5.1 Top 10 physical and sporting activities among Norwegian adults and children and youth

In the population (15+) at least once a month in the season (2007)		Among children and youth (8–15) on their own (2009)		Among children and youth (8–15) in a sports club (2009)	
Hiking in fields and forests	67%	Cycling	43%	Football	36%
Cross-country skiing in forests and mountains	36%	Skiing	41%	Skiing	10%
Cycling to work or on a trip	32%	Swimming	32%	Handball	10%
Weight training	31%	Football	23%	Dance	6%
Hiking in mountains and plateaus	29%	Skating	19%	Swimming	6%
Jogging for exercise	25%	Jogging for exercise	18%	Combat sports	3%
Swimming	21%	Dance	16%	Riding	3%
Cycling as exercise (on roads/in terrain/ spinning)	21%	Hiking	16%	Ice hockey/ bandy/ indoor bandy	3%
Cross-country	17%	Bowling	14%	Gymnastic and turn	2%
Gymnastic/ jazz ballet/ aerobics/freestyle	13%	Snowboard	14%	Jogging for exercise	2%

Sources: *Norsk Monitor* (SynovateMMI); *Barn og ungdom 2009* (Synovate)

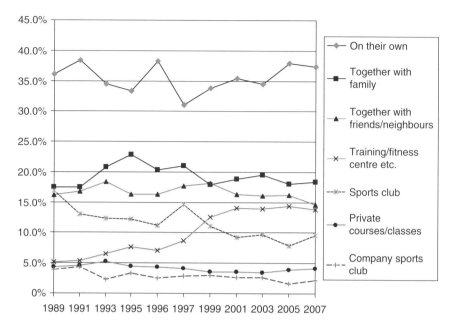

Figure 5.2 The most regularly used organizational frame for physical activity and sport during the last year in the Norwegian population, 15 years or older (N = 18986)

and sport most regularly at gyms or training/fitness centres has nearly tripled, while the number that engage in physical activity and sport most regularly in sport clubs has decreased by 7 percentage points. More than a quarter of the population went to gyms or training/fitness centres in 2007. Together with 'private courses/ classes', this form of engagement could be termed 'commercial organized sport'. Eighteen per cent of Norwegians have engaged in most of their physical activity and sport in this way during the last year, and more than one-third have exercised in gyms or training/fitness centres. The decrease in people engaged in sporting activity in local and in company sport clubs is substantial. This is by far the least important form of organized physical activity. Women are more active in gyms and fitness centres while men prefer sport clubs; older people of both genders are exercising more on their own, while the youth tend to belong to sport clubs.

Sport and exercise have to take place somewhere, and as such this place could be the 'sport facility' (Bale 1989; Tangen 2004a; Tangen 2004c). Most people use 'footpaths or tracks' as their main sporting facility (74 per cent), according to the *Norsk Monitor* for 2007, while 'outlying fields or outdoor recreational areas' are the second most important facility (67 per cent). 'Indoor swimming pool' is the most used ordinary sport facility (48 per cent), while 'ski track with flood lights' is used by 44 per cent of the population over the age of 15. 'Training centre' is used almost as much (30 per cent) while 'facilities for weight training' are used by 32 per cent of the population. 'Football fields' are the preferred facility for 17 per cent of the population. However, some of these facilities, like swimming pools and ski tracks with flood lights, are used infrequently, unlike training centres and facilities for weight training. Children and youth (8–24) are most often using more ordinary sport facilities like gymnasiums/sport halls (58 per cent in 2007), football fields (46 per cent), indoor swimming pools (48 per cent) and tracks for cross-country (33 per cent) (Synovate 2009).

Health is the main motive for being physically active and playing sports. More than two-thirds of the population report that they are physically active because it 'gives physical and mental energy' (68 per cent state that this motive is of very great importance), while more than six out of ten claim that physical activity 'prevents health problems'. 'Fun' and 'experiencing social community' are the next most important motives (40 per cent and 31 per cent respectively). 'Competing or meas-uring strength' is the least important motive among Norwegians over 15 years of age, according to *Norsk Monitor*. Only 8 per cent cite this as their reason for being physically active.

In a study conducted in 2007 on *leisure time and sport*,[4] a sample of the adult popu-lation in Norway (19 years of age or older) were asked if they agreed or disagreed with some general statements on sport. Table 5.2 reports the results, indicating the significance of sport in Norwegian society.

Taken together, the results show that the people in Norway have a fairly opti-mistic view of sport's potential to serve other purposes (utility value), whether this is to build children's character or bring people together. They do not believe that international sport competition creates more tension than goodwill among coun-tries; a slight majority does not want the government to put more money into sport, while they also believe that there is too much televised sport. The interpretation of these findings is that sport is first and foremost seen as a positive leisure activity within voluntary sport organizations, not as a core issue for the welfare state.

In conclusion, sport participation in Norway is by and large initiated and prac-tised individually. This 'self-organized' activity relies only to a limited degree on

Table 5.2 Percentage of people's agreement or disagreement with the following statements on sport (N=1128)

	Agree strongly	Agree	Neither agree nor disagree	Disagree	Disagree strongly	Can't choose
Taking part in sport develops children's character	20.1	60.4	14.2	1.2	0.3	3.8
There is too much sport on TV	20.5	30.1	29.8	13.3	3.9	2.4
Sport brings different groups and races inside Norway closer together	8.1	51.5	26.5	5.4	0.8	8.1
International sport competitions create more tension between countries than good feelings	0.8	6.5	24.1	44.1	14.7	9.8
Norway's government should spend more money on sport	6.0	20.7	30.9	23.8	10.6	8.0

the public sector. The significance of the public sector is substantially larger when it comes to the delivery of sport through the non-governmental sector, the voluntary sport organizations, owing to the substantial government funding for the construction of ordinary sport facilities and for the operation of sporting bodies at different levels. Above all, children and youth are the designated target groups for voluntary organized sport (aged 6–19), and thus benefit from the organized sport system and consequently from publicly funded sport. Less than one-fifth of the population belongs to this target group. Moreover, even if the membership rate for children in organized sport is quite high, there is a downward trend in children's and youth's active participation in sport clubs. The figures indicate that the commercial sector is becoming more important in the delivery of sport; nearly one-fifth of the adult population (15 years of age or older) uses private gyms/fitness centres and private classes/courses as their main arena for sporting activity.

The culture of sport

The value of sport has been a burning issue in Western societies from the time of Solon 2500 years ago.[5] Most of the discussion has revolved around sport as a value in itself or as a benefit for society at large. The direction and intensity of the discussion in the Norwegian context have been influenced by local, regional and national peculiarities, resulting in the country's unique sport culture.

Before British sports and German gymnastics entered the Norwegian scene in the late 1870s, children, youth and adults engaged in skiing, skating, shooting, rowing and wrestling, sometimes recreationally, sometimes competitively (Olstad and Tønnesson 1986). The British, German and Norwegian forms of sport represented three separate cultures. From the time of the Vikings, Norwegians have participated in local boasting matches or trials of strength. From the Middle Ages to the nineteenth century, wrestling, rowing and skiing were popular ways to determine who 'the better man' was. Under the rule of Denmark and in the union with Sweden, target shooting become a popular activity owing to its defensive, political and military value. German gymnastics was compatible with this military value and gained popularity in the larger cities. The strict and orderly regimen disciplined the participants' bodies and minds and prepared them for military service. British sport, in contrast, did not have the same military appeal. British sport was more in line with traditional leisure activities, where excitement over an uncertain outcome, and the possibility of winning and earning the opponent's esteem and recognition, were the ultimate goals. British sport also emphasized competition, training and breaking records. Clubs and associations were established for all these forms of sport. With these three sport cultures as a basis, and mixed with rural–urban differences, political ideologies and a growing tendency to organize leisure time activities in voluntary organizations, a unique sport culture developed in Norway.

In this context two antagonistic poles or cultures strengthened in the course of the nineteenth century (Bergsgard 2005). One culture was found in the regions or rural areas, emphasizing sport for all and versatility, which focused on the use of sport for national defence, health and social benefits. The other was more centralized, had its foothold in the cities, and focused on more specialized and elite sport. These poles found themselves organizational frames in nationwide federations: 'Centralforeningen for Udbredelse av Legemsøvelser og Vaabenbrug' (CF, Central Federation for Bodily Movements and the Use of Arms) was established in 1861. 'Norges Riksforbund for Idræt' (Norwegian Sports Federation) was established in 1910. The latter, together with specialized federations for different sports, were advocates for elite sports. The disagreement was seemingly solved when they joined forces and merged into one confederation, 'Landsforbundet for Idræt' (National Confederation of Sport), in 1919.

Between the First and Second World Wars, a new separation took place. This time the disagreements were grounded in political and ideological differences. The middle class, or bourgeoisie, dominated the National Confederation of Sport. The working class did not see this federation as fit for their sport participation and their goals, so the 'Arbeidernes idrettsforbund' (AIF, Workers Sports Movement) was established in 1924. Some historians, including Olstad & Tønneson (1986), have viewed the AIF as a continuation of the CF's sport ideology with regard to the utilitarian aspect of sport. After the Second World War, in 1946, the more bourgeois sport association (National Confederation of Sport) and the Workers Sports Movement merged into a new organization, the 'Norges idrettsforbund' (NIF, Norwegian Confederation of Sport). This organization assumed an important role in the emerging social-democratic welfare state.

However, the two cultures remained and in a way were institutionalized in the new organization (Bergsgard 2005). They now took the form of two administrative pillars within the organization. One pillar consisted of the central administration of NIF and the regional confederations responsible for sport for all and servicing the clubs. The other pillar consisted of the specialized sport federations, on both the national and regional levels, the tasks of which were to popularize and promote the sport. These opposing cultures seethed in the organization, competing for legitimacy and power. When the Norwegian Confederation of Sport and the Norwegian Olympic Committee merged in 1996, all organized competitive sport, at the elite or grass roots level, fell under its auspices. Sport in Norway became synonymous with organized sport within the Norwegian Confederation of Sport and Olympic Committee (NIF). Other forms of sport participation became what sport leaders, politicians and social scientists called 'un-organized'. In reality, the term just described the activity taking place outside the NIF. As we discussed previously, the participation rate in self-organized sport activity is quite high, and has in some cases been connected to organizations that have not been able to mobilize any large public support or significant organizational weight.

This pragmatic situation had political implications. The dominance of a single organization in the field of sport, as in many in other spheres (Mangset 1992; Mangset and Rommetvedt 2002), has given the NIF a virtual monopoly to represent sport. The NIF became *the* symbol of how sport should be carried out and organized. Those who disagreed achieved neither attention nor money and therefore remained marginal. The NIF had the hegemonic power to define what kinds of facilities were necessary for participation in sport, not only for their members but for the population at large. Facilities for organized sports within the NIF were prioritized by the public authorities at the expense of facilities more suitable to the less skilled population.

Four values serve as guidelines for sport policy in Norway: (1) sport should contribute to health and wellbeing; (2) sport should be for all; (3) sport facilities should facilitate sport; and (4) elite sport creates sport for all. Traces of these values can be found in policy documents and official speeches, both of sport bodies and of public administration and in the statements of politicians. In its most recent policy document, the NIF stated that sporting activities should be based on joy, community, health and honesty (NIF 2007: 6). The government, in the first White Paper on sport in 1991 (St. meld. 41 1991–92), noted: 'The utility value of sport from the government's point of view is related to the health perspective. The positive effect of physical activity as a part of preventive health work contributes to strengthen the legitimacy of government support' (p. 8; our translation). Its second White Paper stated that sport and physical activity for all is the superior vision for government sport policy (St. meld. 14 1999–2000). This vision is also the mission of the NIF: 'The Norwegian Confederation of Sport should be the leading contributor to achieve "sport for all"' (NIF 2007: 5). The values of sport for health and sport for all are mirrored in plans and documents on the municipal level in Norway; however, local sport is to a large degree linked to other issues in a cross-sectoral perspective (Opedal and Bergsgard 2009; Tangen and Rafoss 2009).

Sport facilities are considered to be the major vehicle for the realization of the values of government and the NIF. In its White Paper from 1999 the government underscored that the goal for the building of sport facilities is that it should contribute to sport for all (St. meld. 14, 1999–2000). The premise for this view was that 'the more facilities the more activity is created'. This understanding has roots in the beginning of the twentieth century, and became an accepted 'truth' both in the new organization in 1946 and the new Government Office for Youth and Sport (STUI). When the Minister of Culture, Trond Giske, stated at a sport conference in 2007 that 'more facilities means more activity', few if any in the audience doubted him. To many, he was only stating an obvious relationship.[6] To the majority, the understanding that elite sports create sport for all is similarly obvious. At least it could be seen as an attempt to build a bridge between the two cultures that is embedded in the Norwegian Confederation of Sport. However, the professionalization and commercialization of sport, and the distance between these two forms of sport participation, have increased. This has been documented by Bergsgard (2005); according to some the relationship between elite sport and sport for all is a kind of double-entry bookkeeping: 'You say something and do something else.' This holds for the top administrative level and for the club level. At the club level this is evident in the dilemma of paying salaries to athletes and coaches on elite teams when members do enormous amounts of volunteer work to keep children and youth active.

In conclusion, the culture of sport became the culture of a single sport organization. Some forms of sport participation, like gymnastics and shooting, have more or less disappeared. Others, like outdoor recreation, still hold a strong position in the daily life of the population, but never acquired the strong organizational basis that would regulate and strengthen the activity and facilitate cooperation with the authorities in any significant way.

Organized sport participation

To take part in organized sport, one has to be a member of a club. Membership gives the member the right to engage in certain activities, the right to use certain sport facilities and the right to compete against others. In 1999, 35 per cent of Norwegians claimed to belong to the NIF (Vaage 1999). Since 2005 over 2 million memberships have been registered in the NIF. In 2008, nearly 40 per cent of the members were women (NIF 2008).

As will be explained later, both the authorities and the sport organization (NIF) consider children and youths as target groups for organized sport participation. How are children and youth represented in the organization? Twenty-one per cent of the members in 2007 were 6–12 years of age, according to Statistics Norway.[7] The age group 13–19 years makes up 16 per cent. The adult group (20 years old or over) makes up 60 per cent of the memberships.[8] Still, when the active members in the sport federations are considered, approximately half of them are under the age of 20, and this indicates that the younger people are more active than the older. As mentioned above, 14 per cent of the Norwegian population above 15 years of age train and compete in a sport club.

In 2007, 86 per cent of children and youth in Norway belonged to a sport club (compared with approximately 40 per cent in the 1970s). However, double and triple memberships are included. The survey from Synovate shows that 53 per cent of children aged 8 to 15 years old and 25 per cent of youth aged 16 to 19 years old exercised and competed in a sport clubs in 2009 (Synovate 2009: 19). These numbers have dropped by 7 and 12 per cent respectively since 1992. In the last seven years the decline seems to have stopped; 53 per cent of children between 8 and 15 years old exercised and competed in sport clubs in 2009 compared to 46 per cent in 2002.

The organized sporting activity takes place by and large in 7,760 local sport clubs. In addition there are approximately 4,176 company sport clubs (NIF 2008). The vast majority of sport clubs are relatively small: in 2000, 54 per cent had fewer than 100 members, while 10 per cent had more than 500 (Enjolras and og Seippel 2001). Approximately 70 per cent of the clubs are organized around only one sport, while the remaining 30 per cent are multi-sport associations (Skirstad 2002).

Single-sport clubs and specific sport disciplines in the multi-sport associations are members of 55 national sport federations such as the Norwegian Football Federation, the Norwegian Golf Federation and so forth. On average these federations organize 27,000 members, according to Statistics Norway.[9] Football is by far the largest federation, followed by skiing, corporate or company sport, golf, handball and gymnastics. The five largest specialist federations (company sport excluded) account for nearly half the total amount of members in all the federations. The other pillar in the Norwegian sport system is the 19 regional confederations of sport clubs. Both the 55 federations and the 19 regional confederations are members of the NIF.

Government intervention

In sport policy, as in other political sectors in Norway (Nordby 2000; Slagstad 1998), it is fair to say that power has been concentrated in the hands of the executive. When the Money Game Act was adopted and the National Gaming Corporation (*Norsk Tipping*) was established in 1946, it was decided that the gaming profits earmarked for sport should not be included in the fiscal budget of the state. Consequently, decisions regarding financial allocations to sport organizations were made at the Ministerial level and not by the Norwegian Parliament.

From 1950 to 1982, sport policy was the responsibility of the Office for Youth and Sport under the Ministry of Education and the Ministry of Culture. Today the main responsibility for public sport policy is concentrated in the hands of the Ministry of Culture and Church Affairs, specifically in the Ministry's Department of Sport Policy. It should be noted that most Ministers of Cultural Affairs have shown little interest in sport policy and consequently the sport bureaucrats in the Ministry, in collaboration with the NIF/NOC, have assumed the dominant role. In fact, some of the leading bureaucrats of the sport department of the Ministry have been de facto Ministers of Sport, partly because of the political leaders' lack of interest and knowledge, and partly because of the strong personalities of some of the deputy secretaries at the sport department (Bergsgard 2005; Goksøyr *et al.* 1996; Olstad and Tønnesson 1986). In summary, national sport policy is dominated by the Department of Sport Policy within the Ministry of Cultural Affairs and, with some important exceptions, Parliament plays a minor role.

Until 2002, nearly 20 billion NOK had been allocated from gaming profits to sport, and in the last few years the annual average allocation has been 1.2 billion NOK. The gaming/lottery profits are the primary source of revenue for the Norwegian Olympic and Paralympic Committee and the Confederation of Sport. Since the 1990s, between 80 and 90 per cent of the NIF's income has come as revenue support from gaming profits (Bergsgard 2005; Enjolras 2004). Gaming profit also accounts for a substantial proportion of the total budget of some national sport federations. Although the average contribution is only 10 per cent of the income, for one-third of the national sport federations gaming profit accounts for as much as 70 per cent (Enjolras 2004). The central government is also a significant contributor to the development of sport facilities across the country, with around 20 per cent of capital support coming from lottery money, which is often used to leverage additional funding from local authorities, the sport clubs themselves or commercial interests (Dåsnes and Langkaas 1997).

The discussion above focused on the national level, but in the Norwegian political system there are two other governmental levels: the counties (*fylker*) and the municipalities. Although counties are marginal to the sport policy process and to the delivery of sport services, the same is not true of the municipalities. The municipalities support sport with around 1.5 billion NOK, both as capital support for building facilities and as revenue support to cover the running expenses of sport clubs (Opedal and Rommetvedt 2007). The municipalities also own about half the sport facilities, and are the dominant actor when it comes to building and operating bigger and more expensive facilities (Dåsnes and Langkaas 1997; KKD 2003). Municipal financial support accounts for around 55 per cent of the total public support for sport.

In the mid nineteenth century, defence requirements legitimized public involvement and support for sport in Norway. However, from 1929, responsibility for sport was given to the Ministry of Social Affairs, and social and health benefits became the dominant public motive for supporting sport (Goksøyr 1992). After World War II, public support for sport was related to sport's function of cultivating good citizens. Later, in the 1970s, sport became a part of the 'extended concept of culture' (Mangset 1992). The essential perception of sport that legitimizes public support is the phrase 'sport for all' or 'the opportunity for as many as possible to have equal access to sport', as stated in the first White Paper on culture in 1973, which also included sport (cited in Olstad and Tønnesson 1986: 282, vol. 2, authors' translation).

As we stated earlier, the utility value of sport exemplified by its prominence in volunteer work, its role in the social development of children and especially its capacity to generate health benefits is highlighted by the government. However, the intrinsic value of sport is emphasized as the utility value by the government: 'Sport is legitimized both by its intrinsic value and its utility value. This implies that sport is both an end and a means' (St. meld. nr. 41, 1991–92: 12). The second and most recent government report on sport was titled *Sporting life in transformation – Concerning the government's relation to sport and physical activity* (St. meld 14 1999–2000). Its introduction explains why the government has to justify its involvement in sport: 'Previously sport was seen as a united movement. A detailed definition of the motives for government participation in the area of sport has consequently been seen as unnecessary. Today this unity is under pressure from internal and external forces which has resulted in a more ambiguous picture of sport' (p. 5). Thus, to realize the vision of sport and physical activity for all, and to fulfil the government's responsibility to facilitate the possibility for each individual to do sport, as it is emphasized in the two White Papers on sport, sports carried out in local membership clubs and self-organized sport should be supported: it is 'important that government money also contributes to secure the possibility for self-organized physical activity in the population' (St. meld. 14 1999–2000). In other words, the policies that deal with organized sport participation and those that deal with informal or unstructured physical activity are strongly connected. They are, so to speak, two sides of the same coin.

In summary, the implementation of the policy of sport rests on a division of labour among the state, the NIF, and the municipalities. The government considers both organized and unorganized sport participation as their responsibility. The building of sport facilities is the main political instrument in this policy; as Bergsgard *et al.* (2009: 128) phrased it: 'The policy of sports equates the policy of sport facilities.'

Policy success?

Whether or not sport participation policies have been a success in Norway is a matter of dispute. The fact that almost three-quarters of the population participates regularly in sport and physical activity should be indicative of success. On the other hand, only 10 to 15 per cent of the population above 15 years of age participates in organized sport, even though the government prioritizes organized sports and builds sporting facilities that are most suited to organized sports. It is also questionable whether the large decline in participation in organized sports among children and youths indicates a successful sport policy. To estimate the success of policy implementation more in depth, we will take a closer look at three important issues: Do sport facilities increase sport participation? Will participation in organized sport result in lasting physical activity habits? Are the procedures and decision-making processes behind the planning and building of sport facilities best suited for the realization of the governmental goals? Answers to these questions are indicative of the success of government policies.

As pointed out earlier, the most important policy instrument for the government is the financing and building of sport facilities: national government funding has increased from about NOK 340,000,000 in 1985 to more than NOK 650,000,000 in 2005, an increase of 95 per cent (see Figure 5.3). In the same period the activity rate has risen from 57 per cent to 74 per cent, an increase of 30 per cent (Tangen 2007).

Behind this funding lies the strong assumption that facilities create activity. There is, however, no such simple connection between the number of facilities in Norwegian society and the participation rates in the population. Facilities for football make up more than a quarter of all sport facilities in Norway, but only 7 per cent of the population (15 years of age or older) uses this kind of facility at least once a week. By contrast, more than one-third of the population uses footpaths regularly. However, these facilities account for only 13 per cent of all sport facilities (Rafoss and og Breivik 2005; Tangen 2007). There are 652 multi-sport halls in Norway, one for every 5,588 people. There are 1,204 public swimming pools, one for every 3,024 people. In comparison, there are 4,329 football fields, one for every 841 people. If we divide the number of these sport facilities by the number of people who use these facilities regularly, we find that there are 586 active users per multi-sport hall, 230 per swimming pool and 49 per football field (Rafoss and og Breivik 2005). In other words, even accounting for differences in the amount of people who can use a particular type of sport facility at any one time, there is a strong discrepancy between the number of facilities and the number of people using them. From this perspective, the sport facilities do not reflect the population's activities and needs, which the White Paper from 1999–2000 stated was the main goal in the construction of sport facilities.

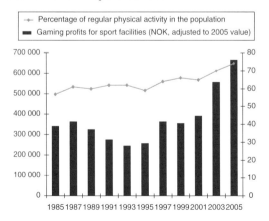

Figure 5.3 Gaming profits to sport facilities versus activity rates in Norway, 1985–2005

A key pillar of the Norwegian sport policy is the role of sport clubs; the clubs should run the activities and create a lasting interest in sport and physical activity. Some studies indicate that joining a sport club at an early age increases the probability of being physically active in adulthood (Kjønniksen 2008; Kjønniksen and Wold 2007). These studies focused on how to establish good habits, and concluded that sport organizations offer some possibilities of establishing such habits. They do not, however, appear to take into consideration the selection process that is involved in organized sports. As young athletes mature, they are expected to train more and more often and teams are chosen on the basis of skills and performance. Studies indicate that those who are born in the beginning of a year are more likely to end up in the elite squad than those who are born at the end of the same year ('The Relative Age Effect') (Helsen *et al.* 2005; Munsch and Hay 1999). Those who are benched or who underperform will, in due time, withdraw from organized sport (Peterson 2003; Tangen 2004b; Tangen 2010). It is no surprise that those who have enjoyed or endured the demands and expectations of organized sport for some years will continue to participate in sport in one way or another. Those who have less positive experiences will probably not take up informal and self-organized sports because 'sport' for them may very well be synonymous with 'organized sports'. From this perspective, the Norwegian Confederation of Sport might not be the best partner if the goals of sport for all and better health through physical activity are to be reached.

In addition to the selection effect inside organized sport, there may be a selection effect on another level. Among children it is roughly one-third who do not take part in any organized sport at all. It is reasonable to assume that this third are basically less active than the two-thirds who do take part. It also reasonable to assume that the one-third that continue in organized sport beyond the first year as teenagers are basically more active than the others. If this is the case, the effect of participation in organized sport can at best be seen as an intermediate variable with limited explanatory power or at worst as a spurious explanation.

Since the beginning of the twentieth century, the relationship between the state, the sport confederations and the local municipalities has been characterized by conflicts, compromises and consensus (Bergsgard 2005; Rafoss 2009). In the last three decades the dealings between the NIF and the government assumed the characteristics of a 'family relationship' (Selle and Øymyr 1995). A rather strict and formal procedure was established for regulating the planning and building of sport facilities if government money was used for the project. Studies indicate, however, that informal and closed channels of influence have emerged with large consequences for which and what kind of sport facilities are actually built (Bergsgard *et al.* 2009; Nenseth *et al.* 2006; Rafoss 2006). There has been a displacement from government to governance and from formal to informal political influence in Norwegian sport policy. The local club has become a pivot point in the construction of a network and lobbying to reach political goals. As Bergsgard *et al.* (2009) underscore, such a network or growth of coalitions is most effective when it works quietly and behind closed doors. Using the concepts 'light and dark social capital' from Kamberidou and Patsadaras (2007), Tangen and Rafoss (2009) argued that local sport clubs and national sport organizations can dramatically change the political decision process behind the building of sport facilities. This is done partly using light social capital (forging bonds among members and building bridges to the local community), and partly using dark social capital (using the positive value of sport for all to realize a sport facility for the local football team that plays in the upper division). The change from formal to more informal politics may threaten the democratic processes, both in sport and in society.

Conclusion

As shown, sport and physical activity are mainly self-organized activities in Norway; the commercial sector's role as an arena for participation in sport is increasing, while the role of voluntary sport clubs is decreasing. Children and youth are the main target groups for the organized sport movement. The focus on children and youth is also reflected in the government's involvement in sport, by and large organized sport, even though self-organized activity also is highlighted. In this context it is a paradox that since 1992 the training and exercise rates within sport clubs have dropped among children and youths.

It could be argued that the government's sport policy excludes the adult population. Still, the sport policy and government intervention through voluntary sport has made physical activity and health important goals. Building sport facilities seems to stimulate some increase in sport participation, but maybe not to the extent one could expect based on the large amount of money spent on facilities that do not serve the entire population. The political instrument of building sport facilities is beneficial for organized sports; organized sports have facilities that are suitable for producing more competitive sports and elite athletes. This contradicts the goal of physical activity and health and sport for all. Most people choose facilities like 'footpaths and tracks' and 'outfields' and 'areas for outdoor life' for their sporting activity. The time has come to discuss which sport facilities will increase the sport participation rates both inside and outside the framework of organized sports.

It is also doubtful whether or not organized sports participation leads to a lasting interest in sports. Organized sports contribute to the political goal of sport for all, however just to a limited degree. Thus, in our opinion, it is time for a discussion on whether the established division of labour in sport policy is suitable with regard to the growing problem of poor health caused by physical inactivity. We also have to discuss whether other ways of organizing sport and physical activity are more appropriate with regards to increasing participation rates in the population. The close relationship between voluntary organized sport and the government is based on a historical course of events. Should this close relationship be untied? Could a vision of sport and physical activity for all be reached through organizational frames other than organized sport?

The prevailing view among sport politicians and sport leaders also has to change. To most politicians, sport administrators and even sport leaders, 'sport' is 'sport' and 'sport facilities create more activity'. They seem to consider it a waste of time to discuss what sport is and what it is not or how sport facilities work. They are rather pragmatic about what is meant by these terms and are less interested in provoking a contentious and time-consuming discussion. We think that the time is ripe for more reflection and discussion among these agents. This may be difficult since the old proverb '*Facta non verba*' ('deeds, not words') seems still to be greatly valued among these agents.

Notes

1 The data presented are from a study called *Norsk Monitor*. This is a survey that has been administered by SynovateMMI every second year since 1985. SynovateMMI bear no responsibility for the analysis or interpretation of data carried out here.
2 These figures are from Synovates' study of children and youth *(Rapport Barn og ungdom 2009, Synovate 14th of Mai)*.
3 The figure was even lower for young adults aged 20–24 (59 per cent). The discrepancy between the figures derived from this study and from *Norsk Monitor* regarding the number of active youth (16–24) may result from a decrease in activity from 2007 to 2009, but can also stem from slightly different answering options (the question raised, though, was the same in the two surveys).
4 The data that are used comes from Norwegian Social Sciences Data Services' (NSD) study *Leisure time and sports 2007* (ISSP 2007). The study is financed by the Norwegian Research Council and the data was gathered by TNS Gallup and prepared for research purposes by NSD. None of these institutions bear any responsibility for the analysis or interpretation of data carried out here.
5 The dialogue between the Greek politician and lawmaker Solon (638–558 BC) and the Scythian prince Anarcharsis, written by Lukian about AD 180, is illuminating in this respect.
6 Tangen (2004a) and Rafoss and Breivik (2005) have problematized this 'obvious relationship'.
7 The data from Statistics Norway are collected via their website, http://www.ssb.no/emner/02/barn_og_unge/2009/tabeller/fritid/
8 The remaining 3 per cent is the age group 0–5 years.
9 http://www.ssb.no/emner/02/barn_og_unge/2009/tabeller/fritid/

References

Bale, J. (1989) *Sports geography*, London: Spon.
Bergsgard, N. A. (2005) 'Oppløsning eller stabilitiet? Relasjoner og maktkamper innen den nasjonale idrettspolitikken' ['Dissolving or stability? Relationships and power struggle within the national policy of sport']. PhD Thesis, University of Oslo, Oslo.
Bergsgard, N. A., Nødland, S. I. and Seippel, Ø. (2009) '"For den som har skal få?" Makt og avmakt i lokal anleggspolitikk'. In K. Rafoss and J. O. Tangen (eds.), *Kampen om idrettsanleggene: Planlegging, politikk og bruk*, Bergen: Fagbokforlaget.
Dåsnes, M. and Langkaas, L. (1997) *Idrett*, Oslo: Kulturdepartementet.
Enjolras, B. (2004) *Idrett mellom statlig styring og selvbestemmelse: Idrettens bruk av spillemidler*, Oslo: Institutt for samfunnsforskning.
Enjolras, B. and og Seippel, Ø. (2001) *Norske idrettslag 2000*. Oslo: Institutt for samfunnsforskning.
Goksøyr, M. (1992) *Staten og idretten 1861–1991*, Oslo: Kulturdepartementet, Idrettsavdelingen.
Helsen, W., van Winckel, J. and Williams, A. M. (2005) 'The relative age effect in youth soccer across Europe', *Journal of Sports Sciences*, 23(6): 629–636.
Kamberidou, I. and Patsadaras, N. (2007) 'A new concept in European sport governance: sport as social capital', *Biology of Exercise*, 3(1): 21–34.
Kjønniksen, L. (2008) *The association between adolescent experiences of physical activity and leisure-time physical activity in adulthood: a 10-year longitudinal study*, Research Centre for Health Promotion, Faculty of Psychology, University of Bergen, Bergen.
Kjønniksen, L. and Wold, B. (2007) 'Fører organisert idrett i barne- og ungdomsårene til mer aktive voksne?' *Kroppsøving*, (5): 24–26, 29.

KKD (2003) *Finansiering av statlig idrettspolitikk: Rapport fra det regjeringsoppnevnte Sundberg-utvalget*, Oslo: Kultur- og kirkedepartementet.

Mangset, P. (1992) *Kulturliv og forvaltning: innføring i kulturpolitikk*, Oslo: Universitetsforlaget.

Mangset, P. and Rommetvedt, H. (2002) *Idrett og politikk: kampsport eller lagspill?*, Bergen: Fagbokforl.

Morgan, W. J. and Meier, K. V. (1988) *Philosophic inquiry in sport*, Champaign, Ill.: Human Kinetics Publishers.

Musch, J. and Hay, R. (1999) 'The relative age effect in soccer: cross-cultural evidence for a systematic discrimination against children born late in the competition year', *Sociology of Sport Journal*, (16): 54–64.

Nenseth, V., Skogheim, R. and Schmidt, L. (2006) *Kunstgress i vekst: svømmehall i forfall: planlegging og prioritering av idrettsanlegg*, Oslo: Norsk institutt for by- og regionforskning.

NIF (2007) *En åpen og inkluderende idrett: idrettspolitisk dokument: tingperioden 2007–2011*. Oslo.

—— (2008) *Årsrapport*. Oslo: Norges idrettsforbund og opympiske og paralympiske komite.

Nordby, T. (2000) *I politikkens sentrum: variasjoner i Stortingets makt 1814 til 2000*, Oslo: Universitetsforlaget.

Olstad, F. and Tønnesson, S. (1986) *Norsk idretts historie* (Vols. 1 & 2), Oslo: Aschehoug.

Opedal, S. and Bergsgard, N. A. (2009) *Idrettspolitikkens iverksetting: Tre offentlige veier til frivillig idrett*. In B. Enjolras and R. H. Waldahl (eds.), Frivillige organisasjoner og offentlig politikk. Oslo, Novus.

Opedal, S. and Rommetvedt, H. (2007) 'Politikk for norsk lokalidrett'. Paper presented at the Idrottshistoriskt symposium 2005, Stockholm.

Peterson, T. (2003) 'Swedish soccer is seeking for talent, but finding age'. http://www.idrottsforum.org/articles/peterson/peterson040831_eng.pdf

Rafoss, K. (2006) *Spill om spillemidler: en studie av idrettspolitiske beslutningsprosesser knyttet til finansiering, prioritering og lokalisering av store innendørsanlegg i Nord-Norge*, Høgskolen i Finmark.

—— (2009) 'Finansiering og forvaltning av anleggsmidler: konflikter, kompromiss og konsensus'. ['Financing and management of funding for sport facilities: conflicts, compromises, and consensus']. In K. Rafoss and J. O. Tangen (eds.), *Kampen om idrettsanleggene: Planlegging, politikk og bruk [The struggle about sport facilities: Planning, policy and use]*.

Rafoss, K. and og Breivik, G. (2005) *Anleggsbruk: En kartlegging og analyse av anleggsbruk i den norske befolkning*, Alta: Høgskolen i Finnmark.

Selle, P. and Øymyr, B. (1995) *Frivillig organisering og demokrati: det frivillige organisasjonssamfunnet endrar seg 1940–1990*, Oslo: Samlaget.

Skirstad, B. (2002) 'Norske idrettslag: oversikt og utfordringer'. In Ø. Seippel (ed.), *Idrettens bevegelser: Sosiologiske studier av idrett i et moderne samfunn*, Oslo: Novus.

Slagstad, R. (1998) *De nasjonale strateger*, Oslo: Pax.

St. meld. nr. 41 (1991 92) *Om idretten: folkebevegelse og folkeforlystelse* [The Parliament White Paper no 41 (1991–92) About Sport], Oslo, Kulturdepartementet.

St. meld. nr 14. (1999–2000) *Idrettsliv i endring* [The Parliament White Paper no 14 (1999–2000)], Oslo, Kulturdepartementet.

Synovate (2009) *Rapport Barn og ungdom 2009 [Report Children and Youth, prepared for the Ministry of Culture and Church Affairs, by Synovate, 14th of Mai.]*, Oslo, Synovate.

Tangen, J. O. (2000) 'Sport: a social system?', *SysteMexico* (Special Edition 'The Autopoietic Turn: Luhmann's Re-conceptualisation of the Social'), 72–91.

—— (2004a) 'Embedded expectations, embodied knowledge and the movements that connect: a system theoretical attempt to explain the use and non-use of sport facilities', *International Review for the Sociology of Sport*, 39(2004)nr 1, S. 7–25.

—— (2004b) *Hvordan er idrett mulig?: skisse til en idrettssosiologi*, Kristiansand: Høyskoleforlaget.

—— (2004c) 'Making the space: A sociological perspective on sport and its facilities', *Sport and Society*, 7(1): 25–48.

—— (2007) 'Idrettsanlegg som politisk virkemiddel: virker det?' Paper presented at the 'Avslutningskonferanse for programmet idrett, samfunn og frivillig organisering'.

—— (2010) 'Observing sport participation: some sociological remarks on the inclusion/ exclusion mechanism in sport.' In U. Wagner, R. Storm and J. Hoberman (eds.), *Observing sport: Modern system theoretical approaches*, Frankfurt a.m.: Karl Hofman Verlag.

Tangen, J. O. and Rafoss, K. (2009) 'Idrettsanlegg som politisk virkemiddel'. In K. Rafoss and J. O. Tangen (eds.), *Kampen om idrettsanleggene: Planlegging, politikk og bruk [The struggle about sport facilities: Planning, policy and use]*, Bergen: Fagbokforlaget.

Vaage, O. F. (1999) Få svetter alene. *Samfunnsspeilet* (Samfunnsspeilet nr. 3).

6 Hungary

Gyöngyi Szabó Földesi

The present structure of Hungarian sport has been in existence since the political regime change in the country took place in 1989–1990.[1] On the surface the structure exhibits fundamental similarities to those that function in a great number of other countries, which consist of government, non-government, and intermediary structures with divided tasks and shared responsibilities (Hédi and Földesi 2004). In reality, the true nature of the intermediary and the non-governmental sectors, as well as the relationship between the three sectors, are different in many respects. In spite of the seemingly de-centralized division of labour, sport is dominated by the State, and the autonomy of intermediary and not-for-profit organizations is restricted (Bakonyi 2008). This situation is understandable if one considers the historical context.

When modern sport emerged in Hungary in the late nineteenth century, sport organizations were independent from government institutions; sport clubs and sport associations operated on a voluntary basis for half a century. This system was radically transformed after World War II, because Hungary had to join the 'socialist camp'. At that time, in the spirit of the communist ideology, all areas of sport were nationalized: sport facilities were confiscated from private owners and became public properties; besides this, the political influence over sport clubs and federations was significant. Sport organizations at local, regional and national levels, including the Hungarian Olympic Committee (HOC) and other national sporting bodies, were directed and controlled by government and political institutions. In order to be accepted in the international arena, they were allowed to function formally as if they were non-government organizations, but in fact they had to operate in the same way as governmental institutions. This means that in Hungary and in other countries of the Eastern Bloc, sport associations and sport clubs had democratic statutes according to which decisions were formally made by the general assembly, including the election of the executive board. Thus the public image was that these were autonomous organizations. The domestic political reality was quite different. General assemblies were controlled by political commissars who dictated the names to be elected as president or as board member, and the decisions to be made.[2]

Non-government sport organizations regained their independence as a result of Act II on Association, enacted by the Hungarian Parliament in 1989. This Act is considered one of the most important milestones in the process of Hungary's political liberalization, and it also had a strong impact on sport. Not only did it allow, but it compelled the quasi-non-government sport organizations to reorganize themselves and to become genuine non-government bodies. To achieve this objective, the HOC, the national and regional federations of the individual sports, other sport associations, and sport clubs of various sizes amended their statutes, so they could embark on the road towards autonomy. However, this road has been difficult, since the genesis of these new non-government sport organizations was totally different from that of genuine voluntary, not-for-profit sport organizations; they were established 'from above' and not 'from below'. Consequently, they lacked, and most of them still lack, the financial (and some of them even the ethical) foundations which, despite the poor structure of the socialist sport model, and partly just because of it, were guaranteed by the state during the previous regime, the period of so-called state socialism (1945–1990),[3] and which were needed for the continuation of their operation. The contradictory character of sport clubs and federations resulted in their inferior position: *de jure* the non-government sector is independent in sport; *de facto* it is subordinated to state institutions (Földesi 1993). In state socialism the not-for-profit sector had to function as quasi-voluntary because of political reasons. Since the non-government sport bodies emerged in the above mentioned upside-down manner after the political transformation, the majority of them are again quasi-non-government organizations, this time because of not political, but economic reasons.

The public sector also had particular problems to cope with. The 1989–1990 political and economic transformations and their social consequences posed permanent challenges, and instead of successful and adequate answers being given, the structure of sport was changed frequently, in large part because of over-politicization. During the last 20 years the organization of the highest sport authority was restructured eight times, followed by the nomination of nine new national sport presidents/ministers/ministers of state/undersecretaries. In 2009, at the head of the governmental structure there was a state secretariat under the direction of the Ministry of Local Government. This leadership system was introduced one year earlier, but the subordinated regional and local sport councils/offices have existed for many years. Both the present minister and the undersecretary responsible for sport were nominated in the spring of 2009, the previous ones having served for less than a year.

In the early 2000s the organizational restructuring included the establishment of three intermediate umbrella organizations: (1) for national sport federations in competitive sport (National Sports Association); (2) for sport for all, school sport and university sport (National Leisure Sports Association); and (3) for sport for people with disabilities (National Association for People with Special Needs). All three umbrella associations were founded on the initiatives of the Ministry of Sport and Youth, but the actual decisions on their establishment were made voluntarily by their future members. They have special status. On the one hand, they were registered by the Ministry of Youth and Sport, their missions and objectives are governed by the Act CXLV of 2000 issued by the same Ministry, and state financial support is guaranteed for their functioning. On the other hand, from the beginning they have been operating as voluntary organizations.

Intermediary structures between government and non-government structures can be found in sport in many countries. It depends on the government partners whether the emphasis is put on their public or non-government nature. In Hungary, according to the Act of 2000 on Sport, the tasks of the intermediary umbrella organizations are the following:

• To distribute the state subsidies among member federations,
• To co-ordinate the activity of member organizations,
• To represent the interest of members,
• To co-operate with the Minister of sport and with the other public utility umbrella organizations,
• To participate in the activity of the appropriate international bodies.

(Hédi and Földesi 2004: 175)[4]

In post-transformational Hungary intermediary sport structures have often been used to cover attempts at re-centralization. They can be regarded more as semi-public organizations, since in principle they are not subordinated to ministries, national offices, state secretariats, and legally they should be regarded as partners to government bodies; however, in practice they are at the mercy of them. They might have different concepts from the official bodies; they are constrained to do what was/is approved and financed by sport ministries, national offices of sport, and state secretariats for sport (Földesi and Egressy 2005).

The status of the existing intermediary organizations is unstable. According to the Sport XXI National Sport Strategy, the National Leisure Sport Association, which covers the interests of sport for all, might be dissolved. This concept demonstrates that sport policy makers are not really concerned about the population's involvement in organized sport. In spite of some efforts, the Act of 2000 on Sport and the National Sport Strategy have not been truly harmonized, and several ideas of both of them have been neglected in practice. The future of the intermediary umbrella sport organizations depends on what policy will be adopted by the next Act on sport.

There are several reasons why non-government and intermediary sport organizations have not been able to act independently and to contribute effectively to a strategy for solving problems in Hungarian sport, and most of them are not rooted in sport, but in the history of the revival of voluntary movements. Most importantly, as a consequence of the contradictory geneses of the newly established voluntary bodies, in the 1990s most voluntary organizations had been institutionalized in all areas of Hungarian society. They had been over-politicized and had been overwhelmed by bureaucracy in the new democracy (Laskai 2003).

An additional problem in Hungarian sport is that in contrast with many countries not a single field of sport, not even top sport, has counted on the contribution of the commercial sector to support the delivery of sport. Market principles which had been denied under state socialism have become legitimate in post-transformational Hungary, but their growing legitimacy has led only to a modest expansion of the commercial sector. The latter has not been strong enough, and has not been interested in supporting sport, especially not on a one-sided basis. The majority of top and middle managerial sporting personnel have not learned yet to act according to the rules of the market; most of them prefer Maecenas to sponsors, that is to say receiving money without returning service. In spite of the fact that many non-government sport organizations are weak economically, and some of them are in a desperate situation, close to liquidation, relatively few administrators make a serious effort to generate additional income and become self-funding.

The main feature of the contemporary Hungarian sport structure is instability. It can be confidently predicted that in the near future it will be transformed again. An amendment to the Act on Sport in force has already been prepared, suggesting yet another organizational restructuring.

Sport culture: consuming instead of practising

In Hungary there have been long traditions in modern sport. Competitions in swimming, shooting and horse racing started as early as the 1820s and 1830s. The institutionalization of sport also began in this period. Sport clubs and associations were established, and sport-related books were published. The first national sport club was founded in 1860, and the first national sport federation in 1885. The first national championship was launched in 1883, in rowing, followed by more than a dozen sports within a decade (Kutassi 1982).

Although sport was originally introduced by the not-for-profit sector in Hungary, it was not developed with the aim to promote the participation of a large number of people in organized sport independent of government intervention, but to invite selected groups of youth with the view to increasing national pride through their successes (Földesi 1996). There was a strong ambition to demonstrate, at an international level, how gifted Hungarians were in sport. This intention also contributed significantly to the enthusiastic activities of promoting the dissemination of sport in other countries and the rise of international sport, including the revival of the Olympic Games. A few Hungarians were involved in the preparation of the Games and other sport competitions between nations during the late nineteenth century.[5]

The structure of Hungarian sport served the aims of elite sport from the very beginning. University students constituted the biggest pool from which elite athletes were selected. Sport clubs at leading universities were founded very early (Egyetemi Athletikai Club/EAC, 1886; Mûegyetemi Athletikai és Football Club/ MAFC, 1897), and in 1907 the Hungarian University Sport Federation was the second national association in the world established for students (Szikora 2007). At that time most Hungarian university students belonged to upper-middle or upper classes, and members of other sport clubs had similar socio-economic backgrounds. There were a few sport movements for blue collar workers, but attempts to involve everybody in sport activity were not made until several decades later. People at large were socialized to be spectators rather than participants.

During the twentieth century, sport for most Hungarians meant various forms of sport consumption: attending sporting events, reading sport journals and listening to sport news on the radio. These activities were especially important in the years of 'hard' dictatorship of the so-called socialist era in the 1950s and 1960s. At that time, as a consequence of the isolated position of the country, the limitation of human rights and widespread poverty, consuming sport was one of the favourite pastimes in Hungary. Football, the most popular sport, was at the centre of interest in everyday life. Football stadia were crowded not only in the first league championships but in matches at all levels, while national, regional and local competitions in other sports were also attended by many spectators. The single daily sport journal had a wide circulation, and most Hungarian men started reading other daily papers at the back page where they found the sport section. Television was not yet used by many people; the two channels of the Hungarian Public Radio were the major sources of information. Sport reporters were well known and their popularity rivalled that of the film stars. The days of Olympics and other international championships were considered as holidays. More men were among the committed fans, but most people supported Hungarian athletes regardless of their gender, age, residence, occupation and education. National victories in sport were celebrated all over the country, and failures were interpreted as a national tragedy. It is believed that the population's deep disappointment in 1954, when the Hungarian soccer team missed the gold medal in the final of the World Cup in Bern, significantly contributed to the nationwide dissatisfaction which led to the 1956 revolution against the local dictators and their Soviet allies.

According to the findings of a recent study the number of sport-loving people in Hungary has decreased. In the late 2000s, 45 per cent of Hungarians were not interested in sport; about 90 per cent generally do not attend sporting events, 80 per cent never read sport journals, 45 per cent do not watch sport programs on television and 40 per cent do not cheer for Hungarian athletes (Földesi 2008). A great number of Hungarians are still proud of the achievements of national athletes in international competitions, especially in the Olympic Games, but many do not follow athletic accomplishments with unremitting enthusiasm, and are no longer disappointed by defeat (Dóczi 2008).

Unequal access to sporting activity

In Hungary until the late 1980s sport and educational institutions were obliged to give an account of their main activities to the sport authorities to whom they were subordinated. On the basis of these reports statistical year books were published containing data on the population's participation in organized sport. These data were not always reliable; in some respects they might even have been manipulated. Nevertheless, the data showed some major trends that occurred in sport. Following the 1989–1990 political transformation, in the spirit of freedom, the autonomous sporting bodies did not have the obligation to provide sport authorities with facts concerning their operation; a new system to get numerical information about sport involvement on a national level has not yet been developed. In this discussion the Hungarian population's sporting activity is presented via other sources; this section is based above all on the findings of research and polls, complemented by statistical data issued by sport federations.

According to the results of an investigation carried out at the end of 2007 in a randomly selected sample, representative of Hungarians aged 18 years or over (N=1027), almost half the adult population either never practise sport or are totally inactive physically (32 per cent); 16 per cent of them are involved so seldom, less than once or twice a week, that it does not have the desired physiological effect on their body (Gál 2008). The term 'sport' was used in the widest possible sense of the word; it included traditional sports, exercise, walking, excursions, and any new kinds of physical movements performed in institutions or at home or in the open air, with the aim of recreation or competition, whether registered with a federation or not. Various forms of casual walking and going for an excursion were mentioned as the most frequent physical activities. These were followed by aerobics, muscle-building by electronic methods, conditioning gymnastics, cycling, cross-country motorcycling, playing soccer, jogging and swimming.

The results of the Special Eurobarometer No. 213 poll, conducted at the request of the European Commission, Directorate-General Press and Communication on the practice and the image of sport within the European Union showed that only 20 per cent of Hungarians played sport at least once a week in 2004 (N=1014). This proportion was significantly below the European average of that time (38 per cent). Another 20 per cent practised sport less than once a week. According to these data Hungarians, together with the Portuguese (22 per cent), were among the least sporting citizens in the European Union. As Table 6.1 illustrates, preceded by Portugal (66 per cent), Hungary (60 per cent) was the second least athletic country as measured by the proportion of people who never do exercise or play sport.

The differences in the participation rate found by the study of Gál and by the Eurobarometer are due to the dissimilar interpretation of the concept of sport.

Table 6.1 How often do you practise or play sport? (answer: NEVER)

Country	Percentage
Portugal	66
Hungary	60
Italy	58
Greece	57
Latvia	48
Lithuania	48
Spain	47
Cyprus	47
Poland	46
Malta	43
EU25	40
Luxembourg	40
Estonia	40
Belgium	36
Germany	36
Slovakia	36
France	35
Austria	34
Czech Republic	34
The Netherlands	31
United Kingdom	31
Ireland	28
Slovenia	24
Denmark	17
Sweden	7
Finland	4

Source: Special Eurobarometer No. 213 (2004: 5)

Namely, during the poll the meaning of sport was used in a narrower sense: casual walking and excursion were not taken into account.

Both studies state that most people in Hungary exercise outside the 'classic' sport facilities (except swimming pools): at home or in open air public places, occasionally in fitness centres, and they choose activities which can be performed individually. Students play sport at schools or universities as well. Although the conditions for sporting activities in educational institutions are limited, community sport clubs are seldom the place of their sporting activities.

Registration with a federation is remarkably low; it is under 1 per cent (Gál 2008). This proportion tends to be much higher in several other countries of the European Union: for instance, in the Netherlands it is 34 per cent, in Denmark 28 per cent and in Germany 25 per cent. The European average is only 16 per cent, due to the fact that sport is often played 'elsewhere' in the ten new member states, including Hungary, that joined the EU in 2004 (Special Eurobarometer No. 213 2004).

The latter data correspond to information provided by the Hungarian Sports Federation. Approximately 300,000 athletes are members of this umbrella organization, which comprises 75 national sport federations. This is equivalent to about 3 per cent of the inhabitants in Hungary, but it includes youth and children under 18, who constitute a large proportion of registered athletes.

As in Europe generally, the rate of sporting activity decreases with age in Hungary. Gál's data indicate that more than half of those aged over 62 years of age are inactive physically; the relevant rate in the 18–29 age group is 15 per cent (see Table 6.2).

Other demographic and social characteristics affect sport involvement of younger and older people alike. The strongest impact is made by socio-economic factors. In all ages and with both sexes, the lowest participation rates were registered in social groups with low education, low income, and with low-ranking blue collar occupations and living in villages or small towns of an agricultural nature. Concerning the latter issue, inhabitants of rural areas are in a gravely disadvantageous situation; about one third of the women living in urban settlements and half the women from the country never participate in any sport or exercise. The relevant data with men are somewhat better: one third versus one quarter (Gál 2008).

Table 6.2 Hungarians' sport participation according to age (%)

Frequency	Age			
	18–29	*30–45*	*46–62*	*Over 62*
Never	14.8	25.2	37.1	51.8
Hardly ever	8.1	9.6	6.2	3.7
1–2 times/month	11.0	10.6	7.5	4.7
1–2 times/week	18.1	17.5	10.9	4.7
3 times/week	17.6	12.9	14.0	8.9
Every day	30.5	24.2	24.3	26.2
Total	100.0	100.0	100.0	100.0

Source: Database of Gál's study (2008)

As Table 6.3 and Table 6.4 show, the practice of sport is linked first to the level of education and second to the amount of income. The tendency seems to be similar in the other EU member states, but social distances are of greater significance in Hungary than in most former Eastern Bloc countries in the Union.

Surprisingly, Hungarian women do exercise a little more regularly than men: 51 per cent of the latter claim to play sport at least once a week, in contrast to 54 per cent of women; men are somewhat more interested in participating in organized sports where they are registered, while women practise at home and in fitness rooms or clubs. More women use sport for overcoming the ever increasing tension which is typical in transitional Eastern European societies. They perform sport mostly to improve their quality of life, to promote health, to shape their body and to meet friends. Men's involvement in sport is motivated mainly by improving their health condition and by building muscles. Three-quarters of the interviewees complained about being exhausted frequently both physically and mentally. In their case, the lack of time as a main reason for the absence of sporting activity is definitely not a pretext. In order to survive their grave economic problems they are under continuous stress. Their worsening financial situation accompanied by worsening health condition also hinders their participation in sport. The lack of suitable sporting facilities is not mentioned as an important barrier for their

Table 6.3 Hungarians' sport participation according to income (%)

Frequency	Monthly income (HUF)			
	Less than 40,000	*40,001–70,000*	*70,001–100,000*	*More than 100,000*
Never	33.9	31.6	26.7	17.9
Hardly ever	10.2	4.9	7.8	17.9
1–2 times/month	5.9	8.3	14.4	7.1
1–2 times/week	12.7	10.2	8.9	17.9
3 times/week	9.3	15.0	13.3	21.4
Every day	28.0	30.1	28.9	17.9
Total	100.0	100.0	100.0	100.0

Source: Database of Gál's study (2008)

Note: The minimal monthly wage in the year of the data collection was officially HUF 69000

Table 6.4 Hungarians' sport participation according to education level (%)

Frequency	Level of education				
	Primary school or lower	*Technical school*	*High school*	*High school + vocational*	*College/ university*
Never	57.1	34.8	23.7	14.1	12.2
Hardly ever	6.5	8.2	6.7	9.4	5.8
1–2 times/month	2.6	8.2	9.7	16.5	12.2
1–2 times/week	5.2	10.9	17.7	11.8	21.6
3 times/week	8.2	12.7	17.0	17.6	13.7
Every day	20.3	25.1	25.3	30.6	34.6
Total	100.0	100.0	100.0	100.0	100.0

Source: Database of Gál's study (2008)

absence from sport: they do not even notice it because of the other reasons that prevent them from practising (Gál 2008).

Comparison of today's data with former research findings must be made with reservations, since the methods used by the individual investigators might differ to some extent. A French–Hungarian study on the time spent on sport carried out two decades ago (Földesi *et al.* 1991, 1994) may be suitable for this purpose. This investigation intended to discover the population's opinions, attitudes and behaviours related to sport, and was made in randomly selected samples both in Hungary (N=2050) and in France (N=3000).

According to the results of the survey that took place at the end of the 1980s, 43 per cent of the Hungarians and 74 per cent of the French between the ages of 12 and 74 years old played sport during the year preceding the research, but less than half of them did so at least once a week. The term 'sport' meant every kind of physical activity practised by people thinking that they were performing sport. The majority of the physically active Hungarians practised sport at home. Nine per cent had registered with clubs/groups for non-competitive sporting activity and 3 per cent had registered with a federation.

Socio-demographic factors had a considerable impact on Hungarians' sport involvement twenty years ago. On average, 11 per cent more men (49 per cent) played sport than women (38 per cent), but the gender differences increased from the youngest to the oldest participants. Sixty-nine per cent of those aged 12 to 17 years and 10 per cent of those aged 65 to 74 took part in at least one physical activity in the preceding year.

The differences due to occupation and education were the most remarkable. These data were collected in the so-called socialist regime when the dominant ideology was based on the principle of equality. Moreover, sport then had special social functions and all areas of sport were declared to be equal. It could reasonably have been expected that sport as a social sub-system was egalitarian and even more open than other social institutions. Contrary to this assumption, social differences in the sporting habits of people belonging to different occupational and educational categories proved to be enormous. The disparity between the participation rates of white- and blue-collar workers, especially agricultural workers, was much greater in Hungary than in France, although the latter was regarded in the Eastern Bloc as a Western 'capitalist' state. Eighty per cent of the French and 78 per cent of the Hungarian white-collar workers played sport. On the other hand, 67 per cent of the industrial workers and 53 per cent of the agricultural workers practised sport in France, while in Hungary the respective figures were 51 per cent for industrial workers and 10 per cent for agricultural workers (Földesi *et al.* 1994).

Földesi's findings can be compared only with the results of Gál's research, since they used the meaning of sport in a similar way in their studies. Based on their data, it appears that the proportion of totally inactive people within the Hungarian population decreased in the two decades following the 1989–1990 political and economic transition. The differences in physical activity according to gender, age and location also seem to have lessened. On the other hand, nothing changed favourably concerning the impact of socio-economic status on sport involvement. As in other sub-systems of Hungarian society, social distances have been growing in sport. The differences in the rates of sporting activity due to education, occupation, and income have become greater. This is surely the major reason, that although there has been a step forward, it manifests itself only in the growing number of people trying to be active physically without cost or with the lowest cost possible, that is to say going for a walk or for an excursion. Participation rates in 'real' sport, especially in organized sport and exercise, did not increase at all, as is shown by the data of the Special Eurobarometer No. 213.

Social class affiliation influenced individuals' sport involvement in the past; those with higher income and higher education then had a better chance of playing sport (Földesi *et al.* 1991; Gáldi 2002). In the new political system, sporting habits according to social strata differ even more owing to the rapid growth in socio-economic differences observable at a macro level in society since 1990. This was probably not a necessary consequence of the political transformation. In some other countries of the former Eastern Bloc there are not such huge social distances in 'sport for all' participation levels (Wolanska *et al.* 2002).

Unequal access to sport occurs in most countries, and it can be witnessed even in prosperous democratic states. However, in those countries the proportion of people living in hopeless poverty and the degree of social inequality are much lower than in present-day Hungary. According to the so-called 'two thirds society' theory, in the Western European countries one third of the population are close to poverty or are already poor, while two thirds are comfortable, and have access to desirable social, cultural (and sporting) benefits (Headey *et al.* 1994). In Hungarian sport an opposite tendency is present. One third of the population can afford to practise sport regularly, and the situation of the other two thirds can be best described by social exclusion. The already narrow middle class has been shrinking; increasing impoverishment can be observed in its lower strata, and again in the working and lower classes. Polarization in Hungarian society has been accelerated. The access to sport is so atrocious that it cries out for institutionalized, organized public help.

Powerful government intervention

The dominance of the state in sport has been indisputable throughout the history of modern sport in Hungary. When modern sport was born, the country was a part of the Austro-Hungarian monarchy; nevertheless, her athletes could participate in international championships as the representatives of an autonomous state. Hungarian athletes were eager to demonstrate the independence of the country. They won a great number of medals in the Olympic Games as well as at other international events, and received public support for their efforts. As a result, Hungary became known as a sporting nation, although very few people were engaged in sport (Földesi 1996).

During the entire twentieth century sport remained a matter of political interest in Hungary. Its functions in terms of interior and foreign policies were particularly exaggerated during the decades of state socialism, when sporting success played a surrogate role. Gold medals were supposed to compensate the population for missing national success in economy and politics. At that time internationalism was a guiding political principle and patriotic feelings could be voiced only in sporting stadia. Consequently, the integrative force of sport events was witnessed at macro and micro levels. Leading politicians made use of the athletes' achievements and aspired to preserve an image of the country in the international arena as a sport superpower (Grawátsch 1989). Thus government intervention was very strong in high-level competitive sport. Sport politics focused on Olympic competitions, and Hungarian Olympic athletes were given substantial financial support even in those years when the Olympic Charter strictly prohibited it. Like other elite athletes in the Eastern Bloc, they were regarded as state-amateurs.

State intervention took place in other fields of sport, but only the method was similar; the support was not really serious. A few mass sport 'movements' were planned, initiated and controlled centrally at schools, universities and work places by government organizations. There was no chance at all for the population's involvement in the promotion of its own sporting activity. In theory, the development of sport for everybody was regarded as equal to the promotion of top sport in the socialist sport model. In practice, it was overshadowed and pushed into an underprivileged position. As a result, generations grew up in Hungary without learning how important physical activity is in one's way of life, and without experiencing the pleasure that can be derived from sporting activity.

Following the 1989–1990 political and economic transition, the dominant role of the state was theoretically diminished, since the not-for-profit sector was reborn and the commercial sector had started to develop. However, strong government intervention did not cease; rather, its method became less direct and more sophisticated. Political ambitions to recentralize sport as a social sub-system and paternalistic attitudes which encouraged the state to keep a firm hand on sport survived. On the other hand, paternalistic expectations were observed in the case of voluntary sport organizations. The latter have been willing to give up their autonomy in exchange for financial support by the state (Földesi and Egressy 2005).

The fact that sport was run mostly by public money made it possible that government intervention could be powerful and one-sided. It has been experienced in all fields of sport and in quite various issues, but as far as participation in organized sport is concerned it has been mostly related to elite sport. Government intervention meant above all the distribution of the central state budget allocated to sport, and the majority of it was used to provide Hungarian international-level and high-level national athletes with the necessary conditions. The latter has been regarded as the true duty of the state and has resulted in ensuring access to sporting facilities for recreational athletes being neglected. The regional and local governments paid somewhat more attention to their population's involvement in organized sport, but their budget seldom allowed serious investment in this area.

At the same time, some groups of mostly young people have started to manage their own sporting activity on a voluntary basis, but they have faced serious difficulties. They had neither money nor experience to operate sport clubs, and they did not receive government assistance. The opportunities for recreational athletes to be involved in organized sporting activity have not been expanded; in fact, they have been diminished. The circumstances in the existing sport clubs were going from bad to worse, and they were interested invariably in dealing with elite athletes alone. The not-for-profit sector was mainly able to promote outdoor sporting activity, in particular running and cycling. The efforts of cyclists requesting local governments to build adequate routes have met with only modest success.

The approach to sport by the individual governments in power from 1990 to 2009 was different in terms of their ideological reasoning, political culture and style. However, the very essence of their sport policies was similar, since only policies related to elite sport were fully delivered. In all sport conceptions the guiding principles comprised more or less the same positive core values: unity of sport, equality, promotion of excellence, health, and quality of life with the help of sport. In the spirit of all these principles, government interventions should have offered more help for participation in organized sport at large, with greater emphasis on children, youth, and people in an underprivileged position. In spite of encouraging declarations, it did not happen. All governments in power from 1990 to 2009 missed the historical opportunity to radically change the traditional sport policy trends. Although scientific evidence indicates clearly that it is an illusion to believe that the former nationwide interest in elite sport is still alive, even nowadays most decisions in sport start from the assumption that high-level sport holds the same place in the population's value system as it used to during state socialism (Földesi 2008).

Contradictory government policy

Establishing the conditions for top sport was the first priority in Hungarian sport politics during the four decades of 'socialism'. Equal opportunities for other areas of sport were not guaranteed at all (Földesi 1993). Following the 1989–1990 political transition there were attempts to change these policies but, with the exception of a few episodes, they failed. When the socialist sport model collapsed in the early 1990s, a new sport model did not emerge, and sport as a social sub-system was not modernized. Until the late 2000s sport policy was based on short-term concepts in which equity of all areas of sport has been professed but never truly realized.

At first there were serious intentions to change political attitudes. At the beginning of the 1990s an important campaign was launched with the aim of promoting the construction of indoor sport facilities for schools with governmental financial aid. Within a few years more than 450 gyms were built at public schools and universities. Parallel to these government actions, measures were implemented which guaranteed per capita economic support for schools and universities according to the number of students. Some years later this rule was withdrawn, putting sport at educational institutions into a worse position, but a few years later similar measures were implemented again.

In the late 1990s the position of sport for people with special needs was upgraded. For a short period this interest was represented at a deputy state secretariat level. At the next restructuring this level was downgraded purely because of political considerations. Most of the relevant measures served the promotion of elite disabled athletes' participation in organized sport. Sporting practice for all disabled persons received much less attention. Nevertheless, this field is rightly regarded as a true winner of the political regime change in sport.

After a long delay, another area, namely the care of sport talent, has benefited highly from government policy. After facing problems rooted in the collapse of the former recruitment system introduced in 1963, a new Sport Talent Care program was launched in 2001 in twenty Olympic sports with the aim of supporting the sporting career of those talented young sportsmen and sportswomen aged 14 to 23 years who are to be the future hopes of the country. This program was given huge financial assistance. However, it could reach its objectives only partly: the recruitment base for talent care was narrower than planned, since the children's socio-economic background strongly determined their chance to join the program (Velenczei *et al.* 2008).

In the post-transformational period an urgent need for a comprehensive sport policy was recognized. After long debates a National Sport Strategy was accepted by the Hungarian Parliament in 2007. It comprises a lot of attractive ideas but it has some major deficiencies. First, the main aim in the Strategy set up for the next fifteen years is twofold: (1) to maintain the high status of Hungarian sport in world sport; and (2) to promote regular participation in sport by all Hungarians (Sport XXI National Sport Strategy 2007). It has to be admitted that the first objective is unrealistic, as in the era of economic and cultural globalization Hungary is not in a position to preserve her former status as a sport power. Second, the Strategy is not complemented by financial guarantees, and in want of the latter it might remain a dream. Third, the action plans issued in the last two years related to the Strategy are rather poor, as far as the promotion of the population's participation in organized sport is concerned. According to this philosophy, the demand for organized sport should be promoted while the supply should not. This means that the government department and local authorities responsible for sport should popularize the importance of regular exercise and encourage people to participate, but they are not expected to take responsibility for broadening sporting opportunities, e.g. by supporting the building or running of public sport centres or subsidizing special programs. This is a mistake, since even the existing demand cannot be satisfied, to a great extent owing to the lack of sport facilities and programs accessible for everybody. Without developing the actual supply with the assistance of the public sector, people in general have little chance to be involved in organized sport.

Sport policy is again at a crossroads. Either the old way will be continued in the usual hypocritical manner, with half-measure arrangements, or there will be at long last a radical change, and the gap between the slogans and actions will lessen. Unfortunately, the present National Sport Strategy does not give sufficient impulse and 'ammunition' for this to be achieved.

Moreover, although the importance of the cooperation between the individual ministries concerning the population's health promotion and physical activity has been regularly emphasized in various state documents, only the sport sphere was expected to take serious actions. In spite of the huge efforts made by the not-for-profit sector, high-level authorities in education have not implemented effective policies in the area of school sport. Similarly, in the declarations made by the ministries dealing with health and welfare issues, how significant sporting practice is in health promotion was often outlined. However, only investigations were carried out, and the solutions related to the problems were transferred to sport authorities. It is believed that without a more comprehensive government approach and greater state responsibility for changing sport culture within the nation, participation in organized sport at large cannot be improved.

Notes

1 In 1989–1990 a velvet revolution took place in the Eastern European communist countries. It started in October 1989 when the Hungarian reform communist leaders allowed the opening of the border with Austria, offering tens of thousands of East Germans an opportunity to escape to the West. This was followed by the fall of the infamous Berlin Wall and by the rise of various movements all over the Eastern Bloc which led to the collapse of communism in Eastern Europe and to the disintegration of the Soviet Union. The Cold War came to an end (Meyer 2009). The states of the Eastern Bloc became independent and their political regimes were democratized.

In Hungary free elections were held in the spring of 1990, and in the following years, instead of a centrally planned and controlled 'socialist' economy, a market economy was introduced. The democratic process affected all sub-systems of society, including sport (Földesi 1996).
2 The commissars were not simply advisors; their instructions had to be followed. They were involved in the everyday life of sport clubs and associations; they even accompanied sporting teams abroad to control the athletes' and officials' communications and to prevent their emigration. International sport bodies were more or less familiar with this contradictory situation, but in a hypocritical way; they pretended that it was an internal affair. People in democratic societies may have difficulties in understanding why the majority of the population in Hungary, and in other Eastern European countries, did not protest, but cooperated with political commissars. It has to be kept in mind that in that time in these states there was dictatorship based on a large network of secret agents, spies and informers. The latter reported all signs of resistance, which were punished very severely. People made moral compromises since they wanted to survive and/or protect their families.
3 During state socialism sport, mainly elite sport, had outstanding functions both in foreign and in domestic politics in Hungary; therefore it was generously financed by the state. The preponderant majority of sport clubs and associations dealt with top sport. The fact that the non-government sport organizations were not autonomous, but were under state control, made it easier to provide them with public financial means directly and/or indirectly. The direct way meant that sport always had a significant share from the national budget. Indirect financial support was given by state-owned firms, factories which were compelled to be connected to sport organizations. They maintained and ran the clubs' sporting facilities, employed 'amateur' athletes with good salaries for which they did not have to work at all, and covered the cost of several competitions at home and abroad. Since in the years following the 1989–1990 political transformation much of the state-owned property was privatized, the indirect financial sources got stopped and the national budgets could not compensate the deficit.
4 In 2002 the Ministry of Youth and Sport was succeeded by the Ministry of Children, Youth and Sport (2002–2006), then by the National Office for Sport (2006–2008), and by the State Secretariat for Sport (2008–). Since that time there have been several attempts to change the legal status of the intermediary umbrella organizations with the declared aim to merge them, without success. Consequently, the actual position of the intermediary umbrella sport organizations weakened. State financial support for their operation decreased, and it is not guaranteed any more. Generally speaking, they cannot accomplish all of their duties stated by the Act of 2000 on Sport, which, with a few amendments, is still in force.
5 E.g. Ferenc Kemény (1860–1944), who made friends with Baron Pierre de Coubertin at the Sorbonne University in the 1880s, was a member of the first board of the National Olympic Committee, which consisted of only seven members at that time (Takács 1998).

References

Bakonyi, T. (2007) *Állam, civil társadalom, sport*, Budapest: Kossuth Könyvkiadó.
Dóczi, T. (2008) 'Magyar sport és nemzeti identitás a globális sportszíntéren', *Magyar Sporttudományi Szemle*, 4: 3–7.

Földesi, S. G. (1993) 'The Transformation of Sport in Eastern Europe: The Hungarian Case', *Journal of Comparative Physical Education and Sport*, 15: 5–21.

—— (1996) 'Sports Policy in Hungary'. In Chalip, L., Johnson, A. and Stachura, L. (eds.) *National Sports Policies. International Handbook*, Westport, Connecticut–London: Greenwood Press.

—— (2008) 'Sportfogyasztás, mint a kulturális fogyasztás válfaja'. In Földesi, S.G., Dóczi, T. and Gál, A. (eds.) *Társadalmi riport a sportról 2008*, Budapest: ÖM – MSTT.

Földesi, S. G. and Egressy, J. (2005) 'Post-transformational Trends in Hungarian Sport (1995–2004)', *European Journal for Sport and Society*, 2: 85–96.

Földesi, S. G., Irlinger, P. and Metoudi, M. (1994) 'East–West: The Practice of Sport as Revealing Aspects of French and Hungarian Society', *International Review for the Sociology of Sport*, 29: 149–170.

Földesi, S. G., Louveau, C. and Metoudi, M. (1991) 'A sportolásra fordított idõ Franciaországban és Magyarországon', *A Testnevelési Egyetem közleményei*, suppl., 1: 1–111.

Gál, A. (2008) 'A magyar lakosság egészségtudatossága és szabadidõ-sportolási szokásai'. In Földesi, S.G., Dóczi, T. and Gál, A. (eds.) *Társadalmi riport a sportról 2008*, Budapest: ÖM – MSTT.

Gáldi, G. (2002) 'Fizikai aktivitás Magyarországon az ezredfordulón', *Magyar Sporttudományi Szemle*, 3–4: 16–18.

Grawátsch, P. (1989) 'A szocializmus utolsó mítosza a sport', *Hitel*, 11: 48–50.

Headey, B., Krause, P. and Habich, R. (1994) 'Long and Short Term Poverty: Is Germany a Two-Thirds Society?', *Social Indicators Research*, 31: 1–25.

Hédi C. and Földesi S. G. (2004) 'Sport Structures in Hungary'. In Tokarski, W., Steinbach D., Petry, K. and Jesse, B. (eds.) *Two Players One Goal? Sport in the European Union*, Aachen: Meyer and Meyer Sport.

Kutassi, L. (1982) *A magyar testnevelés és sport története*, Budapest: Sport.

Laskai, Z. (2003) 'Állam és civil társadalom viszonya', *Politikatudományi füzetek*, 12: 3–35.

Meyer, M. (2009) *The Year That Changed the World: The Untold Story of the Fall of the Berlin Wall*, London: Simon & Schuster.

Special Eurobarometer No 213 'The Citizens of the European Union and Sport' (2004). <http://www.ec.europa.eu/public_opinion/archives/ebs/ebs_213_summ_en.pdf> (accessed 14 November 2007).

Sport XXI Nemzeti Stratégia 2007–2020 (2007) Budapest: ÖTM, Sport Szakállamtitkárság.

Szikora, K. (2007) 'A hazai egyetemi-fõiskolai sport elõzményei és fejlõdése az 1950-es évek derekáig'. In Földesi, S. G. and Krasovec, F. (eds.) *100 év az egyetemi-fõiskolai sport szolgálatában*, Budapest: MEFS.

Takács, F. (1998) *A modern olimpiai játékok*, Budapest, Útmutató Kiadó.

Velenczei, A., Kovács Á., Szabó T. and Szabó A. (2008) 'Társadalmi változások a magyarországi sportutánpótlás-nevelésben egy sportegyesület tükrében', *Magyar Sporttudományi Szemle*, 4: 25–30.

Wolanska, T., Salita, J., Jung, R., Mikolajczak, Z., Pastwa, M. and Zylko, J. (2002) 'Poland: Sport for All as Physical Culture and Social Value'. In DaCosta, L. P. and Miragaya, A. (eds.) *Worldwide Experiences and Trends in Sport for All*, Aachen: Meyer and Meyer Sport.

7 Bulgaria

Vassil Girginov and Ivan Sandanski

This chapter addresses sport participation policy in Bulgaria from 1990 to the present day, a period that marks the transformation from a socialist to a market-oriented society and the building of a new state. More specifically, it seeks to examine the making of sport participation policy as a field of state activity that involves various projects, agents and transformations. The chapter first provides a background to Bulgaria's social, political and economic development in order to place sport policy making in context. The second section offers a discussion of sport participation policies as specific state activities, while, in the final section, five implications of state selectivity for sport participation policy are analysed.

Social, political and economic context

Bulgaria is situated in South-Eastern Europe and has a population of 7.5 million people, the great majority of whom (85 per cent) are Orthodox Christians. It has kept its name since 681, the longest period of continuity of national identity of any country in Europe. Between the end of the Second World War and 1989 Bulgaria was in the former Soviet bloc of influence and created an egalitarian society with highly developed infrastructure, education and sport. The transformation from state socialism to a market economy has significantly altered the political, social and economic fabric of society. In 1993 Bulgaria was given the status of an associate member in the European Union and became a full member in 2007. The country's Gross Domestic Product (GDP) per capita in 2008 was $12,372 compared to $7,330 in 1989 (Economy Watch 2009). Since 1989 the population has declined by 2.4 million (down from 8.9 to 6.5 million) and is ageing, with 18 per cent of people being 65 and older, which is set to increase to 35 per cent by 2020. Administratively, the country is divided into 28 districts and 273 municipalities. These sub-national level units enjoy a degree of relative autonomy with regard to local affairs, but financially they are still heavily dependent on the central government.

In the space of 130 years Bulgaria has undergone three massive social and political transformations: from Ottoman oppression to early capitalism (1878–1944); state socialism (1945–1989); and Europeanization (1990–present). Each transformation has caused enormous shake-ups of the state system and the lives of individuals and society. As a result, a new state has had to be built every 40 to 60 years, and different interpretations were given to events, to actors' roles (both individual and corporate), and to outcomes. This poses significant challenges to researchers analysing sport policy.

Modern sport emerged in Bulgaria at the beginning of the nineteenth century and was largely modelled after the Russian and German sports doctrines, which enjoyed the state's political patronage. Although the English and Swiss concepts of sport diffused in most European countries, they did not succeed in Bulgaria because they lacked state backing. Sport was originally envisaged to become a truly civil movement possessing a political and social unifying force and important educational functions (Girginov and Mitev 2002). Although this vision never fully materialized, sport was built around the notion of the holistic development of man, which is reflected in the term 'physical culture' and came to dominate both political and academic discourses.

Between the late 1950s and the beginning of 2000, the sports development model of the country could most accurately be described as a pyramid. Mass participation formed the base of the pyramid, which was supposed to provide the pool for identifying and nurturing athletes capable of excelling at elite levels. However, the link between mass and elite participation was never truly established as a set of policies and practices. In terms of international results, the most successful Bulgarian sports never enjoyed mass membership or a large participation base. For example, between the 1968 Mexico and 1988 Seoul Olympic Games, with fewer than 20,000 gymnasts, Bulgaria has won 30 medals, including one Olympic title and multiple World and European championships, while during the same period some 4,000 weightlifters have brought in more than 400 medals (Girginov 1998).

Organized sport in Bulgaria currently appears limited in scope and comprises 98,000 registered members in 3,668 sport clubs affiliated to 93 National Sport Organizations (NSOs). This is an average of 27 members per club, which is relatively low compared to an average of 45 club members in the United Kingdom and 260 in Germany. Sport participation is mainly delivered through a network of public and voluntary bodies. Although over the past twenty years private clubs and fitness centres proliferated in the main cities, there is no reliable information about their operations and membership. There is also virtually no coordination or partnerships in delivering participation between the public and voluntary sectors on one hand and the private sector on the other.

It should be stressed that large-scale surveys on people's physical activity have not been carried out since the mid 1980s and even less is known about the key drivers and participation levels in different sports, target groups and regions of the country. Therefore, no reliable participation figures exist, which renders analyses dealing with sport participation trends problematic. What does exist, however, is data on the number of registered athletes and clubs as the latter represent legal entities and are required to keep a register of their members. The top ten sports by athletes and club network respectively are football (32,424/544), martial arts (6,281/183), volleyball (5,751/134), basketball (5,201/136), handball (5,106/78), wrestling (3,383/132), swimming (3,231/56), rhythmic gymnastics (2,956/47), athletics (2,843/131) and field hockey (1,717/37) (SAYS 2008). Those figures are largely consistent with the most popular participation activities in 1990 as reported by Girginov and Bankov (2002). The only new entry in 2008 was field hockey, as it was introduced in the country in 1990, while table tennis had dropped from being the fifth popular sport to a fifteenth position in terms of registered athletes.

General sport participation patterns have been similar to those in other European countries, with school students the most physically active (25 per cent regular participants), followed by the 25–40 age group (17 per cent), and people living in villages and the elderly (7 per cent) (Girginov 1989; Girginov and Bankov 2002). Recently, there have been growing concerns about the low level of participation and general interest in sport. A national representative survey of people aged 15 to 35 years revealed that sport was the fifth preferred leisure pursuit (13.5 per cent) after going out with friends (68 per cent), watching TV (66 per cent), listening to music (49 per cent) and surfing the Internet (37 per cent). It is also concerning that 70 per cent of young people aged 20 to 35 have not done any sport at all in the past year (Mediana 2008). The above and the 'Youth in Action' survey (NCSSO 2005) have confirmed a well-established global trend that higher education and income, and urban environment are associated with greater participation in sport (Collins 2008; Cushman *et al.* 2005; Kamphorst and Roberts 1989; Van Bottenburg *et al.* 2005).

Sport participation policy as state activity

This section considers the making of sport participation policy as state activity. Historically, the state, irrespective of its socio-political form, has always been instrumental in determining the strategic orientation and implementation of sport policies (Girginov 2001, 2009). More specifically, building on those previously mentioned studies the role of the state is analysed as the site and the generator of sport strategies. Those strategies can be viewed as designed to address wider social, political and economic issues with implications for sport, as well as participation-specific agendas. In both cases they become possible through a process of strategic selectivity where the structure and the operations of the state provide the site for playing out this selectivity. For example, between the 1960s and 1980s the state selectivity favoured the use of sport for military training, enhanced work productivity and patriotic education of young people in particular. As a result, structural and material privileges were provided to policies and initiatives promoting those aims. The state becomes the generator of strategies because it offers the strategic terrain where the state system's formal unity (e.g. as a sovereign state) and substantive unity (e.g. as the social basis of support and a hegemonic project) can be established. However, it is also important to note that current sport participation policies should be considered as the product of past political strategies and struggles. The notion of state selectiveness is informative for analysing sport policy because it helps to identify the key preconditions for instigating the policy process (the pursuit of specific strategies), establishing two domains: membership (social identities) and structure (social relations). In addition, the significance of specific historical settings in which state–society relations evolve asserts the idea that previous contests form the conditions for recent/current struggles. Thus, an understanding of state activity in the field of sport participation entails considering the following points:

(1) Sport participation policy making represents a strategic terrain where its orientation has to be established through struggles; its outcomes are always

uncertain and contingent on specific historical settings (i.e. sport policy has a relational character).

(2)   The nature of those struggles is the pursuit of state and sport formal (as an institution) and substantive (as a hegemonic project) unity. Sport participation policies are put together by individuals and groups trying to assert their interests and knowledge while competing for core positions in the domain and for greater privileges (i.e. state hegemonic and sport project).

(3)   If the state is the site of competing sport strategies, it is the state managers who act within the state system, thus their interpretations of the struggles are crucial for the materialization of state policies (i.e. managers' interpretations of sport policy).

(4)   Past and present struggles and their outcomes create various socio-political environments that presuppose the forms of state intervention in sport (i.e. forms of state intervention in sport).

(5)   State selectivity in sport may be class, gender, regional and local, or elite and mass sport, and needs to be established rather than taken for granted (i.e. strategic selectivity in sport policy).

The above five points will be employed to guide the analysis of Bulgaria's sport participation policy. Policy making is not a linear and logical process where policy makers identify a problem, undertake research, consider the results and make rational policies which are then implemented. Policy analysis therefore, as Majchrzach (1984) pointed out, includes recognition that policy is not made but accumulates and implies a series of successive approximations in which policies are constantly suggested, implemented, evaluated and revised, and that the process of making policies is as complex as the social problem itself. Moreover, people's participation in sport is a multifaceted phenomenon that cannot be attributed to a single factor such as the availability of free time, funding or facilities. Sport participation has been defined from a number of perspectives including psychological, behavioural, social, organizational and ecological (Cale and Harris 2006; Compass 1999; Foster *et al.* 2005; Plotnikoff *et al.* 2005), and there is no agreement between academics and policy makers on how best to define and measure this construct. Ecological approaches to physical activity promotion emphasize the need to intervene on multiple levels (individual, organizational, and policy or societal) if sustainable behavioural change is to be achieved (Cale and Harris 2006; Plotnikoff *et al.* 2005). Thus, using single measures such as participation rates as evidence for the success of sport policies becomes problematic.

Sport policy as a social relation

The events of 1989 heralded a major state reshaping – the launching of the new Europeanization project designed to replace state socialism. With it came a number of paradoxes – there were no legitimate political parties to take the lead, a distinct middle class capable of promoting and guaranteeing the key values of the project did not exist, and there was no market economy in place capable of producing democratic institutions for the state. The transformation was designed and implemented by the only significant political and economic actor – the Communist party elite – and its key aim, as Minev (1997: 75) argued, was 'the re-creation of the elite's eroded power, and chiefly of reconcentrating its economic power, which had been lost in the process of industrial development'. The new stateness, which comprises a system and practices or rules as well as patterns of organization and authority, and consists of different elements, resources and social institutions, was politically and socially constructed in an atmosphere of secrecy, obscurity and uncertainty. The civil society was grossly excluded from this process, which did not allow clear group interests and strategies to be expressed, apart from those of the key actors (Kolarova 1994). The state's economic and social policies have been substantially dictated by external agents, such as the European Union, the International Monetary Fund and the World Bank.

The state's response to the events in the field of sport was ambiguous and politically motivated as all pre-1989 strategies, structures and achievements were labelled 'communist' and bound to be demolished. For three years, from being a clearly defined area of state policy, sport became a 'no-man's-land' with no well-articulated policy from ruling or opposition parties. Establishing a new policy and institutional order in sport followed two classical steps of discrediting the institutions to be replaced (e.g. the Bulgarian Sport Union (BSFS), an umbrella voluntary organization, and multi-sport societies at local level (DFS)) and offering an alternative order including a state agency and a network of single-sport clubs. DFSs played an important coordinating role at municipal level by supervising and providing a range of services to all sport clubs within their catchment area. They also used to own and run most of sport facilities on their territory. More importantly, DFSs represented the collective voice of sport to the local state and party committees. In 1992 the government effectively dismantled the BSFS and DFSs (not for being ineffective but as ideologically discredited) and set up a State Committee for Youth and Sport (between 2002 and 2005 it changed to a Ministry of Youth and Sport, before becoming the State Agency for Youth and Sport until August 2009, when it became again a Ministry of Physical Education and Sport, henceforth SAYS). However, SAYS did not publish its strategy until 1996, thus subjecting the sport domain to a four-year conceptual vacuum, replete with uncertainties and leadership improvisations. The average tenure of a SAYS Chairperson has been two years, indicating the political volatility of the post and the institution. No coherent national sport participation policy emerged in this period.

The complete demise of the BSFS in 1998 (after 40 years of operation) was a major change within the sport domain, which resulted in the end of an established sport participation delivery system. As a result, institutions and individuals lost their identification with projects previously promoted by the state, which guaranteed their position in the system. The sport policy domain had to be re-established, which constituted a complex process involving legal, economic, organizational and personal struggles. As the former president of the Bulgarian Gymnastics Federation (1992–98) pointed out: 'Despite the international reputation of gymnastics, the federation was considered non-legitimate by the new (anti-Communist) government administration and had to struggle for six years to gain a formal registration as a governing body' (personal communication, 17 June 2001). His concern was echoed by his successor, who indicated that in the ideological and economic climate of the 1990s and early 2000s, 'from being a well-established profession before 1989, now coaching does not appear on the national register of professions' (personal communication, 26 July 2001). Although between 1990 and 2009 no government ever ceased funding sport, the transformations urged reconfiguration and renegotiation of sport participation policies as well as the place of all actors in the domain. As the rest of this chapter demonstrates, this has turned sport participation into strategic terrain and a relation between the state and various voluntary and commercial agencies.

State and sport hegemonic projects

The launch of the Europeanization project created a specific conjuncture between old and new. As the projected new state had to be built on a new terrain, priority number one of each incoming state apparatus became denouncing previous policies and dismantling the remnants of the past. In doing so, traditional cultural, personal and economic links were cut, thus creating a vacuum in policy formulation, relations and institutions. This made projects' and actors' places in political, economic and sport domains highly uncertain. Pettigrew *et al.* (1992) observed that the concept of legitimacy is central in linking political and cultural analyses essential to the understanding of continuity and change, and provides support to the main premise of the hegemonic project. It suggests that the search for, or restoration of, one's tarnished legitimacy has become an essential part of the behaviour of various group and individual actors in the sport sector.

The restoration of actors' legitimacy in the sport domain needs to be analysed in relation to the prevailing balance of power of the state. The idea of the sources of organized power in society is intertwined, and corresponds closely with the idea of human interactions and interests in different settings, and how it is articulated by the state in enhancing its capacity. Hall (1985) identified three types of power and argued that '[w]here ideological, political and economic powers move in the same direction, it is extremely likely that great social energy will be created . . .', resulting in societal change, or what he calls 'enabling power' (p. 47). The process of channelling the three powers in one direction determines the state hegemonic project (Jessop 1990). It involves the organization of various forces under the political, moral and intellectual leadership of a political actor.

It also constitutes an ideological mechanism through which subjects are endowed with specific identities, social positions and interests (i.e. interpellation). This mechanism is grounded in the accumulation of cognitive and organizational learning capacities (developed through agents' interaction), which are released during crises in the old social order. As modern Bulgarian sport history demonstrates, the ideological agenda of the three hegemonic projects, capitalism (1878–1945), socialism (1945–1989), and Europeanization (1990–present) promoted, as central, the need to increase sport's dependency on the state, and to instil a culture of administrative supremacy in sports policy making, as opposed to public consultations and encouragement of local initiatives (Girginov 2001). A similar approach to Thatcherism, as a hegemonic project, in relation to leisure policy in the UK is argued by Henry (2001).

Table 7.1 shows the relationship between state hegemonic projects, sport projects and specific policy instruments used for interpellation (1987–2008). The

Table 7.1 State and sport projects and main policy instruments (1987–2008)

Year	State project	Sport project	Main policy instruments
1987	Reconstruction of socialism	Greater voluntarism and democracy in sport; sport participation should assist the state in achieving its strategic objectives.	Directives promoting state professionalism and sport services.
1992	Europeanization (joining European structures and accepting commonly established political, economic and social principles and standards)	Democratization of sport; implementing state policy in preserving and improving nation's health and developing the achievements of Bulgarian sport; clear orientation towards elite sport; sport participation seen as a basic human right.	Restructuring national sport domain through licensing, funds allocation and administrative intervention.
1996	Europeanization (compliance with a wide range of common European policies)	Democratization of sport; implementing state policy in preserving and improving nation's health and developing the achievements of Bulgarian sport; clear orientation towards elite sport; sport participation seen as a basic human right.	Conception of Sport and Sport Law (1996).
2008	Europeanization (meeting specific standards in social and economic policy making)	Tackling wider social (e.g. lack of participation, obesity, anti-social behaviour) and organizational agendas (poor coordination between different levels of government) through sport; sport participation seen as inherently good thing.	National- and area- (e.g. Sport for All, Learn to Swim) specific programs; a project-based approach; funding allocated against agreed targets and by meeting certain criteria.

Europeanization project has been hegemonic in nature, as it sought to endow specific identities and interests, and to mobilize wide social support by offering structural and other privileges to various classes and groups. The forging of the institutional unity of the state was presupposed both by the need to deregulate the totalitarian state and by strategies promoted by the former Communist Party elite in attempts to stabilize their economic power. Closely related to that was the process of building the state's substantive unity. Whether seen as a political or a civil project, social unity was not sought through the support of particular social groups, but rather was based on clientelistic relations[1] between political parties, state or foreign agencies and the third sector, including sports associations. Until the late 1990s the sport project had been clearly linked to an anti-communist political agenda, which was largely responsible for dismantling the delivery base of participation and for driving out of the field scores of qualified athletes, coaches and administrators. The state hegemonic project was equally responsible for the dissolution of the other two main Sport for All providers – the Youth League and the Trade Unions. It was not until 2005 when the sport project became associated with wider social and organizational issues that it transcended single political ideologies. In particular, the state, through SAYS, has been instrumental in establishing two domains critical for the policy making process: membership (social identities) and structure (social relations), which are discussed below.

Managers' interpretations of sport policy

State, voluntary and commercial organizations' managers' interpretations of sport policy have been critical in shaping the course of different (in)actions. The Europeanization project in sport began with a major rift between the state and the voluntary sector. It was indicative of the national umbrella voluntary sport organization's leadership interpretation of sport policy. In 1990 the seventh BSFS congress portrayed the party–state policy in sport as 'voluntaristic' (BSFS 1990: 7), because it charged a voluntary organization with the main responsibility for implementing sport in people's daily lives. Thus, the BSFS acknowledged that there was a gap between the state's expectations and the system's capabilities. Pettigrew *et al.* (1992: 290) referred to this type of situation as 'crisis-as-opportunity' where actors' perceptions of crisis push a problem up the policy agenda. Consequently, all NSOs declared their commitment to elite sport and discarded the units dealing with mass participation. In this way they actively initiated two related processes by: (1) translating the crisis into a political and social discourse presupposing incremental changes, and (2) restoring their tarnished legitimacy by displacing Sport for All from the crisis in the economy (lack of resources) to the political system (the new democratic state) by calling for more state intervention.

Equally illuminating was the view of the SAYS's chairman, who was instrumental in dismantling the BSFS and DFS on ideological grounds. In a 1998 interview for the biggest daily newspaper *24 Hours*, Mr Bartchovski portrayed this episode as an achievement for sport. The specific interpretations of sport participation policy by three NSOs have been detailed elsewhere (Girginov and Sandanski 2008). It is worth noting here that those interpretations tend to change in line with changing political, economic and social contexts. The case of swimming is particularly informative as it has come full circle. Before 1990 swimming was a major participation sport heavily supported by the state, and by voluntary and commercial agencies. Between 1990 and 2006 mass swimming disappeared from the policy agenda, to the point where the Secretary General of the governing body of this sport considered the clubs dealing with recreational swimming to be unwelcome members of the federation. As she put it, 'We cannot be concerned with supporting those who are in the business of bathing children. We can only finance those who are producing elite athletes' (personal communication, 17 February 2004). A similar attitude to sport participation is shared by other NSOs and was shaped both by the government pressure for international success and by sport organizations' low delivery capacity. However, the 2006 national initiative 'Learn to Swim' acknowledged the importance of building on past experiences (e.g. the popular 'Learn to Swim' campaign from the 1970s and 1980s). Similarly, it was funded by SAYS and the Ministry of Education, but this time clubs were invited to apply for projects on a competitive basis.

The above two examples illustrate the interplay between actors' legitimacy and managers' interpretations of political and social environment. They also demonstrate that, despite political rhetoric, from a strategic point of view (i.e. visions, resources and delivery capacity) sport participation has been assigned a secondary position to elitism.

Forms of state intervention in sport

Between 1992 and 2004 the rationale for state intervention in sport was based on concerns about democratization of sport, promotion of healthy lifestyles and enhancing the international standing of Bulgarian athletes. However, as Table 7.2 demonstrates, the focus and delivery mechanism of the national sport policy (1997–2000) were very vague and wishful and open to interpretation. The main priority was the reconstruction of the sports domain, which had detrimental effects on mass participation policies. The 2001–2004 policy put a clear emphasis on school-aged boys and girls and gifted young athletes. The state interest in school sport was, of course, not new. Historically, school sport was undoubtedly the first policy area affecting sport identified for state intervention, as early as the 1880s. Since then, with no exceptions, every state and sport administration has expressed concern about pupils' health and fitness and has tried to promote strategies to tackle them. These issues have been regularly placed on the agenda of various responsible national agencies, including the Ministries of Health, Education and Defence, youth organizations and sport associations, and none was complacent about them. This made schools a strategic terrain for implementing sports initiatives, and a large number have been produced. Interestingly, from a state point of view school sport has never been seen as a product for sale, as in the case of aerobics, but as a strategic terrain with a firm state commitment. It has to be noted, though, that despite various ideological rationales, all major national programs have tried to place school sport in a broader concept, like enhancing pupils' military preparation, good citizenship, or health and fitness. School sport, therefore, has been seen rather selectively as an instrument for achieving external objectives rather than as self-expression, development, and fulfilment of individual

Table 7.2 National policies for physical education and sport (1997–2008)

Program	Rationale	Objectives	Target groups	Delivery mechanism	Funding mechanism
1997–2000	Democratization of sport; concerns about health and physical activity of population and poor international performance.	Reconstruction of national PE and sport delivery system; universal access and benefits; promote healthy lifestyle; enhance international successes.	All social groups; youth talents; elite athletes.	Concerted efforts by all stakeholders; sport organizations as delivery partners of the state; sector-specific target programs.	Mixed economy (state, plus voluntarism, market and commercial support).
2001–2004	Same as above.	Improve health and fitness of all, especially young people; increase sport participation rates; raise the number of medals from prestigious sporting events.	School boys and girls; people with disabilities; youth talents; elite performers.	Same as above, plus facility management programs and coaching qualification schemes.	Mixed economy (state, plus voluntarism, market and commercial support).
2005–2008	Concerns about decreasing participation levels, especially school and university students; poor coordination between public authorities and NSOs in providing free access to facilities; decreasing number of elite athletes due to poor selection system; loss of qualified coaches; poor quality of sport facilities due to unclear ownership.	Increase the number of people doing physical exercises, sport activities and social tourism; assert PE and sport as a means of a healthy way of living for young people; sustain and enhance nation's international sporting prestige; modernise sporting infrastructure in line with EU standards; increase sport funding and put in place effective control mechanisms for their spending.	School boys and girls; people with disabilities and deprived social groups; youth talents; elite performers schemes aimed at attracting additional investments for sporting infrastructure; school–sport clubs–local authorities partnerships.	Same as above, plus local and national programs/ campaigns; health–sport initiatives (on a competitive basis – all eligible non-profit sport governing bodies can apply for funding for projects related to the program priorities and outcomes); public–private partnership.	Governmental grants; Sports Lottery grants (through SAYS); local governments subsidies; sport organizations' own sources.

youngsters (Girginov 2001). The 2001–2004 policy has also given special attention to facility management and coaching development, as two critical issues in the delivery of the main policy objectives.

The national sport program (2005–2008) marks a departure from previous approaches towards better governance, greater effectiveness and accountability. Sport participation has increasingly been framed as a service which is delivered through contractual obligations between the SAYS and various clubs and NSOs. However, none of SAYS's performance indicators for funding allocation are actually concerned with service delivery and participants' experiences. Instead, they are very broad and include both qualitative (popularity and accessibility of sport) and quantitative (e.g. number of participants and athletes, clubs, events held and medals won) indicators. It should also be pointed out that no national sport program produced by the state has been informed by specific policy research. In this regard the National Strategy and Programme for Youth Football Development (2009–2014) can be seen as an exception. Initiated by the Bulgarian Football Union (BFU), it builds on a representative survey conducted among all key stakeholders and delivery partners including 52 per cent of football clubs, coaches, administrators, SAYS's regional sport directors, community sports administrators, PE teachers and selected sponsors (Sandanski *et al.* 2008). However, as noted, no reliable data for participation in different activities exist. This is not a trivial issue and, as Piggin *et al.* (2009: 87) argued in the context of New Zealand, 'public policy is a fertile cultural terrain for examining how policy-makers gather such evidence and come to know about sport and recreation'. Despite their limitations, the three consecutive national programs have created a sense of direction and ensured a more systematic involvement of regional state sport administrations in promoting participation.

Since the mid 1990s the central role of the state in sport policy making was reasserted by the Conception for the System of Physical Education and Sport (CYPES 1996a), a Sport Law (CYPES 1996b) and Council of Ministers decree (CM 1997). At the same time, voluntary sport organizations were largely marginalized in matters of policy and strategy and put under central control. The above documents constitute political and structural mechanisms for shaping the sport domain in line with the state's hegemonic project. However, the centralization of sport governance did not positively affect participation, as the concerns about growing obesity, physical inactivity and unhealthy living, expressed in two consecutive (2001–2004 and 2005–2008) national sport programs, suggest. Smith and Swain (1998) noted that the emergence of a great diversity of unarticulated social practices tends to accentuate the crisis of governance in post-socialism, rather than providing solutions to it. They identified three types of processes affecting the network and institutional legacies: (1) the dissolution of networks and isolation of institutions; (2) the reconfiguration of networks in which institutions interact and learn new forms of action; and (3) the endurance of pre-existing networks and the insulation of institutions. Table 7.3 shows the three types of network transformation processes in the sport sector in Bulgaria. Critical national, regional and local networks established between the sport sector and state agencies responsible for the delivery of sport participation were dissolved and new configurations emerged. The only enduring networks, although in different format, have been between three branches of government

Table 7.3 Dissolution, reconfiguration and endurance of major networks in the sports domain in Bulgaria 1989–2009

Dissolution of networks	Reconfiguration of networks	Endurance of pre-existing networks
BSFS–NSOs–DFSs (1990–1998) DFSs–Sport Clubs (1990–1994)	Disbanding DFSs into single Sport Clubs BSFS and NSOs concentrates on elite sport, Sport for All – out	Ministry of Internal Affairs–Sport Club 'Levski' Ministry of Defence–Sport Club 'CSKA'
NSOs–DFSs (1990–1994)	New personal networks of Sport & Business Executives (1994–2009)	Ministry of Education–School Sport Federation
BSFS–Party/Central Government (1989–1992)	Organizational learning – EU policies, seminars, migration of athletes and administrators (1997–2009)	
DFSs–Party/Local Government (1989–1992)		

– defence, police and education – and various sport associations. Traditionally, sport has always been well-organized within these three spheres of government and a change in ideology was not sufficient to upset the existing networks.

Three basic mechanisms were used in deconstructing the membership of the sports domain with huge implications for the planning and delivery of sport participation policies: (1) structural (a compulsory licensing of all associations in the domain granted by the state agency); (2) financial (allocation of sport facilities previously owned by BSFS and funding); and (3) functional (a direct administrative intervention in voluntary organizations' affairs). For example, in 1997 the state subsidy offered to a sport club for an Olympic gold medal ($3,000) exceeded the annual contribution made to any sport club in more than 120 municipalities (of 160 financed in total) (SAYS 1998a, 1998b). Similarly, in 1991 only four swimming and weightlifting clubs obtained a licence and were eligible for state subsidy. In 2009 the number of licensed swimming and weightlifting clubs was 56 and 51 respectively. Privatization seriously affected participation in swimming, as 93 per cent of the pre-1989 swimming pools were lost to private interests or poor maintenance owing to ongoing court battles over their ownership. The lack of facilities also played a structural-constructive role in shaping the organization-specific domain and directly affected participation. In Varna, one of the leading centres, thirteen clubs operate in the only indoor swimming pool in that area. Thus, the number and quality of sport facilities, which in this case has been determined by a politico-economic process of privatization, has been impacting on the number of participants and their experiences.

In 1993, the Council of Ministers (CM 1993) delegated unrestricted rights to the SAYS to override all voluntary sport organizations' collective decisions. This is what Hausner (1995) termed an imperative strategy to change in Eastern Europe, where the key question is 'how to shape the consciousness of the system's participants such that their behaviour becomes compatible with the views of the central authority' (1995: 251).

State interventions in sport participation have been marked with a great deal of political clientelism, which was just as strong as but less oppositional than that found in Greek sport policy, as demonstrated by Henry and Nassis (1999). Unlike Greece, where historically the political life has been dominated by the rivalry between two main parties, in Bulgaria the past twenty years have seen the rise and fall of many political formations. At the beginning of 2000, the presidents of six national federations (equestrian, ski, jet ski, pentathlon, volleyball and boxing) were acting ministers. Between 1992 and 1999 three ministers and five members of the parliament served as presidents of the Basketball Federation, two ministers presided over the Tennis Federation and Swimming Federation, while a major crisis in the Volleyball Federation was solved by the election of the Minister of Agriculture as president. At present the governing bodies of chess, car modelling, aikido, police sport and the Bulgarian Tourist Union have active politicians (members of parliament and ministers) as presidents. It is interesting that there is no Olympic NSOs among these bodies, which is in contrast to the situation from the 1990s. Mingling politicians with sport was encouraged by former Prime Minister Kostov, who did not see this as a political intervention, but rather as a 'healthy process' which aims to 'help sport, and keeps the mutri (ugly faces, a slang for the mafia) away from it' (Ivanov 1999). However, political clientelism and lobbying have been having 'spin-off' effects on sport participation, as in the case of the 2008 'Learn to Ski' program. It is a legacy of the successful staging of the Women's World Cup in Bansko by the Bulgarian Ski Federation and has been enjoying great take-up by young people. The governing body of skiing could not have successfully bid and organized the World Cup without the political and material support of the socialist government at the time, and in return they launched a mass participation program, which is partly delivered by private providers close to the government.

Following the poor performance of Bulgarian athletes at the 2004 Athens, 2006 Turin and 2008 Beijing Olympics, there have been indications that a reversal to the pre-1990 model of sport is imminent. As SAYS's chairperson Lecheva put it at a press conference upon returning from the 2008 Games, 'The liberal model in Bulgarian sport is gone' (SAYS 2008). This implies that in addition to health and social benefits, and similar to the pre-1989 model, the new sport participation policies will be expected to make a significant contribution to the selection and nurturing of gifted young athletes.

Strategic selectivity in sport policy

Strategic selectivity in sport policy could take a number of forms including being gender, ability, national or local, elite and mass sport oriented. It is established through past and present struggles involving various actors. At a more general or conceptual level, state strategic selectivity in sport has changed from seeing participation as a major contributor to enhancing health, work productivity and defence of the country (1950s–1980s) to a matter of choice (1990s–2005), and more recently as a way of life. Each orientation represents specific values which bear directly on the planning and delivery of sport participation programs. For example, the national PE & Sport Strategy (2005–2008) makes 22 references to physical education in the wider sense of a healthy way of life and only one to sport participation. Similarly, the national program for PE & Sport refers 24 times to physical education and 15 times to participation. This suggests an ecological and comprehensive approach to sport participation demanding a high level of coordination between various providers at national, regional and local levels. A similar approach is at odds with SAYS's preferred project-based model of funding participation initiatives because of its short-term span.

The case of football provides an example for a different strategic selectivity. The National Strategy and Programme for Youth Football Development for young people aged 4 to 17 years (2009–2014, BFU 2009) has been built around the goal of increasing sport participation (43 references) and the overall development of sport (103 references). Much of state and NSOs' selectivity has been presupposed by political priorities and demands from external agencies. The targeting of particular groups of young people by SAYS has been encouraged by the European-wide 'Youth in Action' program sponsored by the European Commission to the tune of $3 million in 2008. The National Programme of Youth Football was developed in response to pressure from a network of local football clubs and calls from FIFA and UEFA which also partly sponsor its implementation. Similarly, the sport participation and development orientation of the National Hockey Federation (BHF) was encouraged by grants from the IOC and the International Hockey Federation (IHF). The IOC and the IHF declared 2001 to be the International Year of Children's Field Hockey, which allowed BHF to receive free equipment that was sufficient to support all clubs. In 2003 the IHF urged BHF to present a five-year development plan on the basis of which it became the only European country to be nominated to receive a $US100,000 grant to build the first artificial hockey pitch in Bulgaria (Girginov and Sandanski 2008). State strategic selectivity is manifested most obviously in the funding allocations to different sports. These are made on the basis of sports' international success; a wider participation base does not guarantee greater funding.

Strategic selectivity can also be discerned in the forming of local authorities' sport budgets. State selectivity has not changed since the launch of the Europeanization project and funds continue to be allocated on a per-capita basis where every preschool child and student gets $1.30 and $2 per year respectively.[2] In this way the state bonus of $93,000 for a gold medal at the 2008 Beijing Olympics equalled local authorities' annual sport participation budget for 71,500 children. Although the state funding for sport in the past four years has increased in absolute terms, the actual per-capita allocations for local authorities' budgets remained the same and these are not likely to make any significant impact on participation.

Conclusions

This chapter considered Bulgarian sport participation policies as a state activity, and strategic relations between different public, voluntary and private actors over time. The building of the new stateness represented a structural-creative process with critical implications for the conceptualization, construction, production and consumption of sport. For twenty years no sports policy properly considered the effects of political, economic and social factors on participation of various groups. As a result, national sport policies were grounded more in ideology than needs, evidence or common interests.

The state control of sport is a dominant process in the social construction of sport participation policy because this process has occurred within the framework of building a new stateness. Thus, sport policies developed alongside the constitution of a new democratic state, which advanced a hegemonic project that was not interested in promoting other powerful actors such as voluntary or private groups. Sports' formal and substantial unity was forged not around strategic visions but around ideological constructs such as the Europeanization project. Voluntary sport associations were granted limited autonomy and non-negotiable contracts, both ensuring their place in the domain and giving a formal unity to the sport democratization project. SAYS retained full central control over major strategic resources – finance, facilities and legal leverage for intervention. The autonomy given to sport associations by SAYS implies that this governmental agency currently directly negotiates and supervises 3,668 sport clubs and 93 NSOs. This is indicative of a high level of centralization and bureaucratization of sport policy making.

The interpretation of sport policy by state and NSO managers proved critical both for ensuring the new legitimacy of those organizations and for framing sport participation as a responsibility of the political system and the individual. The state favoured imperative strategies of intervention in sport participation, comprising a three-pronged approach of compulsory licensing, funds allocation and direct administrative control over sport organizations. Recently, direct interventions have been complemented by a more contractual and targeted approach to participation where NSOs and clubs receive funding against the delivery of agreed targets. Similar practices exist in Canada and the UK (Girginov *et al.* 2009; Green 2008).

Generally, sport participation policies were disjoined (1990–1996) and too broad (1997–2009), and were highly selective in that they continuously identified young people as the main beneficiaries of sport and promoted elitism over mass participation. They also promoted a centralized mode of delivery and only recently started to focus on building organizational capacities at local level. Central and local authorities' sport budgets provide per-capita annual funding only for pre-school children and students, and make no provision for working, unemployed or elderly people and those with disabilities (Bankov 2005). The success of various Sport for All programs continues to be determined by clientelistic relations where those organizations with influential leaders and a powerful political lobby enjoy greater privileges. For seven years (1992–1999) SAYS failed to produce any report informing society and policy makers of the outcomes of national sport participation policies. Although SAYS has since started to publish its annual reports, no evaluation of sport participation policies has ever been carried out. Equally, no sport policy was ever informed by research. There is a lack of knowledge about what works and what does not in promoting sport participation. Annual reports are still exceptions for the majority of NSOs, while such documents simply do not exist at grass roots level. Similar practices not only hinder research, but deprive the leadership of these organizations from having realistic ideas about past policies and a clear direction for new ones, thus dooming the policy process to constant improvisation.

In answering the question 'does policy determine politics?' with regard to elite sport, Houlihan and Green (2008: 19) have argued that 'nationally distinct political characteristics were only very weakly correlated with particular policies and that the dominant developmental process in advanced industrial countries was one of convergence'. There is ample evidence to suggest that in Bulgaria state selectivity determines politics in the field of sport. Bulgarian sport participation policy has been following a line of path-dependency and path-shaping. Nielsen *et al.* (1995: 6) argued for the former Eastern European countries that 'path-dependency suggests that the institutional legacies of the past limit the range of current possibilities and/or options in institutional innovation'. In contrast, 'the path-shaping approach implies that social forces can intervene in current conjunctures and actively re-articulate them so that new trajectories become possible' (1995: 6). Participation policies in established, mostly Olympic sports, were path-dependent and preferred elitism, whereas newly emerging sports such as field hockey and martial arts benefited from the political and social conjuncture and pursued more inclusive strategies for sport development and participation. The path-dependency character of participation policies also explains the absolute dominance of the public sector in the delivery of various programs and the relative weakness of the voluntary and private sectors.

Notes

1 The term 'clientelistic relations' refers to an interdependent economic and political relationship, where firms (or sport organizations) provide political support to politicians, and in exchange politicians distribute economic benefits to client firms.
2 All $US amounts are based on the current exchange rate of $1=1.50 BGN.

References

Bankov, P. (2005) Upravlenie na Sporta v Svobodnoto Vreme [Managing Sport in People's Leisure], B Ins: Sofia.
BFU (2009) *Nacionalna strategia i programa za razvitie na detsko-junosheskia i devicheski futbol 2009–2014* [*National Strategy and Programme for Youth Football Development 2009–2014*], Sofia.
BSFS (1990) Otcet za dejnosta na BSFS [BSFS Report], Sofia.
Cale, L. and Harris, J. (2006) Interventions to Promote Young People's Physical Activity: Issues, Implications and Recommendations for Practice, *Health Education Journal*, 65 (4): 320–337.
Collins, M. (2008) Social Exclusion from Sport and Leisure. In B. Houlihan (ed.), *Sport and Society: A Student Introduction*, London: Sage, pp. 77–98.
Compass (1999) *Sports Participation in Europe: A Joint CONI, UK Sport, Sport England Initiative*, London: UK Sport.
Council of Ministers (1993) *Postanovlenie* No 27–27/7 [Decree]. Sofia: Ministerski Savet.
—— (1997) *Nacionalna programa za razvitieto na fiziceskoto vazpitanie i sporta v Balgaria prez 1997–2000* [*National Programme for Physical Education and Sport in Bulgaria 1997–2000*], Sofia: Ministerski Savet.
—— (1998) *Memorandum for Extended Agreement between the Government of Republic of Bulgaria and the International Monetary Fund (1998–2001)*, Sofia: Ministerski Savet.
Cushman, G., Veal, A. and Zuzanek, J. (eds) (2005) *Free Time and Leisure Participation: International Perspectives*, Wallingford, UK: CABI Publishing.
CYPES (1996a) *Conception for the System of Physical Education and Sports in Republic Bulgaria*, Sofia: CYPES.

—— (1996b) *Zakon za Fiziceskoto Vazpitanie i Sporta* [*Law on Physical Education and Sport*], Sofia: NSA.

Economy Watch (2009) Retrieved from http://www.economywatch.com/economic-statistics/Bulgaria/GDP_Per_Capita on 26 June 2009.

Foster, C., Hillsdon, M., Cavill, N., Allender, S. and Cowburn, G. (2005) *Understanding Participation in Sport: A Systematic Review*, London: Sport England.

Girginov, V. (1989) Trends in Sport Participation in Bulgaria. In T. Kamphorst and K. Roberts (eds), *Trends in Sport: A Multinational Perspective*, Voorthuizen: Giordano Bruno, pp. 185–199.

—— (1998) Capitalist Philosophy and Communist Practice: The Transformation of Eastern European Sport and the International Olympic Committee, *Culture, Sport, Society*, 1 (May): 118–149.

—— (2001) Strategic Relations and Sports Policy Making: The Case of Aerobic Union and School Sport Federation Bulgaria, *Journal of Sport Management*, 15 (3): 173–195.

—— (2009) Bulgarian Sport Policy 1945–1989: A Strategic Relation Approach, *The International Journal of the History of Sport*, 26 (4): 515–538.

Girginov, V. and Bankov, P. (2002) Sport for All in Bulgaria: From a Way of Life to a Matter of Choice. In L. Da Costa (ed.), *Worldwide Experiences and Trends in Sport for All*, Aachen: Mayer & Mayer Sport.

Girginov, V. and Mitev, L. (2002) Modernizing Bulgaria: Todor Yonchev: Middle Class Patriot and the Assertion of a Nation, *The European Sports History Review*, 4: 162–185.

Girginov, V. and Sandanski, I. (2004) From Participants to Competitors: The Transformation of British Gymnastics and the Role of the Eastern European Model of Sport. In V. Girginov and M. Collins (eds), *Sport in Eastern European Society: Past and Present*, Taylor & Francis, London, pp. 815–833.

Girginov, V. and Sandanski, I. (2008) 'Understanding the Changing Nature of Sports Organisations in Transforming Societies', *Sport Management Review*, 11: 21–50.

Girginov, V., Taks, M., Boucher, B., Martyn, S., Holman, M. and Dixon, J. (2009) Canadian National Sport Organisations' Use of the Web for Relationship Marketing, *International Journal of Sport Communications*, 2: 164–184.

Hall, A. (1985) How Should We Theorise Sport in a Capitalist Patriarchy, *International Review for the Sociology of Sport*, 20 (1/2): 109–116.

Hausner, J. (1995) Imperative vs. Interactive Strategy of System Change in Central and Eastern Europe, *Review of International Political Economy*, 2(2): 249–266.

Henry, I. (2001) *The Politics of Leisure Policy*, 2nd edn, Basingstoke: Palgrave.

Henry, I. and Nassis, P. (1999) Political Clientelism and Sports Policy in Greece, *International Review for the Sociology of Sport*, 34 (1): 43–58.

Houlihan, B. and Green, M. (2008) Comparative Elite Sport Development. In B. Houlihan and M. Green (eds), *Comparative Elite Sport Development: Systems, Structures and Public Policy*, Oxford: Butterworth-Heinemann, pp. 1–21.

Ivanov, D. (1999) An Interview with the Prime Minister Kostov, *Capital*, 16 December, p. 11.

Jessop, B. (1990) *State Theory: Putting Capitalist States in their Place*, University Park, PA: Pennsylvania State University Press.

Kamphorst, T. and Roberts, K. (eds) (1989) *Trends in Sport: A Multinational Perspective*, Voorthuizen: Giordano Bruno.

Kolarova, R. (1994) Neglasni sporazumenia pri balgarskia prehod kam demokracia [Tacit Agreements in Bulgarian Transition to Democracy], *Politiceski izsledvania*, 1: 2–13.

Majchrzach, A. (1984) *Methods for Policy Research*, Sage: London.

Mediana (2008) *Mladezta v stranata: sastojanie, problemi, promeni, tendencii, vazmozni parametri i nasoki za mladezka politika* [*Youth in the Country: Status, Issues, Changes, Trends, Possible Parameters and Guidelines to Youth Policy*], Sofia.

Minev, D. (1997) Prehodat-Iluzii i realnosti [The Transition: Illusions and Reality]. In K. Bachijska (ed.), *Prehodat v Balgaria prez pogleda na socialnite nauki* [*Bulgarian Transition as a Subject of the Social Sciences*], Prof. M. Drinov: Sofia.

NCSSO (2005) *Mladite v deistvie* [*Youth in Action*], Sofia.

Nielsen, K., Jessop, B. and Hausner, J. (1995) Institutional Change in Post-Socialism. In J. Hausner, B. Jessop and K. Nielsen (eds), *Strategic Choice and Path-Dependency in Post-Socialism: Institutional Dynamics in the Transformation Process*, Aldershot: Edward Elgar.

Pettigrew, A., Ferlie, E. and McKee, L. (1992) *Shaping Strategic Change: Making Change in Large Organizations, the Case of the National Health Service*, Sage: London.

Pettigrew, A., Woodman, R. and Cameron, K. (2001) Studying Organisational Change and Development: Challenges for Future Research, *Academy of Management Journal*, 44 (4): 697–713.

Piggin, J., Jackson, S. and Lewis, M. (2009) Knowledge, Power and Politics: Contesting 'Evidence-Based' National Sport Policy, *International Review for the Sociology of Sport*, 44 (1): 87–101.

Plotnikoff, R., Prodaniuk, T., Fein, A. and Milton, L. (2005) Development of an Ecological Assessment Tool for a Work Place Physical Activity Programme Standard, *Health Promotion Practice*, 6 (4): 453–463.

Sandanski, I., Dimitrov, L. and Bankov, P. (2008) *Prouchvane vav vrazka s razrabotbaneto na nacionalna strategia i programa za razvitie na detsko-junosheskia futbol v Bulgaria 2009–2014* [*Research Commissioned to the Producing of the National Strategy and Programme for Youth Football Development in Bulgaria 2009–2014*], Executive summary for the BFU board.

SAYS (1998a) *Naredba za fiansiraneto na sportnite organizacii v Balgaria* [*Regulation for Financing Sports Organisations in Bulgaria*], Tip-Top Press: Sofia.

—— (1998b) *Pravilnik za materialni vaznagrazdenija na sportistite* [*Regulation for Financial Rewards of Athletes*], Tip-Top Press: Sofia.

—— (2008) *Registar na sportnite klubove i sportisti v Balgaria* [*Registry of Sport Clubs and Athletes in Bulgaria*], Sofia: SAYS.

Smith, D. and Swain, A. (1998) *Theorising Transition: The Political Economy of Post-Communist Transformations*, London: Routledge.

Stark, D. (1995) Not by Design: the Myth of Designer Capitalism in Eastern Europe. In J. Hausner, B. Jessop and K. Nielsen (eds.), *Strategic Choice and Path-Dependency in Post-Socialism: Institutional Dynamics in the Transformation Process*, Aldershot: Edward Elgar.

Van Bottenburg, M., Rijnen, B. and Van Sterkenburg, J. (2005) *Sports Participation in the European Union: Trends and Differences*, Nieuwegein: W.J.H Mulier Institute and Arko Sports Media.

8   Finland

Shane Collins

Over the last 30 or so years, the number and array of government policies for sport development related activities has increased across countries as diverse as Canada, the United Kingdom, Singapore, Australia, Germany and New Zealand (Bergsgard *et al.* 2007; Collins 2008; Green and Houlihan 2005; Stewart *et al.* 2004; Teo 2008). The trajectory of sport development may have varied between nations, but there has been strong commonality across a range of diverse policy areas such as health, social inclusion, social development, economic development and elite sporting success (Houlihan 1997). Finland's early use of sport as part of social policy stands in contrast to the sport policy development of many other Western countries. Since the early 1960s Finnish sport activities and policies have focused on the promotion of sport for all (SfA) over and above elite sport (Green and Collins 2008). A consistent approach to supporting and developing opportunities for all Finns to participate in sport has resulted in Finland achieving participation levels that are the envy of other countries (cf. DCMS/Strategy Unit 2002).

The aim of this chapter is to examine the development of SfA policies and programs in Finland, along with the current structure and cultural environment within which the policies have been developed. The analysis of the developments in Finnish sport policy has been drawn from empirical research conducted over the past four years; this has included a review of documents on sport development activity along with a series of interviews with senior officials in government agencies and non-government sporting organizations. This chapter is divided into three main sections. The first section provides an overview of the culture and structure of Finnish sport, highlighting the emergence of SfA as a key ethos in sport development and the close web of relationships between the various sporting organizations. The second section discusses current data which highlight the comparatively high levels of sporting activity in Finland. The third section reviews the level of state intervention, in particular the policies and programs which have supported and prioritized SfA over and above elite sport objectives.

Culture and structure of sport in Finland

Finland has a long and rich cultural history, with sport acting as a crucial dimension of self-definition (Meinander 1997). From the early part of the twentieth century, class division played a critical role in the emergence of political parties and the development of sport. The civil war of 1917 resulted in a political chasm between the left and right for both political and sporting organizations. The left–right divide evident in the formation of Finnish politics was reflected in the composition and distribution of sporting clubs and organizations (Kiviaho 1981). As a result, the emerging sporting organizations were closely aligned with political ideologies and impacted upon by extrinsic interests; the Finnish Central Sports Federation (SVUL), members of which were predominantly white-collar workers, held a centre right political ideology and the Workers Sport Federation (TUL), members of which were predominantly blue-collar workers, held socialist orientations (Heinila 1989). Other sporting organizations that emerged in the early part of the twentieth century included the Central Swedish Sports Federation and the Finnish Football Association. It was not until the reforms of 1993 (discussed later in this chapter) that the structure of Finnish sport was altered in an effort to streamline and professionalize sport and remove the political influence involved in funding.

The events of the 1912 Stockholm Olympic Games not only identified Finland as a strong sporting nation, but also had a major effect on the independence of Finland five years later (Heikkala *et al.* 2003; Heinila 1987). The success of Finnish athletes at Stockholm made the Finnish people more politically aware and above all increased their interest in sport (Heikkinen 1987). The role of sport in promoting nationalism led Seppanen to observe that

> Finland was probably the first country in the world in which international success in competitive sports was systematically organized to serve purposes of national integration of society. There is hardly any doubt that sports and sports success in international events served as an important instrument not only in the nation building process of Finland but also in the establishing of Finnish nationalism.
>
> (Seppanen 1970: 17, cited in Woodward 1986)

Meinander (1997) posited that an explanation as to why Finland placed special emphasis on sport in promoting nationalism was the lack of ambition with regard to international politics; as a result sport became an important dimension of national identity and self-definition. In the minds of the Finnish people it was sport, in particular the success of the Finnish middle distance athletes, that 'ran Finland onto the world map' (Heikkinen 1987).

The 1952 Olympic Games were considered a great success by Finland yet, despite frequent expressions of nationalism and a large medal tally, concerns were raised regarding the impact of the Olympic Games on SfA. There was a fear that elite sport would dominate the minds of the Finnish people and as a result SfA would be neglected (Heinila 1989). It was about this time that a shift in focus emerged, with a move towards the ideals of SfA and a reduced emphasis on competitive and elite sport.

During the 1960s, with the emergence of the welfare state, many aspects of social life became part of the political sphere. As a result, sport began to be considered by the Finnish government as an activity that could be used for social policy purposes, particularly in relation to health. The emergence of the welfare state assisted in providing a favourable environment for SfA to develop, with 'sport and physical activity seen as part of building a welfare society where sport and physical culture were part of our social policy' (Interview: A senior government official, 2 June 2005). As a more coherent and systematic approach to sport policy emerged during the 1960s, the dominant discourse of competitive sport began to be challenged and the wider values of physical fitness and health became part of the government's social goals. Political parties began to become involved in sport and, with the modernization of Finnish society, new connections between the state and voluntary organizations, including sport, began to develop (Heikkala *et al.* 2003).

A change in the way sport was defined in Finland also occurred in the 1960s; sport policy development and sport itself were increasingly framed in the language and context of SfA. Traditional expressions that encapsulated the more traditional view of sport were replaced; the term 'urheilu' (= sport), which implied competitive sport, was replaced by 'liikunta' (= movement). Liikunta includes top-level and competitive sport as well as sport for everyone in all its forms, including outdoor activities and recreation. Titles of academic chairs and departments within universities were changed to use the prefix 'movement' instead of sport, as were certain sporting organizations, which in effect demanded that the diverse interests of all people were acknowledged (Heinila 1988). This changing discourse was accompanied by an increasing emphasis on health and well-being, supported by an increasing number of sport-related government policies.

From the 1960s onwards, a strong culture of sport participation developed in Finland. A rapid increase in facility development signalled significant investment in sport in an effort to provide equal opportunities for all groups of the population; between 1964 and 2002 the number of sporting facilities in Finland increased from 14,148 to 29,280 (Stahl *et al.* 2002). Mass sport grew in popularity during the 1970s and 1980s, with increases in health-related activities, adventure sport and experiential physical exercise (Heikkala and Koski 1999). During this time the dominant values of competitive sport were challenged and values of physical health and fitness were promoted (Vuori *et al.* 2004). From this point on Finnish sporting culture shifted to one whereby the values associated with mass participation dominated sport participation policies and activities; a culture described as 'deeply rooted in competition blended with recreation' (Savola 2002: 337). While 'sport nationalism' is not unusual in many countries with regard to elite sport, in Finland sport is understood 'to establish a decisive part of a special spirit of the community' in terms of everyday outdoor activities (Meinander 1997: 6).

Along with the changing ethos towards sport, the structure of sport within Finland was significantly changed in 1993. A number of external events played a role in creating the impetus, most importantly the economic recession and the collapse of the Soviet Union. A desire by the SVUL to westernize and unite Finnish sport was combined with the recognition that sport needed to have one voice and one set of agreed values and priorities. Allied to this was the wish of government to remove the political influence involved in the funding of sport, which was based upon the political support of the sport federations by different political factions. A central component of the restructuring was the formation of the Finnish Sports Federation (SLU) and the disbanding of the SVUL. Not only did the structural reform seek to reduce the influence of political ideologies on the structure and funding of sport but it also sought to move Finnish sport away from its traditional hierarchical structure so that sport was controlled from the bottom, not the top (Heikkala and Koski 1999).

Government organizations

The contemporary structure of sport in Finland, which includes both government and non-government organizations, operates within a legislative framework which reinforces and supports the values, beliefs and policies associated with SfA (referred to later in this chapter). The two key government organizations are the Ministry of Education, within which the Sport Division is located, and local municipalities. At the centre of the non-government organizations are the sport clubs which are responsible for delivering sporting activities to the Finnish public. It is through the extensive sport club network that the majority of Finnish people begin their sports career and are involved in sport at some stage during their life. However, while the club network plays an important role in providing sporting activities to children and young people, with regard to older people they are not such strong actors (Vuori 2009). Other major non-government organizations are the national governing bodies (NGBs),[1] the Finnish Sports Federation (SLU – Suomen Liikunta ja Urheliu), domain organizations (DOs) and the Finnish Olympic Committee (FOC), which plays the dual role of a DO and the independent National Olympic Committee.

The Ministry of Education is the government agency responsible for sport and physical activity policy development in Finland. There are three departments within the Ministry of Education: the Department for Cultural, Sport and Youth Policy, the Department for Education and Science Policy and the Administration department. The Department for Cultural, Sport and Youth Policy is responsible for sport and physical culture within the political system, other government organizations and Finnish society in general. Under the Sport Act (1998), the Ministry is required to create and maintain the preconditions for physical activity, ensuring that all citizens have equal access to public services. This is achieved by securing public subsidies for sports organizations and the coordination of building new sports facilities (Heikkala and Koski 1999).

The National Sport Council acts as an advisory board to government and is a strategic unit of the sport division. The appointment, composition and term of the Council are mandated under the Sport Act (1998), with members being appointed by the Minister after each parliamentary election. A key role of the National Sport Council is to provide comment and recommendations on key sporting issues.

Within the Sport Council there are a further four separate divisions. The sport policy division acts as a preparatory group for the Council, raising issues and preparing recommendations for decisions to be made by the Council. Recently it acquired a new role of evaluating changes in Finnish physical culture. The facilities division oversees the subsidizing of facilities and is responsible for developing a facility subsidy strategy. The two remaining divisions are the sports science division, which prepares recommendations on the level of state funding for research institutes, and the division responsible for physical activities for disabled people.

The municipalities create the administrative framework for the delivery of sporting activities throughout Finland with over 30,000 sport facilities provided and about 95 per cent of them owned and managed by the municipalities (Sjöholm 2002). The dense network of sporting facilities is perhaps somewhat surprising given the large percentage of municipalities with a relatively small population base; more than 200 municipalities have fewer than 4,000 inhabitants while only 6 municipalities have more than 100,000 inhabitants. In 2002, the total budget spent by all municipalities on promoting physical activity was about €670 million, consisting of about 1.5 per cent of the total municipal budget. It is the municipalities that provide significant resourcing to the sport club infrastructure, mainly through the provision of free or reduced-rate facilities (Sjöholm 2002).

The significance of municipal investment in sport in comparison to the state is illustrated by the operations expenditure for Helsinki city, which was about €64 million with an additional figure of about €11 million invested in Helsinki city sport facilities. This is in comparison to a total state investment in sport of €91,397,000 for 2005. Recent legislative change has increased the autonomy of municipalities, resulting in the extent of state control over sport at a municipal level gradually decreasing. Prior to 1993, municipalities were required to allocate funding to the areas defined by the state; however, in 1993 this changed and municipalities gained total independence, allowing them to allocate state funding according to their own priorities (Interview: A senior local government official, 2 June 2005). To assist in achieving their priorities, municipalities have developed cross-sectoral cooperation, with sports boards working far more closely with other policy areas such as transport, health, environment, youth and education. This in part reflects the move towards a wider definition of sport and the purpose of sport, shifting from the narrow view of competitive sport towards a more holistic view of health-enhancing physical activity (Interview: A senior advisor in Regional Government Authority, 3 June 2005).

Municipalities provide support to sport clubs and sport organizations through maintenance, development and building of sport facilities, and the frequent provision of facilities free of charge or with heavy subsidies. The relatively small market for the provision of sports service in Finland also creates issues. There is very little private sector provision of sport facilities or programs although this is increasing in areas that are normally considered to be more expensive such as horse-riding or golf. As discussed by a senior local government official, municipalities also try to control the price of activities provided by the clubs by charging moderate fees. Because of this, sporting organizations, including clubs, are unable to exploit their relative monopoly in the market.

Non-government organizations

The umbrella organization for Finnish sport is the Finnish Sports Federation (SLU), membership of which comprises about 126 organizations including NGBs (approximately 76), regional sport organizations, the Swedish Language Sport Association, sport organizations for special groups, student sport groups, TUL, the FOC, DOs and a number of health-related organizations (see Figure 8.1).

The SLU works at both national and international level on policy that affects sport in general, rather than specific issues related to a particular sport, and is considered a key partner of the government. The five main functions of the SLU are:

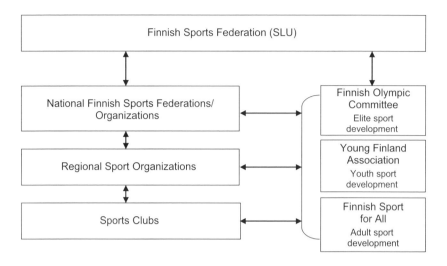

Figure 8.1 Key Finnish non-government sport structure

(1) to support member organizations' interests and activities by influencing political decision-making; (2) to enhance the reputation of sport and physical activity in the minds of both citizens and decision makers, ensuring that children's and youth sports as well as voluntary activities are visible and recognized; (3) to improve the preconditions in sports and support organizations; (4) to provide and support education and training at local, regional and national levels, and conduct international activities to promote tolerance, equality, environment and ethical values; and (5) to perform administrative work and fund-raising, to enhance the sense of community among member organizations (Finnish Sports Federation 2007).

Funding for the SLU is received from three main sources, with approximately 30 per cent from government (approximately €1.4 million in 2006) and additional funding for specific projects, 50 per cent from sport federations and 20 per cent raised by the SLU itself (Interview: A senior Finnish Sports Federation official, 9 March 2006). A key role of the SLU is working closely with a range of government departments including the Ministry of Justice, Ministry of the Interior and Ministry of Social Affairs on matters that are of national importance for sport such as taxation and insurance, or labour legislation. The purpose behind the establishment of the SLU was twofold: first, to provide services to the member organizations; and second, to represent the interests of its member organizations and the Finnish sport culture (Heikkala and Koski 1999).

Three domain organizations operate within the Finnish sport sector. They are focused on the areas of youth sport, top-level sport and recreational sport and health-related activities. Young Finland (YF) is responsible for youth sport, the Sport for All Association (SfAA) and Central Associations for Recreational Sport and Outdoor Activities are responsible for recreational and health-related activities, and the Finnish Olympic Committee (FOC) has responsibility for elite sport. While Young Finland and the SfAA were established in 1988 and 1961 respectively, it was not until the structural change of 1993 that recognition of their role strengthened. It was because of the overlap and duplication of work carried out by the NGBs in relation to youth sport, SfA and elite sport that the DOs were given responsibility for coordinating and overseeing activity across each of these areas. Given the comparatively small size of the DOs – each has between 10 and 26 staff – cooperation, influence and communication are the keys to them achieving their goals. All the DOs work through and with a variety of organizations, but the sporting organizations and the club network are the central partners for all three.

Since 1995 both the level of funding and political support for YF has steadily strengthened, mirroring the growing focus on youth sport in Finland. While increasing participation is a key focus of YF, the organization also works closely with the Finnish Olympic Committee in planning and supporting talent development. In 2006 the strategy of YF focused on the 6 to 18 age group with the intention of extending to include the pre-school group, which includes children 3 to 6 years of age. The key objective of YF is to 'promote children's and youth's well-being and joy of life by means of physical activity' (Interview: A senior Young Finland official, 8 March 2006). This goal further extends the way in which sport is being used beyond the health agenda and towards the wider positive social impacts of sport.

Similar to Young Finland, the Sport for All Association (SfAA) was also established by sport organizations, primarily the SVUL. The goal of the SfAA is to promote well-being and health among citizens by providing knowledge with regard to recreational sport and health-related physical activity in Finland (Interview: A senior SfAA official, 9 March 2006). The SfAA has articulated health as a key objective but has also extended their role by using 'well-being' as a goal, although this has not been clearly defined. There are three key areas through which the strategy is delivered: organized sport, corporate fitness and gym activities. While the target group of the SfAA is the 19 to 63 age group, a key focus is the working population who have below average fitness levels (Interview: A senior SfAA official, 8 March 2006). Contrary to providing sport for all adults, the SfAA is targeting those individuals whose fitness is at a level that impacts adversely upon their ability to work effectively. While adults already participating in sport are the backbone of the SfAA and are provided with programs, there is now an emphasis on delivering programs for people 'who need sports' (Interview: A senior SfAA official, 8 March 2006). Increasingly the SfAA is working with other government departments such as the Ministry of Social Affairs and Ministry of Health, which also have members on the SfAA Board of Trustees. Through agreements with private gymnasiums, there are extensive programs aimed at increasing the fitness levels of employees. Assisting employers in promoting sport and physical activity is a €200 tax-free subsidy (per employee) for providing physical activity programs or facilities. Of the programs that are organized by SfAA, about 50 per cent are focused on physical activity and 50 per cent on sport.

The Finnish Olympic Committee has played a key role in promoting and supporting elite sport in Finland. However, it was not until the mid 1990s that it was recognized as the DO for all elite sport (Interview: A senior FOC official, 7 March 2006). As an independent organization, the FOC is responsible for Olympic member sports; however, as the domain organization for elite sport this responsibility extended to non-Olympic sports, particularly with regard to the Management by

Results (MBR) process introduced by government with the aim of increasing efficiency and enhancing evaluation of performance. The duality of roles does have the potential to create tensions within the FOC with regard to its role as an NOC and being able to accommodate the wider Finnish elite sport sector. The decision to expand the role of the FOC to include non-Olympic elite sport was prompted by concern regarding the role of the state in elite sport and the organization of elite sport. As a result, the Elite Sport Working Group was established with a key aim of clarifying Finland's elite sport development strategy, the distribution of operational responsibilities and the division of labour (Nieminen 2004).

The role and importance of the DOs has steadily grown, with each playing an integral role in the Management by Results (MBR) process. The DOs assist in preparing data relating to the performance of NGBs and provide comment to the Ministry of Education regarding the performance of different sports. This places DOs in an unusual position, as on the one hand they are assisting in the evaluation of sport organizations, while on the other they are selling a service (such as education material and programs) and need to work with NGBs to achieve their own organizational goals.

Historically the NGBs have been oriented towards elite and competitive sport. With about 1,300,000 members Finnish clubs are the core of Finnish sporting culture (Koski 1999). The registration of sports clubs has been steady, with the most active period of growth being the 1980s when about one fifth of all sport clubs were founded (Heikkala and Koski 1999). It is difficult to establish the exact number of sport clubs in Finland but it is estimated that currently over 1 million Finns participate in activities provided by 7,800 sport clubs (Ministry of Education 2009). In 1999 about 36 per cent of children between the ages of 3 and 18 years were members of a sport club, while about 24 per cent of the adult population held a sport club membership (Heikkala *et al.* 1994). What is significant, however, is the number of Finns who participate outside the sport club structure. The Ski Association estimated that between 1.2 million and 2.2 million Finns participate in cross-county skiing outside a club, while in orienteering it is estimated that between 10,000 and 20,000 Finns participate but are not members of a club. This is in contrast to the total club membership of 15,000 and 50,000 for skiing and orienteering respectively.

Approximately 35 per cent of all NGB resources are absorbed by elite sport and 29 per cent of resources are absorbed by youth sport, which has typically been considered part of competitive/elite sport (Heikkala and Koski 1999). As highlighted earlier, lack of focus on youth sport and SfA appears to have been the catalyst for the formation of YF and the SfAA. Furthermore, the narrow focus by NGBs on youth and elite sport was a catalyst for the government in establishing an organization that deals with public health and utilizes sport as one of its means of increasing physical activity levels (Haukilahti, cited in Vuori 2009).

Participation in sport

Finland has been held up as a country that other European countries should aspire to emulate with regard to levels of sport participation, and a number of authors have identified Finland as being distinctive with regard to its ability to achieve and maintain high levels of sport participation (Sport England 2002; Stahl *et al.* 2002). Among young people, surveys indicate that between 1991 and 2005 frequent participation in sport and physical activity gradually increased, due primarily to increased participation in organized sport (Vuori 2009). Furthermore, according to the National Physical Activity Survey, nearly half the children who participated in sport and physical activity did so in activities organized by sport associations (Kansallinen liikuntautkimus 2005–2006, 3 to 18 years, representative sample of 5,505 persons).

With regard to adult participation in sport and physical activity, surveys indicate that Finns are physically more active than the people of many other Western countries. A comparative survey (referred to as the Compass report) of seven European countries (Italy, Finland, Sweden, United Kingdom, Ireland, Spain and the Netherlands) indicated that Finland had achieved levels of sport participation across various age groups and between gender groups that few other countries had been able to achieve (UK Sport, Sport England, and Comitato Olimpico Nazionale Italiano 1999). The Compass report classified sporting activity into seven categories: competitive, organized and intensive; intensive; regular, competitive and/or organized; regular recreational; irregular; occasional; and non-participant.[2] In comparison with the other European countries in the survey, Finland has been able to achieve high levels of participation in 'regular recreational' and 'intensive' categories, indicating not only high participation but also high levels of frequency (see Table 8.1).

Furthermore, Finland stands out from the other countries in having a high percentage of sport participation in groups where activity is undertaken outside of the sport club setting. When we combine the two categories of 'regular

Table 8.1 Sport participation across seven European countries among adults 16+ years†
(%)

	Finland	Ireland	Italy	Netherlands	Spain	Sweden	UK
Competitive, organized, intensive	6	7	2	8	2	12*	5
Intensive	33	11	33	8	7	24*	13
Regular, competitive and/or organized	5	7	2	10	2	5	4
Regular recreational	28	3	3	6	4	17	6
Irregular	6	15	8	25	10	11	19
Occasional	2	21	5	6	6		20
Non-participant; participation in other physical activities	16	10	37**	38	43**	8	15
Non-participant: no physical activities‡	3	26	40		26	22	19

Adapted from UK Sport *et al.* 1999

Notes
† Finland uses 19 years+ as definition for adults and, therefore, was not able to provide information on 16–19 year age group.
* Issues with pre-coding mean that the figures for intensive groups may be inflated.
** Issues with data collection are likely to lead to a serious under-estimation of sport participation in comparison with other countries.
‡ In the reporting of this data, the non-participant category was separated into two groups.

recreational'and'intensive'(categorieswhichinvolveparticipationinsportingactivity undertaken outside of a sport club) we find that 61 per cent of all sporting activity is undertaken in this way, supporting the claim that much of Finland's sporting activity (for those aged 19 years and over) is based outside the formal structure of clubs (UK Sport *et al.* 1999). This is considerably higher than for any of the other European countries surveyed (see Table 8.1). Participation surveys conducted by Suomen Gallup reinforce the Compass report findings; in 2001, it was found that 16 per cent of the Finnish population took part in sport and physical activity within a sport club or sport organization while 75 per cent of Finns took part in sporting activity on their own initiative (van Bottenburg *et al.* 2005).

The high percentage of Finns participating in sport and physical activity outside the club structure has been a consistent phenomenon over a six-year period. In 1991, 1994 and 1997, the percentage of Finns participating in sport and/or physical activity in a sport club or organization remained stable at 15 per cent. Over the same time period the percentage of Finns undertaking sport and physical activity on their own initiative was 77 per cent, 76 per cent and 82 per cent respectively (van Bottenburg *et al.* 2005).

The level of sport participation by females in Finland also contradicts trends in other countries where female participation is often lower than for males. The Compass report indicated that females in Finland had higher levels of participation than males in the 'intensive group', which contrasts with the levels in the six other European countries with the exception of Sweden. While the level of female participation in the 'competitive, organized, intensive' groups is lower, if we take the two groups combined (both reflecting participation at the highest frequency) the participation rate is considerably higher for women (42 per cent) compared to men (34 per cent). In regular, recreational sport participation, female participation was only slightly lower than for men, indicating that gender disparity with regard to participation in sport is not as great in Finland as in the other European countries surveyed (with the exception of Sweden).

The annual survey of the leisure pursuits of Finns reported in 2006 supported the earlier Compass survey by reporting that about '30 percent of both men and women participated in [30 minutes of moderate intensity] physical activity at least four times per week' (Vuori 2009: 122). Furthermore, participation by women in leisure-time physical activities (at least two times per week) has increased steadily since 1978, indicating that participation in sport and physical activity has also been maintained over a period of time. In contrast, participation by men has remained stable since the mid 1990s (Vuori 2009).

Finland's ability to maintain levels of sport participation across various age groups is also in stark contrast to other Western countries. However, with regard to competitive, organized and intensive sport, Finland's declining levels of participation with age indicate that it has not been able to alter the trend which is prevalent in other countries such as the UK, Italy and Ireland. In spite of this, Finland has been able to maintain relatively stable rates of participation in relation to 'competitive organized and intensive', and 'intensive' sport participation (see Table 8.2). The level of sport participation across different age groups, and in particular older age groups, in Finland is noteworthy, given the lack of success in the other European countries in increasing the levels of sport participation among older age groups.

Table 8.2 Sport participation by age group in Group 1 (Competitive, organized and intensive) and Group 2 (Intensive) (%)

Age group	Finland	Ireland	Italy	Netherlands	Spain	Sweden	UK
16–19		36	14	32	17	62	53
20–24	46	33	11	26	14	59	44
25–29	40	23	10	20	13	39	35
30–34	35	13	6	17	7	38	34
35–39	34	17	5	14	7	33	30
40–44		12	4	13	8	32	25
45–49		10	3	11	8	26	21
50–54	38	9	3	13	8	26	20
55–59	41	8	3	16	5	24	18
60–54	46	6	3	8	5	19	14
65+		4	1	7		28	10

Adapted from UK Sport *et al.* 1999

Note: Data was unavailable for some age groups

In summary, the results of the 1999 Compass survey and other supporting research indicate that levels of sport participation in Finland are high in comparison with other European countries' surveys, especially in relation to sporting activity outside the structure of clubs or competition, particularly for adults. It is interesting to note that Finland, along with Sweden, had the highest participation levels among adults and also has high levels of participation among the younger age groups. This may suggest that the foundation for achieving lifelong practice in sport is based upon establishing high levels of participation in children. That Finland is able to achieve high levels of participation not only among younger age groups and females but also across the adult population indicates that they may be some way towards achieving lifelong participation in sport, a goal which many countries have articulated in their respective sport policies but which many have been unable to achieve.

Government intervention: programs and policies

A paradox arises in relation to government intervention in Finnish sport development where at times the government has directly intervened in sport matters while maintaining a strong commitment to ensuring that sport organizations retain their autonomy. As explained by a senior government official:

> the whole idea in our civil society is the idea of autonomy, even though it's a little of a paradox that the state is subsidizing volunteer [sporting] activity we are trying to maintain a partnership but still have them [retain] their own autonomy in these issues.
>
> (Interview: 2 June 2006)

While the rapid construction of facilities during the 1960s illustrated government's commitment to mass participation, the introduction of legislation formally indicated the direction of government policies. At the highest level the Constitution of Finland requires public authorities to guarantee and provide basic rights; while sport is not directly referred to, the requirement for local authorities to provide the preconditions for exercise is interpreted as a basic educational right guaranteed under the Constitution (Sjöholm 2002). The Sports Acts (1980, 1998) and the Finnish Local Government Act (1995) placed requirements on local government to provide sporting opportunities to the community, while the Reform of Provincial State Office Act (2000) mandated an evaluative framework for municipalities in relation to the basic services they provide, including sport for all. The existence of such a legislative framework places sport in a strong position with regard to support at the state and municipal level, as it incorporates sport within the health and social policy framework.

Alongside the legislative framework a number of policies have been developed that further support and encourage mass participation in sport. The late 1970s and 1980s witnessed a number of government policies and strategy documents, which reinforced SfA. A key document in the development of the sport policy in Finland was the Report of the Sports Act Committee in 1976, which provided the foundation for the passing of the Sports Act in 1980. While the 1980 Sports Act clarified and legitimized the already existing informal structures of sport in Finland (where the state and municipalities take responsibility for ensuring that facilities are available for the Finnish people while sport organizations manage and deliver sporting activities), it also officially recognized the social significance of the sports movement (Heinila 1988; Vuori *et al.* 2004; Woodward 1986).

Furthermore, the 1980 Sports Act reaffirmed support for SfA and provided increased resources for SfA activities and programs. Subsidies were allocated to municipalities for the express purpose of providing 'sports secretaries' (local organizers) in the municipality along with funding directed toward facility development (Vuori *et al.* 2004). This intervention by the state, in directing the way in which municipalities must allocate capital and organize their sport division, was an interesting contrast to the hands-off approach taken towards sporting organizations. The passage of the Sports Act may also have reduced the risk that sporting bodies or organizations would change the focus of sports policy away from SfA towards another area such as the development of elite sport.

State policies continued to reflect the emphasis of the government in providing sporting opportunities for all regardless of ability as well as promoting health and well-being. As stated in the national document *Directions of Finnish sports policy in the 1990s*, the main aim of sport policy was 'well-being through exercise and sports – sports for all' (Vuori *et al.* 2004). While SfA was the dominant term from the 1960s to 1980s, Health Enhancing Physical Activity (HEPA) was to emerge as a new term, which would encompass sporting activity as well as other forms of physical activity.

The structural change of 1993 was followed by the introduction of managerial processes to the sport sector. The introduction of the Management by Results (MBR) system in the 1990s reflected a desire of government to achieve increased efficiency and transparent evaluation. MBR is used to assist the government in allocating funds to NGBs based upon their performance in three areas: youth sport, SfA and elite sport. State funding is allocated according to the NGBs' result in each of those areas with 50 per cent allocated to youth sport, 25 per cent to SfA and 25 per cent according to results in elite or top-level sport (Heikkala and Koski 1999). Every four years a national survey is conducted involving over 11,000 respondents to determine the type of sport activities that are being undertaken by the public. This information is then presented to the Ministry of Education by the domain organization, and in conjunction with other information is used to determine levels of funding. Unlike more prescriptive management evaluation processes, the MBR process used in Finnish sport is not a strict or inflexible system as factors outside the MBR process are taken into consideration in allocating funding.

The introduction of MBR has had a significant effect on NGBs, and has resulted in a growing emphasis on youth sport and SfA (Heikkala and Koski 1999). However, this change has been gradual and elite-level sport remains a key focus for many sport federations. This may be explained by the fact that despite the introduction of MBR, NGBs still retain considerable autonomy in terms of how they spend state funding. While it is allocated according to performance in the three domain areas, NGBs are able to allocate funding wherever, or on whatever, they wish. There is no compulsion for them to spend the funding on those areas for which the funding was allocated, allowing sports to retain a high level of autonomy in relation to their own direction and focus.

There is a paradox, however, as despite increasing levels of evaluation by government the autonomy of sport has been retained. Sport federations are not required to allocate their spending according to MBR, and can allocate state funding according to their own priorities. While it is necessary for NGBs to provide an annual report, there are no detailed requirements for federations to report back on how government funding is allocated unless it was allocated for a specific project. As discussed by a senior sport official:

> it [MBR] may be a good system. Anyway it's up to federations to decide how to use the money, even if the money comes 50 per cent SfA, the federations can decide how to use the money. So in that regard it is quite OK.
>
> (Interview: A senior NGB official, 7 March 2006)

Increased autonomy was given to municipalities by the state in the 1990s. Legislative change altered funding arrangements, allowing funds given to municipalities by the state to be spent as they wished. However, although the funding by municipalities for sport has increased since 1993, the level of state support both in actual values and as a percentage of the total municipal budget has been steadily decreasing. The extent of the investment in sport by municipalities is unclear, with estimates between €670 million and €368,307,000 by the Ministry of Education (Ministry of Education 2005). What is evident is that the level of investment by municipalities is significant in comparison with that by central government. With the increased autonomy of local government and the increased investment in sport, the influence of the municipalities in delivering sport policy objectives is steadily growing whereas the direct influence of government appears to be lessening. A steady change has, nevertheless, occurred as municipalities move towards supporting SfA principles rather than focusing on competitive sport as they had previously.

The second Sports Act, enacted in 1998, continued to reinforce SfA principles and further increased the emphasis on health and well-being. The purpose of the act was to

> promote recreational, competitive and top-level sports and associated civic activity, to promote the population's well-being and health and to support children's and young people's growth and development through sports . . . to promote equality and tolerance, cultural diversity and sustainable development of the environment through sport.
>
> (Liikuntalaki 1998)

In reinforcing the principles of the preceding legislation, the 1998 Sports Act set out two underlying rationales for government investment in sport: the promotion of health and well-being and the promotion of the broader social benefits of sport, both of which require continued participation in sport or physical activity to achieve their goals. Interestingly, while top-level sport is included under the main purpose of the legislation, it is only directly referred to under section 9 of the Act relating to subsidies for research and development.

While the rapid development of facilities during the 1970 and 1980s slowed, changes to the criteria for state subsidies for construction of facilities and sites for exercise and sports emphasized the need for increased access for 'ordinary people'. The government continued to invest in facilities as mandated under the 1998 Sports Act, with funding for facilities modestly increasing between 1995 and 2003 from €10,596,000 to €14,386,000 (Ministry of Education 2005). To assist in achieving the aims of the second Sports Act (as stipulated in the purpose of the Act) the Ministry of Education directed that over a five year period a major proportion of state resourcing for facility development would be directed at sites that served 'ordinary people in their daily environments' (Vuori *et al.* 2004: 334).

In conjunction with legislation, the Finnish government also established national projects to stimulate support and promote SfA. Two national programs, *Finland on the Move* in 1991, and its successor *Fit for Life* in 1995, were implemented with the aim of motivating ordinary citizens, over 40 years of age, to participate in regular activity. The need to introduce such projects was in part due to the recognition by government that clubs were unable (or unwilling) to deliver this type of service to members (Wuolio 2003) and the need for government to continue steering sport and sport organizations towards the promotion of SfA:

> the Ministry of Education is directly influencing the Federations in this area [SfA] . . . with project money, special money and trying to convince them also by giving money to the local system for sports related activities, and [because of this] our clubs are more and more interested in this matter [SfA].
>
> (Interview: A senior Finnish Sports Federation official, 9 March 2006)

The projects were also the first time that a number of government Ministries cooperated towards achieving a common goal. The multi-sector approach adopted by the *Fit for Life* project was later formalized in the *2001 Government Resolution on Policies to Develop Health-Enhancing Physical Activity*.

Despite Finland being recognized as one of the most active countries in Europe in terms of sport participation, it is impossible with any certainty to determine what effect national and local government policies have had upon achieving this. Finland's success in achieving high levels of sport participation across a range of age cohorts appears to have occurred despite the lack of an overarching policy. By creating the preconditions for sport through an extensive facility network, participation by adults has been left primarily to their own initiative. As one senior state official explained:

> basically the adult mass sport or SfA is very dependent on individuals and their own motivation. There are various projects that we have that subsidize health or [physical activity/sport for] whole of life projects. But they are like pressure points in various municipalities, here and there and here and there. But there is no overall programme or overall institution like that.
>
> (Interview: 2 June 2006)

Conclusion

Finland is a country that has achieved participation levels in sporting activities across all age groups that few other countries have been able to replicate. The shift towards policies and a culture that supported SfA values during the 1960s appears to have strengthened and developed, and little deviation from this path since that time is evident. Social democratic values inherent in Finnish society, such as egalitarianism, have supported and provided a favourable environment for SfA policies (Green and Collins 2008). The increased emphasis on 'physical activity stimulating well-being, fitness and health' has also supported the establishment of SfA policies (Vuori 2009: 145). While initial government policies focused upon ensuring that the preconditions for sport and physical activity were in place, more recent policies reflect a shift towards multi-sector policies and programs. Supporting these policies is the strong cultural tradition for Finns to participate in some sort of physical exercise and/or sporting activity and the consistent approach towards supporting mass participation. While the passing of the two Sports Acts in 1980 and 1998 reinforced sport as a part of social policy and formalized the roles and responsibilities of the state and municipalities with regard to sport policy, the legislation merely recognized practices that were already in operation within Finnish sport.

The level of government intervention with regard to influencing the direction of Finnish sport policy has oscillated between a hands-off approach and one of direct intervention; however, a common theme has been the desire of government to ensure the autonomy of volunteer organizations. Despite this, the influence of government on the direction of NGBs and local government has been significant. The establishment of a legislative framework, the adoption of sport as part of social policy, the prioritization of funding for community-based facilities and the establishment of national SfA programs reinforced to NGBs and local government that SfA was to be prioritized. In contrast, the establishment and funding of the Finnish Sports Federation (SLU) by government ensured that NGBs and other sporting organizations were able to provide a united and influential voice through which to lobby government and shape the direction of sport policy. The level of government intervention and interaction with regard to municipalities has been considerably less than that with NGBs. Nevertheless, through legislation, government has ensured that municipalities are responsible for providing community-based facilities. Therefore, while it may be considered that the government has adopted a less interventionist approach to municipalities with regard to influencing sport policy, the legislative framework and dominant discourse of SfA has meant that the central values evident at national level are also reflected at local government level. Given the structure, culture and political ethos embedded within Finnish society it would appear that Finland will be able to maintain its comparatively high participation levels in sport.

Notes

1 National governing body refers to the lead national organization for a particular sport.
2 Group 1 – Competitive, organized, intensive: (i) Practice of sport ≥ 120 times per year AND (ii) playing at a competitive level in at least one sport AND (iii) member of a sport club.
   Group 2 – Intensive: (i) Annual frequency of participation ≥ 120 times per year AND either not playing at a competitive level in any sport OR not a member of a club OR neither (ii) nor (iii).
   Group 3 – Regular, competitive and/or organized: (i) Annual frequency of participation ≥ 60 and <120 AND either (ii) playing at a competitive level in at least one sport OR (iii) member of a sport club OR both (ii) and (iii).
   Group 4 – Regular recreational: (i) Annual frequency of participation ≥ 60 and <120 AND (ii) not a member of a sport club AND (iii) not playing competitively in any sport.
   Group 5 – Irregular: (i) Annual frequency of participation ≥ 12 and <60.
   Group 6 – Occasional: (i) Annual frequency or participation ≥1 and<12.
   Group 7 – Non-participants: (i) No recorded participation over the last 12 months.

References

Bergsgard, N.A., Houlihan, B., Mangset, P., Nødland, S.I. and Rommetvedt, H. (2007) *Sport Policy: A Comparative Analysis of Stability and Change*, Oxford: Butterworth.

Collins, S. (2008) 'New Zealand'. In B. Houlihan and M. Green (eds.), *Comparative Elite Sport Development: Systems, Structures and Public Policy*, Oxford: Butterworth-Heinemann.

Finnish Sports Federation (2007) *The Finnish Sports Federation Strategy*, http://www.slu.fi/eng/finnish_sports_federation/finnish_sports_federation_s_stra/ (accessed 20 December 2007).

Green, M. and Collins, S. (2008) 'Policy, politics and path dependency: Sport development in Australia and Finland', *Sport Management Review*, 11: 225–251.

Green, M. and Houlihan, B. (2005) *Elite Sport Development: Policy Learning and Political Priorities*, Oxford: Routledge.

Heikkala, J. and Koski, P. (1999) *Reaching Out for New Frontiers: The Finnish Physical Culture in Transition in the 1990s*, Finland: University of Jyvaskyla.

Heikkala, J., Koski, P. and Puronaho, K. (1994) *The Organization and Economy of Finnish National Sport Organizations*, International Sociological Association.

Heikkala, J., Honkanen, P., Laine, L., Pullinen, M. and Ruuskanen-Himma, E. (2003) *The Story of Exercise and Sport*, Helsinki: Finnish Sports Federation.

Heikkinen, A. (1987) 'The role of sport in the history of Finland'. In Shimizu and Shigeo (eds), *ICOSH Seminar Report: Civilizations in Sport History*, Kobe Japan: Maiko Villa.

Heinila, K. (1987) 'Social research on sports in Finland', *International Review for the Sociology of Sport*, 22(1): 3–24.

—— (1989) 'The sport club as a social organization in Finland', *International Review for the Sociology of Sport*, 24: 225–248.

Hornbuckle, A. R. (1996) 'Helsinki 1952: The Games of the XVth Olympiad'. In J.E. Findling and K.D. Pelle (eds), *Historical Dictionary of the Modern Olympic Movement*, Westport, Conn: Greenwood Press, pp. 109–118.

Houlihan, B. (1997) *Sport Policy and Politics: A Comparative Analysis*, London: Routledge.

Koski, P. (1999) 'Characteristics and contemporary trends of sports clubs in the Finnish context'. In K. Heinemann (ed.), *Sports Clubs in Various European Countries*, Stuttgart: Schorndorf Hofmann.

Laasko, L. (1976) 'Characteristics of the socialization environment as the determinants of adults sport interests in Finland'. In *Proceedings of the International Congress on Physical Activity Sciences*, Quebec, July 11–16, 1976, vol. 9: 103–111.

Liikuntalakai (Sports Act) 18.12.1998/1054, http://www.finlex.fi/fi/laki/ajantasa/19981054 (accessed 14 March 2008).

Meinander, H. (1997) 'Prologue: Nordic history, society and sport', *International Journal of the History of Sport* (14): 1–10.

Ministry of Education (2005) *Sports in Light of Statistics: Basic Statistical Information 2003 (liikuntatoimi tilastojen valossa: perustilastot vuodelta 2003)*, http://www.minedu.fi/julkaisut/liikunta/2005/opm24.pdf (accessed 12 April 2006).

Nieminen, L. (2004) 'Elite sport: In search of a future', *Motion: Sport in Finland (Helsinki)*, (1): 28–29.

Savola, J. (2002) 'Finland, the country where sport is for all'. In L.P. DaCosta and A. Miragaya (eds), *Worldwide Experiences and Trends in Sport for All*, United Kingdom: Meyer and Meyer Sport.

Sjöholm, K. (2002) 'Municipal sport and youth sport in Finland'. Paper presented at the conference *Out of Bounds: An International Idea Exchange on Sports, Rrecreation and Youth Programmes*, Boston, USA.

Sport England (2002) *Game Plan: A Strategy for Delivering Government's Sport and Physical Activity Objectives*, UK: Strategy Unit/DCMS.

Stahl, T., Rutten, A., Nutbeam, D., and Kannas, I. (2002) 'The importance of policy orientation and environment on physical activity participation: A comparative analysis between Eastern Germany, Western Germany and Finland', *Health Promotion International*, 17(3): 235–246

Stewart, B., Nicholson, M., Smith, A., and Westerbeek, H. (2004) *Australian Sport: Better by Design? The Evolution of Australian Sport Policy*, Oxford: Routledge.

Teo, L. (2008) 'Singapore'. In B. Houlihan and M. Green (eds), *Comparative Elite Sport Development: Systems, Structures and Public Policy*, Oxford: Butterworth-Heinemann.

UK Sport, Sport England, and Comitato Olimpico Nazionale Italiano (1999) *COMPASS: A Project Seeking the Co-ordinated Monitoring of Participation in Sports in Europe*, London: UK Sport.

van Bottenburg, M., Rijnen, B., and van Sterkenburg, J. (2005) *Sports Participation in the European Union: Trends and Differences*, Nieuwegein: Michel van Troost.

Vuori, I. (2009) 'The contribution of sport to community health in Finland'. In H. Westerbeek (ed.), *Using Sport to Advance Community Health: An International Perspective*, Arko Sports Media: Nieuwegin.

Vuori, I., Lankenau, B., and Pratt, M. (2004) 'Physical activity policy programme development: The experience of Finland', *Public Health Reports*, 119: 331–345.

Woodward, S.C. (1986) 'Finnish sport structures: An overview', *Momentum*, 11(1): 51–61.

Wuolio, T. (2003) 'Money and labour in elite sports: Justifying public funding is the question', *Motion: Sport in Finland*, 1: 10–12.

9   South Africa

Cora Burnett

By the late 1800s the African continent had become a major political game for colonial 'masters' where European powers amalgamated some 10,000 African polities into forty European colonies and protectorates by treaty and/or conquest (Meredith 2006). The modern states of Africa are thus largely a result of European political negotiations, where boundaries were created along geometric lines enclosing diverse populations to establish colonial territories for France, Germany, Belgium, Portugal and the British Empire. In South Africa, the British Empire subjected the two independent Boer republics and sowed the bitter seed of Afrikaner nationalism that would flourish after the formation of the Union of South Africa, which received independence in 1910 under white minority rule (Allen 2003). The Afrikaner sporting culture became predominantly associated with rugby, when in 1908 a national team competed under the emblem of the springbok (Nauright 1992, 1997). The politics of race, ethnicity and sport was thus tied in the very nexus of rugby symbolism.

High performance or elite male sports such as rugby and soccer in the South African context are considered to be the national sports and thus carry the symbolism of the formation of a national identity through advocacy and by association. This is also true for international events (Lee and Maguire 2009). The media inevitably plays a dominant role in mediating event rhetoric and event symbolism, with various degrees of potency and effect to nation-states and key political stakeholders (Houlihan 1991). In South Africa, the importance of being the host nation for several world cups since hosting and winning the Rugby World Cup in 1995 has in this sense conveyed a message of 'nation building' and 'reconciliation'. This was vividly captured by Nelson Mandela supporting the predominantly white national team (under the slogan of 'One Team, One Nation'), as a political gesture of reconciliation between white and black South Africans. Yet, this gesture of statesmanship did little to transcend the persuasive media imagery to heal the manifested racial divides and inter-racial conflicts eroding the very fabric of South African society (Steenveld and Strelitz 1998). The 2010 'Africa FIFA World Cup' similarly carried the symbolic imagery of African countries being recognized as a continent of stature, with South Africa celebrating the event 'on behalf of its African brothers', in recognition of their political support during the struggle for freedom and democracy. International relations are thus at the heart of participation in elite sport and hosting such mega events while profiling the state within the global and national context and ideology it wishes to portray.

Piggin *et al.* (2009) make a convincing case to illustrate how policy makers draw on a wide range of knowledge sources in the formulation of policies. By utilizing Foucault's conception of governmentality or 'art of government', they explore the myriad ways in which the state manipulates power relations, implements strategies and passes legislation to influence the values and behaviours of citizens to achieve national and global outcomes. At an international level, the United Nations declaration of 2005 as the International Year of Sport and Physical Education resulted in nation states increasingly directing their intervention towards mass participation. Resources were allocated for health benefits, to enhance the quality of life of citizens and to include marginalized groups (e.g. women, impoverished communities and groups, and 'youth at risk') in structured physical activity (Schultz 2007). In 2006, the South African Deputy Minister of Sport and Recreation acknowledged UNESCO's leadership in addressing 'wellness and development'. He pledged the government's commitment to 'massifying participation in sport and recreation' through the government's flagship community-based mass participation program (*Siyadlala*, a Zulu word meaning 'Let us Play') (Oosthuizen 2006).

In recognizing that the state machinery is pivotal to facilitating national and global sport, this chapter provides a historical overview of policies, structures and consequential practices in South Africa. The national discourse of race is central to the thrust for transformation and sports-related development in state-funded mass and elite sporting practices and structures. Two case studies will be presented in this regard.

Historical overview

The political union in 1910 represented a colonial system in South Africa that paved the way for apartheid, which was implemented after the white-dominated National Party came to power in 1948. Segregation between various 'racial categories' was awarded socio-political merit and was legally constituted (Lapchick 1979). Various 'apartheid laws' were instituted, such as the Prohibition of Mixed Marriages Act (1949) and the Urban Areas Act (1955), which reserved sport facilities for special racial groups and set the scene for discrimination (Gemmel 2007) and politically inspired violence (Burnett 2005). The 1960s signified an era of well-organized domestic and international political resistance led by the Supreme Council for Sport in Africa. Anti-apartheid activists within South Africa and abroad successfully elicited political support to ensure the country's exclusion from major competitions and representation on international sporting bodies, and also placed a moratorium on rebel sporting tours (Guttmann 1992; Kidd 1988). International political action was taken in which international political leaders increasingly played an important role in ensuring sporting boycotts against South Africa and implementing punitive actions against rebel tours, particularly in rugby and cricket, regarded as white male bastions of superiority (Bose 1994). Major stakeholders such as the International Olympic Committee, the Commonwealth Games Federation and the International Amateur Athletics Federation were mobilized against apartheid (Guelke 1993).

International political pressure and isolation contributed to some internal reforms under the National Party's regime (Booth 1998). However, superficial changes and persisting racial segregation met with severe opposition from the

South African Council on Sport (SACOS). This body followed in the footsteps of SANROC (South African Non-Racial Olympic Committee) which, under the charismatic leadership of Dennis Brutus, stepped into the breach vacated by the outlawed African National Congress (ANC) to facilitate anti-apartheid unity under the slogan of 'No normal sport in an abnormal society' (Merrett 2003). The leaders rejected multinationalism, represented by the division of sport federations into African, coloured, Indian and white associations; only members from the latter institution could qualify for Springbok honours and thus represent the country at international competitions (Archer and Bouillon 1982).

During the 1980s SACOS maintained an 'uncompromising ideological grip on sport', while a pro-collaboration group formed the National Sports Congress in 1989 to successfully broker a new sports order. In removing the bans on the ANC, the Communist Party and the Pan African Congress (PAC) in February 1990, President de Klerk fundamentally changed South African politics and new non-racial umbrella controlling bodies were structured in Olympic and non-Olympic sports. The ANC leadership supported negotiations and most international federations lifted their boycotts by 1992 after the ruling National Party (NP) had repealed the legislative foundations of apartheid (Booth 1998).

South African sport entered a new era when the first democratic elections of 1994 spelled the end of SACOS, which was still entrenched in an ideology of resistance politics and non-cooperation. The Constitution of a democratic South Africa and its Bill of Rights provided the basis for sporting unity and solidarity. South Africa's participation in the 1992 Barcelona Olympic Games was met with internal disillusionment over the racial composition of the team, which comprised 80 per cent white athletes. The lack of a national identity was also evident as spectators still waved the old tricolor flag despite Nelson Mandela's (president-in-waiting) claim of unity (Masao 1992). New symbolism about unity and nation building emerged in the wake of the 1996 Atlanta Olympic Games, captured by the President of the National Olympic Council of South Africa (NOCSA) Sam Ramsamy's slogan of 'Simunye' ('We are one') (Kersting 2007), echoed by the nationalistic rhetoric surrounding the Olympic medallists (Penny Heyns, Hezekiel Sepeng and Josiah Thugwane) who competed as 'rainbow warriors' (Merret 2003).

In the aftermath of a new democratically elected sport structure, alliances were formed that would unite the African continent in a brotherhood of anticolonialism and political agency. Regional unity set the scene for the FIFA World Cup 'coming to Africa' (for the first time) in 2010. Football being widely considered as the sport of the masses in African countries implied a sense of ownership for the 'black majorities' on the continent. However, 'transcendental euphoria' evoked by South Africa's athletes and teams at international events has not eradicated the racial divides embedded in entrenched socio-cultural differences and hegemonic structures and practices. The politics of race is still acutely embedded in all spheres of South African society, including the different sectors of sport.

The socio-political dynamics of culture

According to the latest demographic data, South Africa had an estimated population of 48.7 million in mid 2008. Classification based on four major racial groups (according to the apartheid categorization) still serves as a guiding principle for state interventions in the setting of 'transformation targets' according to the Transformation Charter of Sport and Recreation South Africa that stipulates that sport teams at all levels (e.g. schools, clubs, regional, provincial and national levels) should reflect the racial demographics of the country. Selectors at all levels of competitive sport are thus bound to select racially representative teams in the name of sport development and nation building. Racial representation is guided by the fact that the African population is the largest (80 per cent), followed by white and coloureds (9 per cent each) and people of Indian decent (2 per cent) (Kane-Berman and Macfarlane 2008: 5–6). This is further diversified into nine main ethnic groups, identified according to the preferred language as mother tongue, of which the Zulu (23.8 per cent), Xhosa (17.6 per cent) and Afrikaans speakers (13.3 per cent, predominantly coloured and white) are in the majority (Kane-Berman and MacFarlane 2008: 45). Much public debate relates to the inclusion of 'ethnic black' players in national teams as proof of the successful state intervention and the penetration of sport development into previously disadvantaged areas.

South Africa is considered to be a developing country according to the United Nations Development Programme's (UNDP) Human Development Index (HDI, which measures broad social welfare and gave the country a score of 0.674 in 2005). South Africa is relatively well off compared to other African countries such as Nigeria, Zambia and Mozambique, which fell in the lowest percentile of human development. South Africa ranks among the richest countries of sub-Saharan Africa, yet poverty is widespread, measuring as high as 49 per cent at the one-dollar-a-day poverty line (Elbers *et al.* 2003). The income inequality as expressed in the Gini coefficient (0 for complete equality and 1 for complete inequality) is relatively high for the African (0.14) and coloured population (0.14), compared to their Indian (0.65) and white counterparts (–0.063) (Roodt 2008: 235–236). The indication of income and economic inequality is a proxy for wider socio-economic inequalities such as the relative lack of access to physical resources (e.g. housing, well-equipped schools and sport facilities), poor health and low levels of education evidenced in impoverished communities and people who have been exposed to chronic poverty for most of their life. It is thus evident that the redress of the unequal distribution of resources and development, including in the sectors of sport, should be focused on these disenfranchised impoverished communities where the majority inhabitants fall into the racial categories of being considered black or coloured.

Modern sport is very much a cultural activity with socio-political nuances embedded in the very fabric of institutionalized participation. The legitimate sport/cultural activity binary is one that has been constructed out of colonial discourses and requires deconstruction to recognize that contemporary sports are still reflections of the cultures from which they stem. Giles and Baker (2008) have commented on the diverse social dynamics and potential conflicts that have become part and parcel of sport as social construct. According to them, cultural dominance might blind groups to the inherent cultural and political nature of sport. They explained:

> The position that sport is apolitical and acultural is one that can only be taken
> by those who exist in the main/white stream and are able to see themselves

and their practices as being divorced from culture and politics because sport is congruent with their own particular cultural politics.

(p. 162)

The prominence of football as the world's most popular game generates passionate and deeply rooted feelings of local and national pride (Hunter 2003). In South Africa, passion and emotional involvement contribute to the structuring of a unique cultural milieu that presents segmented quasi-political formations around prominent Premier Soccer League (PSL) teams (such as Kaizer Chiefs and Orlando Pirates), as well as the national male team, Bafana Bafana (meaning 'the Boys') (Burnett 2005). The 2010 FIFA World Cup on South African soil is politically significant as it acknowledges South Africa as a country of prosperity, possibility and freedom – a far cry from the days of its suspension from the Confederation of African Football (CAF) in 1958 (Milan 1997). It is, however, still a long way off from optimally providing and capitalizing on opportunities for all within the football fraternity, which in South Africa has increasingly become associated with black leadership and empowerment.

According to a national survey that revealed the participation patterns in South African sport, only 25 per cent of South Africans actively participate in sport on a regular basis; factors such as age, inadequate training facilities and lack of interest are the main contributors to this state of affairs (HSRC 2006). Sport is being defined as:

> Any activity that requires a significant level of physical involvement and in which participants engage in either a structured or unstructured environment, for the purpose of declaring a winner, through not solely so; or purely for relaxation, personal satisfaction, physical health, emotional growth and development.

(HSRC 2005: 2)

It is a matter of concern that 75.0 per cent of the sample (n=5,639) representing 500 census enumeration areas (EAs) in all nine provinces were considered to be sedentary, of which the coloured respondents were proportionally the highest with 84.8 per cent, followed by Asian/Indian respondents (75.6 per cent), black (75.0 per cent) and white citizens (63.4 per cent).

Participation in sport is dominated by males (42.6 per cent) following an active life style compared to females where 88.8 per cent are considered to be sedentary. A breakdown by age categories shows the highest incidence of participation of people aged between the ages of 16 and 20 years (51.7 per cent) with a sharp decline to 34.4 per cent (age group 21–25 years), 18.8 per cent (age group 26–60 years) and 5.7 per cent (age group older than 60 years). Younger children were excluded in this survey, yet a similar pattern of decreased participation in structured school sport and physical activity was reported in a baseline study of the School Sport Mass Participation Programme (Burnett and Hollander 2008). National data was collected from 161 schools, from 1,848 secondary school and 2,233 primary school learner respondents, confirming a sharp decline in active participation at school level – from an average of 71.0 per cent to 31.0 per cent in primary schools, and from 63.5 per cent to 10.0 per cent in secondary schools in impoverished areas across the country. The average of girls' participation in the secondary schools was 3.5 per cent (Burnett and Hollander 2008: 86).

Class divisions are still evident, with the more affluent whites predominating in participation in tennis, swimming and cricket, which are respectively rated as having the fourth, fifth and sixth largest number of participants (HSRC 2006). Participation in different sporting codes made accessible through the two national Mass Participation Programs contributed to the fact that black juniors (between ages 13 and 18 years) account for 60 per cent of the participation figures in 18 different sporting codes, followed by 17 per cent white and coloured (respectively), and 6 per cent Indian (Anon, 2006: 10–12). Yet, the vast majority of girls (98.2 per cent) mainly participated in netball, as the other codes such as soccer (80.2 per cent male participants), rugby (89.5 per cent male participants) and cricket (85.6 per cent male participants) were relatively exclusionary owing to cultural dynamics, participation preferences and limited resources (Burnett and Hollander 2008).

Rugby is still largely perceived as belonging to the Afrikaans-speaking rural folk (Boers) who united around common values and an ethos of toughness, physical prowess and patriarchal values (Van der Merwe 1998). The sport symbolized Afrikaner values and became contested territory when international boycotts against rebel tours in the 1970s and 1980s succeeded in isolating the once 'national sport' of the white minority (Kidd 1988). International success (winning the World Cup in 1995 and 2007) did not bridge the racial divide that continued to widen due to enforced racial quotas being implemented since 1997 at schoolboy level and in 1998 at senior level (Nel 2000). Racial stacking is evident in over-representation of black players on the wing position to reach transformation targets of 'black ethnic players' (Coetzee 2007). The Portfolio Committee on Sport and Recreation in Parliament has increasingly become a voice of discontent directed at national sport federations not meeting 'transformation targets' (Wyngaard 2007). In his Budget Speech, the Minister of Sport and Recreation identified transformation as a major challenge and critically reflected on the racial composition of the national cricket team to Bangladesh and India, stating that 'transforming sport is not negotiable', whilst applauding Pieter de Villiers who became the first black national rugby coach (SRSA 2008).

Cricket and rugby are considered to be 'white sports'; however, there has been increased representation at elite levels by coloured players, while Indian cricket players from Kwa-Zulu Natal have broken through the ranks to represent the provincial and national team. Soccer is mostly played by blacks, with a vast support base for Professional Soccer League (PSL) teams. The national and racial discourse thus finds expression in the political profiling of the 2010 FIFA World Cup – an event where the political power is vested in a black majority, while celebrating football as a sport of the African working class (Merrett 2003).

Delivering on national objectives

The current dispensation of the state in delivering sport and recreation to the South African public is largely the result of the Ministerial Task Team on Sport that was brought together after the country's dismal performance at the 2000

Sydney Olympic Games (Ministerial Task Team on Sport 2002). Key stakeholders undertook a comprehensive analysis of the high performance sport sector in South Africa and came up with a blueprint of national structures that would stream-line and professionalize service delivery to elite athletes. It would also ensure a clear pathway from talent development at school level to nurturing talent through coaching and scientific support provided by the national sport federations in col-laboration with provincial academies (SRSA 2009a).

A synergy of stakeholder collaboration was envisaged, guided by strategic planning and optimal performance, focusing on excellence in service delivery and professionalism, and in accordance with national objectives in providing the opportunity for all sectors to reach their sporting potential (access and equity). National federations have been identified as the 'bedrock of the sports system' that should be athlete-centred and coach-driven, supported by sports science and guided by principles of fair play and 'drug-free sport' (Ministerial Task Team on Sport, 2002). Coach education was prioritized and the need voiced for appropriate training programs and formal accreditation qualifications, linked to the national accreditation system through the Tourism, Hospitality and Sport Education and Training Authority (THETA). This body is tasked with the accreditation of unit standard qualifications to ensure quality and alignment of education and training courses that may progressively build towards a qualification recognized by them according to the different levels identified by the South African Qualifications Framework. Clear role demarcations between Sport and Recreation South Africa (the national government department) and other national, regional and provin-cial sporting bodies were to be structured to afford a skilled labour force through accredited education, training and workplace experience.

By absorbing the South African Sports Commission (SASC) into Sport and Recreation South Africa (SRSA) and the South African Sports Confederation and Olympic Committee (SASCOC) structures, role demarcation became apparent with the former body mainly focusing on creating and enabling environments for sport participation, policy formulation, international cooperation and social development. SASCOC was tasked with the delivery of elite sport development and facilitating international competitions for Team South Africa's participation in events such as the Olympic Games, Commonwealth Games and All Africa Games. These key stakeholders collaborated to draw up a national strategy that would focus on the development of potential individual medal winners rather than team sport. In doing so, funds could be optimized in addressing the reality of wide-spread poverty. It was further envisaged that the National Lottery (of which 70 per cent supports Higher Performance Sport) and tax concessions could supplement government funding for sport (SRSA 2009a). The concept of Team South Africa was born to attract commercial funding and facilitate nation building through racially representative teams that would reflect the demographics of the broad South African society. As a political keyword, 'transformation' not only replaced the 'quota system' (of enforced ethnic representation), but 'became the clarion call of a nation seeking to effect a fundamental change in sports and ensure that sport reflects the demographics of our country and on merit produces excellence in performances drawing from all the talent in our country, black and white' (SASCOC 2005).

The Steering Committee that was to implement the recommendations of the Ministerial Task Team culminated in the formation of SASCOC in 2004, acting as the controlling body for all high-performance sport as a Section 21 Company (SASCOC 2009). This body is responsible for the delivery of Team South Africa by maximizing resources and synergizing services between SRSA and other sporting bodies at national, provincial and regional levels (SASCOC 2005). The current National Academy Programme (NAP) is being coordinated by SRSA and SASCOC with the strategy to support athletes in certain priority codes in preparation for the 2012 and 2016 Olympic Games (SRSA 2009b). In view of South Africa's 71st place at the Beijing Olympic Games and relatively poor team performance, SRSA called for a Sports Science Conference, followed by a National Sports Indaba (a forum where major stakeholders could voice their opinions) in October 2008 (Du Rand 2009). During the former Indaba, key stakeholders proposed a High Performance system based on the alignment of sport structures that would place the athlete and coach at the centre of the development (see Figure 9.1 for the organogram of proposed sports structures, Du Rand 2009: 27).

The Minister of Sport and Recreation identified that the scientific services and expertise at regional tertiary institutions should be utilized in the development of high-performance sport, talent identification and long-term athlete development (SRSA 2008). The South African long-term athlete development model (LTAD) is based on the Canadian model that focuses on identifying and developing talent from a broad or mass participation base which is fostered at school and club level, for which Sport and Recreation South Africa takes responsibility in collaboration

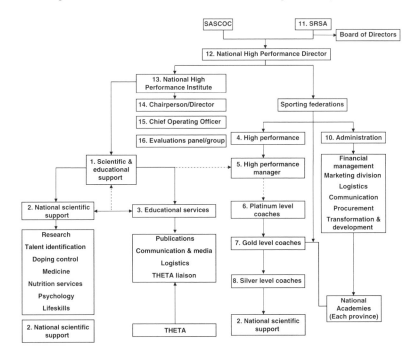

Figure 9.1 Proposed South African sport structure

with the national sport federations and Regional and Provincial academies for a throughput of athletic talent (SRSA 2009b).

Revisiting the framework of sport and recreation in South Africa, the White Paper is in the process of being revised in line with a National Plan for Sport. SRSA embarked on a consultative process, yet agreed to retain the 'development triangle' as a conceptual guideline for sport, based on the vision of 'Creating an active and winning nation' (see Figure 9.2, Anon. 2007).

To achieve the goal of broad-based participation and specialization at school and club levels, other government departments were drawn into the loop, such as the Department of Provincial and Local Government (DPLG) that took over the Building for Sport and Recreation Programme from SRSA and SA Tourism. The Building for Sport and Recreation Programme focused mainly on providing the necessary facilities in impoverished communities to facilitate active participation in sport and structured physical activity programs. The implementation of the *Siyadlala* and School Sport Mass Participation programs was a national initiative to optimally use these facilities – changing some from white elephants to 'work horses' (Burnett and Hollander 2006). During the four-year period starting in 2001, SRSA initiated the building of 363 basic sport and recreation facilities in impoverished communities, yet the program lost momentum as only 45 facilities were erected before a facility audit and needs analysis delayed further development (SRSA 2008). At the other end of the scale, world-class facilities are being built for the 2010 FIFA World Cup and the government at all levels has a key role to play to ensure post-event usage by lobbying for major events that could have a significant economic impact (such as the Indian Premier League, contributing an

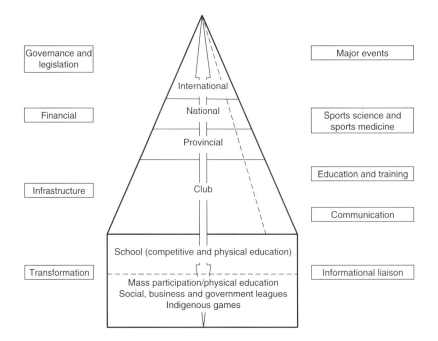

Figure 9.2 Sport development continuum

estimated R1 billion to the local economy). Mashishi, the then President of SASCOC, emphasized government's involvement in the bidding process for mega events and explained the potential value of hosting the 2010 FIFA World Cup by stating that 'the overall contribution of sport to the international marketing and GDP of the country will place sport amongst the foremost sectors in terms of positioning South Africa for growth and prosperity, and for facilitating harmonious and constructive relationships between all the people of our country' (SASCOC 2005).

Sport and Recreation South Africa is represented in three of the five government clusters (i.e. each cluster consists of several different government departments), namely the Social Cluster, the International Relations, Peace and Security Cluster and the Governance and Administration Cluster. SRSA provides support in hosting major events, leaving a legacy that ensures 'a better life for all South Africans' (SRSA 2007a). A most recent collaboration is with the South African Police Services, Department of Basic Education and other international stakeholders such as the British High Commission and British Airways on the 'sport for safety' project (SRSA 2009a).

As signatory to the Millennium Development Goals, South Africa increasingly views sport as a vehicle to address political objectives in terms of contributing to social cohesion, enhancing health for all, improving international relations, enhancing peace, development, tourism, human empowerment, the development of infrastructure and hosting a successful 2010 FIFA World Cup (Jordaan 2007; SRSA 2008). The Minister of Sport and Recreation has the legislative powers, as reflected in the National Sport and Recreation Amendment Act (Act No. 18 of 2007), to oversee the development and management of sport and recreation in South Africa at the macro-level. Transformation, inclusion and equality are the main thrusts for the five-year Strategic Plan of SRSA in line with the Constitution of the Republic of South Africa, Act 108 of 1996 (Anon. 2008: 17). This directive is supported by five program areas, of which key deliverables include delivery on the guarantees signed with FIFA (e.g. training of volunteers and mobilizing South African support that will leave a lasting legacy), and delivering mass participation programs in impoverished communities (*Siyadlala*) and schools (School Sport Mass Participation Programme) (SRSA 2007b). These priorities are captured in the mission statement of SRSA – 'To improve the quality of life of all South Africans, foster social cohesion and enhance nation building by maximizing access, development and excellence at all levels of participation in sport and recreation' (Anon. 2008: 19).

International stakeholders with political clout such as UNICEF South Africa, the Australian Sports Commission, GTZ (the German Development Cooperation), the European Union and the British Sports Council are increasingly forging strategic partnerships with SRSA (Burnett 2008). In support of community transformation and grass roots development, these organizations mainly promote sport for development initiatives. In most cases, schools and community-based clubs are the channels of delivery and relations are established at different levels with SRSA's 2010 Legacy Programme, *Siyadlala* and/or the School Sport Mass Participation Programme.

In a meeting on school sport with the Provincial Coordinators, the Deputy Minister paid tribute to the Department of Education for their collaboration in offering the School Sport Mass Participation Programme to 3,000 of the poorer schools in the lower three quintiles. He elaborated on the political significance of the framework of their agreement, stating that 'the transformation of sport and recreation in South Africa is integral to the overall transformation of the South African society' and being 'catalysts in the promotion of national reconciliation, social cohesion and national identity' (SRSA 2009c). In his Budget Vote Speech, the Deputy Minister of Sport and Recreation drew attention to the social benefits in terms of the reduction of self-reported 'soft-fabric' crimes, and up to a 15 per cent decrease in crime in several communities as a positive impact of the two national mass participation programs (SRSA 2008).

The degree of success and/or impact is inherent in the cost–benefit analysis of government spending and delivery on national outcomes. The case study that will be discussed entails the national community-based program *Siyadlala*, where the most significant changes were traced during pre-, mid- and post-impact assessments over a two year period – from September 2004 to September 2006 (Burnett 2007; Burnett and Hollander 2006).

Siyadlala

By introducing a community-based sport mass participation program (*Siyadlala*) in 2004, the government intended to provide widespread opportunities for active participation in sport and recreation that could change the relatively low profile of active participation in impoverished communities, identified as 'hubs' (HSRC 2006). Initially, seven provinces each delivered the program in four of their impoverished communities, with Gauteng Province launching it in eight hubs or communities and the Free State Province implementing it in 22 hubs. The number of hubs increased from 60 in 2004 to 131 in 2005 and 256 in 2006. In addition to providing a pool of talent from which future elite athletes could be recruited, the program set out to stimulate social and community development that could address national development priorities and contribute to the Millennium Development Goals (Burnett 2007). An impact assessment according to a pre-post research design (2004–2006) was undertaken to determine 'change' according to 13 indicator fields. According to the Sport in Development Impact Assessment Tool (S·DIAT) designed and developed to trace change according to two main indicator bands, namely (i) Program management and delivery, and (ii) Individual and community development or social development, impact of the program was determined in a sample of one urban and one rural hub in each of the nine provinces (Burnett and Hollander 2006).

A mixed method approach was followed, with quota sampling according to a Participatory Action Approach where indicators were refined through reciprocal agency between researchers and research participants at the community level (Burnett and Hollander 2006; Cunningham and Beneforti 2005). Extensive data was obtained through the following methods and sample:

- 470 interviews with various community-based stakeholders
- 479 case studies of activity and hub-coordinators and participants
- 54 different focus group sessions with different sets of participants, namely

all coordinators and a representative purposive sample of all groups of participants, community leaders and representatives of households, totalling 2,107 participants

- 1,476 questionnaires that were completed by coordinators and participants
- 1,040 participants and non-participants (as control group) who completed a self-esteem questionnaire.

The delivery system was established under the provincial departments of Sport and Recreation responsible for contracting 'unemployed youth' in the different communities to deliver it at community and/or school facilities in collaboration with local stakeholders (such as schools and sport clubs). Initial sporting codes (2004) entailed indigenous games, general gymnastics, aerobics and street ball games (football, basketball and handball), as well as fun run/big walk or road running. In 2005, two more sports were added with an allowance for regional selections (such as sky ball in some regions of the Western Cape Province).

The results indicated that two main models of implementation emerged, namely sport for development (+sport) and sport for performance (sport+). The models were interrelated, yet differed in the respect that in the second model, sport in the community was mainly structured on a club basis with sport federations being involved. On the other hand, the sport for development model mainly focused on school-based delivery (forming part of the school curriculum) and/or where the program was offered at informal spaces (e.g. open grounds) in communities.

Staging regional, provincial and national events boosted participation numbers prior to such competitions and, despite fluctuations, the program added to an overall increase in active participation. The increase was consistent with the increase in the number of hubs (from 60 to 256, representing a 573.7 per cent increase). This in turn impacted on the increase in practice sessions per week (from 144 to 563, or a 291.0 per cent increase); the number of participants (an increase from 1708 to 6,267, or 266.9 per cent) and an increase in the number of activities as an average of 5.8 per hub (from 41 in 2004 to 104 in 2006). However, community-based impact remained low as the program only contributed to an increase in active participation from 8.1 per cent (n=2,547, school sport only) to 11.8 per cent (n=3,720, added participation due to the program), representing 37 target schools and 31,559 learners in the sample schools.

Although the program also focused on 'out-of-school youth' as participants and volunteers, school children accounted for most of the participants (80.9 per cent), with an increase of 618.7 per cent during the first interval (pre- to mid-impact) and a slight fall in numbers over the last interval (32 per cent decrease) evident in the fluctuation and interest generated through events and competitions.

On the one hand, the increase in participation enhanced the functionality and utilization of community-based facilities, yet it caused overuse and discriminatory practices, and boys and older groups were awarded a higher status and mostly dominated practice schedules. However, gender equity was addressed, as 47.4 per cent of the activity and hub coordinators were men and 52.6 per cent women, and 40.6 per cent boys compared to 59.4 per cent girls participated in the program. However, there was a bias towards male participation (65.6 per cent) among volunteer presenters joining the program because of the perception that experience as a volunteer would lead to employment.

The program had a low impact (below 39 per cent) on bringing about change on the poverty-related health profiles, as only five hubs (27.7 per cent) had established partnerships with organizations that provide health services. A more positive impact was registered on sense of well-being and feelings of self-worth, with from 50 per cent to 89 per cent of research participants reporting an increase.

Having access to education and training is highly valued in impoverished communities (Terreblanche 2002). The impact varied in terms of respondents being satisfied with the quality and availability of formal training (low impact of 39 per cent, according to the rating register of the S·DIAT), informal training (medium impact of 58 per cent) and gaining job-related experience (medium impact of 71 per cent), yet they wanted the courses to be credit-bearing.

In the face of extreme poverty, earning a stipend of R1,200 per month (about 171 USD) contributed to the survival of 54 households (representing 42.7 per cent of the activity coordinators). The program thus contributed to poverty alleviation as 22.4 per cent coordinators have obtained permanent employment.

Seven South African police station commanders attributed the decrease of local 'crime statistics' and 'petty crimes' to the program, proclaiming that 'boys were kept busy and had less time to do crime'. Most participants (53.0 per cent) reported a decrease in 'soft-fabric crimes', but 'scientific proof' of a reduction in the 'crime rate' could not be substantiated owing to the lack of reliable records and myriad of variables that might have impacted on recorded and reported cases – a widely recognized dilemma (Coalter 2005).

In terms of social networking, the outreach to schools and local municipalities seems to have been relatively successful as the program was supported by an average of four schools per hub as main points of delivery, and in most cases municipal facilities were made available. The collaboration of government institutions provided a network of mutual service delivery and community entitlement despite many obstacles impacting on optimal program delivery and participation.

The community-based program was intended to unearth sporting talent at school level, but the vast resources needed for the delivery of a quality program were underestimated. Sustainability was compromised as local implementers (Hub and Activity Coordinators) had to rely on personal relationships with schools to deliver the program at school level. Unemployed youth attached themselves to the program as players and/or volunteers often just prior to a provincial or national event and then would cease participation because of a lack of interest or delivery on perceived expectations such as finding employment in the sporting sector. Without a clear vision and directives for delivery, *Siyadlala* did not deliver athletic talent, especially in sporting codes such as indigenous games and road running. Diverse models of implementation and lack of coherent service delivery of government departments at local level negatively impacted on the sustainability and formation of independent community clubs under local leadership.

The focus of developing sporting talent led to the implementation of the School Sport Mass Participation Programme by SRSA in collaboration with the National Department of Education. The Memorandum of Understanding signed at national level had little effect at local levels, where Provincial and Cluster Coordinators had to ensure delivery through School Sport Assistants in primary and secondary schools. Again, the lack of synergy between government departments and local stakeholders, as well as poor physical resources at schools, did not create an enabling climate for optimal social development or the development of sporting talent. It seems to be unrealistic to expect optimal delivery on strategic outcomes without a clear vision, strategic leadership, well-trained human resources and adequate local infrastructure.

Conclusion

State intervention in sport is imperative as the latter is viewed as an effective vehicle towards nation building, the formation of a national identity and addressing national priorities such as community regeneration and racial transformation. Hosting high-profile international sporting events and developing infrastructure, especially in previously disadvantaged communities, are some of the interventions that were used in post-apartheid South Africa to address racial and class inequalities. International relations, national unity and the prestige on the global stage of sport are important signifiers of good governance and political validation to be recognized at all levels of engagement.

It is clear that the state has a central role to play in the development of 'enabling' policies, representative structures and adequate resourcing for the different agencies and role players in a mutually beneficial partnership to deliver on national targets for both elite performance and increased mass participation. An even more significant role has emerged during the last five years, namely for sport as a vehicle to contribute to the achievement of the Millennium Development Goals. The challenge for developing countries such as South Africa is to address issues of national priority in which sport might serve as an appropriate and accountable means of delivery on the different agendas for development. Yet, the implementation of a national sporting program such as *Siyadlala* could not mature and develop into sustainable community club structures owing to the severe lack of resources and the inability of impoverished community members to pay membership fees or volunteer on a continuous basis. The lack of synergy and cooperation at local levels between different government sectors contributed to conflict and territorial claims. Top-down development initiatives do not always address local needs, and neither is the government always a responsive partner sensitive to local dynamics and discourses.

No single program can deliver on a myriad of objectives and expectations, as in the case of *Siyadlala*. Collaborative planning, funding and service delivery between government and private partners with an optimal buy-in from local institutions (e.g. schools and municipalities) are essential for providing sustainable and optimal opportunities for an active life style for all citizens. Strategic partnerships and networking are thus essential for multi-level articulation of programs that could counter the current silo effect of service delivery by the public sector.

References

Allen, D. (2003) 'Beating them at their own game: Rugby, the Anglo-Boer War and Afrikaner nationalism, 1899–1948', *International Journal of the History of Sport*, 20(3): 37–57.

Anon (2006) 'Kids at play: Who plays what in SA', *Your Sport*, July: 10–12.
—— (2007) 'Revisiting the framework of sport and recreation in South Africa', *Your Sport*, 3rd Quarter: 18–19.
—— (2008) 'SA sport: The way forward', *Your Sport*, 3rd Quarter: 16–20.
Archer, R. and Bouillon, A. (1982) *The South African Game: Sport and Racism*, London: Zed Press.
Booth, D. (1998) *The Race Game: Sport and Politics in South Africa*, London: Frank Cass.
Bose, M. (1994) *Sporting Colours: South Africa's Return to International Sport*, London: Robson Books.
Burnett, C. (2005) '"Violence-by-proxy" as a recent trend of soccer violence in South Africa', *African Journal for Physical, Health Education, Recreation and Dance*, 2(11): 104–111.
—— (2007) 'The social impact of *Siyadlala*: A national mass sport participation programme in South Africa', report prepared for Sport and Recreation South Africa. Johannesburg: Department of Sport and Movement Studies, University of Johannesburg.
—— (2008) 'Accounting for sports development'. In V. Girginov (ed.), *Management of Sports Development*, London: Elsevier (pp. 259–275).
Burnett, C. and Hollander, W.J. (2006) 'The impact of the Mass Participation Project of Sport and Recreation South Africa (Siyadlala) 2004/5'. Pretoria: Sport and Recreation South Africa.
—— (2008) 'Baseline study of the School Sport Mass Participation Programme: Report prepared for Sport and Recreation South Africa, 1/8/5/2 (021/06)'. Pretoria: Sport and Recreation South Africa.
Coalter, F. (2005) 'Sport, social inclusion, and crime reduction'. In G.E.J. Faulkner and A.H. Taylor (eds.), *Exercise, Health and Mental Health*, London: Routledge (pp. 190–209).
Coetzee, G. (2007) 'Politici kry Bok-koors' ['Politicians get Bok-fever'] <http://www.die-burger.com/Stories/news/15.0.3203702397.aspx> (accessed 16 January 2009).
Cunningham, J. and Beneforti, M. (2005) 'Investigating indicators for measuring the health and social impact of sport and recreation programs in Australian indigenous communities', *International Review for the Sociology of Sport*, 40(1): 89–98.
Du Rand, C. (2009) 'Getting to a holistic solution for improving high performance sport', *Your Sport*, 1st Quarter: 24–27.
Elbers, C., Lanjouw, J.O. and Lanjouw, P. (2003) 'Micro-level estimation of poverty and inequality', *Econometrica*, 71(1): 355–364.
Gemmell, J. (2007) 'South African cricket: "The Rainbow Nation must have a Rainbow Team"', *Sport in Society*, 10(1): 49–70.
Giles, A.R. and Baker, A.C. (2008) 'Culture, colonialism, and competition: Youth sport culture in Canada's North'. In Michael D. Giardina and Michele K. Donnelly (eds.), *Youth Culture and Sport: Identity, Power, and Politics*, London: Routledge (pp. 161–174).
Guelke, A. (1993) 'Sport and the end of apartheid'. In L. Allison (ed.), *The Changing Politics of Sport*, Manchester: Manchester University Press.
Guttmann, A. (1992) *The Olympics: A History of the Modern Games*, Chicago: University of Illinois Press.
Houlihan, B. (1991) *Sport and International Politics*, London: Harvester-Wheatsheaf.
HSRC (2005) 'HSRC client survey 2004: Draft report to Sport and Recreation South Africa'. Pretoria: Sport and Recreation South Africa.
—— (2005, 2006) 'Participation patterns in sport and recreation activities in South Africa'. Pretoria: Sport and Recreation South Africa.
Hunter, J.S. (2003) 'Flying the flag: Identities, the nation, and sport', *Identities*, 10(4): 409–425.
Jordaan, D. (2007) 'South Africa is ready: 2010 National Communication Partnership'. Johannesburg: 2010 Partnership.

Kane-Berman, J. and MacFarlane, M. (2008) *South Africa Survey 2007/2008*, Johannesburg: South African Institute of Race Relations.

Kersting, N. (2007) 'Sport and national identity: A comparison of the 2006 and 2010 FIFA World Cups', *Politikon*, 34(3): 277–293.

Kidd, B. (1988) 'The campaign against sport in South Africa', *International Journal*, 43(4): 643–64.

Lapchick, R.E. (1979) 'South Africa: Sport and apartheid politics', *Annals of the American Academy of Political and Social Science*, 445 (September): 155–65.

Lee, J.W. and Maguire, J. (2009) 'Global festivals through a national prism', *International Review for the Sociology of Sport*, 44(1): 5–24.

Masao, R. (1992) 'Non-racial sport: Real commitment or white ticket to Barcelona', *Mayibuye*, July, p. 43.

Meredith, M. (2006) *The State of Africa: A History of Fifty Years of Independence*, London: Free Press.

Merrett, C. (2003) 'Sport and nationalism in post-liberation South Africa in the 1990s: Transcendental euphoria or nation building', *Sport History Review*, 34: 33–59.

Milan, R. (1997) 'Stop the slaughter: Give Africa back to the tribes', *Sunday Telegraph*, 8 June, p. 33.

Ministerial Task Team on Sport (2002) 'A High Performance Sports System for South Africa'. Unpublished document, Pretoria: Sport and Recreation South Africa.

Nauright, J. (1992) 'A besieged tribe? Nostalgia, white identity and the role of rugby in a new South Africa', *International Review of the Sociology of Sport*, 31(1): 69–86.

—— (1997) *Sport, Cultures and Identities in South Africa*, Cape Town: David Philip.

Nel, B. (2000) 'Bulls to be quizzed on the quota scandal', *Pretoria News*, 9 September, p. 5.

Oosthuizen, G.C. (2006) 'Sport and youth wellness in South Africa'. Paper presented at the International Conference on Sport and Development, University of the Western Cape, 10 April.

Piggin, J., Steven, J.J. and Lewis, M. (2009) 'Knowledge, power and politics: Contesting "evidence-based" national sport policy', *International Review for the Sociology of Sport*, 44(1): 87–102.

Roodt, M. (2008) 'Business and employment'. In John Kane-Berman and Marco MacFarlane (eds.), *South Africa Survey 2007/2008*, Johannesburg: South African Institute of Race Relations (pp. 173–331).

SASCOC (2005) 'Towards equity and excellence in sport: 2005–2014: A decade for fundamental transformation and development'. Paper presented by Moss Mashishi, President of SASCOC at Annual General Meeting of SASCOC, 30 August.

—— (2009) *History* <http://www.sascoc.co.za/about-2/history> (accessed 11 July 2009).

Schultz, W. (2007) 'The relevance of sports in the context of quality of life and consequences of social policy'. In Hannu Itkonen, Anna-Katriina Salmikangas and Eileen McEvoy (eds.), *The Hanging Role of Public, Civic and Private Sectors in Sport Culture*, Research Report No. 3/2007, University of Jyväskylä: Jyväskylä (pp. 196–208).

SRSA (2007a) 'Revisiting the framework of sport and recreation in South Africa', *Your Sport*, pp. 18–19.

—— (2007b) 'Sport and Recreation South Africa: Strategic Plan 2007–2011'. Pretoria: Sport and Recreation South Africa.

—— (2008) 'Sport and Recreation Budget Speech by Minister M.A. Stofile'. Paper presented at the National Assembly, 27 May.

—— (2009a) 'Draft strategy for delivery of integrated support services for priority sport codes in advance of 2012 and beyond'. Unpublished document, Pretoria: Sport and Recreation South Africa.

—— (2009b) 'School Sport'. Speech delivered on school sport at a meeting with provincial counterparts by Gert C. Oosthuizen MP, Deputy Minister of Sport and Recreation, 9 March.

—— (2009c) 'Budget Vote Speech' by Mr. Gert C. Oosthuizen MP, Deputy Minister of Sport and Recreation South Africa, 1 July.

Steenveld, L. and Strelitz, L. (1998) 'The 1995 Rugby World Cup and the politics of nation-building in South Africa', *Media Culture & Society*, 20: 609–629.

Terreblanche, S. (2002) *A History in Inequality in South Africa, 1652–2002*, Pietermaritzburg: University of Natal Press.

Van der Merwe, F. (1998) 'Rugby in the prisoner-of-war camps of the Anglo-Boer War', *Occasional Papers in Football Studies*, 1(1), 76–83.

Wyngaard H. (2007) 'Transformasie, nie getalle, moet getakel word. ANC se laaste woord: Vermoë, nié kwotas' ['Transformation, not numbers must be taken on. ANC's last word: Ability, not quotas'], *Rapport*, 24 June, p. 12.

10 India

Packianathan Chelladurai, D. Shunmuganathan and Sheila Stephen

The first thing that comes to mind for many foreigners when they think of India is its immense population of more than one billion people, crowded in a land mass of 3,288,000 square kilometres, which results in a population density of 336 people per square kilometre. It is also well known that India is a country of great religious, ethnic, linguistic and cultural diversity. Eighty per cent of the people are Hindus, 11 per cent are Muslims, and the remaining 9 per cent is made up of Sikhs, Buddhists, Jains and Christians. The Indian population is composed largely of two ethnic groups: Indo-Aryans (72 per cent) and Dravidians (25 per cent), who are found in the southern States of Andhrapradesh, Karnataka, Kerala and Tamilnadu.

There are 18 official languages recognized by the Government of India and 4 more are being considered (Languages of India 2009). Among these Indo-Aryan (n = 18) and Dravidian families (n = 4) of languages, Hindi is the official language of India and English is designated an associate language. English is the only language spoken across all of India, and although a smaller percentage of the population speak English, they still constitute the largest English-speaking population in the world outside the United States of America.

Most of the State boundaries were drawn on the basis of language, so that people who spoke the same language and its dialects were placed under one administration. Prior to independence, the British government created provinces that had more than one language group each, which was one way of enacting the 'divide and rule' policy. After independence, however, the boundaries were redrawn to reflect the dominant languages.

In 2008 India ranked twelfth in the world in terms of gross domestic product. Its total output was estimated to be equivalent to US$1.237 trillion. Furthermore, when this absolute dollar amount is converted to purchasing power parity (PPP) (i.e. the sum value of all goods and services produced in the country valued at prices prevailing in the United States), India's GDP rises to 3.304 trillion dollars and ranks fifth behind the European Union, United States, China and Japan (*The World Factbook* 2008). But this positive trend must be viewed with caution because of the huge population (estimated at 1.166 billion people as of July 2009) that needs to be sustained by this enormous output of products and services. Thus, India is ranked 167th in the world in terms of per capita income, which is a meagre US$2,700. But we must remember that this figure is only an average and it masks the fact that more than 30 per cent of the population are middle class and that they have a lot of purchasing power. In addition, we must also bear in mind that the rate of growth of the Indian economy at 7.45 per cent is much higher than for most of the industrialized nations.

Sometimes conflicts arise among groups defined by religion, ethnicity, language and caste; such hostilities often capture media headlines all over the world. These hostilities are in stark contrast to the fact that India is the largest effectively functioning democracy in the world and is modelled after the British parliamentary democracy. The Indian Union is made up of 28 States run by an elected government and 7 Union territories which are administered by the President through an appointed Administrator (*Know India* 2009).

While religion, ethnicity, language and even gender play a part in local elections, they do not seem to matter when leaders of the nation are chosen. India was one of the first countries to have a woman, Indira Gandhi, as its Prime Minister; the current President of India, Pratibha Devisingh Patil, is a woman; while the Prime Minister, Manmohan Singh, is a Sikh. There are several Muslims in the Central Cabinet of ministers. What is even more impressive is that the most politically powerful person in the nation at the moment is Sonya Gandhi, an Italian born Catholic. It would be hard to find similar instances of tolerance and acceptance of diversity elsewhere in the political world.

Sport culture in India

India has a tradition of sports and physical fitness. From the Vedic times, sport, fitness, and competitions have always been part of the Indian culture and folklore. Hinduism promoted the virtues of physical perfection or *kaya sadhana*, which is based on an understanding of the body and its functions. It is believed that the practice of *yoga* results in 'strength, stamina and supreme control of the body' (India Press 2010). In *yoga*, meditation is combined with physical movement that involves both breathing control (*prnanayama*) and body posture (*asanas*). Of all the physical activities, *yoga* is truly of Indian origin and is now practised all over the world.

The epics of *Maha Baratha* and *Ramayana* describe the physical fitness and competitive successes of their heroes. The five Pandava brothers of Maha Baratha specialized and excelled in specific physical activities. Dronacaharya was the mentor and coach of these five heroes. In fact, the highest award granted by the Government of India for a sports person is the *Arjuna Award*, named after the famous archer and one of the Pandava brothers. The highest award for a coach is named the *Dronacharya Award*. *Maruthi*, one of the heroes of Ramayana, is idolized for his physical prowess. The senior author of this chapter was a lecturer in a physical education institution named Maruthi College of Physical Education in South India, named after the hero of Ramayana.

Kabaddi is a team sport originally from the State of Tamilnadu and its roots can be traced to prehistoric times when humans defended themselves against animals in groups (Kabaddi 2010). This ancient game of India is gaining popularity around the world. In fact, the World Kabaddi Federation was founded in 2004. Kabaddi is a simple and inexpensive game which requires only a small playing area (12.5 metres by 10.0 metres for men and 11.0 metres by 8.0 metres for women) with 4 metres of free space surrounding the playing area. No equipment is used in the game, and the players are restricted to wearing a jersey and shorts. These minimal requirements are the main reason for the popularity of the sport in rural India. The game has gained popularity in other countries, as evidenced by the fact that 14,000 spectators watched the first World Kabaddi Championships held in Hamilton, Canada, in which teams from India, Pakistan, Canada, England and the United States participated (Kabaddi 2010). India has remained world champion since it was included in Asian Games and South Asian Federation Games. The Amateur Kabaddi Federation of India (AKFI), founded in 1973, is the national sport governing body for Kabaddi in India.

The advent of British rule in India saw the introduction of the modern games of field hockey, football (soccer) and cricket (Culture of India 2010). The Indians took to these sports whole-heartedly and even excelled in these activities. The Indian field hockey team won six consecutive gold medals from the years 1928 to 1956, and again in 1964 and 1980. Although India cannot boast of much success in international soccer, it is a very popular sport in India. India has the distinction of having the second largest soccer-specific stadium in the world, at a capacity of 120,000, in Kolkatta (Football Stadia 2010).

India's most phenomenal success in modern sport is its exploits in international cricket. India has successfully competed with all the cricketing nations of the world and is considered the powerhouse of cricket. As of December 2009, the Indian national cricket team was ranked first by the International Cricket Council in Tests (five-day matches) and second in One Day International matches. Up to that date, the Indian team had played 430 Test matches (101 wins, 136 losses, 195 draws, and one tie). India has won over 50 per cent of its One Day International matches (Indian Cricket 2010).

India has and is producing world-class cricketers and continues to fill the financial coffers of local and international governing bodies with its many and varied cricket competitions. The Board of Control for Cricket in India (BCCI), the richest cricket board in the world, allocated a grant of Rs. 25 crores (roughly US$530,000) to the All India Football Federation (AIFF) to promote the game (BCCI Grants 2009). This is a reflection not only of the popularity of cricket in India, but also of the power of its governing body.

In contrast to its demographic, economic and political prominence, India's status in international sport is rather low except in the case of cricket. For instance, India's performance at the Beijing Olympics was meagre: one gold medal in shooting (Men's 10m Air Rifle) and two bronze medals in wrestling and boxing. However, this was an improvement on performances in previous games. India's performance in the previous four Commonwealth Games is an indication that its performance is improving relative to the rest of the world. As shown in Table 10.1, India's total number of gold medals was 6 in 1994 and 7 in 1998, whereas in 2002 and 2006 it ranked third and fourth respectively.

Government involvement in sport

The Government of India has taken several steps to encourage relevant organizations to promote sport under their respective jurisdictions, and it has initiated its own programs to increase participation in sport and enhance India's

Table 10.1 Comparative performance of India in successive Commonwealth Games

Games entered	Gold	Silver	Bronze	Total
1934 British Empire Games	–	–	1	1
1938 British Empire Games	–	–	–	–
1954 British Empire & Commonwealth Games	–	–	–	–
1958 British Empire & Commonwealth Games	2	1	–	3
1966 British Empire & Commonwealth Games	3	4	3	10
1970 British Commonwealth Games	5	3	4	12
1974 British Commonwealth Games	4	8	3	15
1978 Commonwealth Games	5	5	5	15
1982 Commonwealth Games	5	8	3	16
1990 Commonwealth Games	13	8	11	32
1994 Commonwealth Games	6	11	7	24
1998 Commonwealth Games	7	10	8	25
2002 Commonwealth Games	30	22	17	69
2006 Commonwealth Games	22	17	10	49
Total medals	102	97	72	271

Source: India – Medals Tally by Games. Retrieved from www.thecgf.com/countries/tally.asp on 10 February 2010.

standing in the international sport arena. These types of government involvement are described in the following sections.

Sport governing bodies

The Government of India recognizes that the primary responsibility of the promotion of sport lies with the Indian Olympic Association, the national sports federations that govern their respective sports within the country, and their State-level counterparts (Department of Sports 2009). The major role of the government in this regard is to provide financial assistance to these independent entities. However, the National Sports Policy of 2001 envisaged that these organizations would become more efficient and transparent in their operations. They must become result-oriented and be accountable for their actions. Accordingly, the policy proposed a model of by-laws and organizational structures to be followed by the national sports federations while respecting the Olympic Charter.

The National Sport Policy urged the national sports federations to hold annual championships for all categories of participants – seniors, juniors and sub-juniors (for both men and women) at the District, State and National levels with greater emphasis placed on competitions for the juniors and sub-juniors. The policy also envisaged that the national sports federations would draw up long-term planning documents incorporating details of standards of performance, targeted levels of performance, participation in competitions at national and international levels, sports exchanges, scientific support and the holding of international competitions in the country. More significantly, the policy stipulated that government support to these organizations was to be based on how well the federations carried out the plan and how well they had performed in relation to the plan.

Government of India initiatives

The National Sports Policy of 2001 has the twin objectives of broadening the base of sports and achieving excellence in sports. The policy emphasized that the primary responsibility for propagating sports at the grass roots level resided with the State governments. More specifically, State governments were encouraged to fund Panchayat Raj Institutions (governing systems at the village level) and Local Sport Clubs and prompt them to promote sport culture at the grass roots level. The policy also emphasized that the Indian Olympic Committee (IOC) and national sports federations (NSFs) should strengthen their efforts regarding talent identification, athlete development and competition systems.

While the policy referred to the promotion of sports tourism, it also urged the relevant sports bodies to be innovative and creative in generating resources, especially from corporate houses (i.e. businesses). Accordingly, it envisaged the upgrade and development of infrastructure, supporting national sport federations, strengthening scientific research and coaching, offering incentives to athletes, increasing the participation of women, involving the corporate sector in the promotion of sports, and increasing the 'sports mindedness' of the public.

Schemes of the Department of Sports

With the above in mind, the Department of Sports initiated the following schemes:

1. Scheme for Sports Infrastructure Development. The *Panchayat Yuva Krida aur Khel Abhiyan* (PYKKA) is the sub-scheme which aims at providing basic infrastructure and sports competitions in all villages and *block* (a group of villages) panchayats (governing councils); the Scheme offers one-time grants for infrastructure and operational grants for organized sports competitions.
2. Schemes for Promotion of Excellence in sports, which includes grants to national sports federations, talent search and training programs, contribution to the National Sports Development Fund, which includes contributions from the corporate sector.
3. Schemes for giving incentives to athletes (see Table 10.2), which includes schemes for national awards, and awards to winners in international competitions and meritorious sportspeople.
4. Schemes designed to promote sports among people with disabilities and organizing national championships for women.
5. Schemes for providing assistance to institutions, which include the National Anti-Doping Agency, the Sports Authority of India (SAI) and the Lakshmibai National University of Physical Education.

In 2009, the Department of Sports created two new units – the National Playing Fields Association of India (NPFAI) and the Commonwealth Games Division. The NPFAI was launched in February 2009 in order to create public awareness and support for the development and protection of public play spaces. The Commonwealth Games Division was created to handle all affairs relating to the organization and conduct of the 2010 Commonwealth Games in New Delhi.

Table 10.2 Incentive schemes of the Department of Sports, Government of India

Level	Award	Criteria
National awards	Rajiv Gandhi Khel Ratna Award	For most spectacular performance in that year
	Arjuna Awards	For outstanding sportspersons for their performance in the previous three years
	Dhyan Chand Award	For sportspersons who continue to contribute even after retirement
	Dronacharya Award	For eminent coaches who have trained successful athletes in international competitions
	Rashtriya Khel Protsaha Purushkar	Instituted in 2009, recognizes corporate entities for promoting and supporting (a) community sports, (b) sports excellence, (c) sports academies, and (d) employment of sportspersons
Special awards	Awards to winners and their coaches in international events	Awarded to medal winners in the Olympic Games, World Championships, Asian Games, and Commonwealth Games
	Pensions to Meritorious Sportspersons	Awarded to medal winners in international competitions and who have since then retired
	Maulana Abdul Kalam Azad (MAKA) Trophy	For the university securing first place in interuniversity competitions
	National Welfare Fund for Sportspersons	For former outstanding sportspersons who are in indigent circumstances

The Comprehensive Sports Policy of 2007 aimed to address the emerging challenges of India in the twenty-first century. On the basis of empirical evidence from the Commonwealth Advisory Body on Sports (CABOS), it recognized the contribution of physical education and sport to personal development, especially youth development, community development, health and well-being, education, economic development and entertainment, and in the promotion of international peace and brotherhood. It also addresses the pursuit of excellence in sports and high performance on the international scene.

Development of infrastructure

Prior to 2001, the Ministry of Youth Affairs and Sports had in place four schemes to develop sports infrastructure in the country: (a) Grants for the Sports Infrastructure; (b) Grants to Rural Schools for sport equipment and playgrounds; (c) Grants for the Promotion of Games and Sports in Universities and Colleges; and (d) Grants for the Installation of Synthetic Surfaces. However, these schemes have since been transferred to the State governments, and thus the Central government is not involved in these initiatives. This move is unfortunate since less than 5 per cent of the population has access to sporting facilities and organized sports.

In addition, there is the Sports Authority of India (SAI), which was set up as a Society under the Societies Act for the purposes of promoting sports and games.

It also has the responsibility of maintaining and utilizing the stadia in Delhi (Jawaharlal Nehru Stadium, Indira Gandhi Stadium and Yamuna Velodrome, Major Dhyan Chand National Stadium, Dr Shyam Prasad Mookherjee Swimming Pool Complex and Dr Karni Singh Shooting Ranges). The major objectives of SAI are to promote sports at the grass roots level, implement programs to achieve excellence in sports, maintain and utilize the stadia on behalf of the government, act as a link between the Ministry of Youth Affairs and Sports and other agencies involved in sports, produce high-calibre coaches and sports scientists, maintain and utilize sports infrastructure and facilities in the country, and encourage sport-related research projects.

National institutes

The Department of Sports is the supervisory body for the two national institutes set up by the government in 1957. The first is the Lakshmibai College of Physical Education, which has become an autonomous university with the name Lakshmibai National Institute of Physical Education. The second institution is the Netaji Subhas National Institute of Sports, which is monitored by the Sports Authority of India. It is important to note that these two institutes serve two different purposes. The Lakshmibai Institute is devoted to training and certifying physical education teachers, whose major thrust is the promotion of participation in sport among the nation's youth. On the other hand, the Netaji Subhas Institute is devoted to promoting the pursuit of excellence in sports by training and hiring coaches as well as training elite athletes.

Sport in India's Five-Year Plans

The economy of India is largely shaped by the Five-Year Plans initiated and monitored by the Government of India. The Five-Year Plans were initiated in 1951 and the current Eleventh Five-Year Plan (2007–2012) is underway. The successive Five-Year Plans funded the growth of sport and physical education in progressive steps. The First Five-Year Plan emphasized the integration of physical education and sports with formal education. The Second Five-Year Plan sanctioned and facilitated the creation of two separate institutes to promote excellence in sport and to foster physical education and sport in educational institutions described earlier – Netaji Subhas National Institute of Sports (NIS) in Patiala and the Lakshmibai National Institute of Physical Education (LNIPE) at Gwalior. The National Coaching Scheme and the Rural Sports Programme were started in the Third Five-Year Plan and expanded during the Fourth and Fifth Five-Year Plans. The Sixth Five-Year Plan focused on identification and fostering of talent in sport. The creation and maintenance of infrastructure for sport was emphasized in the Seventh Five-Year Plan. The thrust of the Eighth Five-Year Plan was the development of Rural Sport and organization and conduct of Special Area Games. The Ninth Five-Year Plan recognized and funded the creation of modern sport infrastructure

The Tenth Five-Year Plan (2002–2007) emphasized the need to create a network of basic sports infrastructure at the rural level as well as a higher level of infrastructure at the District, State, and regions of the country (Tenth Five-Year

Plan 2010). The major thrust of the plan was to facilitate high-level performance in international competitions by providing modern equipment; improving coaching skills; training sport scientists, judges, referees and umpires; creating a drug-free environment; and providing incentives for sportspersons in the form of job reservation and awards. The plan also envisaged that the Central government would be focused on achieving excellence at the national and international level while the State governments would focus on mass sports with a high priority placed on the promotion of sports in schools and rural areas.

The Eleventh Five-Year Plan (2007–2012) proposed the launching of a new program labelled *Panchayat Yuva Krida aur Khel Abhiyan* (PYKKA) providing for basic sport infrastructure at the grass roots level in the villages and blocks of villages, over a period of ten years, with a budget of Rs. 1500 crores (US$30 million approximately). *Panchayats* are councils elected to govern the affairs of a village at the lower level and/or a block (a group of villages) at the higher level. This budget will cover grants for acquisition of land, maintenance of the fields, cost of competitions, and prize monies. The scheme is expected to cover 250,000 villages and 6,373 blocks. The proposed scheme, if continued, will cost nearly Rs. 4,500 crores (US$90 million approximately) in the next two Five-Year Plans. There is also a proposal to have similar schemes for urban areas in the country labelled *Nagar Palika Yuva Krida aur Khel Abhiyan.*

PYKKA was intended to link sports and youth development and make it a national priority at the same level as health and education because they are all intrinsically linked. The proposal was to spend Rs. 5,000 crores (approximately US$ one billion) in the Eleventh and Twelfth Five-Year Plans (2002 to 2012). The money was to be allocated to village panchayats (governing councils of villages) and block panchayats (governing councils of groups of villages) for both the construction of infrastructures and the organization of sports competitions at the rural level. The scheme is expected to extend the opportunities for sport participation to nearly 700 million youth, adolescents and children who currently lack such opportunities (PYKKA 2010a).

The budget allotted to this scheme was Rs. 82 crores (approximately US$16.4 million) in 2008–2009 and Rs. 145 crores (approximately US$29.0 million) in 2009–2010 (India Budget, 2010). These amounts are transferred to the State governments, which distribute their allotments to the villages and panchayats in their respective jurisdictions (India Budget 2010).

Funding for sports

While the foregoing aims of the successive Five-Year Plans to promote sports are laudable, the finances allocated to these projects and programs are meagre. For instance, the Tenth Five-Year Plan (2002–2007) allocated Rs. 1145.36 crores to sport, which is equivalent to 0.073 per cent of the total Union Budget (Comprehensive Sport Policy 2007). In 2007–2008, Government of India expenditures on sport and games totalled Rs. 494.56 crores (Ministry of Youth Affairs and Sport 2008). This amount converts to about US$110 million, which is lower than the US$123 million expended by one NCAA Division I university athletic department in the USA (NCAA 2009).

The funding provided to the national sport federations in US dollars in 2008 is shown in Table 10.3. The total amount of the grants allocated by the Government of India to sport governing bodies, including the Indian Olympic Association and

Table 10.3 Department of Sports Grants to National Sports Federations

Federation	Rupees in lakhs	US dollars
All India Carrom Federation	5.87	12 708
All India Chess Federation	106.92	231 481
All India Karate Do Federation	—	—
All India Sports Council of the Deaf	30.37	65 751
Amateur Baseball Federation of India	7.50	16 237
Amateur Handball Federation of India	34.76	75 255
Atya Patya Federation of India	10	21 650
Ball Badminton Federation of India	—	
Basketball Federation of India	25.40	54 991
Cycle Polo Federation of India	13.72	29 703
Fencing Association of India	5.52	11 950
Gymnastics Federation of India	7.80	16 887
Indian Body Building Federation	—	—
Indian Kayaking & Canoeing Association	29.24	63 304
Indian Polo Association	3.17	6 863
Indian Power lifting Federation	8.00	17 320
Judo Federation of India	41.11	89 003
Kho kho Federation of India	—	—
Korfball Federation of India	4.97	10 760
All India Tennis Association	59.24	12 8254
National Rifle Association of India	311.20	673 748
Netball Federation of India	16.28	35 246
Roller Skating Federation of India	—	—
Rowing Federation of India	33.54	72 614
Sepak Takraw Federation of India	9.00	19 485
Shooting Ball Federation of India	—	—
Softball Federation of India	—	
Squash Racket Federation of India	32.90	72 614
Swimming Federation of India	8.09	17 514
Table Tennis Federation of India	7.66	16 583
Taekwondo Federation of India	—	—
Tenni Koit Federation of India	15.79	34 185
Tennis Ball Cricket Federation of India	9.00	19 485
Tug of War Federation of India	8.50	18 402
Volleyball Federation of India	8.38	18 147
Yachting Association of India	12.33	26 694
Wushu Association of India	11.27	24 399
Throwball Federation Of India	—	—
Para Olympic	27.30	59 104
Archery Association of India	56.56	122 452
Billiards & Snooker Federation of India	13.03	282 209
Indian Amateur Boxing Federation	129.35	280 042
Indian Hockey Federation	103.81	224 748
Indian Women Hockey Federation	75.17	162 743
Indian Amateur Kabaddi Federation	15.42	33 384
Indian Weightlifting Federation	—	—
Athletics Federation of India	148.77	322 087
Badminton Association of India	143.95	322 651

Table 10.3 continued

Federation	Rupees in lakhs	US dollars
Equestrian Federation of India	44.71	96 797
Football	21.64	46 764
Indian Golf Union	1.06	2 294
Wrestling Federation of India	141.06	305 395
Winter Games Federation of India	0.63	1 363
Women's Cricket Federation of India	9.98	21 606
Cycling Federation of India	—	—
Special Olympic Bharat	—	
Indian Olympic Association	201.6	436 464
Sports Authority of India	500	1 082 500
Malkhamb	1.25	2 706
Total	2512.38	5 439 302

Source: http://indiabudget.nic.in/ub2009-10/bag/bag1.htm

the Sports Authority of India, was equivalent to US$5,439,302. The Government of India's total expenditures in the same year were nearly 20 billion dollars; the small proportion allocated to sport is indicative of its absolute and relative importance within the larger scheme of challenges faced by the Government of India.

Programs at the local level

Almost every State government in India has replicated the efforts of the Union government in promoting sport participation and excellence in its jurisdiction. The policies and organizational structures instituted by the State governments mimic the Union government's actions.

Infrastructure at the local level

With a view to promoting participation at the grass roots level, the Government of India was to furnish funds to the State governments for construction of sports infrastructure at the District levels of every State. In general, the Government of India would provide 25 per cent of the cost of such infrastructure and the State government 50 per cent of the cost. The remaining 25 per cent of the cost was expected to be generated at the local level by a stadium committee headed by the District Collector (the government representative at the District level).

While the objective of building infrastructure at the local level is laudable, the financial resources allocated both at the Central and State levels are inadequate to meet this objective. Further, even such meagre amounts are not properly spent (CAG, 2008). Insofar as the Central government distributes its funds for sport and physical education to the State governments, it is the responsibility of the State governments to monitor their sport and physical education programs and the expenses thereof. Accordingly, we looked at one particular State, Tamilnadu, and its program of sport development.

Tamilnadu (the land of the Tamils), the southernmost part of India, is the eleventh largest State in India and the seventh most populous, and the most urbanized

State in India. Its contribution to India's GDP is the fifth largest in the nation, and it has the highest number (10.56 per cent) of business enterprises in India. In essence, Tamilnadu ranks very high among the States of India in overall development (Tamilnadu 2010).

Tamilnadu is divided into 30 Districts which are, in turn, split into 206 *Taluks* for administrative purposes. The Department of Youth Welfare and Sports of the Government of Tamilnadu set up in 1992 the Sports Development Authority of Tamilnadu (SDAT) as the apex body to implement all government policies on sport and youth welfare. The SDAT proudly announced that its clients are: (a) all persons with outstanding sports potential; (b) all persons who would like to have access to sports infrastructure subject to availability and the guidelines fixed by SDAT; (c) all Sports Associations recognized by SDAT; (d) all educational and non-profit institutions engaged in promotion of sports and youth activities; and (e) all organizations eligible to utilize the existing infrastructure under the prevailing rules and guidelines (Government of Tamilnadu 2009). The list of clients is illustrative of the breadth and the depth of the SDAT's objectives.

The SDAT has formulated several schemes that include academies specializing in specific sports, sports schools and hostels, sports development centres in colleges, talent development centres, special development centres, coaching centres, and a champions development scheme (Policy Note 2009–2010). However, the attainment of these objectives is somewhat constrained by the total budget for the Department of Youth Welfare and Sports Development. Its total budget including the grants from the Central government for the years 2003 to 2008 was Rs. 172.93 crores (CA 2008). This amount converts approximately to US$34.586 million overall and an average of $6.92 million per year.

Effectiveness of State-level schemes

The following assessment of the operation of the SDAT and some of its programs is drawn from the Audit Report of the Comptroller and Auditor General of India for Tamilnadu (CAG 2008). The Audit found that there was a great need for more sports infrastructure at the District and Taluk levels in order to serve everyone. More significantly, the Audit was quite critical of the (a) ineffective use of grants for new infrastructure, (b) lack of planning in this regard, and (c) the meagre provision for the maintenance of the infrastructure. The major barriers to implementation of infrastructure policy were delays in identifying suitable land for the infrastructure, securing the services of consultants for the design of infrastructure, and calling for tenders. It is not clear why SDAT failed to assign any funds for maintenance and care of the facilities that have been built. The report also noted the lack of coordination among the authorities of SDAT, the State government, and the officials at the District and Taluk levels in managing sport development within the State.

Physical education in schools

The State is also responsible for promoting sport and physical education in the schools. According to the CAG report, there are 17,957 government and private schools categorized as middle, high and higher secondary schools which come under the auspices of the Tamilnadu State government. Given its overarching mandate over all schools, the government of Tamilnadu does have considerable sway over the promotion of sport and physical activity. Yet, there does not appear to be any concerted effort toward this end. For instance, in 2002 the government launched a scheme for spotting talent appropriately named 'World Beater Talent Spotting Scheme' (WBTSS). The scheme envisaged that all schools will require their students in classes VI, VII and VIII to undergo a battery of physical tests once in a year in 2002 and thrice a year beginning from 2004. The tests included the conventional 50-metre race to test speed, running 800 metres for boys and 600 metres for girls to test endurance, shot put to test strength, broad jump to test explosive power, and 6 × 10 metre shuttle to test agility. It turns out that more than 32 per cent of the schools did not implement the program in the years 2004 to 2008. Most of the schools that ran the tests did so only once a year as opposed to thrice a year as planned. The report says that 35 per cent of headmasters polled noted that lack of physical education teachers and the playing fields prevented them from carrying out the tests in their schools. Many of the headmasters of schools were not even aware of the WBTSS scheme (CAG 2008).

Noting that the information has not filtered down to all the schools, the SDAT launched in 2004 the web-based Tamilnadu School Mail System with a view not only to informing all schools throughout the State but also gathering the results of the tests. Of the 150,000 schools expected to participate, only about 400 schools did so. What is interesting is that most of the schools did not have internet connection at that time. This is an instance of embarking on a scheme without due consideration of its feasibility.

From the perspective of the thrust of the present book on participation in sport and physical activity, the policies of the Central and State governments are not consistent with the goals of mass participation. Even the documents that relate to physical education underscore the notion that physical education is the breeding ground for athletic talent. Consider the opening paragraph of the Audit Reports of the CAG (2008):

> Government recognized the importance of Physical education and made it compulsory in schools. Physical education in schools has a direct bearing on achievements in sports. Identifying and encouraging talented sports persons has to ideally commence from early childhood, much before the designated agency for sports development intervenes with expert coaching techniques. The synergy created between sports development programmes and Physical education programme therefore could help the State to achieve laurels in the sporting arena.
>
> (Chapter III: 68)

Thus, physical education in schools is emphasized only because it might promote excellence in sport. Unfortunately, there is no attention paid to sport and physical activity contributing to health and fitness of the populace in this report or elsewhere in government policies. It is not surprising, therefore, that the practices associated with physical education emphasize competitions with other entities rather than intramural competitions.

Government policy states that there should be one physical education teacher for a high school with 250 students and another physical education teacher for every 300 additional students subject to a maximum of three physical education teachers in a high school. Yet, the CAG Report (2008) says that several of these positions are not filled. Further, 20 per cent of the schools could not carry out intramural sports programs for lack of physical education teachers as well as playgrounds. In addition, while the Tenth Five-Year plan set up the goal of one physical education teacher in every middle school, the Government of Tamilnadu had not yet taken firm steps in this regard. In addition, only 582 of the 8,126 middle schools had a physical education teacher. Even more alarming is the fact that none of the 35,146 primary schools in the State had a physical education teacher.

A recent trend to restrict the number of physical education teachers in schools is reflected in the Tamilnadu Government Order of 29 December 1997 which restricted the number of physical education teachers in a school to three even when the number of students may exceed 2,500 (Sangameswaran 2009). This order runs counter to the movement in India to make physical education a compulsory subject in all high schools (Manikandan 2008; *Times of India* 2009).

While the number of physical education teachers is being debated, there is a more serious problem affecting the fruitful practice of sport and physical education – the dearth of playgrounds and other facilities within the schools. While the National and State governments have been successful in approving and financing more primary and secondary schools in the country, much less attention has been paid to the infrastructure within these schools. This neglect is more serious in the case of physical education and sport.

An added constraint in the promotion of sport and physical activity is the lack of playing fields in schools. The Audit reported that the meagre funds provided by the Government of India and the State of Tamilnadu for constructing playing fields had helped only 91 of 12,305 government schools in the State. Further, 52 per cent of 1,034 headmasters responding to a survey reported that they could not conduct intramural games owing to the want of adequate playing fields, paucity of funds, lack of PETs and the academic timetable. This state of affairs does not point to the cultivation of an active lifestyle among the students of the nation. If the Central and State governments are keen on promoting physical activity among the students of the nation, much more needs to be done in terms of providing playgrounds, equipment and physical education teachers.

The rise of the middle class and sport development

Despite the extensive policies of the Central and State governments promoting and governing sport in India, the financial resources allocated to sport by these governments have been meagre. This is understandable given the governments' higher priorities of education, health and the eradication of poverty. Allied to this, the average household in India does not have the discretionary income to spend on sport. In recent years, however, the middle class is growing fast. Some estimates note the size of the middle class in India as 300 million people (Standard of Living in India 2009) and some others note that it will grow to be 583 million people by 2025 (*Business Week* 2007). Such a scenario might suggest that the middle class, with its discretionary income, will be the engine that drives the future development of sport in India. An indication of this trend is the sudden growth in the last few years of private, profit-oriented sport and fitness clubs, as well as professional leagues in basketball, cricket, field hockey, kabaddi and soccer. The emergence (and success) of such professional leagues is likely to result in a large population 'spectating' at sport events rather than participating in sports. However, it cannot be denied that the advent of professional sports may encourage the youth of the country to practise in sports of their choice with a view to emulating their heroes on the professional circuit. This has been the case with soccer around the world, basketball in the US, and cricket in India. Both the Central and State governments need to view the inevitable emergence of professional leagues as a blessing in disguise and persuade the professional leagues to promote the actual participation of their fans in their respective sports.

Sport in the educational sector

As recently as August 2009, the Union Sports Minister called for compulsory physical education in all schools (*The Hindu* 2009). Further, both the Union and State governments stipulate that every school and university must have an adequate number of physical education and sport personnel based on the number of students. As noted earlier, not all sanctioned positions in physical education have been filled. Further, even those who have been hired are not fully utilized for three significant reasons. First, in most States physical education is not yet a compulsory subject and thus there are not regularly scheduled classes. Second, adequate playing fields and equipment are not available, particularly in urban schools. Finally, the teachers and parents place a far greater emphasis on academic subjects, at the expense of physical activity, sport and other leisure-time activities.

Sport and physical education in colleges and universities

Tertiary education in India is offered by universities, and independent colleges affiliated with a university. Typically, each university has a sport board which organizes sport competitions among the colleges affiliated with it. After the completion of competitions in a given sport, the university will form a representative team comprised of the best players from among all its member colleges. This team represents the university in competitions against other universities.

The Association of Indian Universities (AIU) is the parent organization that promotes sports in Indian universities and colleges in the country. As of the end of 2008, 460 universities and 22,000 colleges are members of the AIU (Association of Indian Universities 2008). One of the objectives of the Association of Indian Universities is to establish and maintain a sport organization for promoting sport among member universities (Association of Indian Universities 2009). Accordingly, it has established the Interuniversity Sports Board of India which organizes and conducts sports competitions among the member universities. For this purpose, universities are organized into four zones – North, South, East and West. The winners of competitions in each zone advance to national competitions.

The Interuniversity Sports Board of India had also identified 12 sports as priority disciplines for selection, training and participation in the World University Games of 2009. These disciplines are:

> For both men and women:
> Athletics, Hockey, Basketball, Volleyball, Swimming, Tennis, Football, Handball, Gymnastics and Table Tennis
> For men only:
> Boxing and Wrestling

Unfortunately, the AIU and the Interuniversity Sports Board of India have not initiated any program to promote participation in sport by all students instead of focusing exclusively on elite athletes.

Conclusion

We have outlined the various policies promulgated by the Union and State governments aimed at the promotion of sports. As policies, they have been well articulated. However, the rationality of any policy needs to be judged on the basis of the planning preceding the policy, and the financial allocation for the implementation of the policy. We noted earlier that the budget allotments for sport by various governments were not commensurate with the lofty ideals set forth in the policies relating to sport. Based on the meagre budget allocations towards sport, one can surmise that the policy statements are simply official statements to appease the various constituents interested in sport and not a true reflection of government intent to really promote participation in sport. As noted, it is quite understandable that any government burdened with other more critical concerns would not and should not elevate sport to a higher priority. However, it is surprising that there has not been a serious effort on the part of the governments to ensure the proper implementation of the enunciated policies and the effective disbursement of the allocated funds. The report of the Comptroller and Auditor General of India (CAG 2008), confined to the State of Tamilnadu, clearly shows that the policies are trivialized in their haphazard implementation. If such lapses are found in one of the more advanced States in India, the situation is arguably much worse in less advanced States.

It is also disappointing that the policies of both the Central and State governments tend to focus on talent identification and development in the pursuit of victories in international competitions. Even when there seems to be an emphasis on sport and physical education for all, the rationale is always talent identification. It is unfortunate that the sport policies do not link participation in sport and physical activity to the health issues confronting India. Policy makers may seriously consider advocating sport and physical activity for fun and health. Such a policy would 'churn' the masses into physical activity and the 'cream would rise to the top'. As it stands now, there is no research or database on the activity patterns of the Indian people. It is to be hoped that the governments in India extol the health benefits of sport and physical activity, and facilitate and finance mass sport in their respective jurisdictions.

References

Amateur Kabaddi Federation of India (2009) http://www.indiankabaddi.org/rules/##NPKL.doc (accessed 19 November 2009).

Association of Indian Universities (2008) *Long Term Development Plan: 2009–2012*, New Delhi: AIU House.

—— (2009) Objectives. http://www.aiuweb.org/Objectives/objectives.asp (accessed 5 December 2009)

BCCI Grants (2009) http://www.goal.com/en-india/news/136/india/2009/08/13/1438041/bcci-grants-rs25-crores-to-all-india-football-federation (accessed 30 October 2009).

CAG (2008) Comptroller and Auditor General of India: Audit Report (Civil), Tamilnadu for the Year 2007–2008. http://www.cag.gov.in/html/cag_reports/tn/rep_2008/civil_chap_3.pdf (accessed 6 February 2010).

Comprehensive Sport Policy (2007) http://yas.nic.in/writereaddata/mainlinkfile/File371.pdf (accessed 27 October 27).

Cricinfo staff (2009). Indian Premier League. http://www.cricinfo.com/ipl2009/content/story/396758.html (accessed 20 November 2009).

Culture of India (2010). Recreation and Sports. http://en.wikipedia.org/wiki/Culture_of_India#Recreation_and_sports (accessed 2 February 2010).

Department of Sports (2009) http://yas.nic.in/index1.asp?langid=1&linkid=10 (accessed 7 December 2009).

Farrell, D. and Beinhocker, E. (2007) 'Next big spenders: India's middle class', *Business Week*, May 19, 2007. http://www.mckinsey.com/mgi/mginews/bigspenders.asp (accessed 25 September 2009).

Football stadia (2010) List of association football stadia by capacity, Wikipedia. http://en.wikipedia.org/wiki/List_of_association_football_stadia_by_capacity (accessed 6 February 2010).

Government of Tamilnadu (2009) http://www.tn.gov.in/citizen/sdat.htm (accessed 13 October 2009).

India Education Diary (2009) Sports Ministry revised guidelines for selection procedures for Maulana Abul Kalam Azad award. http://www.indiaeducationdiary.in/Showlatest.asp?newsid=2216 (accessed 8 December 2009).

Indian Cricket (2010) Indian National Cricket Team (2009) http://en.wikipedia.org/wiki/India national cricket team (accessed 25 January 2010)

Kabaddi (2010) Kabaddi. http://en.wikipedia.org/wiki/Kabaddi (accessed 25 January 2010).

Know India (2009) http://www.india.gov.in/knowindia/state_uts.php (accessed 30 October 2009).

Languages of India (2009) http://en.wikipedia.org/wiki/Languages_of_India#Official_languages (accessed 1 November 2009).

Manikandan, K. (2008) Plan to make physical education compulsory. *The Hindu*, Jul 30, 2008. http://www.hindu.com/2008/07/30/stories/2008073060510500.htm (accessed 15 October 2009).

Ministry of Youth Affairs and Sport (2008) Demand No. 104. http://indiabudget.nic.in/ub2007–08/eb/sbe104.pdf (accessed 15 November 2009).

NCAA (2009) Revenues and expenses of Division I intercollegiate athletic programs. http://www.ncaapublications.com/Uploads/PDF/Revenues_Expenses_10_208acb1ac8-caf1–42ad-9e1e-dc6c399c227b.pdf (accessed 6 November 2009).

NCERT (2002) Seventh All India Educational Survey. http://7thsurvey.ncert.nic.in/ (accessed 1 October 2009).

Nightengale, B. (2008) Novice pitchers from India sign with Pirates. USA Today, 12/1/2008. http://www.usatoday.com/sports/baseball/nl/pirates/2008–11–24-indian-pitchers-sign_N.htm (accessed 11 October 2009).

NSINS (2009) About us. http://www.nsnis.org/ (accessed 25 Septmber 2009).

Policy Note 2009–2010 http://www.tn.gov.in/policynotes/pdf/ywsd.pdf (accessed 15 November 2009).

Sangameswaran, K.T. (2009) Schools can have more physical education teachers. *The Hindu*, December 13, 2009. http://www.thehindu.com/2009/12/13/stories/2009121353220500.htm (accessed 1 February 2010).

Standard of Living in India (2009) http://en.wikipedia.org/wiki/Standard_of_living_in_India (accessed 15 November 2009).

Tamilnadu (2010) Tamilnadu. http://en.wikipedia.org/wiki/Tamil_Nadu (accessed 5 February 2010).

The Hindu (2007) Physical education teachers demand withdrawal of Government Order 525. http://www.hindu.com/2007/05/04/stories/2007050402450500.htm (accessed 12 October 2009).

The Hindu (2009a) Gill for compulsory sports, physical education in schools. August 31, 2009. shttp://beta.thehindu.com/education/school/article12635.ece (accessed 2 February 2010).

Times of India (2009) Compulsory physical education in govt schools. http://timesofindia.indiatimes.com/Bangalore/Compulsory-physical-education-in-govt-schools/articleshow/4764333.cms (accessed 20 October 2009).

World Factbook (2008) https://www.cia.gov/library/publications/the-world-factbook/rankorder/2001rank.html (accessed 22 November 2009).

World Kabaddi Federation (2004) Rules of Kabaddi. http://www.kabaddiinternational.org/rules.php?pagename=rules (accessed 19 November 2009).

11 China

Fan Hong and Lu Zhouxiang

Sport has, in general, played an important role in China's political, economic, cultural and social life since the People's Republic of China was established in October 1949. Since the 1980s Chinese society has undergone dramatic transformations, from planned economy to market economy, and from orthodox Leninist society to neo-liberal socialist society with Chinese character. Sport has played its part, as have education, the economy and other social institutions, in reflecting and stimulating the change. In order to understand the change, a review is necessary of sports policies developed in response to different political, economic and cultural agenda in different historical periods. This chapter will examine the structure of the sports governing bodies and organizations and analyze the dominant pattern of sports policy making and particular policy issues in China between 1949 and 2009.

Nationalism and national defense: Chinese sports policy in the 1950s

The People's Republic of China (PRC) was established in 1949 under the Chinese Communist Party's (CCP) leadership, creating a viable administrative structure and becoming the first truly unified government after the collapse of the Qing Dynasty in 1911. The new China included various social classes and 56 ethnic groups. Its major objective was to build a strong nation state in order to end the hundred years' humiliation brought by the foreign powers from the first Opium War in 1840 to the Second Sino-Japanese War in 1945.

Sport and physical education became an important tool for the PRC to build a strong nation state. From the beginning, the sports policy of the PRC was colored by nationalism and self-strengthening sentiment. The CCP continued its sports policy during the war times. Training healthy and strong bodies for national defense and the building of the socialist state were the major themes. At the All-China Sport and Physical Education Congress held in October 1949, Zhu De (1886–1976), the Commander-in-Chief of the People's Liberation Army and Vice Chairman of the central government, explained:

> Physical education and sport (*Tiyu* in Chinese) is an important part of education and health. The central government must pay attention to it. It should serve the people, serve the national defense and serve the purpose of people's

health. Chinese people including students, peasants, workers, citizens and soldiers all should participate in physical exercise and sport activities.

(*New Sport* 1950 (1): 7)

At the conference, Feng Wenbin (1911–1997), Secretary of the Communist Youth League, stressed Zhu De's view further: 'In order to serve the construction of the new democratic economy, the new democratic culture and contribute to the national defense, we must build up people's physical strength and improve their health by promoting mass sport' (Feng 1950).

The All-China Sports Federation (ACSF 中华全国体育总会) was founded in Beijing in June 1952 to implement this policy. It was a semi-government organization. Its objectives were as follows:

The Federation is under the leadership of the central government and the CCP. It follows rule 48 of the 'Common Program of the Chinese People's Political Consultative Conference', and helps the government to organize and promote physical education and sports. The objective is to improve people's health and serve the national defense and state-building.

(All-China Sports Federation 1952)

Mao Zedong (1893–1976), Chairman of the Chinese Communist Party, wrote an inscription for the inaugurating meeting of the ACSF on June 10, 1952, to show his support: 'Promote Sport, Build up People's Physical Strength'. Vice Chairman Zhu De also wrote an inscription to the meeting: 'Popularize Mass Sport, Serve the Construction of the Socialist Country and National Defense'. These two inscriptions were regarded as the supreme command from the CCP leadership, and thus became the guideline for the government's sports policy. Also in this period, the booming nationalism triggered by the Korean War between 1950 and 1953[1] consolidated the mission of sport and physical education of training strong bodies for the purpose of national defense.

China's experience at the Helsinki Olympic Games in 1952 stimulated the government's determination to utilize sport as a valuable tool to project the New China in the international politics. The central government decided to send a team to the Helsinki Olympics on February 4, 1952. The Organization Department of the CCP Central Committee and the Central Committee of the Communist Youth League of China (共青团中央) jointly established a notification entitled 'Select and Train Elite Athletes' on February 18 to prepare for the Games. The notification stated:

International sports competitions are flourishing worldwide. International friends hope China can participate in these events. Recently, we have announced that China will send a team to the Helsinki Olympics. Sport in China was poorly developed in the past. After competing at a few international sporting events in recent years, we are well aware of the low standard of the Chinese athletes, which does not match China's international status. We must change this situation! Sport must be promoted and the standard of the athletics must be improved.

(Tan and Li 1996)

Tan Hua argued that the Helsinki Olympics saw a major transformation of the Chinese government's sport policy. Competitive sport was utilized as a vehicle to enhance China's international reputation and inspire the Chinese people's national self-confidence (Tan and Li 1996).

After the Helsinki Olympics, Rong Gaotang (1902–2006), secretary-general of the ACSF, reported to the CCP Central Committee in April 1952 and made suggestions on the future development of sport and physical education in China. Ma Xulun (1885–1970), the Minister of Education supported Rong's view and submitted a similar report to the Government Administration Council in September. The two reports stated:

> The ACSF is only a semi-government organization and it does not have the power to lead sport and physical education activities in China . . . In order to promote sport, we must have a powerful organising body. We suggest the central government establish a national governing body for sport under the Administration Council of the Central Government (中央人民政府政务院) and appoint He Long (1896–1969) to be the Chairman.
>
> (Wu 1999: 49)

The reports were submitted to the central government. On November 15, 1952, the central government decided to establish a new national sport governing body. Following the Soviet Union model, the new State Physical Culture and Sports Commission (SPCSC) was established in Beijing in 1954 with Marshal He Long as the Minister.[2] The SPCSC was a government ministry with the same status as other ministries such as Education, Finance and Commerce, all directly under the leadership of the State Council. At the same time, local sport commissions were established at provincial, municipal and county levels throughout China. These sport commissions were under the supervision of the SPCSC in terms of sport policy making and implementation, but received direct leadership from local government in terms of human resource, budgeting and operation (*China Sports Daily* 2009).

The formation of the SPCSC and local sport commissions established governments' direct control of sport in the nation, physical education in schools and pastimes in the communities. A centralized organization system for sport took shape. Organized by the sport commissions, sport and physical education activities were carried out in cities, villages, schools, service sectors, industry sectors, commerce sectors, armies and government institutions at all levels.

In order to 'provide physical exercise for the masses and train them to be healthy, brave, optimistic national defenders and socialist builders' (Policy Research Centre of the Sports Ministry 1982c: 218), the SPCSC adopted the Soviet Union's Labor Defense System (LDS 准备劳动与卫国体育制度) in 1954. At the beginning, the LDS was promoted in middle schools, vocational schools and universities. Students were required to participate in track and field, gymnastics, weight lifting and other physical exercises. Once the level of performance reached a certain standard, they would be honored with medals or certifications (Wu 1999).

Also in 1954, the Administration Council of the Central Government issued the 'Notification of Carrying out Sports Activities during Breaks' to 'improve cadre members' health condition, build up their physical strength and enhance the work efficiency' (Policy Research Centre of the Sports Ministry 1982c: 353). Cadre members in government departments at all levels were required to undertake physical exercise for ten minutes in the morning and afternoon during working days.

In the same year, the All-China Federation of Trade Unions (全国总工会) issued 'The Instruction of Promoting Sports in Industrial Factories'. The Instruction called for the promotion of mass sport in industry sectors to 'improve workers' health, reduce illness, ensure the attendance rate, enhance the work efficiency and thus assure successful completion of their work tasks' (All-China Federation of Trade Unions 1954). It required the Trade Union at all levels to 'organize physical exercises during breaks based on the principle of serving industrial production and serving the people' (All-China Federation of Trade Unions 1954).

Guided by the above policy documents, 30,505 sport associations were established around the country to promote sports and physical activities. The membership of these associations reached 915,150 by 1956.

In cities, led by the Union, there were 3,200 basketball teams in the railway sector by 1952. About 1,200 work units built their own sports fields. Sport meetings were held frequently in major cities (Fu 2007). In the countryside, basketball, volleyball and football were introduced to peasants. For example, there were 30 football teams and 120 village level sport clubs in County Yanbian, Jilin Province, by the end of 1953. Thirty-nine basketball teams were established in County Chao, Anhui Province, in 1953. In County Taishan, Guangdong Province, volleyball became popular among villagers (Zhang 1984).

At the Preparation Meeting of the 8th Congress of the CCP in August 1956, Mao Zedong was pleased with the progress of mass participation in sport. His speech clearly indicated that sport was seen as the backbone of the nation, and the development of sport was crucial for the strengthening of the country. He claimed that

> China used to be a country which was regarded as a 'decrepit empire', 'the sick man of East Asia'. The economy was backward and the culture was inferior. [Chinese] People didn't care about hygiene. They were not good at ball games and swimming. Women bound their feet. Men had pigtails and eunuchs still existed. People always thought that the moon in foreign lands was brighter than in China. In short, there were more bad things in China than in foreign countries. However, after six years reformation, we have changed the face of China. No one can deny our great achievements.
>
> (Zedong 1956)

In addition to the development of mass sport, a competitive sports system was established by the SPESC to train elite athletes and prepare for international sports competitions. When the SPESC issued 'The Competitive Sports System of the PRC' in 1956, the competitive sports system was formally set up. Forty-three sports were officially recognized as competitive sports; rules and regulations were defined; professional teams were set up at provisional and national levels, which competed with each other at regional and national championships; the National Games would take place every four years to promote competitive sport and to unite the nation through this event. At the same time the Sports Ministry issued 'The Regulations of the Youth Spare-Time Sports Schools' in 1956. The Soviet Union's spare-time sports school model was adapted to train and foster talented athletes from a very young age. By September 1958 there were about 16,000 spare-time sports schools (业余体校) with approximately 777,000 students throughout the country (Wu 1999).

Great Leap Forward of Sport: unrealistic sports policy and practice (1958–1960)

The First Five-Year Plan had substantially promoted industrialization by the end of 1957 (Jing 2004). However, agriculture lagged behind: 'The disparity between the industrial progress and the relative stagnation of agriculture presented a large number of serious problems, especially when the latter had to serve as the principal source of accumulation for the development of the economy as a whole' (Rodzinski 1991: 403). At the same time there was a rapid growth of the population which raised the demand for food supplies. Facing these problems, Mao believed that the power of China's labor force should be realized. The fast development of agriculture could be the solution, which could be achieved by mobilizing the entire nation 'with the aid primarily of ideological and political means' (Rodzinski 1991: 403). He also hoped that the mass mobilization 'would make possible a simultaneously rapid and equal progress of all branches of the economy, industry as well as agriculture, and eliminate the dangers inherent in the widening gap between the cities and the rural areas' (Rodzinski 1991: 403). In order to achieve this goal, the Great Leap Forward was launched at the eighth CCP National Congress in December 1957. Its slogan was 'Go all out, aim high and achieve greater, faster, better and more economic results'. 'Surpass Great Britain in 10 years and the US in 15 years' in terms of steel production and heavy industry were set as the objectives of the campaign (Guo 1995).

The Great Leap Forward was derived from CCP leaders' desire to drag the country out of the mire of poverty and backwardness. However, this approach led to 'the cherishing of totally unrealistic expectations and the formulation of grandiose, but badly planned and clumsily implemented schemes, the execution of which heaped insupportable burdens on the Chinese people' (Rodzinski 1991: 407). The campaign ended in November 1959, and was followed by the Great Economic Crises and the Great Famine which resulted in millions of deaths (Li 1998; National Bureau of Statistics of China 1983).

Although the Great Leap Forward was primarily focused on agriculture and heavy industry, it touched every aspect of Chinese society. The Great Leap Forward of Sport began in February 1956 when the SPCSC issued the 'Ten-Year Guideline for Sports Development'. It aimed to promote mass sport and competitive sport simultaneously and to reach world levels within a decade. The major target was to 'have four million people achieve the standard of the LDS. Cultivate eight million active athletes and five thousand elite athletes in ten years time' (SPCSC 1958a). By mid 1958, inspired by the booming campaign in agriculture and heavy industry, the SPCSC believed that 'the goal of surpassing the capitalist West has encouraged the development of sport . . . the old Guideline could no longer suit the current situation and will reduce people's enthusiasm' (Fu 2007: 161).

Therefore, the SPCSC revised the Guideline in September 1958 and required '150–200 million people to achieve the standard of the LDS, cultivate 50–70 million active athletes and 10–15 thousand elite athletes' (Fu 2007: 161).

In September 1958, the revised Ten-Year Guideline for Sport and Physical Education was approved by the CCP central committee. It defined the role of sport and physical education in serving the Great Leap Forward:

> The fundamental task of sport and physical education is to build up people's physical strength, and thus contribute to the construction of the country and serve the national defense. It can serve the Great Leap Forward by providing it with strong and healthy workers. To achieve this goal we must promote mass sport.
>
> (*New Sports* 1959a: 1)

Stimulated by the policy, mass sport developed rapidly in China. Participants in the LDS programs and physical activities increased dramatically in factories, schools and the countryside. Programs, such as 'National Physical Exercise Month' and 'National Physical Exercise Week', were especially designed to mobilize the masses. People were encouraged to participate in track and field, gymnastics, weightlifting, swimming, basketball, volleyball, badminton, wushu and other physical exercises.

According to the Ten-Year Guidelines, 'the LDS would be promoted among 80 percent of the trade union and expect 2.79 million workers to achieve the standard levels' (Jarvie *et al.* 2008: 77). Although the signs of an oncoming crisis caused by the Great Leap Forward were visible in the spring of 1959, the SPCSC continued to trumpet its mass sport campaign. In January 1959, an editorial of the *New Sport*, the mouth organ of the SPCSC, argued that

> In order to promote mass sport, we must go all out and aim high. Conservatism and superstition should be avoided; the spirit of daring to think, to speak and to act must be advocated. Based on the great achievement of mass sport in 1958, we must achieve a greater and all-around success in 1959.
>
> (*New Sports* 1959b: 3)

Unrealistic sport policies were applied to physical education in primary, secondary and higher education sectors. The Ten-Year Guidelines required 10 percent of the students to reach the first level of the LDS, 50 percent to reach the second level, and 40 percent to reach the third level during the Second Five-Year Plan period (1958–1962) (SPCSC 1958b). Students who reached level 1&2 of the LDS were honored as 'Double Red'. Those who reached level 1&2 of the LDS, and had qualified as athletes and standard shooters, were honored as 'Four Red' (Yang and Wang 2006).

The campaign resulted in chaos in education sectors. Physical education classes were occupied by unscientific training and tests. In order to reach the standards of the LDS, some students trained at night; some got up at four o'clock in the morning to practice long-distance running. Students ate their lunch while they undertook training. Some of the boys ran 16,000 meters per day, girls 9,900 meters per day. Over-exercise resulted in damage to students' health (Fu 2007).

Promoting sports in the countryside was also a major goal. An essay entitled 'Promote Rural Sports Immediately' published in the *New Sport* in 1958 claimed that

> If we ignore the rural population, promoting sport, organizing mass sport activities to serve the construction of the country would be empty talks. Sport development depends on 500 million peasants. Rural sport should be our major concern.
>
> (Fang 1958: 3)

With the support of local sport commissions, peasants were mobilized to participate in 'broadcast exercises', track and field, football, basketball and volleyball. Sport meetings were organized by sport commissions at village level and town level. Officers in the People's Communes composed folk songs to introduce the LDS program to the peasants:

> Labour Defense System,
> Clear and simple,
> Every event has its own standard,
> Run, jump, throw and climb.
> It is good to achieve the standard,
> Medals in front of the chest,
> Certificate in the pocket,
> Build up the physical strength,
> Contribute to the construction of the country.
> (*New Sports* 1958 (14): 142)

According to the figures in the *History of Sport in China* published in 2007, during the Great Leap Forward 67 counties in China adopted the LDS. About 100,000 peasants reached different levels of the LDS. Five percent of the rural population (about 20 million) participated in sports activities. In Liaoning, Shanxi and Hunan provinces, 40 percent of the rural population participated in physical exercise. In some regions where sport and physical education were well developed, such as Naxi, Xuyong, Jiangbei in Sichuan Province; Tengchong in Yunnan Province; Gaotang in Shandong Province; County Yu in Henan Province; Xiangtan in Hunan province and Changzhi in Shanxi Province, the proportion of participants reached 70 percent (Fu 2007).

A report published in 1958 stated, '160,000 sport associations were established in the countryside around China by the end of 1958. There were 1,800,000 sports teams and physical exercise groups. 300,000 play grounds were built in the countryside. More than 50,000 sport meetings were held at village level. More than 100 million peasants participated in sports activities frequently' (*New Sports* 1958 (19): 4). Although, like those in other reports published during the Great Leap Forward, the figure in this report was largely exaggerated, the achievement of the campaign should not be neglected. It was the first time that modern sport was introduced to peasants on a large scale.

Although the Great Leap Forward ceased at the end of 1958, the sport policy continued to take effect. The 'Report on the State Physical Culture and Sports

Commission Conference for the Works in 1960' clearly reflected this trend. It stated: 'Encouraged by the policy of the Eighth Congress of the CCP, great leaps in promoting sports and physical education were achieved in 1958 and 1959. Mass sport and competitive sport have been developed, sport has been popularized' (Policy Research Centre of the Sports Ministry 1982b: 48).

In January 1960, the SPCSC announced, 'The mission in 1960 was to develop mass sport with great effort, enhance the level of performance in a short period of time, use sport to build up people's physical strength, and thus serve the purpose of national construction and national defense' (Policy Research Centre of the Sports Ministry 1982b: 52).

Besides the SPCSC, other organizations also supported the policy. The All-China Federation of Trade Unions announced in January 1960, 'The campaign of developing workers' sports will be advanced into a new stage. A new upsurge in physical exercise will be achieved' (Li 1960: 1). The Trade Union called for workers' participation in 'broadcast exercise', long-distance running and a 'ten thousand people table tennis competition'. The Communist Youth League of China also accounted that: 'In order to let the youth embrace the 1960s with a strong and healthy body, the Youth League and the Young Pioneers should engage actively in physical exercises, and cooperate with the SPCSC and schools to organize sport competitions' (Lu 1960: 4). The CYLC, the SPCSC and the Ministry of Education jointly established a notification on April 20, 1960, to encourage students to participate in track and field events (Fu 2007: 157).

Pompous and formal sport programs and activities such as the 'National Sports Competition Month', 'Ten Thousand Teams Basketball Tournament', 'Ten Thousand Teams Football Tournament', 'Ten Thousand People Athletic Meeting', 'Ten Thousand People Shooting Team Competition', 'Sport Commune' and 'Sport Village' took place around the country. Participating in physical exercise became a political task. Exaggerated reports on the development of mass sport can be found in all the newspapers, journals and government reports in the late 1950s and early 1960s.

As the great famine and economic crisis continued in the second half of 1960, survival became the priority. The campaign of sport promotion had to stop. Mass sport programs were, therefore, brought to a halt. Sport meetings were no longer held. In schools and universities, physical education hours were reduced, and some physical classes were even canceled. 'Reduce or Cancel' became the guideline for sport and physical education throughout the country.

Together with the recovery of agriculture and economy, mass sport and school physical education recovered slowly in 1963 and 1964. The previously radical sport policy was replaced by a less radical one. The LDS was replaced by the 'Training Standard for the Youth' in 1964. People were no longer forced to reach certain levels of physical exercise. However, the influence of the Great Leap Forward was still apparent. From 1964, formal and unrealistic mass sport programs emerged again. For example, in 1965 the CYLC in Jinan organized the 'Ten Thousand People Long-distance Running', the 'Ten Thousand People Mountain Climbing' and the 'Ten Thousand People Swimming'. Guangzhou city government and sport commission organized a 'Ten Thousand People River Swimming' (Hao 2006).

Prepare for war: sport policy between 1962 and 1965

Ten years after the Korean War (1950–1952), the Sino-India Border Conflict in 1962 and the Sino-Soviet split in the 1960s revived the anti-imperialist sentiment. Threats from the Soviet Union and India 'made calls for defense of the nation more credible and emotional' (Townsend 1992: 121). The Vietnam War (1959–1975), which was regarded as the United States' offensive against China, further consolidated fears of an invasion from the US and resulted in the rise of Chinese nationalism. 'Prepare for the War, Fight against the Invaders' was a slogan, and China's domestic policy changed accordingly. National defense became a central focus. Mao Zedong called for the development of militiamen in June 1962 (He 2006). A nation-wide campaign to promote mass military training was initiated to 'Turn Everyone into Soldier' for the war (He 2006).

Lu Dingyi (1906–1996), Minister of the Publicity Department of the CCP Central Committee, explained the importance of sport in serving the national defense at the Second National Games in 1965:

> Recently, the United States is expanding the Vietnam War. India is invading Pakistan and continues to make troubles at the Sino-India border. Therefore, we must be alert and be prepared for the War. Sport must adapt to the situation both at home and abroad. We must promote mass sport and military physical exercises. The aim is to mobilize all the Chinese people to exercise their bodies and their minds to enable them to be ready to protect our country and to contribute to our socialist construction.
>
> (Guo 2009: 138)

In 1964, the SPCSC called for mass participation in swimming, shooting, radio sport and mountain climbing and other military-related sports activities (SPCSC 1964). The SPCSC and the PLA jointly established the 'Notification of Promote Swimming for the Masses' in 1965. Consequently, swimming and aquatic military training became the major theme of mass sport. Camping was another popular military exercise. For example, between May and September 1965, 2.5 million people in Shandong province participated in camping activities.

In addition to the boom of military sports and physical exercise, the first half of the 1960s saw the consolidation of the competitive sport system. The government was determined to use the best of limited resources to provide special and intensive training for potential athletes in a particular sport so that they could compete on the international sporting stage. Consequently, professional sports teams increased from 3 in 1951 to more than 50 in 1961. The SPCSC issued the 'Regulations of Outstanding Athletes and Teams' in 1963 to improve the competitive sports system. Under the instruction of the SPCSC, a search for talented young athletes took place in every province (Policy Research Centre of the Sports Ministry 1982a). Meanwhile, 10 key sports were selected from the 43 sports that had been defined as competitive sports in 1956. They were: basketball, volleyball, soccer, table tennis, track and field, gymnastics, weightlifting, swimming, skating and shooting (Policy Research Centre of the Sports Ministry 1982a). The country concentrated all the resources on a few elite athletes in order to produce high performances on the international sports stage.

Following the Maoist road: sports policy during the Cultural Revolution (1966–1976)

China gradually recovered from the disasters brought by the Great Leap Forward from 1963 to 1965. The economy grew steadily under the moderate and realistic domestic policy, and living standards gradually improved. However, the progress proved to be merely a period of respite before the storm. From 1966 a widespread social and political upheaval, the Great Proletariat Cultural Revolution, swept over China, resulting in nation-wide chaos and economic disarray.

The Cultural Revolution was initiated by Mao Zedong in early 1966 as he believed that he was losing control over fundamental Party decisions. The principal aim was to regain and consolidate his power (Rodzinski 1991). In addition to the power struggle, Mao and his supporters also wanted to use the Cultural Revolution to prevent China from changing its color from Red (Communism) to Black (Capitalism and Revisionism) (Fan 1999).

The turbulence of the Cultural Revolution also reached the field of sport. The confrontation ultimately concerned the relationship between competitive sport and mass sport. The former was regarded as representative of bourgeois and capitalist ideology and the latter as communist and proletarian. He Long, the Sports Minister, was accused of neglecting mass sport participation and for supporting the revisionist and capitalist sports policy of Liu Shaoqi (1898–1969) and Deng Xiaoping (1904–1997). He was condemned, jailed and died in prison in June 1969.

The Revolutionary Communist Central Committee, the State Council and the Central Military Commission jointly issued a Military Order on May 12, 1968, to disband local sports commissions. PLA officers and soldiers were sent to replace the cadres. Most of the sports officials were attacked by the Red Guards and revolutionary rebels. More than 1,000 cadres from the SPCSC were sent to a 'May Seventh Cadre School' (五七干校) in Shanxi province to be 'Re-educated' by doing physical labor (Fan 1999). Administrators and coaches of local sports commissions were sent to the countryside to be 'Re-educated' as well. The whole training system in China was dismantled. Sports schools were closed down. Most sports teams were dismissed. National squads stopped participating in international competitions. Sports competitions ceased. Sports facilities were destroyed by the Red Guards. Sports stadiums became the venue for denunciation meetings. Top athletes, outstanding coaches and scientists/scholars were condemned as counter revolutionaries, capitalist-roaders and rightists, and suffered mentally and physically (Fan 1999). Some of the athletes died in the violent revolutionary storm, and three famous world-class table tennis players even committed suicide in 1969 to avoid further torture.

Competitive sport suffered because of Mao's decision to wipe out his political enemies and to consolidate the Maoist ideology between 1966 and 1970. The situation began to change owing to political and diplomatic reasons in 1971 when China felt the threat from the Soviet Union and sought a new ally in the US. Sport was a pleasant and efficient way to make approaches to Western powers through a medium which benefited from a non-political image (Fan 1999). Ping-Pong Diplomacy played its part to establish the relationship with the United States. At the same time, under the slogan 'Friendship First, Competition Second', sport was used to strengthen the relations between China and its old allies including socialist countries, African countries and South American counties (Fan 2001). For example, in 1972 the Chinese Table Tennis Teams visited Asia, Africa, South America, Europe and America, and 72 countries and regions communicated with China through Chinese sports delegations' visits (Yuan 2002).

The rise of mass sport

Different from the competitive sport and elitism that were smashed by the Cultural Revolution, mass sport survived the violence and developed under the slogan 'Sport for the People'. The Cultural Revolution was an accessible introduction to modern sport in a patriotic and politically unimpeachable form, supported by the full might of the Chinese state (Fan 2001). Since the early 1970s, the government's sports policy 'pushed the roots of sport deep into Chinese society and raised the sporting standards throughout the whole population' (Fan 2001: 159).

With the change of the political atmosphere in the early 1970s, the adoption of a new sports policy and the enforcement of the revised revolutionary guidelines resulted in the rapid growth of mass sport. In 1972 the sports ministry held a national conference on the promotion of rural sports. It argued that the development of sport among peasants was an important role of the Maoist sports policy. In 1973, an editorial entitled 'Take Vigorous Action to Promote Physical Exercise and Sport in the Countryside' was published in *New Sport* to call for the promotion of physical exercises in the countryside. It emphasized, 'We must understand that the promotion of sport and physical exercises in the countryside is vital to implement Chairman Mao's revolutionary sports policy' (Fan 1999).

The systematic promotion of mass sport came in 1974 when Mao's wife, Jiang Qing (1914–1991), launched the Anti-Confucius Campaign, which aimed at assaulting the Prime Minister Zhou Enlai (1898–1976) and his successor Deng Xiaoping by means of quite obvious innuendoes (Rodzinski 1991). During the campaign, Jiang initiated a national campaign of 'Learn from Xiaojinzhuang', a village in Hebei province in Northern China that had an impressive record of combining mass sport and ideological education, to use sport to disseminate proletarian ideology and propagandize the Maoist Road. Therefore, promoting sport among peasants became an important mission of provincial and county sports commissions. Villages were required to have their own sports teams, and sports meetings became an official agenda of local authorities (Fan 1999). For example, Yuchan Commune of County Hu in Shanxi Province mobilized 70 percent of its adults to participate in sports activities. It also established 12 basketball teams, and competitions between the teams took place frequently. In Tianjian, all the communes were required to establish sports teams including for basketball, volleyball, table tennis and swimming (Yuan 2002).

Peasants were mobilized to follow the 'Mao Zedong Thought' and the 'Maoist Sports Road' by participating in sport and physical exercise. Sports activities were usually connected with political and economic commitment. In some villages, peasants had to participate in certain physical exercise or sports competitions, otherwise they would not get their working points. For example, peasants at Lengzuitou Brigade, Zhuihua County, in Hebei province were required to do morning exercise every day to get their working points (Fan 1999). In addition to daily physical exercises, politicalized mass sport programs such as 'Ten Thousand People Sports Show', 'Thousand People Gymnastics Show', 'Mass Cross-River Swimming' and 'Mass Cross-Lake Swimming' were frequently held in the countryside across China (Fu 2007).

Following the previous attempts to promote rural sports (the policy that called for the promotion of rural sports in the 1950s and during the Great Leap Forward and the Cultural Revolution), the early 1970s saw the popularization of sport and physical exercise in rural China: 'Untold millions of peasants watched and played. Most of them had never before participated in any modern form of exercise. This was a cultural education project involving sport of historically unprecedented scope' (Fan 2001: 159).

In urban areas, mass sport was restored after a national sports conference held in 1973. The conference demanded a nation-wide restoration of sport commissions at every level. From then on, the sports administrative system began to operate after suffering seven years of disorder. The Anti-Lin Biao and Anti-Confucius Campaign and Jiang Qing's 'Learn from Xiaojinzhuang' Campaign consolidated the political significance of mass sport and brought it to another peak. Mass sport activities were frequently held to commemorate important days or events such as the birth dates of the CCP and the PLA, the National Day, the International Women's Day, the International Workers' Day and the revolutionary Spring Festival. During the Spring Festival in 1974, *Tiyu Bao* (*Sports Daily*) reported: 'Millions of people participated in various sports activities . . . In Beijing, 700,000 young people joined the long-distance running to commemorate the Long March' (*China Sports Daily* 25–01–1974). It reported again in July 1974: 'In order to respond to the call of the Anti-Lin Biao and Anti-Confucius Campaign, 5,000 citizens and soldiers participated in the Cross-Yangzi River Swimming in Wuhan city. In Beijing, 90,000 citizens practiced swimming, diving, water polo and other aquatic activities. In Changsha, citizens and soldiers joined the Cross-Xiang River Swimming' (*China Sports Daily* 17–07–1974). A newspaper article entitled 'Following Chairman Mao and Marching Forward in Gig Storm and Surge' reported in July 1975: '7,000 citizens and soldiers swam in the Cross-Gulangyu Channel Swimming in Xiamen' (*China Sports Daily* 18–07–1975).

These mass sport programs were closely linked to political campaigns such as the Anti-Lin Biao and Anti-Confucius and the 'Learn from Xiaojinzhuang'. Sport was regarded as 'an important approach to promote people's health, to attack the bourgeois and help socialism to take over the field of ideology and culture' (*China Sports Daily* 01–02–1975). The objective was to 'serve the proletarian politics' (*China Sports Daily* 01–01–1975). For example, in February 1975, 'in order to support the campaign through sport' (*China Sports Daily* 04–02–1975), Shanghai Trade Union and Shanghai Sport Commission organized 'broadcasting gymnastics', 'work gymnastics' and 'Taiji convention' for workers and cadres. However, in order to suit the anti-tradition nature of the Cultural Revolution and to follow the Maoist Road, traditional sports, such as dragon boat race and dragon dance, were banned by the authorities as they represented 'feudalism' and 'revisionism'.

The promotion of military physical education in schools and universities

Nationalism was another major force that changed the government's sports policy during the Cultural Revolution. Influenced by the rising Chinese nationalism which was filled with nationalist, anti-imperialist and anti-Western xenophobic sentiment, sport was a vehicle for national defense and national construction. Military physical education in schools was one of the characteristics of the Cultural Revolution.

The CCP Central Committee issued the following regulations in February 1967: 'The Notification of Cultural Revolution in Primary Schools', 'The Regulations on Cultural Revolution in Primary and Secondary Schools' and 'The Regulations on Cultural Revolution in Colleges and Universities'. These regulations required students to participate in military training as compulsory in the curriculum for national defense purposes. The CCP Central Committee issued another requirement instruction by Mao Zedong on March 8, 1967, which required the army to help the education sectors to carry out military training.

Following the Party's instructions, physical education in schools was renamed as 'military physical education'. Modern sport events were condemned as part of capitalist education and were replaced by military physical exercises including formation drills, grenade throwing, shooting, military hiking, camping and field training. Track and field and swimming became supplementary exercises as they were closely related to military training. Veterans and soldiers entered schools to be military physical education instructors. PE teachers were required to be 'Re-educated' to be equipped with basic military knowledge and skills before they could be assistants to the military instructors.

After the Sino-Soviet Border Conflict in 1969, anti-imperialist nationalism stimulated further development of military physical education in China. The slogans were 'Be prepared against the war, be prepared against natural disasters, do everything for the people', 'An entire nation in arms' and '800 million peasants are 800 million athletes and soldiers'. According to a military physical education text book published by Beijing Education Bureau (北京市教委) in 1970, the objective of military physical education was to 'cultivate the spirit of revolution, reinforce the organizational discipline, equip students with basic knowledge and skills of military exercise, train their bodies and serve the great revolution with class struggle consciousness, production skill and scientific experiment' (Fu 2007: 313). The content of the text book included drill, grenade throwing, shooting, military hiking, camping, field training, mountain climbing, swimming, rope climbing, gymnastics, single/parallel bars, basketball, supplementary ball games (soccer, volleyball and table tennis), running, obstacle race, jumping, shot put, military boxing and hygiene (Li 1982).

Military physical exercise was also introduced to universities. A policy document approved by the CCP Central Committee in June 1970 re-emphasized that military physical education must be included in the university curriculum as a compulsory course (CCP Central Committee 1970). It was also implemented in people's communes in order to train peasants to 'prepare for the war' (Hao 2006: 409).

However, with the change of the political atmosphere and the restoration of the SPCSC in the early 1970s, military physical exercise began to decline. On February 1, 1973, the State Council required the SPCSC at all levels to promote physical education in schools and to encourage students to practice broadcast gymnastics, basket ball, soccer and volleyball, and organize sport meetings (State Council 1973). The purpose of school physical education was changed from producing future soldiers to producing healthy students. Therefore, the SPCSC and the State Council jointly issued 'The Fifth Broadcast Gymnastics for Children' on June 1, 1973, which required all the primary schools to participate in this exercise for 15 minutes every school day. New text books which focused on track and field, ball games, gymnastics and swimming were ready for students and teachers. By the end of the Cultural Revolution in 1976, physical education classes began to return to the school curriculum.

Elite sport as the priority: Chinese sports policy from 1977 to 2008

The Cultural Revolution ended in 1976. The post-Cultural Revolution period 'witnessed the continuation of intensive efforts to rebuild the country and to make up for the self-inflicted damage of the tragic decade from 1966 to 1976' (Rodzinski 1991: 432). The Third Plenary Session of the 11th Central Committee which was held in September 1978 marked a new era for China. The 'Class Struggle-oriented' political policy was abolished. Socialistic modernization became the new guideline. Therefore, 'Economy Construction-oriented' domestic and foreign policies were adopted to serve the goal of modernization (Jing 2004).

Sport policy also underwent transformation in the new era. The SPCSC held a national sports conference in Beijing in February 1979 to discuss the future development of sport. Following the guidelines of the Third Plenary Session of the 11th Central Committee, the SPCSC abolished the class struggle-oriented sports policy which was applied during the Cultural Revolution and a new sports policy was born which was to serve the four modernizations.[3]

The SPCSC held another national sports conference in 1980 to consolidate the 'modernization construction-oriented' sports policy, and officially established its strategy for the future development of sport. According to the strategy, both mass sport and competitive sport should be promoted. However, competitive sport should be the major focus. Wang Meng (1919–2007), the Sports Minister, explained the reason. He stated, 'On the one hand, China was still a poor country and was restricted in the amount of money it could invest in sport. On the other hand, elite sport was an effective way to boost China's new image on the international stage. Therefore, the solution was to bring elite sport into the existing planned economy and administrative system, which could assist in the distribution of the limited resources of the whole nation to medal-winning sports' (Wang 1982: 150). It was hoped that the international success of Chinese athletes would, in return, bring pride and hope to the nation, which were badly needed in the new era of transformation (Rong 1987).

Based on this strategy, the conference drafted the blueprint for Chinese sport in the 1980s and 1990s. Elite sport was set as the priority. The short-term plan required the national team to be placed among the top ten at the 1980 Olympics, and to be placed among the top six at the 1984 Olympics. The long-term plan required China's elite sport to reach top world standards by the end of the 1980s (Hao 2008).

China's success at the 1984 Los Angeles Olympics proved the validity and the necessity of the 'elite sport first' strategy. The national squad's remarkable achievements (Chinese athletes won 15 gold medals and China was placed fourth in the Olympic medals tally) excited many in China and stimulated a stronger call for the promotion of elite sport from both the central government and ordinary Chinese people. 'Develop elite sport and make China a superpower in the world' became a popular slogan in China (Fan *et al.* 2005).

The central government issued 'A Notification about the Further Promotion of Sport' in October 1984. The mission of making China a world sports power was born (Tan 2005). The notification stated that

> Sport has a close relationship with people's health, the power of the nation and the honor of the country. It plays an important role in promoting people's political awareness, achieving modernization targets, establishing foreign relations and strengthening the national defense. Therefore, the Party and the society have recognized the importance of sport in our society and will develop sport in China further . . . The remarkable achievement in sport, especially the success at the 1984 Olympics, has restored our self-confidence and national pride. It has stimulated a patriotic feeling among all the Chinese both at home and abroad and enhanced China's international influence . . . Our policy is to develop both mass sport and elite sport, and strive for greater success in the international sport arena.
>
> (CCP Central Committee 1984)

Following this guideline, the Society of Strategic Research for the Development of Physical Education and Sport (体育发展战略研究会) produced the 'Olympic Strategy' (奥运战略) for the SPCSC in 1985. The new strategy aimed to use the nation's limited resources to develop elite sport. The ultimate goal was to build up China's international image by transforming China into a leading sports power (Fan *et al.* 2005). One year later, the SPCSC issued the 'Decisions about the Reform of Sports System (Draft)', which confirmed the importance of sport in serving the modernization construction. The major objective of the policy was to raise the standard of elite sport (State Sports Commission 1986). The clauses of the policy clearly indicated its elite sport-oriented nature. Six out of nine of them were directly related to elite sport:

1   Improving the level of sport leadership and confirming the SPCSC's overall role of leadership, coordination and supervision;
2   Establishing a scientific training system;
3   Improving the system of sport competitions;
4   Enhancing and promoting Chinese traditional indigenous sports;
5   Developing sports scientific research gradually;
6   Reforming the sport and physical education system;

7   Enhancing political thought on sport;
8   Improving the sport prize system;
9   Developing flexible open policies in relation to international sport.

> (SPCSC, Decisions about the Reform of the Sports System (Draft),
> 1986, cited in Jarvie *et al.* 2008: 100)

The rise of elite sport

Supported by the new sports policy, China's elite sport experienced a rapid growth in the 1980s and 1990s. Since 1980, the famous 'Ju Guo Ti Zhi' (whole country support the elite sport system, 举国体制) has been applied to promote elite sport. Based on the professional training and selection system that was officially created in 1963, a well-organized and tightly structured three-level pyramid system was developed to meet the needs of the 'elite sport first strategy' (see Figure 11.1).

Athletes were selected and trained from when they were very young. When boys and girls between the ages of 6 and 9 years old were identified with some talent in particular sports, they were encouraged to join local sports schools throughout the country on a voluntary basis. After a period of training, young people with potential were selected for the provincial sports academies or training centers. Provincial and local sports teams and commissions took the responsibility of nurturing and training elite athletes for the national teams and rewarding them when they won medals. In 2004 there were 372,290 young athletes in more than 3,000 sports schools around China. The number of professional athletes was 46,758; 15,924 athletes were titled national athletes; and 3,222 people were in the Olympic Squad.

In order to serve the 'Ju Guo Ti Zhi', the nation's limited economic resources, education resources and human capital were channeled to this system. All efforts were being made to serve the goal of winning Olympic medals. As the Minister of Sport, Wu Shaozu, stated in 1994, 'The highest aim of Chinese sport is to achieve

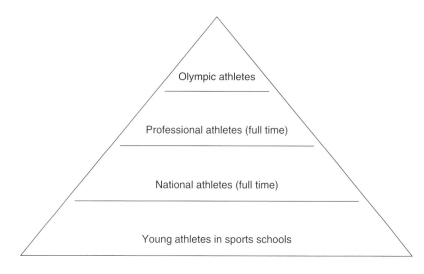

Figure 11.1 China's selective system for elite sport pyramid

success at the Olympic Games. We must concentrate our resources on it. To raise the flag at the Olympics is our major responsibility' (Wu 1999).

The 'Ju Guo Ti Zhi' brought China remarkable success on the international sports stage. From the 1984 Los Angeles Olympic Games to the 2008 Beijing Olympics, Chinese athletes climbed the ladder of the gold medals with a world record speed (see Figure 11.2). After the Chinese squad won 32 gold medals and was placed second at the 2004 Athens Olympics, CNN commented that

> In the six Olympic Games they have competed in, China has moved up the medal tally in world record time. Their first gold medal came only 20 years ago. In Barcelona 92 they climbed to 5th spot on the medal tally, in Atlanta 96 they moved into fourth place, in Sydney 2000 they took third and this year in Athens they finished second. Another Games, another rung up the ladder. Undoubtedly China wants to reach the top spot in Beijing 2008.
>
> (Holmes 2004)

The CNN commentator was right. In 2008, China's dream came true with being first on the gold medal table. It had beaten the USA and become a world sports power.

Economy reformation and sport: policies for mass sport and sport industry since the 1990s

While the 'Ju Guo Ti Zhi' played a major part in ensuring the development of elite sport, economic reform in China stimulated the development of mass sport. The turning point came in 1992 when a major reform policy was initiated by Deng Xiaoping. On his South Patrol in February 1992 Deng urged the central and local governments to speed up economic reformation at all levels in Chinese society. To answer the call, the SPCSC held a conference in Zhongshan, Guangdong province, in November 1992 to discuss how to speed up sports reformation. At the conference, Wu Shaozu, Minister of Sport, pointed out that the major focus of the reform was the transformation of the sports system, which was based on a

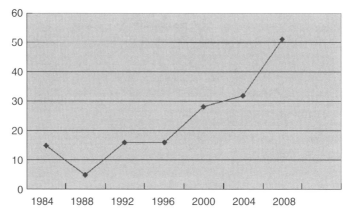

Figure 11.2 Gold medals won by China in the Summer Olympics (1984–2008)

planned economy, to a new system that would be based on a market economy. Sport should not only be regulated and supported by the government but should also stand on its own feet.

Based on the principle of the Zhongshan Conference, the SPCSC issued the 'Suggestion on Moving Further Ahead in Sports Reformation' on May 24, 1993. It officially announced a market economy-oriented reform policy. In this policy document, the SPCSC, for the first time, publicly advocated the commercialization of sport and the promotion of the sport industry. As Wu Shaozhu claimed, the 'Chinese sports system must reform without delay. The strategy of the reform is to commercialize sport and to integrate sport into people's daily life. This includes people paying for sports and exercise; privately sponsored sport; the club system and promotion of sports commercial market' (Fan 2009).

After the official approval of the establishment of the socialist market economy system at the Third Plenary Session of the 14th Central Committee in November 1993, the SPCSC set the framework of the future development of sport in an increasingly market-oriented economy. It issued three decrees in June 1995: the Olympic Strategy (奥运争光计划纲要), the National Fitness for All Programme (全民健身计划纲要) and the Development of Sport Industry and Commerce Outline (体育产业发展纲要). These decrees were designed to be integrated, and were expected to support each other and to form a new sports policy and practice in China. They were approved by the China State Council in June 1995. Although elite sport still held the dominant position and continued to be supported by the government, mass sport and the sport industry were highlighted for special attention. It was also the first time that the government established a work plan for the promotion of the sport industry.

Since the mid 1990s, mass sport and the sport industry have supported each other and have experienced a rapid growth. In 2009, Wei Jizhong, Chairman of the China Sport Industry Co Ltd, commented, 'Compared with the situation ten years ago, people's awareness of sport and leisure increased, thanks to the development of the sports and leisure industry in China . . . The demands of people and the market will further push the development of the sport and leisure industry' (*China Daily* 18–05–2009).

Fifteen years after the establishment of the market economy system, China has become the world's biggest sporting goods factory as well as the world's largest sporting goods market. By 2008, 65 percent of the world's sporting goods were made in China (Chinese Market Network 2008). In 2009, the US Commercial Service anticipates that China will become the largest sporting goods market by 2010, surpassing the United States (*China Digital News* 20–07–2008).

At the same time, China's sports service industry (fitness and leisure industry, and professional sport industry) is growing rapidly. According to the General Administration of Sport of China (国家体育总局, the former SPCSC), prior to 2010 the annual growth rate of China's sport industry is approximately 20 percent. It is estimated that by 2010 the total output value of the industry will account for 0.5 percent of the GDP (Li 2007).

China's sport industry has 'stood on its own feet' during the past 15 years with little dependency on the government. For example, in the sporting service industry, nearly all the fitness clubs are privately owned. In the sporting goods industry, the majority of the manufacturers are joint ventures, privately-owned enterprise and foreign-funded enterprise. By 2007, only 14.07 percent of the export market share in the sporting goods industry belonged to state-owned enterprises. In recent years, the proportion of state-owned enterprise has continued to decline (MOSTGROUP 2008).

At the same time, economic reform has stimulated the development of sports and leisure recreation among ordinary people. With the rapid growth of the Chinese economy since the 1980s (see Figure 11.3), people's living standard has improved, leisure time has increased and health awareness has been enhanced. Consequently, the demand for sport and leisure activities has emerged. From the mid 1990s, more and more Chinese people have spent their time and money on sport and leisure activities. According to a survey conducted by the General Administration of Sport of China in 2008, about 340 million people in China participate in physical exercise regularly; 250 million of them spend an average of 593 yuan per year on sport and leisure activities. The survey also showed that 28.2 percent of the population spent more than 30 minutes on physical exercise and leisure activities at least three times a week (*People's Daily* 18–12–2008). Compared to the 1970s and 1980s, mass sport activities have changed from being government-led to taking place on a voluntary basis.

Health and fitness as the focus: physical education in schools

Influenced by the modernization policy, school physical education changed accordingly. At the National School Physical Education Conference held in 1979, the SPCSC and the Ministry of Education announced that the policy for school physical education should be focused on 'Fitness and Health Promotion' (Hao 2006: 434). The SPCSC and the Ministry of Education issued 'The Regulation for Physical Education in Primary and Secondary Schools' and 'The Regulation for Physical Education in Colleges and Universities' on October 5, 1979. In order to standardize school physical education and to mobilize students to participate in

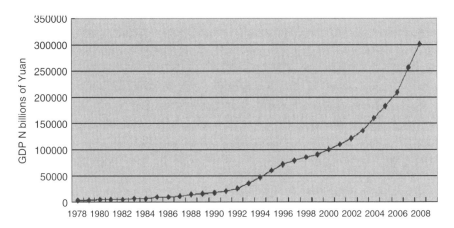

Figure 11.3 The People's Republic of China's National Domestic Product (1978–2008)

Source: National Bureau of Statistics of China

physical exercises, the SPCSC and the Ministry of Education jointly established the revised 'State Physical Training Standards' in 1982. The standards were applied to most primary and secondary schools. Some 280 million students reached the standard by 1988.

The health and fitness-oriented policy continued in the 1990s. The Ministry of Education issued 'The Guidance for Physical Education in Higher Education' in 1992. It stated, 'The objective of physical education is to cultivate students' awareness of sport and exercise and help them to form a habit of participating in physical exercises in their lives. Sport and exercise help to improve their fitness level and turn them into healthy successors for the construction of the socialist country' (Ministry of Education 1992).

In 2000, the Ministry of Education issued two new syllabuses for physical education entitled 'Nine-year Compulsory Education Syllabus for Physical Education and Health Education in Primary Schools' and 'Nine-year Compulsory Education Syllabus for Physical Education and Health Education in Secondary Schools'. These two syllabuses consolidated the principles of health-centered and student-centered policy. They laid the foundation for the future development of physical education in education sectors.

Chinese sports policy post 2008: coda

After the Establishment of the PRC in 1949, China's sports policies were heavily influenced by every major political event and they served political purposes. In the early 1950s, policy was focused on training people's bodies for national defense and self-strengthening. In the late 1950s, the Great Leap Forward resulted in the implementation of an unrealistic sports policy which aimed at building up the nation's strength through mass sport. However, the failure of the GLF and the Great Famine brought about a decline in mass sport participation. At the same time, channeling the limited resources to develop elite sport in order to compete against the Western powers on the international stage became a priority. In the early 1960s, the Sino-India Border Conflict and the Sino-Soviet Split made military physical exercise a central theme. During the Cultural Revolution (1966–1976), competitive sport suffered but mass sport and military education were developed because of class struggle-oriented politics and anti-foreign nationalism. In short, prior to 1978, mass sport, school physical education and competitive sport traversed a tortuous course of development. A sustainable sport industry had failed to emerge under the planned economy system.

The end of the Cultural Revolution in 1976 brought a new era of economic reform. The goal was to achieve four modernizations and restore China as a powerful country in the world by the end of the twentieth century. The government's sports policy reflected the change and the goal. It identified elite sport as a priority for improving China's new image and joining the rank of the great sports powers in the world.

The development of the market economy created a new dimension for Chinese sport in the 1990s. Commercialization and globalization of the sport industry and economy became a focus of the new policy for sport. After 15 years' development from 1994 to 2009 the sport industry stands on its own feet without relying on government support. At the same time, mass sport developed with new characteristics in the new era. With the increase of leisure time and improved living standards people willingly participated in physical exercise and leisure recreation. Fitness and lifelong physical activity has become a new trend of mass sport. The government's sports policy in the twenty-first century will pay attention to the area of the health benefits of recreation and sport.

The CCP Central Committee in 2002 issued the 'Proposals on the Further Promotion of Sport' and the State Sport General Administration in 2003 issued the '2001–2010 Strategic Plan for Sport'. These documents declared that the objectives of current and future reform are to 'reduce the degree of government's intervention in sport and make sport rely on the support of the society' (Yu 2006: 16). The National Sports Congress in early 2009 reemphasized the continuation of the implementation of the sports policies issued by the State Council in 1995: the Olympic Strategy (奥运争光计划纲要); the National Fitness for All Programme (全民健身计划纲要); the Outline of Development of Sport Industry and Commerce (体育产业发展纲要).

It is likely that, on the one hand, the government will continue its economic reformation of sport in the areas of mass sport and the sport industry and speed up the commercialization of sport. Sport will be pushed further towards the market. On the other hand, elite sport will continue to develop in the traditional form of 'Ju Guo Ti Zhi', a product of the planned economy, and will receive support from the government. The 2008 Olympics in Beijing proved it was an effective way to make China a sports power. The unique system, which has played such an important role in China's political life, will continue to fulfill China's ambitions to be one of the global economic and political superpowers in the world in the twenty-first century.

Notes

1 Having fought the world's strongest power, the United States, to a standstill, the Korean War greatly enhanced Chinese people's confidence and secured the national unity and sovereignty of the PRC. The war was regarded as a turning point in Chinese history that symbolized the rise of China as an independent nation. Consequently, Chinese Nationalism was consolidated.
2 Since the establishment of the SPCSC, the ACSF stepped aside.
3 At the Third Plenum of the 11th Central Committee, Deng Xiaoping announced the official launch of the Four Modernizations. This included the modernization of agriculture, industry, technology and defense.

References

All-China Federation of Trade Unions (1954) *The Instruction of Promoting Sport in Industry Sectors*.
All-China Sports Federation (1952) *General Statutes of the All-China Sports Federation*.
Cai, S. (1958) 'The Spring of Chinese Sports', *New Sports* (19).
CCP Central Committee (1970) *The Central Government's Decision on Tsinghua University's Enrolment Work*.
—— (1984) *A Notification about the Further Promotion of Sport*.
China Daily (2009) 'Sport Industry Bucks Business Downturn', May 18.
China Digital News (2008) 'Adidas CEO Says China to Become Second-Most Important

Market in 2009' http://chinadigitaltimes.net/2008/07/adidas-ceo-says-china-to-become-second-most-important-market-in-2009/ (accessed 17 June 2009).

China Sports Daily (1974) 'A Revolutionary Spring Festival', January 25.

—— (1974) 'Marching Forward in the Storm', July 17.

—— (1975) 'The Promotion of Sport during the Cultural Revolution', January 1.

—— (1975) 'On the Promotion of the Mass Sport across the Country', February 1.

—— (1975) 'Anti-Lin Biao and Anti-Confucius Sports Programmes', February 4.

—— (1975) 'Follow Chairman Mao, March Forward in the Storm', July 18.

—— (2009) 'The History of the All-China Sports Federation', May 20.

Chinese Market Network (2008) *Report on Chinese Sporting Goods Industry between 2008 and 2009*.

Fan, H. (1999) 'Not All Bad! Communism, Society and Sport in the Great Proletarian Cultural Revolution: A Revisionist Perspective', *International Journal for the History of Sport*, 16 (3): 47–71.

—— (2001) 'Two Roads to China: The Inadequate and Adequate', *International Journal for the History of Sport*, 18 (2): 148–167.

—— (2009) 'The Change of Chinese Government's Sports Policy, A Historical Review'. Paper presented at the 2009 International Conference/Workshop at University College Cork, Ireland.

Fan, H., Wu, P. and Xiong, H. (2005) 'Beijing Ambitions: An Analysis of the Chinese Elite Sport System and its Olympic Strategy for the 2008 Olympic Games', *International Journal for the History of Sport*, 22 (4): 510–529.

Fang, Y. (1958) 'Promote Rural Sports Immediately', *New Sports* (17).

Feng, W. (1950) 'Discussions on People's Sport', *New Sports* (3).

Fu, Y. (ed.) (2007) *The History of Sport in China*, Vol. 5, 1949–1979, Beijing: People's Sport Press.

Guo, D. (ed) (1995) *The History of The People's Republic of China (1949–1993)*, Beijing: Beijing Normal University Press.

Guo, L. (2009) 'The Second National Games: Paean for the Revolution', *China Sports* (2): 138–139.

Hao, Q. (ed.) (2006) *History of Sport*, Beijing: People's Sport Press.

He, L. (2006) 'The Origins of the Slogan "Turn Everyone into Soldier"', *Martial Historical Facts* (4): 11–17.

Holmes, T. (2009) 'China Takes the Olympic Limelight'. http://edition.cnn.com/2004/SPORT/08/30/athens.games (accessed 4 June 2009).

Jarvie, G., Hwang, D. and Brennan, M. (2008) *Sport Revolution and the Olympics*, Oxford: Berg Publishers.

Jing, C. (2004) *The History of The People's Republic of China (1949–2004)*, Beijing: CCP History Press.

Li, C. (1998) 'Population Change Caused by The Great Leap Movement', *Demographic Study*, No. 1: 97–111

Li, J. (1982) *The History of School Physical Education in China*, Haikou: Hainan Press.

Li, S., Fan, Y. and Gu, G. (1960) 'Promote Sports in Work Units', *New Sports* (3).

Lin, H. (2007) 'Chinese Sport Industry Welcomes Foreign Investment', *Observe and Think*, 3–16: 55–57.

Lu, Z., Rang, S. and Yong, G. (1960) 'Welcome the 1960s with a Strong Body', *New Sports* (3).

Ministry of Education (1992) *Guidance for Physical Education in Higher Education Sectors*.

MOSTGROUP (2008) 'The Export Condition of Chinese Sporting Goods in 2007', http://www.mostgroup.com/html/Industry/2008912/6726EBFE4B025079.html (accessed 17 June 2009).

National Bureau of Statistics of China (1983) *Yearbook of China Statistics* (1983) Beijing: China Statistics Press, 103–104.

New Sports (1958) 'The First Flag of the Labour Defense System in Rural Area' (14).

—— (1959a) 'The Central Government's Instructions for Sport'.

—— (1959b) 'Carry on the Great Leap Forward in Mass Sport'.

—— (1973) 'Take Vigorous Action to Promote Physical Exercise and Sport in the Countryside' (2)

People's Daily (2008) 'Exercise a Habit with 28% of the People', December 12.

Policy Research Centre of the Sports Ministry (ed) (1982a) *Policy Documents for Sport (1949–1981)*, Beijing: People's Sport Press.

—— (1982b) 'Reports on the National Sport Conference in 1960', *Policy Documents for Sport (1949–1981)*, Beijing: People's Sport Press.

—— (1982c) 'Labour and Defense, Statutes for Sport', *Policy Documents for Sport (1949–1981)*, Beijing: People's Sport Press.

Rodzinski, W. (1991) *The Walled Kingdom*, London: Fontana Press.

Rong, G. (ed) (1987) *The History of Contemporary Chinese Sport*, Beijing: China Social Science Press.

SPCSC (1958a) *The Ten Year Guidelines for Sports Development*.

—— (1958b) *Reports on the Ten-Year Guidelines for Sports Development*.

State Council (1973) *Details of the 1973 National Sports Conference*.

State Sports Commission (1964) *Directives to Promote Swimming, Shooting, Radio Sport and Mountain Climbing*.

—— (1986) *Decisions about the Reform of Sports System (Draft)*.

Tan, H. (ed) (2005) *History of Sport*, Beijing: Higher Education Press.

Townsend, J. (1992) 'Chinese Nationalism', *The Australian Journal of Chinese Affairs*, 27: 97–130.

Wang, M. (1982) 'The Report to the 1980 National Sports Conference', *Sports Policy Documents (1949–1981)*, Beijing: People's Sport Press.

Wu, S. (ed.) (1999) *The History of Sport of the PRC*, Beijing: China Books Press.

Yang, G. and Wang, M. (2006) 'The Development of the Standard for Students' Health and Fitness', *Physical Education in China* (5).

Yu, J. (2006) 'China's "Ju Guo Ti Zhi" in the New Era', *Journal of Physical Education*, 13 (1): 16–17.

Yuan, W. (ed) (2002) *The History of Sport in the People's Republic of China*, Beijing: China Book Press.

Zedong, M. (1956) 'Consolidate the Solidarity of the Party, Continue the Tradition of the Party', Preparation Meeting of the 8th Congress of the CCP, August 30.

Zhang, Y. (1984) 'Sport in Rural China', in National Sport History Material Committee (ed.) *Sport History Materials*, Beijing: People's Sport Press.

12 Singapore

Lionel Teo

Since Singapore gained independence in 1965, the government has invariably featured sport in the development and progress of the island-city-state. Sport as a national policy was adopted as an instrument that fostered social cohesion and national identity (independence up to the 1970s), promoted health, fitness and nationalistic objectives (1980s to 1990s), and more recently facilitated nation-building and international recognition (Horton 2002; McNeill *et al.* 2003; SSC 1998a; SSC 2008a). Like most other aspects of social and political development in Singapore, sport policy has been somewhat 'orchestrated' and engaged under the scrutiny of the ruling government, to the degree that the population has internalized the hegemonic influence in their lives (Horton 2002; McNeill *et al.* 2003).

Since 1965, the People's Action Party (PAP) has continuously governed the republic with a political ideology anchored on 'multi-racialism, pragmatism and meritocracy' (Perry *et al.* 1997: 67; Turnbull 1987). Singapore is now a flourishing and highly developed city-state with a per capita Gross Domestic Product equal to that of the big four West European countries (Central Intelligence Agency 2005). With a cosmopolitan population of 4.3 million, Singapore prides itself on being one of Asia's most stable societies, largely due to an efficient and corruption-free government and a productive and resilient workforce (Chen 1983; Perry *et al.* 1997). It is also a society passionate about academic and economic success; only 48 per cent of the population are involved in some form of sporting activity once a week (SSC 2005). Observers allude to Singapore's 'highly interventionist, single-party-dominant polity' (Chua 2001: 265; McNeill *et al.* 2003; Turnbull 1982) but it is not this chapter's aim to debate the government's style of leadership. Rather, it serves to underline the context within which organized sport participation and development is contingent in Singapore (see Perry *et al.* 1997, for an understanding of the socio-political make-up of Singapore).

According to Soon (2002: 193), sport was seen as an important means 'to bring together different ethnic groups to better understand and accept each other through work and play'. The government's pragmatic and paternalistic style of leadership has guided Singapore from the shadow of colonialism to the status of a developed country in the span of only four decades, and it is this same style of government that has seen sport used as an aspect of this broader development (Horton 2002; McNeill *et al.* 2003; Soon 2002). As observed by Horton (2002: 247):

> No aspect of economic, political and social activity, including sport, was to be left to chance . . . All decisions that concerned national development, whether pertaining to the more dramatic issues of foreign policy or national economic management or the seemingly more mundane aspects of social development involving, say, sport or the arts were to be considered and reactions and responses planned.

The discussions and findings in this chapter are based upon examination of academic, government and national sport association (NSA) documents and are informed by interviews with senior officials from government, NSAs or from newspaper articles. It reviews the national sport participation policies in Singapore and examines the extent and efficacy of government intervention in facilitating participation in organized sport.

Development of sport in Singapore

The development of sport in Singapore has its vestiges in its colonial legacy. From 1819 up to the island's sovereignty in 1965, the British introduced and dominated the sport and recreation landscape, with club membership and privileged participation in sports such as golf, polo and shooting prominent (Soon 2002). Horse racing, hunting, cricket and football were some of the other more common sports played by the British. However, participation was not extended to the local population, who continued to take part in indigenous and traditional games for leisure (Lim 2004). The British repeatedly refused to grant broader access to participation in sport and recreational activities to the growing Chinese population, while the locals continued to challenge colonial authority and maintain links with mainland China (Aplin and Quek 2002; Lim 2004). As a result, sport participation by local groups became secondary and was limited to observation, 'either with indifference or with fascination, from a distance' (Aplin and Quek 2002: 69). Lim (2004a) attributed this to several factors. First, sport did not feature highly in the culture of the residents. While the British brought with them 'a strong work ethic, games for recreation, a dedication to exercise and a respect for sporting . . . and team skills' (Aplin and Quek 2002: 69), the locals were devoted to securing their livelihoods via commercial means. Second, having already experienced limited access to sport it was not surprising that the local population concentrated their energies and productivity on the economic opportunities that were present in the entrepôt. Finally, the apparent divisions present between the elite and the majority Chinese group, notably, the former's administration of the colony and the latter's domination of the economy, was manifest in broader divisions throughout the country. According to McNeill *et al.* (2003: 37), 'from the early years of independence, economy-based values and extrinsic goals were given precedence over the promotion of all other cultural practices and the achievement of continuing success planted a materialistic orientation as part of the Singaporean identity'. As will be shown, this inclination toward materialism would have deep-seated consequences for the fledgling sport culture in Singapore.

By the early 1900s, the population of Singapore had a critical mass that existed for sport participation to expand sufficiently as more people were beginning to participate and enjoy sport for its leisure and productivity gains (Alpin and Quek 2002). The context of segregation and exclusivity indirectly prompted the formation of community-based sport clubs and sports associations by the various ethnic migrant groups in Singapore to cater to their own local interests (Lim 2004; Soon 2002). While it may appear that these developments in sport among the British and locals occurred independently of each other, Horton (2001) argued that both the British and dominant local groups exerted collective influences and dynamics to mould Singapore's evolving sport panorama. For example, aspects of British cultural imposition like administration and efficiency inspired the formation of the Singapore Olympic Sports Council (SOSC) in 1947 and at least nine sports associations to oversee training and selection of *local born* athletes for competitions and facilitate organized sport promotion for Singaporeans (Aplin 2009). This engagement with organized sport represented an increasing shift to a more centralized sport structure and 'facilitated the production and perpetuation of nationalism' (Lim 2004: 176). Therefore, as sport and recreation featured prominently in the social differentiation practices of the colonial settlers, it also became a means to improve social cohesion in post-colonial Singapore (McNeill *et al.* 2003). Notwithstanding the challenges posed in those prevailing social, commercial and political conditions, the colonial era precipitated the beginning of what Lim (2004a) termed the 'sportization' of Singapore.

Contemporary structure and culture of sport

The early years of independence were dominated by the government's concern to establish stability and security amid a period of racial unrest, sectional communalism and uncertainties posed by decolonializaton (Chen 1983; Lim 2004; Turnbull 1982). Sport featured in the PAP's effort to manage this turbulent phase with the establishment of the Sports Division within the Ministry of Social Affairs (SSC 2005). The Division's main task was to organize mass, community-based sport and recreational activities such as the *Pesta Sukan*, or Festival of Sports (SSC 1983), although the then Minister also encouraged the SOSC to 'turn out champions of the future' (cited in Horton 2002: 253). The Ministry advocated a Sport For All policy, characterized by a pyramid model of participation for everyone (SCC 1983), underlining the government's stand toward sport at that time – an emphasis on community-level activities to build a 'Singaporean identity', among a heterogeneous and pluralistic population (Chiew 1983; Perry *et al.* 1997). According to Lim (2004), these moves to establish control and regulate sport by the PAP were aimed at 'systematically and swiftly' dominating resources so as to impose their authority: initial indications of the extent of potential government intervention in organized sport in Singapore.

Between the 1970s and 1980s, with economic progress underway, the government's emphasis turned to providing facilities and activities for mass sport participation and encouraging a healthy and productive society (McNeill *et al.* 2003; SSC 1994). The establishment of the Singapore Sports Council (SSC) by an Act of Parliament in 1973 signalled the government's determination to regulate and provide direction to the promotion of sport amid a low and slow response

Table 12.1 Selected key events and initiatives in the development of sport in Singapore: Independence to 1990s

Date	Key events/sport development initiatives	Impact on sport development
Aug 1965	Singapore gains independence as a Republic led by Prime Minister Lee Kuan Yew and PAP Administration	The government tapped the potential of sport as a means of social cohesion and nation-building
Oct 1965	Sports Division set up within Ministry of Social Affairs	Organized annual sports festivals (*Pesta Sukan* or Festival of Sport), managed existing sports facilities and promoted sport participation
1970	Singapore National Olympic Council (SNOC) established	Formed to encourage and foster the development of sport for the Olympic and other international sport competitions
Feb 1971	National Sports Promotion Board (NSPB) and National Stadium Corporation (NSC) set up	Objectives to develop and promote sports for competitive and recreational purposes, co-ordinate activities of voluntary sports bodies, organize international competitions and maintain sports facilities. NSC responsible for the plans and construction of the national sports stadium (open in July 1973)
1972	Introduction of various sports Training Schemes and Learn-to-Play courses	Aided by corporate sponsors, training schemes aimed to broaden the base of athletes for NSAs, while instructional courses provided opportunities for skill acquisition
Sept 1973	7th South East Asian Peninsula Games, Singapore	First time Singapore hosts the regional games, held in the newly built National Stadium. Singapore athletes win 140 (45 gold) medals
Oct 1973	Singapore Sports Council (SSC) formed through the merger of NSPB and NSC	SSC responsible to organize and administer sport as part of the government's commitment to the main priority of sport for all with limited attention to competitive sport (the pyramid model)
1976	Formation of Constituency Sports Clubs (CSCs)	CSCs to help SSC promote sports and to motivate residents to participate at the community level as part of the Sport For All policy
1983	12th South East Asian Games, Singapore	Singapore athletes win 134 (38 gold) medals
1989	Advisory Council on Sports and Recreation releases its report	Calls for concerted national effort to promote sport for all and enhance sports excellence among others

1990	PM Goh Chok Tong sworn in as Prime Minister	Would play a catalytic role by placing sport higher on the political agenda during his term in office. Promises Singaporeans 'a more caring and consultative style of government'
1992	Launch of National Healthy Lifestyle Campaign	Part of the national effort to raise the health and exercise benefits of sport and healthy living
Dec 1993	Launch of Sport Excellence (SPEX) 2000: Winning for Singapore – a proactive and focused approach to promote sports excellence	SSC announces an extensive list of incentives and schemes to lay the infrastructure for development of sport excellence; 7 core sports and 7 merit sports identified. $10 million annual budget for the next 5 years ($4 million from government, $4 million from Singapore Pools [lottery], $2 million from corporate sponsors)

Source: Singapore Sports Council (SSC) (1983, 1994); SSC (2005a)

from the population and the various voluntary sports bodies (SSC 1983). With the formation of the SSC, independent sport associations established and run by volunteers were brought under the government's centralized control, with the effect that the sports clubs lost some autonomy and control. As another indication of growing interference by the government in sport, Lim (2004) reported that as early as 1970 some national sport associations (NSA) began to be headed by government ministers.

Organized sport programs included corporate-sponsored sport training schemes to support talented individuals while 'learn-to-play' courses provided the public with opportunities to pick up life-long sport skills (SSC 2005). At the community level, Constituency Sports Clubs (CSC) were formed throughout the island as support for the SSC's aim to bring organized sport closer to the grassroots, further realizing the pyramid concept (SSC 2005). The CSCs, administered by management committees comprising volunteers, worked closely with various grassroots organizations to promote sports for residents in general, and lower socio-economic groups in particular, within the vicinity of their precincts (Soon 2002). At this time, the accent of the PAP administration remained undoubtedly on promoting mass sport and the government's statement typified the significance of the then-prevailing socio-political climate:

> There are no national benefits from gold medallists for smaller countries ... For the superpowers with large populations superiority in sports is national propaganda to persuade other people of the superiority of their competing political systems. But it is foolish and wasteful for smaller countries to do it. Singapore's best return is to generate healthy, vigorous exercise for the population ... who will lead better and more satisfying lives if they are fit and healthy.
>
> (Prime Minister Lee Kuan Yew, quoted in Horton 2002: 251)

The persistence of low sport participation levels was exacerbated by the discovery by the SSC and NSAs that the difference in competitive standards between local athletes and those from competing countries was widening (Teo 2002). More alarming was the Singaporean's growing desire for affluence and penchant for social status in the wake of sustained growth in the 1970s and early 1980s (Lim 1983; Perry *et al.* 1997). The growth of affluence is very much tied to the inclination for materialism, a characteristic that is linked with traditional Chinese cultural expectations of wealth and prosperity in Singapore. In spite of the government's early efforts at promoting the benefits of sport and healthy lifestyles, it still remained of relatively low importance for locals, especially parents, who were more intent on grooming their children for more conventional careers (Horton 2001; Turnbull 1982). As noted by Tay (2001: 3),

> Singapore's parents need to be convinced that under the prevailing social climate they would not regret imbuing their children with the sporting ethos of fair play and equality under the laws of the game, rather than simply preparing their charges to survive and prosper in the law-of-the-jungle conditions which currently prevail.

Confronted with these barriers to participation, an Advisory Council on Sports and Recreation was commissioned, and in 1989 it published its report to the SSC 'calling for a concerted national effort to promote constituency sports, enhance sports excellence, improve employment prospects of sportspersons and promote sports that challenge' (SSC 1994: 127). The 1990s were a significant period for the sport community in Singapore, marked by the transfer of political power to second-generation PAP leaders, 'the nature of the discourse of sport used by leading politicians' (Horton 2002: 258) and particularly for a perceptible shift in organized sport policy, with a new emphasis on elite sport development.

Buoyed by 20 years of economic growth and social stability, the country experienced unprecedented levels of affluence and quality of life that stirred expectations of Western ideals and political liberalization from among a growing middle class (Chen 1983; Perry *et al*. 1997). To address high obesity and sedentary levels among school-going children and adults, the Ministries of Health, Defence and Education collaborated to launch, in 1992, the Trim and Fit (TAF) weight-reduction program for students, and the National Healthy Lifestyle Campaign for adults (SSC 1994). These initiatives were implemented in typical paternalistic fashion throughout the community and emphasized the government's concern with the low participation levels in physical activity among an emergent wealthy population. As described by Horton (2002: 257),

> When the Singapore government endorses policies that seek to change behaviour or that promote an aspect of social activity, there are no half measures; the people are left in no doubt as to the government's intentions.

To a large extent, the PAP successfully addressed the social and economic progress with a well-managed transfer of political leadership that professed a 'more caring and consultative' style of governing (Perry *et al*. 1997: 84). In his manifesto, *Singapore: The Next Lap*, the new Prime Minister outlined his vision 'to make Singapore one of the major hub cities of the world' (Government of Singapore 1991: 6) and, more significantly, reiterated the government's categorical support for sport for all and sports excellence. The new government advocated a two-pronged approach to sport policy: one centred on the well-being and collective benefits of exercise through mass sport participation; and the other based on the perception that local sporting champions would contribute to a range of national objectives. However, the Sport For All policy remained a central focus and the National Healthy Lifestyle Campaign became the tool that the government utilized to drive mindset changes about the benefits of sport and health among Singaporeans.

A defining moment for Singapore sport was the publication of *Sports Excellence 2000 (SPEX 2000): Winning for Singapore* in December 1993, accompanied by a fourfold increase in annual funding of S$10 million from the government, the national lottery agency and sponsors over the next five years (MCD 1993). Although SPEX 2000 primarily spelt out an ambitious inventory of schemes to advance elite sport, it also represented a shift in the manner in which sport was to be delivered in the country. For example, there were now concerted strategies to change or review the administrative and operational infrastructure within the SSC and NSAs and to actively tap the resources of organizations within the private and non-profit sectors,

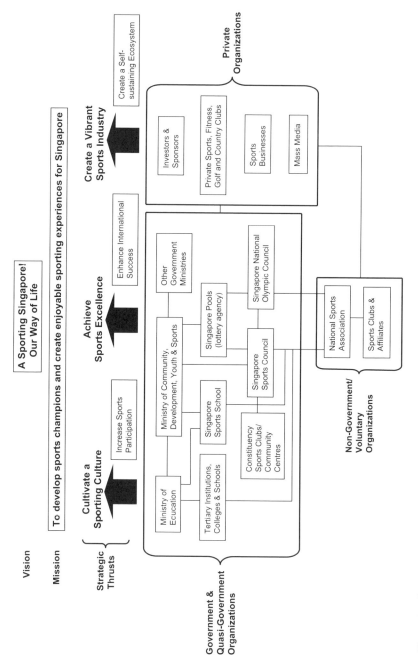

Vision A Sporting Singapore! Our Way of Life

Mission To develop sports champions and create enjoyable sporting experiences for Singapore

Strategic Thrusts

Cultivate a Sporting Culture — Increase Sports Participation

Achieve Sports Excellence — Enhance International Success

Create a Vibrant Sports Industry — Create a Self-sustaining Ecosystem

Government & Quasi-Government Organizations

- Ministry of Education
- Ministry of Community, Development, Youth & Sports
- Other Government Ministries
- Tertiary Institutions, Colleges & Schools
- Singapore Sports School
- Singapore Pools (lottery agency)
- Constituency Sports Clubs/Community Centres
- Singapore Sports Council
- Singapore National Olympic Council

Non-Government/Voluntary Organizations

- National Sports Association
- Sports Clubs & Affiliates

Private Organizations

- Investors & Sponsors
- Private Sports, Fitness, Golf and Country Clubs
- Sports Businesses
- Mass Media

Figure 12.1 Schematic representation of the Sports Community and the Sporting Vision of Singapore

to rejuvenate the sport community. The move was also seen as the government's gesture to 'loosen the shackles' (Horton 2002: 258) of control over sport. The success of the sport development effort now hinged on active engagement of major stakeholders – government, constituencies, educators, employers, media, parents, volunteers, athletes and residents – to contribute to the evolution of modern sport in Singapore. In the age of globalization and international recognition, sport served its malleable function to foster nation building, this time through the exploits of the sports excellence program in Singapore. Put succinctly by Horton (2002: 259), 'achieving sporting success was no longer politically superfluous or to be left to chance. The new policies reflected very direct and orchestrated political attempts to change the whole perception of sport in Singapore'.

Extent of government intervention in sport

The introduction of SPEX 2000 marked an increase in government intervention and was a wake-up call for professionalism and a rejuvenation of the operations and management of NSAs in Singapore, including the need for accountability and responsibility for mass and elite objectives. Realizing that it could not interfere directly in the affairs of these constituted sport governing bodies and yet acknowledging that the NSAs played pivotal roles in the local sport community, the government strategized, through the SPEX 2000 initiative, to institute controls and 'policy dictates' (Green 2004: 377) to stipulate the threshold standards of corporate governance with which the NSAs had to comply as a condition for SSC funding (Wee 2002).

The government's prevailing sport aspirations with regard to NSAs were 'to build on the objectives created with SPEX 2000 but make the NSAs responsible for not only developing elite talent but [also] for administering, marketing and developing the popularity of their sport to the wider community as a measure to achieve the Republic's sporting ambitions' (McNeill *et al.* 2003: 54). With SPEX 2000, a more active and systematic infrastructure was now in place to identify and nurture talented athletes rather than have them simply surface through the pyramid system. Sport continued to have a highly functional social and political purpose in Singapore, and the focus on the unhealthy and unfit remained top of the government's agenda. A significant milestone for Singapore was the decision by the government to elevate sport on the Cabinet agenda and subsequently rename the responsible ministry as the Ministry of Community Development and Sports (MCDS) in April 2000 (SSC 2000; Thomas 2000b). It was a notable landmark for sport development and one that catapulted sport to unprecedented levels. SPEX 2000 was re-launched as SPEX 21 to reflect the challenges faced by the MCDS and the SSC in the new millennium (SSC 2001; Thomas 2000a). According to Lim (2004: 255), the establishment of the MCDS 'represented an intensification of the monopoly of control of the sporting development in Singapore'. With this focused approach to sport development, however, it also characterized the more omnipresent role the government played in the control and nature of sport in nation building and community development.

The drive for modern sport development took another momentous step with the establishment of the Committee on Sporting Singapore (CoSS), which was required

Table 12.2 Selected key events and initiatives in the development of sport in Singapore: 1990s to 2008

Date	Key events/sport development initiatives	Impact on sport development
1994	SSC undergoes corporate restructuring	New corporate identity to reflect new challenges in sport development
Sept 1996	Sports For Life program launched to promote greater participation in sports and physical activities	Continued emphasis on mass sport participation activities among Singaporeans, particularly senior citizens, housewives and working adults
1999	Strategic Management Review releases its report	New mission statement: 'Towards a Sporting Nation'. SSC to promote sports excellence at regional and international sports competitions in tandem with the Sport For All policy
Nov 1999	SSC sets up Women & Sport Working Group (WSWG) to bolster participation among women	WSWG sets up 6 sub-committees, with one specifically for high-performance sport for women
Jan 2000	Launch of SPEX 21 – comprehensive range of athlete, coach, official, sports administrator and sports management programs to help achieve Singapore's aim of becoming one of Asia's leading sporting nations	Government commitment to develop international sporting excellence through a focused and holistic approach and supporting deserving NSAs. Review of core and merit sports, with 3 core sports – football, sailing and badminton – receiving additional attention for setting special targets
Apr 2000	Sport portfolio added to Ministry of Community Development and Sport (MCDS)	Major milestone in nation-building; manifestation of Singapore's status as a developed nation and ambitions for sporting success at international competitions
Sept 2000	Setting up of Committee on Sporting Singapore (CoSS)	CoSS's objectives were to establish the vision and desired outcomes for sport and identify issues impeding sport development
Jul 2001	Publication of CoSS report; Government commits $500 million to the Sporting Singapore Fund to implement the recommendations and build the sports school	40 recommendations proposed; 13 relate to sports excellence while 8 concern management of NSAs. $375 million from government and $125 million from Singapore Pools (lottery) for sport development between 2001 and 2005
2002	SSC launches the (i) NSA Management Development Department – to assist NSAs in planning and executing their vision, mission and goals; and (ii) the NSA Relationship Management Department – to generate more opportunities for sports participation, build management capabilities and further the vision of Sporting Singapore	Management Development identifies and puts in place a basic organizational structure and model for successful NSAs through its 'Professional Sports Manager' program and as well as posting of its staff to NSAs The aim of Relationship Management is to enhance the network and capabilities of sports partners and service providers. Also sees to the review of Partnership Agreement (PA) to facilitate accountability between NSAs and SSC; funding based on agreed performance measured by NSAs

| Feb 2003 | Code of Governance (COG) launched – set of principles of good governance for NSAs to adhere to | All core and merit NSAs to comply with the principles of the COG by Mar 2004 (extended to June 2004 at the request of some NSAs) in order to qualify for elite level funding |
| Jan 2004 | Singapore Sports School opened; a co-ed boarding school with top-class facilities and sports science support in 8 sports | Costing approx $200 million, it is the government's initiative to usher in the era of sporting excellence. Essentially, a hot-house for student athletes with potential to attain elite level status |

by the MCDS to formulate a strategic blueprint for the future of Singapore's sport policy (SSC 2002; Thomas 2000c). Chaired by the Sports Minister himself, the committee's proceedings reflected the familiar PAP priorities established in all aspects of Singapore's development thus far (Horton 2002). Following a ten-month consultation process, the CoSS submitted its report, expounding six targets and forty recommendations that would chart the direction, establish the infrastructure and create a conducive environment for sport development to thrive in Singapore (Chan 2000a; MCDS 2003). The government accepted in full the CoSS report, the crux of which centred on the vision of a Sporting Singapore, to be built upon three strategic thrusts: high performance, high participation and a vibrant sports industry (Franklin 2001; SSC 2002).

One of the main findings to emerge from the CoSS report was the idea that strong and effective sport governing bodies played a considerable role in the sports delivery system in Singapore (Chan 2000b; MCDS 2001b). It acknowledged that NSAs were the cornerstones for raising greater awareness and support for active membership and for the promotion of excellence in their respective sports. On the other hand, it also meant that the relationship between government and the NSAs is expected to become more intense and more significant in shaping the development of sport in Singapore. The CoSS also believed that by strengthening and 'professionalizing' the NSAs through management development and account-ability, the various sports bodies would be able to better serve their elite and mass participation objectives and thereby help to realize the nation's sporting vision (MCDS 2001a; Ng 2000). The Sports Minister emphasized this when he stated: 'I urge the NSAs to set clear directions and goals for themselves. I would encourage all the NSAs, especially the leadership, to see this as a challenge to lead your sport and its development to the highest possible level in Singapore' (Ibrahim 2002).

Improvements in NSA administration and athlete management remain high on the SSC's priority list. The 'half-time' assessment of the CoSS blueprint by the CEO of the SSC revealed that there has been 'good progress in the forty CoSS recommendations' (quoted in Tan 2006d: 55). For example, in moves aimed at commercializing the NSAs and maximizing their limited resources, the SSC introduced an 'outcome-based and multi-year' funding model in August 2005 (Leong 2006a). Based on three strategic thrusts, the new model aimed to 'prioritise and channel resources into critical areas that will create optimum impact and contribute directly to the CoSS objectives' (Oon 2005). Essentially, instead of relying on past performances to establish core and merit levels of funding for the NSAs, the new model requires NSAs to critically establish 'strong governance and sound management policies' (Leong 2006a: 54) to attract funds into their sport. According to the SSC, the new system will permit NSAs greater flexibility and empowerment to manage their budget in addition to strategizing long-term programs for sustained benefits. The SSC will also evaluate NSAs' organizational standards when deciding funding allocations. In general, annual funding for the fifty-eight NSAs will increase by 10 per cent – from S$28.3 million in 2005 to S$31.1 million in 2006 (Leong 2006a), although the SSC's CEO reiterated that 'if there are excellent programmes and good associations, we [the SSC] will be flexible and reprioritize if we have to, to ensure that new opportunities will be funded' (quoted in Leong 2006a: 54–55).

Government intervention is most intensive when governance issues are at stake. Managed and presided over by part-timers, the NSAs' volunteer leadership usually lacked the 'passion, vision and capabilities to be the driving force behind their sport' at the professional level (Tan 2000). An example of the extent of government intervention can be seen in the sport of track and field. Subsequent to a review of the SPEX Programme in 2000, the sport was removed from the SSC list of privileged sports because the Singapore Amateur Athletic Association (SAAA) had not achieved its targets. The SSC leadership argued that 'the SAAA should revamp its management practices and put in place an effective leadership. The SSC hopes that the association and its members will strive to make improvements to revive the sport' (quoted in Thomas 2000d: 75). One of the SSC's main concerns was the failure of the SAAA to modernize and reciprocate by adopting effective organizational and administrative strategies befitting a major sport. The tension between the SAAA and the SSC was expressed by the SSC's Executive Director when he stated:

> We found that they [SAAA officials] were not prepared to listen, not interested in doing any soul-searching. We have nothing in common with them. The SSC is also hoping that the dropping of track and field from the SPEX programme would lead to an injection of new blood into the SAAA's management.
>
> (quoted in Tay 2000: 76)

Of note were the in-house power struggles that ensued in the SAAA's leadership, centred on the reluctance of the incumbent to step aside despite a twenty-three-year reign as President. Two tightly contested elections for the top position in 2000 and 2002 provided the SSC with the excuse to intervene and, following the 2002 annual meeting, the SSC's Deputy Director (Sports Excellence) was seconded to the SAAA to establish a full-time secretariat and assume responsibility for implementing the development plans (Chan 2002). When the incumbent finally agreed to resign in 2004, and after the SAAA had submitted its Strategic and High Performance Plans as required by the Code of Governance, track and field was duly reinstated to the elite sport status (Chan 2002; SAA 2006).

In April 2009, the Senior Parliamentary Secretary of the MCYS reiterated the nature and extent of the government's intervention policy with NSAs when he warned them over poor governance or lack of planning in their respective sport's development:

> If the NSA administration has an issue, it can be dormant, but the training and development must still carry on. So we want to make sure the athletes as well as the coaches continue their training. So if we need to take over, we will take over.
>
> (Channel News Asia 2009)

Building and strengthening the capabilities of the NSAs are the foremost challenges facing the SSC as it endeavours to inculcate best management practices, sport development and athlete management in organizations reliant on unpaid, elected officials (Robert 1998; SSC 2004).

Table 12.3 Selected key events and initiatives in the development of sport in Singapore: 1990s to 2008 (continued)

Date	Key events / sport development initiatives	Impact on sport development
Aug 2004	PM Lee Hsien Loong sworn in as Singapore's 3rd Prime Minister	The new PM continues the rallying call for sporting success and international achievement
Mar 2005	Government announces continued funding for the Sporting Singapore Fund and plans for a new sports hub	Greater focus on sports 'software' – youth and talent identification, training and education clinics. $300 million committed for sport development between 2006 and 2010. New sports hub to comprise world-class multi-purpose arena, stadium and aquatic centre; estimated to cost $650 million and ready by 2011
Mar 2006	SSC releases data from the 2005 National Sports Participation Survey	The incidence of regular sports participants rose since the last survey conducted in 2001. The 2005 survey revealed that 48 per cent of Singaporeans participate in some form of sports or exercise at least once a week with more than half (25 per cent) doing so at least three times per week. Singaporeans are also engaging in a wider variety of sports such as gym workout, in-line skating and beach volleyball
Nov 2006	SSC and SNOC announce Project 0812 'Glory to the Nation' whereby $7 million is set aside for elite athletes	Sailor Colin Cheng, shooter Vanessa Yong, shuttler Ronald Susilo and paddler Sun Beibei are among the 22 athletes identified for special support under Project 0812 which aims to help Singapore achieve success at the Beijing 2008 and London 2012 Olympiads
Dec 2006	15th Asian Games, Doha	Singapore athletes win 27 (8 gold) medals
Aug 2007	Singapore announced its bid to host the 1st Summer Youth Olympic Games in 2010	Together with 9 other cities, Singapore submitted its bid to host the inaugural youth games targeted at youths aged 14 to 18 years
Feb 2008	Sporting Culture Committee releases 23 recommendations to build and develop a sporting culture in Singapore	Headed by PS Teo Ser Luck, the Committee identified 4 strategic thrusts – (i) inspiring the nation, (ii) generating sporting opportunities for all, (iii) building a flourishing sports ecosystem, and (iv) developing champions – to galvanize the sports scene in Singapore
Mar 2008	SSC and MOE open selected school fields for public use	A total of 43 primary school fields are opened for public use free of charge and on a first-come, first-served basis, to encourage participation and maximize facility usage
Aug 2008	2008 Olympic Games, Beijing	Singapore athletes win the first Olympic (1 silver) medal when paddlers Li Jiawei, Wang Yuegu and Feng Tianwei brought an end to Singapore's 48-year Olympic medal drought in the Table Tennis Women's Team event

| Nov 2008 | SSC and MOE jointly announce their hosting of the inaugural Asian Youth Games (AYG) in Singapore in Jun 2009 | The AYG Singapore 2009 is part of Singapore's bid plan to the IOC for the Youth Olympic Games (YOG) in 2010 |
| Dec 2008 | Singapore selected as hosts for the 1st FINA World Swimming Coaches Conference | First ever conference for swim coaches, and is another boost for Singapore's fledgling sports industry |

Source: Foo (2005); Horton (2002); MCDS (2001); Ng (2000); SNOC (2005); SSC (2005a), SSC (2006), SSC (2007), SSC (2008a)

Signalling its unequivocal endorsement of sport development in Singapore, the government and the Singapore Pools (the national lottery agency) jointly committed S$500 million over a five-year period to implement the proposals (MCDS 2001a). In addition, Prime Minister Goh identified three specific goals connected to the pillars of sports: (i) to achieve a 50 per cent nation-wide sports participation rate by 2005; (ii) for Singapore to be among the top 10 sporting nations in Asia by 2010; and (iii) to double the value of the sports industry from S$680 million to S$1.4 billion by 2010 (Chan 2001; SSC 2002).

Despite the emphasis on three sporting areas, the Sport For All model remained the cornerstone of Singapore's sport policy (MCDS 2001a; MCDS 2001b). With more leisure alternatives that people could indulge in, and in recognition of the potential social and economic impact of an ageing population, the government set aside S$315 million to increase sports participation for the period 2000 to 2005 (SSC 2002). This represented a significant investment by the government, signalling its intent to counter the negative observation made by the SSC Executive Director that 'many Singaporeans have very unhealthy and sedentary lifestyles . . . playing computer games, going to the movies or buffets' (Kwan, quoted in Lim 2004: 254).

Organized sport in Singapore: other key influences

One of the strategic aims of the SSC was to provide and manage the provision of sports facilities and services to Singaporeans, and to keep such amenities accessible and affordable. The 1975 Master Plan on Sports Facilities aimed 'to provide all Singaporeans with a stadium, sports hall and swimming complex within 3 km of their homes' (Soon 2002: 199). The intention was to facilitate sports participation, as major transport and supporting service infrastructure were already functioning at residential estates, and to reduce the inconvenience of travel for residents. To its credit, the SSC continually reviewed and revised the master plan, taking into consideration changes in lifestyle habits and residential patterns. For example, Phase 3 of the plan – covering the years 1993 to 2000 – focused on providing 'integrated new generation leisure-cum-recreation complexes which aimed to promote sports participation through family togetherness with a diversified range of amenities' (Soon 2002: 199). By the late 1990s, the SSC had reportedly spent about S$514 million in building or renovating sport facilities, now designated as Regional Sports & Fitness Centres (RSFC), to support the national initiatives of improving sport participation and fostering social cohesion (Lim 2004; SSC 1998a). The modern RSFCs included facilities such as multi-purpose indoor halls, track and field stadia, swimming pools, tennis or squash courts, fitness gyms, outdoor fitness stations and dance studios, and by 2002 there were fifteen purpose-built RSFCs available all over the island (MCDS 2003). In his address to mark the 25th anniversary of the Singapore Sports Council, the Chairman reiterated the government's stand of employing sport to foster social cohesion:

> The change in architecture of our facilities reflects a paradigm shift in terms of the way we as a nation look at sports and play. Clearly, there is an increasing emphasis on things like fun, family togetherness and social interaction. Add

to these our constant efforts to make sports convenient and affordable for our people and one understands the direction we're moving in terms of facilities.
(Ng, quoted in SSC 1998a: 104)

The development of sport policy in Singapore is inherently tied to its economic survival and, invariably, key factors such as the fitness and productivity levels of employees, the improvement of health levels among the population and concerns over national identity take precedence. When the Sport For All drive was launched in 1973, the Prime Minister urged more citizens to participate in sport and 'to make it a habit of daily exercise to keep fit, as this was deemed necessary in an urbanized and mechanized society for a productive workforce' (McNeill *et al.* 2003: 42). Two other significant aspects that are fundamental to the government's mass sport policy are the nation's defence objectives and the physical education of children and youth. As in most PAP-led campaigns, organized sport strategies had the full support of government agencies and stakeholders to ensure that the policy took off. Led by the SSC, the Ministries of Education and Defence would also work with the NSAs to organize events to cater to the varied needs and interests of the population. The importance of a high and sustained level of fitness and 'ruggedness' in the Singapore Armed Forces is obvious and sport played a key role in this preoccupation (Horton 2002). In addition to placing emphasis on individual physical fitness within the ranks, the Armed Forces also added to the nation's sporting calendar by organizing both competitive and sport endurance events such as swim-run biathlons, half marathons and cycling. These socially responsible acts complement the other sport events offered by the SSC, the CSCs and NSAs to provide more opportunities for Singaporeans to be involved in sport. For example, the SSC and the Singapore Amateur Athletics Association jointly organized a mass 'Big Walk' event in 1998 where 69,030 participants were registered (SSC 1999). Other organized sport initiatives included 'inter and intra-constituency tournaments, National Walk/Jog, Swim and Cycling events, water sports, learn-to-play courses and sports that challenge' (SSC 1994: 46).

Another feature that emphasized the government's focus on sport participation and fitness levels was the introduction of fitness tests and schemes such as the National Aerobic Fitness Award in 1976, and the National Physical Fitness Award (NAPFA) in 1982 (SSC 1983). These tests were designed to provide straightforward yet consistent methods for people to assess the basic components of fitness such as aerobic condition, muscular strength and coordination. Introduced by the SSC, the tests were subsequently adopted by the Armed Forces, schools and NSAs for their respective objectives. Owing to its popularity and frequency of implementation throughout the year, the tests quickly became hallmarks of the fledgling Sport For All campaign. In a bid to encourage participation, incentives such as towels and water bottles were distributed, emphasizing the challenges faced by organizers to maintain attendance figures, attract newcomers and make such activities relevant to the participants. Employee Fitness Programmes were also introduced to tackle workplace health and productivity concerns. Spearheaded by the Health Promotion Board and the SSC, the scheme provided subsidies and assistance to companies to encourage their employees to attend fitness-related seminars, in-house sports events and inter-company games among others (Soon 2002).

Schools also introduced fitness tests for students in physical education classes once policy makers noted increasing obesity levels and sedentary lifestyles among pupils (Balasekaran and Loh 2009). The NAPFA test and the body mass index became integral components for the Trim and Fit (TAF) weight-loss program in secondary schools as the results were used to sort and position participants for the TAF Club. Physical education teachers were re-trained to conduct TAF classes and soon physical education sessions became 'dominated by fitness and weight-reduction activities to the detriment of the physical education and sports activities' (Horton 2002: 262). Fitness and exercise was adopted as the most efficient approach to weight reduction with schools building outdoor fitness stations and installing gym machines, further demoting the value of sport participation (Lim 2004). As a consequence, accountability for fitness and TAF Club objectives took precedence over responsibility for the teaching of games and sport participation in physical education classes. Tied in to this complex issue was the increasing numbers of overweight and unfit students enlisting into National Service reported by the Ministry of Defence. As a result, sporting activities took a further step back in schools as 'the emphasis on physical education is given to the improvement of physical fitness of youths to meet the requirements of National Service' (McNeill *et al.* 2003: 48).

To its credit, the Education Ministry has consistently focused on organized sport in the curriculum for the many intangible benefits that sport brings to their pupils, while schools have repeatedly been 'the spawning ground' (McNeill *et al.* 2003: 47) where NSAs can identify future talent. For example, in 1999, the Singapore Sports Schools Council organized a total of 15 sports competitions for primary school pupils and 22 tournaments for secondary schools, and over 26,920 secondary and junior college students (representing about 15 per cent of the cohort) participated in district, zone and national level sport competitions (Ong 2000). Moreover, all schools encouraged and made available opportunities for pupils to engage in structured, sport-related extra-curricular activities such as sports education, outdoor adventure, dance, water sports, and intra/inter-school sport competitions. At the opening of the Chua Chu Kang Regional Sports and Fitness Centre in July 2001, the Prime Minister reiterated the importance of sport in the all-round development of youths, stating that 'lessons from sports cannot always be taught in a classroom – winning and losing gracefully, the killer instinct, compassion, teamwork, fair play, sportsmanship. These are lessons that build character' (Goh, quoted in Lim 2004: 264). However, despite being a compulsory component of the school curriculum, the design of physical education and sport classes in schools 'are structured with very little room for individual differences' (McNeill *et al.* 2003: 49), as the preferred approach centred on student conformity and uniformity to facilitate teaching and resource constraints. Till this day, many schools and tertiary institutions in Singapore still emphasize fitness training and testing as the predominant feature of physical education or sport program offerings, acceding to the wider political obligation to prepare male students for military enlistment.

Sport participation rates

Sport participation, as defined by the National Sports Participation Survey (NSPS), includes 'sports and all forms of recreational physical activities, e.g. "weights/

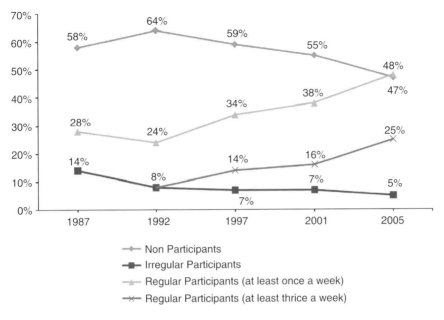

Figure 12.2 Sport participation in Singapore, 1987–2005

Source: National Sports Participation Survey, 2005

gym-workout and various forms of aerobics exercise"' (NSPS 2005: 1). The first survey, commissioned by the SSC in 1987, and conducted every five years thereafter, revealed that 28 per cent of the adult population (defined as those 15 years and above) participated regularly in sports at least once a week. Between 1987 and 1992, the NSPA initially defined regular sport participation rates as those who had participated in sports at least once a week. The provision to include those who participated regularly in sports at least three times a week was added from the 1997 survey onwards (NSPS 2005), perhaps in view of reported increases in attendance at national mass sport events such as walking and running from about 50,000 in 1994 to almost 250,000 in 1998 (SSC 1998b).

When the 1992 survey revealed a drop in the number who participated regularly in sports at least once a week to 24 per cent (National Sports Participation Survey 1992; Soon 2002), the government introduced the Sport For Life (SFL) program. Launched by the Prime Minister in 1996, it aimed to 'instil in Singaporeans life-long habits of adopting a positive attitude to sports and enjoying a better quality of life through sports participation' (Soon 2002: 203; SSC 1996). Backed by a S$360 million financial plan, the SFL program was the government's latest plan under the sport for all strategy to tackle the high sedentary levels by bringing sport and amenities closer to people, and making it convenient for Singaporeans to enjoy the benefits and fun of organized sport (SSC 1999; Tan 1996). The objectives of the SFL were twofold: (1) to raise the percentage of those who participate in sport at least once a week from 24 per cent in 1992 to 40 per cent by the year 2000 and to 50 per cent by 2005, and (2) to raise the percentage of Singaporeans who exercise three times a week from 8 per cent in 1992 to 15 per cent by the year 2000 and to

20 per cent by 2005 (NSPS 1992; NSPS 1997). The SPEX 2000 and SFL schemes reflected the PAP's twin approach to sport policy development, and this was duly endorsed by the SSC's new mission statement, *Towards A Sporting Nation* (SSC 2000: 1), in 2000. The appeal for a well-rounded Singaporean, imbued with a sporting disposition, was underscored by the Prime Minister at the launch of the SFL:

> One who is cultivated, sporty, caring and gracious. Such a Singaporean reads widely, enjoys music and the arts, sings or plays at least one musical instrument, is active in sports, and cares for his fellow citizens. Most of us are not such a complete person . . . But everyone can be competent in at least one sport.
>
> (Goh, quoted in Lim 2004: 254)

In its 1997/98 Annual Report, the SSC attributed the increase in participation in constituency sports and fitness activities from 390,000 in 1996 to 802,000 in 1997 to greater awareness and the diverse program offerings arising from the SFL campaign (SSC 1997). Increases in regular (once a week) sport participation rates were observed – from 24 per cent in 1992, to 34 per cent in 1997, and then to 38 per cent in 2001 (NSPS 2005; SSC 2000). However, the annual report also revealed that the three most popular sports attended by Singaporeans were those that were again fitness-related and performed individually – walking, jogging and swimming (SSC 1997), somewhat predictable as this could be a carry-over from the fitness-oriented mentality internalized from their time in the school system. The survey conducted in 1997 revealed that there were lower participation rates among females (28 per cent who exercised at least once a week). The common reasons cited by women for participating included study commitments, work, family obligations and the lack of interest in sport (MCDS 2001a; SSC 2000). To tackle this segment, the SSC formed the Women and Sports Working Group in 1999 to increase the participation of women and girls in sport and exercise in schools and the workplace (MCDS 2001a; SSC 2000). A variety of organized sport events such as rock climbing, street soccer, martial arts, National Sports Carnival for Women, the International Folk and Recreation Dance Night, and walk/jog programs were also added for other target groups, such as youths and the elderly, to participate in (SSC 1998b).

Regular participation in sport (at least once a week) rose from 38 per cent in 2001 to 47 per cent in 2005 while 25 per cent participated in some form of sport at least three times a week in 2005, as compared to 16 per cent in 2001. The 2005 survey also revealed that the 'young adult' segment (24 to 34 years old) experienced the most significant increase in regular sport participation, and that more people were participating in the assorted range of sporting activities that were made available in Singapore (NSPS 2005). Much of this can be credited to the growing awareness of physical fitness among the better-educated, mounting interests and attendance at organized endurance and multi-sport events, and improvements in the work-life environment. In addition, the impact of the private sector and government partnership in sport delivery has had significant influence in expanding consumer interests in areas such as sports entertainment, elite performance and alternative leisure exploits. For example, Singapore's sports calendar now features three marathons, numerous distance (10 to 21 km) runs, duathlons, triathlons (including a half *Ironman*) and even 84 km ultramarathons as compared to only one marathon offering in 2001. The number of participants at the annual Standard Chartered Singapore Marathon has increased exponentially in recent years and reached a record high of 50,000 runners in various categories – Kids Dash, Team, 10 km, half marathon and the full marathon in 2008, adding further support for the significant growth in sport participation rates (SSC 2009). Other than endurance events and the familiar sports events such as football, basketball and swimming, the local scene now comprises diverse and exotic sporting choices such as wakeboarding, mountain climbing, fencing, archery, yoga, ballroom dancing, *petanque* and *capoeira*, catering to the widening demands of a cosmopolitan and globalized population (SSC 2009). Responding to the findings and expressing the government's level of satisfaction at the organized sport participation rates, the Chief, Industry Development and High Participation at the SSC, remarked that

> We are very encouraged by the 48 per cent sports participation rate as it is an increase of 10 per cent from 2001. More significantly, the increase in the variety of sports played means that Singaporeans are now keen to try out different types of sports. The combined increase in participation rate and interest in a wider variety of sports suggests that sport is becoming a lifestyle option of choice in Singapore.
>
> (SSC 2008b)

Walking, jogging and swimming remain the most popular sports in Singapore, and according to Soon (2002: 204) 'an estimated ¼ million Singaporeans jog at last once a week while more than 250 private and public swimming pools cater to the nation's 180,000 regular swimmers'. As a sign of the growing affluence, golf and tennis, once considered the pastime of well-heeled country club members, were now among the top 10 most popular sports in Singapore (NSPS 2005). It is also noteworthy that Singapore has, in recent years, successfully bid and organized world-class mega-sporting events such as the SingTel F1 Grand Prix, the Volvo Ocean Race and the FINA/Arena Swimming World Cup. In another attempt at boosting the fledgling sporting culture, in August 2010 Singapore hosted the inaugural Youth Olympic Games.

Considering that the Singapore Government has systematically invested heavily in sport facilities, infrastructure and national campaigns to promote sport participation, the findings also highlight an underlying concern that the level of non-participants remains significantly high (64 per cent in 1992, 47 per cent in 2005). For example, the surveys consistently reveal that costs, convenience and availability of organized sports programs and facilities are not impediments to sports participation in Singapore (NSPS 2005). Rather, the most common declared justifications for non-participation is the lack of time as a result of work commitments, which in themselves underscore the Singaporean penchant for academic and economic status. These, plus the 'sports-can-wait' mindset, remain the foremost barriers that the government faces as it strives to influence sport participation in the nation.

Conclusion

Having just marked its 44th year of independence, Singapore's sport policy model is still nascent in its development. On the other hand, the government's sport strategies and programs appear comprehensive and sound, and are aligned to the ideals of a modern city. The omnipresent Sport For All policy has prevailed in the face of increasing affluence and growing national pride from the economic successes of the 1970s and 1980s. On closer inspection, however, the Sport For All model has its share of drawbacks. The official and centralized manner in which many of the mass events were organized bears evidence of the paternalistic authority of the government, and may inadvertently have led citizens to defer individual responsibility for their own regular physical activity and sport participation. According to McNeill *et al.* (2003: 43), 'the one-off nature of these mass events essentially became a visible token of directed play, as many citizens still required extra persuasion to exercise'. Notwithstanding the reported increases in sport participation rates over the years, the main barriers to sport participation remain the populations' inclination toward sedentary lifestyles and alternative leisure pursuits aided primarily by modern technological gadgets and rising standards of living. Furthermore, the time-honoured quest for economy-based values and extrinsic goals continue to overshadow the long-established benefits of sport in a highly competitive society such as Singapore's.

As was shown earlier, the status of organized sport participation in schools may have been poorer at the expense of the convergence of policies triggered by the demands from the Education and Defence ministries. As a result of the pressures placed by school authorities on fitness results and other imposed objectives relevant to military defence, efforts to improve or institute structured sport programs in the curriculum were often hindered or deemed secondary. The positive support and investments cascading from the SPEX 2000 and CoSS initiatives only served to entrench the extrinsically motivated attitude of students with regards to fitness training and testing. In addition, as physical education in schools is a non-examinable subject, it is accorded low priority and is often marginalized. In their study of modern sport and physical education in Singapore, the unique conundrum faced by education policy makers in Singapore was highlighted by McNeill *et al.* (2003):

> Owing to the resilience of traditional values, the physical education programme in many schools still remains shallow and dysfunctional . . . This is difficult to understand at a time when so much political rhetoric is spent on the benefits and importance of sport, physical activity and healthy lifestyles.
>
> (2003: 49)

At the turn of the millennium, sport development strategies were geared towards the extensive global value of sport to the nation. According to Houlihan and Green (2008: 285), 'nation building, national identity and increasing global presence are at the heart of Singapore's attempts . . . to establish itself as a vibrant independent sovereign state'. As a result, all major sport policies, whether mass or elite, would naturally be of utmost concern to the government now that it took on an international stance. As observed by Horton (2002: 261), 'sport now had become not only part of the rhetoric of nationalism in Singapore but also a feature of the portrayal of its image internationally'. It was shown that the extent of intervention and influence in sport increased as government increasingly sought accountability for state investments. For example, the hegemony and central resolve of the PAP to influence policy to suit its political objectives has resulted in the NSA's adherence of market-oriented managerial and organizational demands of the modern era. The struggles by the SAAA in failing to anticipate the planning dictates set by the SSC demonstrate the vulnerability of NSAs when governments flex their political might to influence policy to match its own agenda.

According to Horton (2001: 99), 'the diffusion of modern sport to Singapore and the emergence of the nation's sport culture constituted a complex process, one that should not be simplistically defined or rationalized. The process was the product of disparate and associated and separate and fused influences, and of course, it continues to develop'.

Nevertheless, as it now embarks on a campaign to capitalize on the pervasive global value of sport, the political principles adopted by the Singapore Government will ensure that it continues to deploy sport as a malleable tool to promote community participation, healthy lifestyles, national pride, sporting culture and other non-sport objectives for the good of the nation.

References

Aplin, N. G. and Quek, J. J. (2002) 'Celestials in touch: Sport and the Chinese in colonial Singapore', *International Journal of the History of Sport*, 19(2–3): 11–34.

Aplin, N.G., Quek, J.J. and Kunalan, C. (2009) 'Sport in Singapore: The path to "First-World" Status'. In N.G. Aplin (ed.), *Perspectives on Physical Education and Sports Science in Singapore: An Eye on the Youth Olympics 2010*, Singapore: McGraw-Hill.

Balasekaran, G. and Loh, R. (2009) 'School physical education programmes: Health and fitness issues and challenges'. In N.G. Aplin (ed.), *Perspectives on Physical Education and Sports Science in Singapore: An Eye on the Youth Olympics 2010*, Singapore: McGraw-Hill.

Central Intelligence Agency (2005) *The World Fact Book*. http://www.cia.gov/cia/publications/factbook/ (accessed 11 July 2005).

Chan, T. C. (2000a, 7 September 2000) 'We're serious about sports', *Straits Times*, p. 63.

—— (2000b, 7 September 2000) 'Committee to chart direction', *Straits Times*, p. 63.

—— (2001, 2 July) 'PM spells out 3 sports goals', *Straits Times*, p. 1.

—— (2002, 28 July) 'SSC's Song seconded to athletics association', *Straits Times*, p. 51.

Channel News Asia (CNA) (2009) 'Sports council could take charge of athletes if NSAs are not capable'. http://www.channelnewsasia.com (accessed 20 April 2009).

Chen, S. J. (1983) 'Singapore's development strategies: A model for rapid growth'. In P. Chen (ed.), *Singapore: Development Policies and Trends*, Oxford University Press: Singapore.

Chiew, S. K. (1983) 'Ethnicity and national integration: The evolution of a multi-ethnic society'. In P. Chen (ed.), *Singapore: Development Policies and Trends*, Oxford University Press: Singapore.

Foo, A. (2005, 16 March) 'Govt's $300m carrot cheers NSAs', *Straits Times Interactive*. http://www.straitstimes.asia1.com.sg (accessed 26 July 2005).

Franklin, B. (2001, 2 July) 'At a glance: The recommendations', *Straits Times*, p. S2.

Government of Singapore, 1991. *Singapore: The Next Lap*. Times Editions: Singapore.

Green, M. (2003) 'An analysis of elite sport policy change in three sports in Canada and the United Kingdom'. Unpublished PhD thesis. Loughborough University.

—— (2004) 'Changing policy priorities for sport in England: The emergence of elite sport development as a key policy concern', *Leisure Studies*, 23: 365–385.

Green, M. and Houlihan, B. (2005) *Elite Sport Development: Policy Learning and Political Priorities*, London: Routledge.

Green, M. and Oakley, B. (2001) 'Elite sport development systems and playing to win: Uniformity and diversity in international approaches', *Leisure Studies*, 20: 247–267.

Horton, P. A. (2001) 'Complex creolization: The evolution of modern sport in Singapore'. In J. A. Mangan (ed.), *The European Sports History Review: Europe, Sport, World: Shaping Global Societies*, Vol. 3, Frank Cass & Co Ltd: London.

Horton, P. A. (2002) 'Shackling the lion: Sport and modern Singapore', *International Journal of the History of Sport*, 19 (2–3): 189–212.

Houlihan, B. and Green, M. (2008) *Comparative Elite Sport Development: Systems, Structures and Public Policy*, London: Routledge.

Ibrahim, Y. (2002, 20 April) Speech by the Minister of Community Development and Sports at the Singapore Sports Awards 2002. Singapore Government. http://www.gov.sg (accessed 15 July 2005).

Khoo, P. (1990, 5 January) 'Almost $6 million in Sports Aid Fund', *Straits Times*, p. 41.

Koh, T. (1999, 19 December) 'The celebration', *Sunday Times*, p. 54.

Lee, H. L. (2001) Speech by the Deputy Prime Minister at the Appreciation Dinner for 21st SEA Games participants. Singapore Government. http://www.gov.sg (accessed 15 July 2005).

Leong, W. K. (2006a) 'Tell us why you want the money', *Weekend Today*, 11–12 March, pp. 54–55.

Leong, C. (2006b) 'New code for elite athletes, NSAs', *Today*, 8 September, p. 78.

Lim, C. Y. (1983) 'Singapore's economic development: Retrospect and prospect'. In P. Chen (ed.), *Singapore: Development Policies and Trends*, Oxford University Press: Singapore.

Lim, L. K. (2004) 'The development of sport in Singapore: An Eliasian approach'. Unpublished PhD thesis, James Cook University.

Lim, M. (2006, 15 November) '$7m kitty to develop Olympic champions', *Straits Times*, p. H11.

McNeill, M., Sproule, J. and Horton, P. A. (2003) 'The changing face of sport and physical education in post-colonial Singapore', *Sport, Education and Society*, 8(10): 35–56.

Ministry of Community Development (MCD) (1993) *Sports Excellence 2000: Winning for Singapore (December 1993)*, Singapore, MCD and SSC Publication.

Ministry of Community Development and Sports (MCDS) (2001a) *Report of the Committee on Sporting Singapore (July 2001)*, Singapore, MCDS.

—— (2001b) *Sporting Singapore Report, Summary Version (July 2001)*, Singapore, MCDS.

—— (2003) *Annual Report 2002/2003*. http://www.mcys.gov.sg (accessed 14 July 2005).

National Sports Participation Survey (NSPS) (1992) Singapore Sports Council.

—— (1997) Singapore Sports Council.

—— (2005) Singapore Sports Council.

Ng, S. M. (2000) Opening address by the Chairman, Singapore Sports Council at Sports 21 @ SSC: Towards a Sporting Nation Seminar, 15 January. Singapore Government. http://www.gov.sg (accessed 2 June 2005).

Ong, L. H. (2000) 'Sports in schools', paper presented by Mr Ong Lye Huat at the Sports 21 @ SSC: Towards a Sporting Nation Seminar, 15 January. Singapore Government. http://www.gov.sg.

Oon, J. T. (2005) Speech by the Chief Executive Officer, Singapore Sports Council at the

NSA Networking Session on SSC's New Funding Model, 26 August. Singapore Sports Council. http://www.ssc.gov.sg (accessed 12 October 2006).

Peh, S. H. (2005) 'More cash and space for sports enthusiasts', *Straits Times Interactive*, 12 March. http://www.straitstimes.asia1.com.sg (accessed 26 July 2005).

Perry, M., Kong, L. and Yeoh, B. (1997) *Singapore: A Developmental City State*, Singapore: John Wiley & Sons.

Razali, A. (2006, 9 August) 'A future of world stars and events', *Today*, p. 55.

Robert, G. (1998, 1 January) 'Isn't it time S'pore had a Ministry of Sport?', *Straits Times*, p. 45.

Singapore Athletic Association (SAA) (2005) Annual Report. SAA, Singapore.

—— (2006) http://www.singaporeathletics.org.sg (accessed 21 October 2006).

Singapore National Olympic Council (2009) http://www.snoc.org.sg (accessed 14 July 2009).

Singapore Pools (2005) http://www.singaporepools.com.sg (accessed 8 July 2005).

Singapore Sports Council (SSC) (1983) *Singapore Sports Council: The First Ten Years*. SSC Publication by Times Editions.

—— (1994) *On Track: 21 Years of the Singapore Sports Council*. SSC Publication by Times Editions.

—— (1995) *Annual Report 1994–1995*, Singapore: SSC.

—— (1996) *Sports for Life: It's More Fun than You Think*. SSC Publication by Times Editions.

—— (1998a) *A Nation at Play: 25 Years of the Singapore Sports Council. Leading Sports into the 21st Century*. SSC Publication by Times Editions.

—— (1998b) *Annual Report 1997–1998*, Singapore: SSC.

—— (1999) *Annual Report 1998–1999*, Singapore: SSC.

—— (2000) *Annual Report 1999–2000: Towards a Sporting Nation*, Singapore: SSC.

—— (2001) *Annual Report 2000–2001: Towards a Sporting Nation*, Singapore: SSC.

—— (2002) *Annual Report 2001–2002: Championing the Vision*, Singapore: SSC.

—— (2004) *Annual Report 2003–2004*, Singapore: SSC.

—— (2005) SSC Sports Museum. http://www.ssc.gov.sg (accessed 12 July 2005).

—— (2008a) *Annual Report 2007–2008*, Singapore: SSC.

—— (2008b) SSC Sportsweb. http://www.ssc.gov.sg (accessed 12 July 2009).

—— (2009) SSC Sportsweb. http://www.ssc.gov.sg (accessed 16 March 2009).

Singh, P. (2006) 'Singapore forms committee to aim for gold medal at Olympic Games', *Channel News Asia*, 14 November. http://www.channelnewsasia.com (accessed 15 November 2006).

Soon, M. Y. (2002). 'Singapore: Towards a sporting nation with Sport for All'. In L. P. Da Costa and A. Miragaya (eds.), *Worldwide Experiences and Trends in Sport for All*, Germany: Meyer and Meyer Sports.

Tan, D. (1996, 30 September) 'Sports for all near every home', *Straits Times*, p. 1.

Tan, B. (2000) 'A national athlete's perspective of Sports Excellence', paper presented by Dr Benedict Tan at the Sports 21@SSC: Towards a Sporting Nation Seminar, 15 January, SSC.

Tan, Y. H. (2006a) 'Sports associations set for review', *Today*, 26 June, p. 41.

—— (2006b) 'Green light for Sports Institute', *Today*, 31 August, p. 49.

—— (2006c) 'Expect an upbeat CoSS report today', *Today*, 2 October, p. 34.

—— (2006d) 'Olympic gold beckons', *Today*, 15 November, p. 55.

Tay, C. K. (1993) 'Time to build on Sea Games success by re-assessing the NSAs', *Sunday Times*, 4 July, p. 28.

—— (2000) 'We can't work with Loh, says SSC chief', *Straits Times*, 18 February, p. 76.

—— (2002) 'Sport's best athletes to be taken care of – for life', *Sunday Times*, 17 March, p. 1.

Tay, K. Y. (2001) 'Singapore soul-searching over sports', *Asian Times*, 15 March, p. 3.

Teo, C. H. (2002) Speech by the Chairman, Singapore National Olympic Council at the XVII Commonwealth Games 2002 Flag Presentation Ceremony, 14 July. Singapore Government. http://www.gov.sg (accessed 25 July 2005).

Thomas, L. J. (2000a) 'The dawn of a new beginning', *Sports*, 28(2): 4–11.

—— (2000b) 'The long wait is over for Singapore sports', *Sports*, 28(5): 12–15.

—— (2000c) 'Down to business', *Sports*, 28(9): 4–7.

—— (2000d) 'Athletics gets axed – and what a blow', *Straits Times*, p. 75.

Turnbull, C. M. (1982) *A History of Singapore, 1819–1975*, Oxford: Oxford University Press.

Wee, S. (2002) 'Proposed Code of Governance: Pre-requisite for SSC funding', *Sports*, 30(10): 2.

13 Japan

Kazuo Uchiumi

Japan has a long and distinctive cultural history of sport. Prior to the Meiji modernization the strongest sporting tradition was associated with *Bujutsu*, the martial arts, and was confined to the warrior ruling class. In the nineteenth century, owing in part to the long period of political stability during the Edo period, many martial arts became more sport-like and assumed a greater educational and personal developmental role (Hamaguchi 2006). This evolution in the character of martial arts was accelerated during the Meiji period when *budo* was promoted as training in a 'way of life' and introduced into the education system (for those of higher social status) and gradually into the training of young conscripts for military service, thus spreading it more evenly across society.

In more recent times the practice of *budo* has had to compete with a wide range of Western sports and sport events. The close association with the United States from the middle of the nineteenth century resulted in the introduction of baseball, which spread rapidly from the universities to the wider population and was soon established as the major team sport in Japan. Key agents for the promotion of sports in Japan were the schools into which many sports, such as baseball, tennis, soccer and athletics, were introduced in the late nineteenth century. Currently in Japan there is a rich mix of traditional sports – such as sumo – and Western sports and also a mix of amateur and professional sports. While sport is widely practised in schools, maintaining participation in the post-school years has proved difficult for a variety of reasons discussed in the following sections. However, it is also accurate to state that sport is an important element of contemporary Japanese popular culture, even if the evidence for this conclusion lies more strongly in the passive consumption of sport through spectating and watching broadcast sport than in active participation in sport.

The structure of sport in Japan

Public sector sport in Japan is administered through a hierarchy with the Ministry of Education at the top, to which Prefecture Education Boards are accountable. In turn Local Education Boards are accountable to Prefecture Education Boards. The Local Education Boards have jurisdiction over school sport (physical education and extra-curricular school sport activity) and also over local (municipal-level) sport policy and facilities. However, as will be made clear later, local sport facilities tend to be severely under-resourced, reflecting the low level of welfare investment in Japan. Under-investment by the government has been the greatest obstacle to the growth in sport participation. The organization of voluntary sporting bodies parallels the administrative pattern of the state sector. At the national level there is the JOC (Japan Olympic Committee) and the JSA (Japan Sport Association). The JOC is an organization which aims to achieve improvement in the top-level athletic sphere, including the Olympic Games, and consequently has strong links with the elite athlete sections of national governing bodies (NGBs). The role of the JSA is to promote participation in sport, and thus the Association works in conjunction with the participation sections of NGBs. NGBs also have organizations corresponding to each of the governmental education levels. As regards the network of sports clubs, most are reliant upon public sport facilities, but as these facilities are very limited in number it serves as a severe restriction on the development of the club network and is the most significant factor impeding the spread of local sports.

Alongside the public and voluntary sectors is the private sector, which can be divided into two categories. The first category is company sport, which has two sub-domains. The first of these is where sport opportunities are provided as part of a welfare program for employees. However, this form of provision is possible only in major companies and not in small and medium-sized enterprises because of the costs involved. The second sub-domain is the company team, the origins of which were specific to Japan. Company teams first emerged in the period of high economic growth in the 1960s as part of corporate promotion strategies. Owing to the weakness of the local sport club network, the company team system took the lead and supported the development of top-level clubs in Japan. However, the spread of satellite television viewing, the rise in company bankruptcies due to the economic depression in the 1990s and the globalization of international sport sharply reduced the appeal of domestic 'amateur' (company amateur) sports, which led to a reduction in their propaganda value to companies. The decline in company teams has been steady, with more than 300 top company teams abolished in the last twenty years. Consequently, many leading Japanese sportsmen and women lost their jobs in companies and the standard of top-level sport in Japan declined.

The second private sector category is the management of for-profit/commercial sport facilities, such as fitness gyms and jazz dancing studios, which rely on rapid recruitment of high-volume customer numbers, or golf clubs, which are able to charge high annual membership fees and green fees (playing charges). However, the fortunes of these facilities are, with the exception of the wealthy, directly dependent on trends in consumption, which in turn are affected by employment levels. Between 1985 and 2010, 30,000 commercial sport facilities disappeared through bankruptcy, a development which is discussed more fully below.

The decline in commercial providers has not been matched by a corresponding increase in the provision of school sport facilities and public local sport facilities. Indeed, there has been some support for privatization of public sector sports facilities from the series of neo-liberal governments in Japan. However, in relation to sport for all it is accepted that sports such as soccer, baseball, basketball, tennis, track and field and sailing, which need extensive land and/or built facilities, cannot operate as profit-making organizations. If they were to be privatized the user fees would be too high, making them unattractive to the general public. Consequently, it is acknowledged that privatization of sport facilities is not a suitable strategy for the spread of these sports and the promotion of sports participation and they need to remain under public management.

As in all countries, the attitude of government is important in understanding the opportunities and demand for participation in sport. In Japan the association between rapid post-war economic growth and the expansion of welfare provision, so clearly evident in Western Europe, was conspicuous by its absence. Rapid economic growth in the 1960s in Western Europe was one of the factors which enabled the development and inclusion of public services related to culture, art and sport alongside the conventional elements of a welfare state such as medical treatment, education and social housing. This recognition of sport as an element of welfare contributed to the adoption of the sport for all policy which was subsequently reinforced by the emerging public health concern with the consequences of an increasingly sedentary lifestyle combined with increased intake of calories. Further consolidation of the rising political status of sport within many developed economies resulted from the increased willingness of governments to recognize access to culture, art and sport as fundamental social or 'third generation' rights (Wronka 1998). Consequently, sport for all is a sport policy which is strongest in welfare states where it is considered to be an important element in broader welfare provision (Uchiumi 2006).

Unfortunately, while there was considerable public support for a sport for all policy in the 1970s, which was seen as an element of welfare state provision and an element of the 'new human rights', there was little support from government. Despite the existence of high economic growth in the 1970s, which outpaced that of Europe, the benefits of that growth were used to further strengthen the competitive position of Japan's major companies through the design of a taxation system which was favourable to business, but a heavy burden for the people. Public finances are conventionally divided into four elements, namely security (military affairs and police), investment for industrial infrastructure, investment for life (welfare) infrastructure, and other investment (Miyamoto 1972; Ninomiya 2009). The security element has consistently been allocated less than 1 per cent of the national budget so the main issue is the ratio of investment between industrial infrastructure and life (welfare) infrastructure.

In contrast to many Western European countries, investment in industrial infrastructure (such as roads, harbours, dams and highways) for major companies has been a central focus for Japanese central and local government public finances for many years, while life (welfare) infrastructure (such as hospitals, schools, libraries and sports facilities) has been marginalized. In many Western welfare states, after their major period of high economic growth in the 1960s and 1970s, the ratio of industrial to welfare state investment was approximately 1:2. In many Western industrialized countries the ratio has, in more recent years, moved to almost 1:5 on average, thus justifying the claims of these countries to be known as welfare states. In contrast in Japan, the ratio was 2:1 after the period of high economic growth, with welfare taking second place to preferential treatment for major companies. Admittedly, industrial infrastructure was poor in Japan until around 1960, and there was some justification for this policy, but by the 1980s, the quality of industrial infrastructure had increased dramatically and was beginning to prompt accusations of environmental destruction and fiscal waste. However, in recent years expenditure on industrial infrastructure still exceeded expenditure on welfare infrastructure by a ratio of 2.5:1.

In summary, in the 1980s the adoption of neo-liberal policies by successive conservative governments, an increase in the number of people working additional hours without payment, a decline in employment security and the dramatic growth of part-time working meant that the decade was no more supportive of the promotion of sport participation than the 1970s. Furthermore, social welfare had been cut to such an extent that Japan ranked close to the bottom for percentage welfare spending among developed countries. The overall effect was that people did not have enough disposable income or leisure (free) time to participate in sport.

The period of neo-liberal economic policy in the 1980s was followed by a prolonged period of economic stagnation which lasted at least until 2004, prompted, in part, by the collapse of the real estate market. According to Ito and Patrick (2005: 11), the economy experienced the 'malaise of inadequate growth, a soaring unemployment rate and deepening under-employment'. The economic problems of this period contributed to the high level of political instability in the 1990s (six prime ministers in the decade), both of which combined to make progress in areas of welfare policy such as sport participation even less likely to receive attention. The present century witnessed the return to radical neo-liberal economic policies under Prime Minister Koizumi and also a continuation of the period of slow, and at times even negative, economic growth. During the 1990s and into the present century domestic politics were dominated by economic concerns and by the ideology of neo-liberalism, neither of which were conducive to a sustained focus on issues such as sport participation, which was considered to be on the margin of welfare policy which itself was overshadowed by financial and industrial policy priorities.

Funding for sport

The radical restructuring of the machinery of government in 2001 led to the establishment of the Ministry of Education, Culture, Sports, Science and Technology (MEXT) which remains the lead department on sport policy. However, as is the case in many countries, a number of other central government departments have an involvement in aspects of physical fitness (such as those for health and the armed forces), thus not only making policy coordination complex, but also making assessments of the total public sector investment in the promotion of sport participation difficult to specify with precision. These problems notwithstanding, it is clear that while the budget for sport facilities, including those for physical fitness, increased in the middle of the 1990s, there has been a steady decrease since then (see Table 13.1), despite increases in total public expenditure.

Table 13.2 indicates the change in the total number of sport facilities in Japan. The number increased gradually from 1969 when government statistics started, to about 300,000 in 1985, which was twice as many as in 1969. However, this was still half the number recommended in the 1972 report from the Health and Physical Education Council to the Minister of Education (HPEC 1972). Within the government there was an expectation that any future expansion in the number

Table 13.1 Budget for physical fitness (from all relevant departments, billion yen)

Year	Total	Facility development	Services	Club development	Leadership training
1970	80	22	55	≈0	–
1972	60	30	27	≈0	–
1974	60	60	0	≈0	–
1976	140	100	35	≈0	–
1978	220	165	45	≈0	–
1980	320	260	50	≈0	–
1982	250	190	55	≈0	–
1984	250	180	70	≈0	≈0
1986	249	155	80	8	≈0
1988	300	185	105	8	≈0
1990	330	200	122	8	≈0
1992	400	245	140	12	≈0
1994	430	275	145	20	≈0
1996	450	295	150	20	≈0
1998	410	280	125	20	≈0
2000	395	n/a	n/a	n/a	n/a
2002	335	n/a	n/a	n/a	n/a
2004	285	n/a	n/a	n/a	n/a

Source: The Ministry of Home Affairs. Annual budgets for physical fitness promotion

Table 13.2 Japanese sport facilities (estimated)

Year	School	Public	Private	Workplace	Private non-profit
1969	50,000	50,000	20,000	25,000	5,000
1975	50,000	75,000	30,000	25,000	5,000
1980	135,000	30,000	15,000	25,000	6,000
1985	155,000	60,000	30,000	30,000	20,000
1990	150,000	76,000	n/a	n/a	n/a
1996	160,000	70,000	20,000	10,000	n/a

Source: Department of Education. PE and sport facilities in Japan

of facilities would be driven by the private sector, but since 1990 many private sector sport facilities have gone bankrupt, which explains the significant decrease from the middle of the 1980s to the middle of the 1990s. The number of facilities in 1996 showed there had actually been a decrease of approximately one tenth of the total number of facilities in Japan, and there is little indication that facility provision has recovered during the early part of this century. This deficiency provides further evidence that Japan should be referred to as an 'immature welfare state' in terms of sport.

Table 13.3 details the facilities budget of the Department for Education. From the mid 1990s it decreased slightly, but after 2000 the budget line declined sharply, which reflected the government's expectation that the private sector would make a greater contribution to the provision of sport for all opportunities – an expectation that was not fulfilled.

Table 13.4 shows the historical trend in the rate of the sport expenditure in an average household economy. The rise in the demand for sport can be ascertained by the expenditure of a typical household. Sport expenditure from the 1960s until

Table 13.3 Facility budget of the Department for Education (approximate)

Year	Budget (bn yen)
1970	9,000
1975	33,000
1980	79,418
1985	55,000
1990	65,000
1995	65,000
2000	50,000
2005	19,000

Table 13.4 Household expenditure on sport (approximate) (in yen)

Year	Sporting goods	Entrance fees	Coaching/tuition fees
1963	2,000	–	–
1965	2,200	–	–
1967	2,400	–	–
1969	2,500	700	–
1971	3,200	1,800	–
1973	5,000	2,300	–
1975	7,200	2,300	–
1977	9,200	1,300	–
1979	12,500	2,400	–
1981	14,500	3,000	4,000
1983	17,500	3,000	4,200
1985	18,500	6,000	7,200
1987	18,000	7,000	7,700
1989	20,700	7,500	10,000
1991	24,500	11,000	10,000
1993	25,500	13,000	11,000
1995	22,000	14,000	10,000
1997	20,000	15,000	11,000
1999	20,000	16,000	11,000
2001	18,000	15,000	10,000

Source: Ministry of Home Affairs. Annual Report on the Investigation of Household Economy

1993 increased consistently, but immediately after the 'bubble economy' collapsed total household expenditure on sport began to decrease. Although the data since 2000 are not available, it is extremely unlikely that expenditure has increased due in part to the fragility of the economic recovery in the early 2000s, the cultural preference for saving over expenditure and borrowing among the Japanese, and the continuing relatively high level of youth unemployment (approximately twice the rate for the population as a whole).

In Table 13.5 we can see that 'participation rates in movement and sport' show a gradual increase since 1972. However, the rate of 'sports club membership' has dwindled since the peak of 17.6 per cent in 1982. Furthermore, it is important to look at the different types of activities Japanese people participate in. The top three 'sports' in 2004 were 'going for a stroll', at 34 per cent, 'walking' (fast walking intended as exercise) at 21.6 per cent in second place, and 'light gymnastics' (free-standing exercise) in third at 18.6 per cent. They were followed by 'ten pin

Table 13.5 Participation in sport and exercise, 1972–2004 (%)

Year	Participation in sports clubs	Participation once a week or more	Participation at least once a year (but less than once a week)	Do not participate
1972	7.2	n/a	60.0	40.0
1976	13.0	n/a	65.0	35.0
1979	14.7	n/a	67.9	32.1
1982	17.6	27.9	64.2	35.8
1985	15.3	27.0	63.2	36.8
1988	17.5	26.4	64.1	35.7
1991	17.7	27.8	65.7	34.1
1994	16.2	29.9	66.7	33.0
1997	17.0	34.8	71.7	28.1
2000	15.8	37.2	68.0	31.9
2004	15.8	38.5	68.2	31.4

Source: Ministry of Home Affairs. Survey of physical fitness and sport

bowling' at 16.4 per cent. The top three are forms of exercise that do not require special facilities. Sports that require special facilities rank much lower.

The development of sport in Japan

The modern Japanese nation-state dates from the Meiji Restoration in 1868, one of the goals of which was that Japan would catch up with Europe and the United States in terms of politics, economics and culture. Compulsory education was introduced and, in order to provide physical training for soldiers and manual workers, gymnastics was 'imported' as part of the physical education curriculum. Although sport was also imported at around the same time, it was not generally adopted as part of physical education because it was expensive, except in the elite education institutes such as universities where it formed part of the range of extracurricular sport activity, as was the case in many Western European countries. Gymnastics and sports enjoyed roughly equal popularity until the new education system after World War II, while outside the education system sport was generally available only to the graduates of elite education institutes.

The importance of Western sport should not obscure the strong tradition of indigenous 'sport' that existed in Japan and which was also subject to the drive for modernization. For example, in 1882 Jigoro Kano modernized the medieval martial art of *Jujutsu* to establish *Judo*, a form of martial arts which was given a stronger educational orientation.

During World War II, not only was Western sport prohibited and excluded from society as it was regarded as an enemy culture, but also physical education gradually became militarized. After World War II, sport was reintroduced to schools and as a result of educational democratization became part of the PE curriculum. While there was a shortage of sport facilities and equipment, the experience of sport in some schools and universities laid the foundation on which contemporary sport in Japan was to develop.

Although some organized sports such as baseball quickly re-emerged following the end of the war, the national priorities were the re-establishment of international diplomatic relations and, more urgently, the rebuilding of the economy. Not until the 1960s when favorable diplomatic and economic conditions coincided did sport receive greater attention within Japanese society. The decision by the government to bid to host the 1964 Olympic Games not only put sport, or at least high-performance sport, on the agenda of the government but, more importantly, the hosting of the Games stimulated public interest in sport. The increased public enthusiasm for sport coincided with the growth of the 'company sport teams', formed partly as a means of publicizing companies and partly as a way of improving employee morale. These teams made up the Japan leagues in their respective sports and had a leading role in the development of Japanese sport. At this time, there was very little community sport in Japan, for although the Ministry of Education tried to promote community sport policies it received no support from central government. Part of the explanation for the lack of central government investment was that Japan had no tradition of state investment in welfare.

The limited progress in investing in participation in sport during the 1960s and 1970s was undermined in the 1980s by the government's adoption of neo-liberal economic policies, which not only increased the gap between rich and poor but also negatively affected participation in sport. Neo-liberal economic ideology has, with varying degrees of intensity, dominated Japanese politics since the 1980s, irrespective of prime minister and government. Consequently, the brief period of significant public investment in sport provision appears increasingly as an exception rather than the beginning of a trend towards greater acceptance of the provision of access to sport as part of the normal obligations of government.

Sport policy in Japan

Politics in Japan have been dominated by the Liberal-Democratic Party (conservative) since 1946, and the relationship between central government and local governments has been very hierarchical. Local government has only very limited autonomy, especially when it comes to financial matters. Political independence in local government is weak, and in relation to sport policy the hierarchical structure is particularly pronounced. The section that follows provides a brief history of sport policy in Japan and draws substantially upon earlier research by the author (Uchiumi 2006).

The 1960s

Public opinion and politics in Japan were divided into two groups by the amendment of the Japan–US Security Treaty in 1960. On one side of the division was a conservative group which was in favour of the Treaty and on the other side was a progressive group against the Treaty. Although the latter group's campaign gathered some momentum, the Treaty was finally renewed. However, as a result of the divisiveness of the Treaty, the conservative government was faced with a political and ideological crisis. One response by the government to the need to repair the divisions in society was to position the Tokyo Olympic Games in

1964 as a means for the integration of domestic public opinion. In addition to the strong public appeal of the Olympic Games, they were also considered to be an important opportunity to display Japan's post-war revival to the rest of the world. However, before the Olympics could be held the infrastructure for some domestic sports needed to be improved.

The first step in this process of infrastructure development was the introduction of the 'Sport Promotion Law' in 1961. Although the law did not include a provision for a sport budget at central government level, it was the first sport law in Japan and had a significant impact on sport policy, particularly at local government level. Although there had been a demand for sport by local residents, local government had been in a weak position to increase supply due to the fact that there was no sport law. The law gave local government a legal basis for their sport policies. In addition to the law providing a definition of sport and allocating administrative responsibility to the Ministry of Education, it also required the development of a sport promotion plan in relation to mass participation. However, it would not be until 2000 that this last element of the law would be implemented. In short, while the law was indeed important its primary significance was in confirming the political priority of elite sport success.

The success of the Tokyo Olympic Games in 1964 represented the political revival of Japan in the world and the domestic integration of ideology and nationalism. Furthermore, the hosting of the Games had a substantial economic impact as it led to improved infrastructure in Tokyo. However, the legacy of the Tokyo Games for sport was heavily skewed in favour of spectating and elite athlete development. The Tokyo Olympics accelerated people's demand for sport which had already been steadily increasing because of the rapid economic growth. Stimulated by the Olympics, the market for colour televisions expanded rapidly and supported the development of 'see-sport' or the passive consumption of televised sports events. Many of the 'Japan leagues' for different sports formed by the company teams were a response to this consumer demand, but they only represented the top sports in Japan, not community sport, which was still underdeveloped. The prioritization in central and local government of support for the expansion of major companies, at the expense of people's welfare, led to a build-up of frustration in the 1960s. This frustration exploded in public protest in the 1960s and led to some political innovation by reformist parties regarding the role and autonomy of local government from the second half of the 1960s.

The 1970s

A further result of the political crisis of the late 1960s was that the central conservative government began to pay lip service to welfare in the early 1970s, with the year 1973 declared to be the 'first year of welfare' (Uchiumi 2006). The Minister of Education, as the responsible minister for sport, invited his consultative body, the Health and Physical Education Council, to prepare a fundamental policy to promote physical education and sport. The Council published its report in 1972 (HPEC 1972) and it was the first report from the Ministry that recommended increasing sport in the community. It was consequently said that the report was the first welfare state report on sport, even though it was not clear whether this was intentional. The report identified the 'drastic changes in lifestyle and physical fitness in accordance with economic growth' which necessitated 'creating a healthy society based on human dignity [as] the most important issue for Japan' and the development of a 'comprehensive plan to encourage life-long participation [in sport]' (HPEC 1972: 2, quoted in Yamamoto 2010). In the report, Western sport for all policies and sport facility installation standards were identified as reference points, and the number of sport facilities in relation to the population of a community was calculated. Reference to this calculation was used to encourage the construction of sport facilities by local governments, which were also encouraged to take account of the strength of local demand for sport. Although Japanese welfare development suffered a setback due to the oil crisis of 1973, the number of facilities steadily grew but levelled off in the mid 1980s (see Table 13.2) at a figure which was just 50 per cent of the target proposed in the 1972 report.

Despite the loss of momentum following the oil crisis of the early 1970s, the 1972 report inaugurated a rare, if modest, period of policy innovation in relation to sport for all. In 1974 JSA implemented a mass participation policy, the Nationwide General Sport Promotion Project, which aimed to increase sport club membership from 4.5m to 10m by extending JSA's organizational structure to regional and local levels, creating a National Youth Sport Competition, and organizing training courses for coaches/trainers (Yamamoto 2010). Although JSA's plans were never fully realized, the 1970s were the time when the concept of sport for all entered the public and political consciousness.

The 1980s

In the 1980s, the Nakasone (the then prime minister) administrative reforms were initiated. This was one of the three major worldwide neo-liberal initiatives, the others being those by Ronald Reagan in the United States and Margaret Thatcher in Britain. Japan was still an immature welfare state, and people's welfare levels were low. The promotion of privatization of central and local government's services resulting from the introduction of neo-liberalism reduced welfare levels further. The 1980s were popularly referred to as the 'ten blank years' politically and economically. When economic growth recovered during the 'bubble economy' in the second half of the 1980s, the neo-liberal policy for local government was strengthened further with the consequence that people's opportunity to participate in sport deteriorated.

Twenty years on from the Sport Promotion Law, it is accurate to conclude that by the 1980s there was still neither a coherent nor a substantial sport policy at central government level. The Ministry of Education, which was small and weak in relation to other government departments, was not able to promote sport policy. One reason for this was that sport policy was conceptualized as an element of welfare and the central government had little enthusiasm for investment in state welfare services. As Laratta (2010: 134) noted, in the 1970s the government of Prime Minister Ohira promoted the idea that 'Japan's own hidden assets, such as neighbourhood and family bonds, should be more positively exploited' as a source of welfare support. Not surprisingly, the sport-related budget of the Ministry of Education was steadily reduced throughout the 1980s and the modest momentum developed in the 1970s slowly dissipated. The lack of government enthusiasm and commitment is indicated in a perhaps surprising source, the report from the Health and Physical Education Council, published in 1989, which stated that there were enough community sport facilities in Japan, even though the total was only 50 per cent of that recommended in the report of 1972 (HPEC 1989). In addition, and perhaps partly in recognition of the shortfall in the construction of new facilities, the 1989 report proposed the dual (or community) use of the existing school facilities. The main implication of the report was that the central government was determined to leave future sport facility construction to local government. Since then central government has not been involved in any aspect of facility construction and, in fact, the facility construction budget of the Ministry of Education has been reduced year on year since the mid 1990s (see Table 13.3).

However, the government's reluctance to invest further in sport for all facilities did not apply to elite sport. Although Japan had been in second place in Asia with regard to top-level sport, she was surpassed by South Korea at both the Seoul Asian Games in 1986, and the Seoul Olympic Games in 1988. This created what was known as the 'Seoul shock' among conservative politicians and economists in Japan, and it brought about the reorganization of what was formerly known as the 'sport division', which was split by the Ministry of Education in 1988 into two parts: the 'sport for all division' and the 'competitive sports division'. However, while the budget for the latter increased, the budget for the former declined.

The 1990s

The 1990s was an extremely difficult decade for sport for two main reasons. First, the bubble economy which developed in the second half of the 1980s collapsed in 1991. Second, the government had adopted a strong neo-liberal stance and generally ignored the topic of welfare. During this period the number of incidents of 'Karoshi', that is to say death by overwork, increased because of long working hours, including unpaid overtime work. The value added tax (consumption tax) rose from 3 per cent to 5 per cent in 1995, which affected people's consumption patterns. The combined effect of the decline in people's disposable income and disposable time was that demand for sport services and facilities was reduced with a particularly severe impact on the commercial sector (see Table 13.2).

At the same time the Ministry of Education's budget for sport facility construction all but disappeared. However, despite the economic crisis and the dominance of neo-liberalism within government, two sport development reports by the Ministry of Education, published in 1989 (HPEC 1989) and 1997 (HPEC 1997), did have a small impact on the promotion of community sport. In particular, the 1997 report from the Health and Physical Education Council to the Minister of Education included the unprecedented preliminary statement that the government should give enough money to promote this report. This was a strong statement which reflected not only the desire of the committee which produced the report, but also that of the Ministry of Education for a greater resource contribution from other ministries such as Health and Land, Transport and Tourism. Unfortunately, the Ministry of Education was of relatively low status and influence within government.

Since 2000

The low status of sport within government and the continued dominance of neo-liberal reforms were reflected in the decision to abolish the Health and Physical Education Council. The Council submitted its final report on the 'Sport promotion master plan' in 2000 (HPEC 2000). This report anticipated the use of earnings from the so-called 'soccer lottery' established in 1998. However, there was no mention of sport facility construction in this master plan, and emphasis was placed on the, arguably unnecessary, creation of 'synthesized community sport clubs'. 'Synthesized club' describes a club which provides opportunities in several sports, a model which was copied from the German club system. The failure of the report to propose a facility construction master plan, which would be led by the government, was compounded by the steady decline in income from the 'soccer lottery' to the extent that assistance for community sports was finally reduced to zero. The formation of 'synthesized community sport clubs' has been forcefully advanced as the centrepiece of the new master plan in a top-down fashion from the Ministry of Education to local government. Because the master plan could not provide for the building of new facilities there was a need for a new and unique policy approach – the synthesized sports clubs. However, the membership of 'synthesized community sport clubs' had to bear the cost of the policy as many traditional local single-sport clubs were expelled from the community sports facilities in order to accommodate the new type of multi-sport club.

Because of the current economic recession, people's detachment from sport has increased, not only in terms of 'do-sport', but also in terms of 'see-sport'. Worldwide television broadcasting has enabled Japanese people to see athletic meets at the highest level; however, they are not interested in watching Japanese professional sport. In Japan, professional baseball and the J-League (soccer), which were established in 1993, have not been able to attract enough fans and are having serious financial problems. In 1995 the J-League attracted about 6 million spectators with ten teams, but in 2008 it attracted about 6.5 million spectators with 32 teams. Furthermore, the two professional baseball leagues attracted nearly three times the number of spectators as the J-League but the numbers did not increase in the ten years since the mid 1990s. In addition, hundreds of top company sport teams which had been the engine of top Japanese sport no longer exist since the collapse of the 'bubble economy' in 1991. There are a number of reasons for this, such as the perceived decline in the promotional benefit for the company because fewer people were watching company team matches on television owing to the lower standard of play and the availability of matches from the top leagues in other countries. Moreover, company teams no longer played a part in company consciousness-raising because the employment system of companies had diversified, for example through the employment of an increased number of part-time staff who don't have the same strong feelings of loyalty to the company as full-time employees.

In summary, the 'Sport promotion master plan' would only have the opportunity of being fully realized in a welfare state (Uchiumi 2003). Although the opposition party came to power in the general election at the end of August 2009 it is not yet known whether they will adopt a 'sport for all' policy.

Problems of public sport policy in Japan

The demand for sport in Japan is not great, as is shown by a national survey of demand carried out by the government (Cabinet Office 2009). Consequently, officials of the Ministry of Education can defend, or at least disguise, their policy of negligence. However, the survey data need to be treated with caution as it can be argued that the data conceal a number of problems.

First, people do not feel that they are in a position to demand more sport facilities from the government. This is because Japan does not have a proper welfare system, and people are also faced with a lack of disposable income and free time because of long working hours and unpaid overtime. It is argued that these factors may restrain people's demand for culture, including sport. Second, what has brought about such an oppressive situation originated in the weakness of people's consciousness to demand welfare. With regard to social philosophy, the Japanese did not experience a democratic revolution historically and socially, unlike the Western democracies. So, it is generally said that Japanese people's demand to the government for democracy including welfare rights is still rather weak compared to Western countries (Garon 1997; Miyamoto 2003; Schwartz and Pharr 2003).

Japan has sufficient economic strength to provide taxes to improve people's welfare. If national fiscal expenditure changed from a ratio of 2.5:1 to 1:1 in relation to industrial infrastructures and life infrastructures, Japan would suddenly become a welfare state; the 'sport for all policy' would progress dramatically, and the 'sport promotion master plan' could come to fruition. The improvement of sport policy in Japan will only be possible within the framework of a welfare state.

References

Cabinet Office (2009) *National Survey on Physical Fitness and Sport*, Tokyo: Cabinet Office.

Garon, S. (1997) *Molding Japanese Minds: The State in Everyday Life*, Princeton NJ: Princeton University Press.

Hamaguchi, Y. (2006) Innovation in martial arts. In J. Maguire and M. Nakayama (eds.), *Japan, Sport and Society: Tradition and Change in a Globalising World*, London: Routledge.

Health and Physical Education Council (1972) *A Fundamental Policy to Promote Physical Education and Sport* [*Taiiku-sport no fukyu shinko no kihonhosaku ni tsuite*].

Health and Physical Education Council (1989) *On the Development of Sport toward the 21st Century* [*21 seiki ni muketa sport no shinko housaku ni tsuite*].

Health and Physical Education Council (1997) *Education on Keeping and Promoting Lifelong Health of Mind and Body, and on the Development of Sport* [*Shougai ni wataru shinshin no kenkou no hojizoushin no tameno kongo no kenko ni kansuru kyouiku oyobi sport no shinkou no arikata ni tsuite*].

Health and Physical Education Council (2000) *Sport Promotion Master Plan* [*Sport shinko kihon keikaku*].

Ito, T. and Patrick, H. (2003) Problems and prescriptions for the Japanese economy: An overview. In T. Ito, H. Patrick and D.E. Weinstein (eds.), *Reviving Japan's Economy*, Cambridge, MA: MIT Press.

Laratta, R. (2010) From welfare state to welfare society: Towards a viable system of welfare in Japan and England, *International Journal of Social Welfare*, 19: 131–141.

Miyamoto, T. (2003) Dynamics of the Japanese welfare state in comparative perspective: Between 'Three Worlds' and the developmental state, *Japanese Journal of Social Security Policy*, 2.2: 12–24.

Miyamoto, K. (2009) *On Public Expenditure* [*Shakai shihon ron*], Yuhikaku, 1972.

Ninomiya, Atsumi, Watanabe, Osamu, *et al.* (2009) *Neo-liberalism or Neo-welfare state?* [*Shin jiyushugi ka shin fukushikokka ka*], Junposha.

Schwartz, F.J. and Pharr, S.J. (eds.) (2003) *The State of Civil Society in Japan*, Cambridge: Cambridge University Press.

Uchiumi, K. (2003) *Sport for All in England: Sport Policy in a Welfare State* [*Igirisu no Sport for All: Fukushikokka no Sport Seisaku*], Fumaido Publisher.

Uchiumi, K. (2006) *Sport for All in Japan: Sport Policy in an Immature Welfare State* [*Nippon no Sport for All: Mijukuna Fukushikokka no Sport Seisaku*], Fumaido Publisher.

Wronka, J. (1998) *Human Rights and Social Policy in the Twenty-First Century*, 2nd edn, Lanham MD: University of America Press.

Yamamoto, M.Y. (2010) The influence of non-domestic factors on elite sport development and anti-doping policy: The cases of Japan and UK/England. Unpublished PhD thesis, Loughborough University, Loughborough, UK.

14 Australia

Russell Hoye and Matthew Nicholson

Australia has long been considered a 'sporting nation' that is obsessed with watching and consuming sport, as well as participating (Cashman 1995). In many ways this is true, yet the actual level of participation by Australians in formal organized sport, as well as the lack of consistent effective government policy in this area, might surprise readers of this book. The purpose of this chapter is to briefly explain the structure of the Australian sport system and the place of sport in Australian culture, to review what we know of sport participation rates and trends in Australia, to describe the nature of federal government intervention in matters related to sport participation, and finally to analyse the efficacy of government sport policies designed to influence the nature and extent of Australians' participation in sport.

Structure of sport in Australia

The foundation of the Australian sport system is the 30,000 nonprofit clubs and associations governed by volunteers that facilitate sporting competitions and events, manage development programs for coaches and officials, assist in the identification and development of talented athletes, undertake volunteer training, engage in marketing and promoting their sports, and liaise with governments at local, state and national levels. Sport clubs and associations usually coordinate their efforts through a complex federated model, with national sport organizations (NSOs) funded by the Australian government to deliver its public policy objectives, which are focused on enhancing elite performances and increasing participation in sport. These NSOs work with affiliated state sport organizations (SSOs) to deliver sport development programs in each of the eight states and territories of Australia, which in turn also receive varying degrees of funding support from their respective state or territory government. Within each state or territory, local or regional clubs and associations work at the 'coalface' of sport; coaching teams, recruiting and managing volunteers, developing the skills and abilities of athletes and administering competitions and events. These clubs and associations generally work with local governments, the major providers of stadia and other facilities used by sport.

Operating in conjunction with this complex community club sport system is what can be regarded as 'the most competitive professional sport marketplace in the world, with four major football codes, a national basketball league, a crowded international and domestic cricket calendar, a highly successful Grand Slam tennis tournament, a thriving horse racing industry and a host of other major sports events each year' (Hoye and Nicholson 2009: 234). As noted by Hoye (2005: 90) 'the scale of commercial activity associated with professional sport in Australia and New Zealand is significant', but there is limited government policy that affects these leagues and events; it is typically focused on investment in major stadia at the state level and regulation of broadcast rights at the national level.

At the national level, government policy is set by the federal Minister for Sport, which is then executed via a national sport agency, the Australian Sports Commission (ASC). The ASC works with more than 120 NSOs by supporting their activities, emphasizing elite sport rather than mass participation (Green 2007). The ASC, via funding and service agreements, and through annual reviews that monitor performance and allocate funding on the basis of each NSO's achievements, ensures that NSO planning and activities are aligned with the ASC's strategic objectives and government policy aims. It is worth noting that the ASC, as the lead federal agency responsible for sport, recognizes the importance of the community club system in its most recent strategic plan: 'The critical ingredient of the Australian sports system remains the involvement, commitment and dedication of the many thousands of Australians who participate at the grassroots level as players, coaches, officials, administrators and supporters of our community sporting clubs' (ASC 2006b: 3).

Australian sporting culture

The importance of sport to Australia and its culture was powerfully expressed by arguably Australia's pre-eminent sport historian, Richard Cashman:

> While Australia has inherited or borrowed much of its sporting culture, this culture has been transformed to such an extent as to have become distinctively Australian. Our culture of sport – the character of play, the behaviour of players and spectators, language, architecture and club identity – has become recognizably Australian, and its importance is generally agreed: most Australians would be surprised by any suggestion that sport was not a cornerstone of Australian life.
>
> (Cashman 1995: 205)

Cashman offered several explanations why this should be the case: the outdoors lifestyle of Australians; the gold rush boom of the late 1800s that provided for the development of so many important sport stadia and spaces, ovals and parks; the lack of other common 'social bonding' to link communities – Australia has had no civil war, hostile neighbour or past traditions to unify the population; and the influx of migrants such as Italians and Greeks that used sports (i.e. soccer) to establish their identity in their new country. He concluded that 'sport has become central to Australian life and the business of being Australian. Sporting culture is accessible and provides continuing satisfaction for many Australians . . . Sport is the regular theatre for ordinary Australians' (Cashman 1995: 207).

The ASC (2006b: 4) also believes in the importance of sport to Australia:

Sport occupies a central position in Australian life. It is a source of health and enjoyment for millions who participate as players, coaches, officials, administrators and spectators, the vast majority of whom do so in a voluntary capacity. As an industry, sport contributes significantly to the Australian economy. Within the Australian community, sport also provides a strong and continuous thread through a diverse and widespread population. In short, sport is a binding element in the social and cultural fabric of Australia.

The data for sport spectatorship certainly seems to support both the ASC's and Cashman's view of the importance of sport to Australians and the place of sport in Australian culture. The most recent Australian Bureau of Statistics (ABS 2008) data show that 7.1 million or 44.3 per cent of Australians aged 15 years and over attended at least one sport event during the 12 months prior to interview in 2005–06. The most popular sport was Australian Rules football (15.6 per cent of Australians), followed by horse racing (12.8 per cent), rugby league (9.0 per cent), motor sport (8.9 per cent), cricket (4.6 per cent), rugby union (4.3 per cent), soccer (3.4 per cent), harness racing (2.8 per cent), tennis (1.6 per cent) and basketball (1.4 per cent). Whether this level of sport spectatorship is reflected in the level of sport participation by Australians is important in the context of this chapter. Are Australians merely a nation of sport watchers or is participating in sport also a way of life for Australians?

Sport participation data

There are two organizations involved in gathering data on Australian sport participation: the ABS and the Standing Committee on Recreation and Sport (SCORS). Each organization uses a different method and classification scheme for participation in sport and physical activity. The ABS uses data gathered as part of the annual Multi-Purpose Household Survey (MPHS) and previously used the General Social Survey (2002) and Population Survey Monitor (1993 to 2000). The ABS itself noted that 'each collection may define sports and physical recreation activities in different ways because there is no standard classification for these activities' (ABS 2008: 8). The MPHS for 2005–06 collected data for persons aged 15 years and over and was based on a sample of 14,219 who were asked whether they had participated in a sport or physical activity as a player or participant at least once in the previous 12 months. A participant was defined as a player, competitor or person who physically undertakes the activity; people who participated solely as coaches, umpires or officials were not included. The main source of data from the ABS used in this chapter is the MPHS for 2005–06 reported by the ABS in *Participation in Sports and Physical Recreation, Australia, 2005–06* (cat. 4177.0).

The ABS data for participation in organized sport or physical activity through a club or association in 2005–06 indicates that 29.0 per cent of males and 26.0 per cent of females aged 15 years and over participated at least once in the 12 months prior to being interviewed. Regular participation was defined as participating more than twice per week; 29 per cent of the population claimed to be regular participants. When this figure is considered alongside the fact that the number of Australians participating in non-organized activities (8.6 million or 54 per cent) was almost double that of organized activities (4.4 million or 28 per cent), it can be estimated that less than 10 per cent (i.e. only 29 per cent of these 4.4 million participants do so regularly) of Australians participate in regular sport or physical activity in the context of formal organized sport clubs or associations.

Table 14.1 highlights the most popular forms of sport and physical activities enjoyed by Australians; these include activities predominantly undertaken outside formalized organizational settings (walking, swimming, cycling, running and bush walking), in an organized capacity (aerobics/fitness, tennis, netball and soccer) and in a mixture of settings (golf and aerobics/fitness).

The more precise and frequently collected source of participation data is the Exercise, Recreation and Sport Survey (ERASS), administered by SCORS since 2001, that 'collects information on the frequency, duration, nature and type of physical activities that are participated in for exercise, recreation or sport by persons aged 15 years and over' (SCORS 2009: 1). The most recent report is based on a sample of 17,293 conducted in 2008. Participation is defined as 'active playing participation and does not include coaching, refereeing and being a spectator, or activities related to work, household chores or gardening duties' (SCORS 2009: 4). The ERASS reports focus on those individuals classified as regular participants (participating three times per week or more).

The ERASS data for participation in organized physical activity (sport, exercise or other physical activity) at least once annually show that 40.8 per cent of Australians aged 15 years and over chose to do so. This quickly falls to 28 per cent for weekly participation and 12.1 per cent for three times a week or more, the rate considered to be the minimum to deliver physical health benefits. In general more males than females participate at every frequency level, and participation diminishes with age. Significantly, 59.2 per cent of Australians aged 15 years or older do not participate at all in formal organized settings. In contrast, participation in non-organized physical activity at least once annually is 72.5 per cent for Australians aged 15 years and over. This does not fall as dramatically for weekly participation (59.7 per cent), or for participation three times a week or more (39.8 per cent). It is worth noting that only 25.3 per cent of Australians participate at least once a year

Table 14.1 Top 10 sport and physical activities for participation at least once in 12 months 2005–2006

Sport	% Participation		
	Males	Females	Total
Walking	16.5	32.8	24.7
Aerobics/fitness	9.4	15.7	12.6
Swimming	8.0	10.0	9.0
Cycling	8.8	3.9	6.3
Golf	8.8	2.2	5.5
Tennis	4.9	4.7	4.8
Running	5.4	3.1	4.3
Bush walking	3.1	3.3	3.2
Netball	0.6	4.8	2.7
Soccer (outdoor)	3.9	1.3	2.6

Source: ABS (2007)

through a sport or recreation club or association. This figure falls to 16.9 per cent for weekly participation, and to 6.3 per cent for three times a week or more, the rate, as noted earlier, considered the minimum to deliver physical health benefits. Again, more males than females participate in club based physical activity.

Participation by males for club-based physical activity has increased from 5.9 per cent to 8.2 per cent over the period 2001 to 2008 (but actually diminished between 2001 and 2007), and for females from 3.6 per cent to 4.4 per cent over the same period. The ERASS data also show that while participation for both organized and non-organized physical activity increased over the period 2001 to 2008, the 'increase was greater for non-organized activity' (SCORS 2009: 22). In summary, the ERASS data show that while the level of regular participation in all forms of physical activity has increased between 2001 and 2008, the increase is almost entirely explained by an increase in participation in non-organized activities and participation in organized activities has remained relatively unchanged over the same period. Australians participate far more in non-organized physical activity than club-based physical activity and have been drifting toward this form of participation in increasing numbers over the last decade.

Government policy intervention in sport participation

As Hoye and Nicholson (2009) argued, Australian federal government involvement in sport prior to World War II was limited and sporadic. The majority of government investment in sport was undertaken by local governments providing sporting infrastructure such as sporting grounds and facilities, while some state governments provided assistance to water-safety and lifesaving bodies (Booth 2001). The period after the end of World War II and the early 1970s was 'characterized by the continued funding of travelling Australian teams, lifesaving grants and support of the physical fitness initiatives of the Commonwealth National Fitness Council' (Hoye and Nicholson 2009: 229). Evidence of substantive and meaningful government interest in influencing the nature and extent of Australians' participation in sport only emerged after the election of the Whitlam Labor government in 1972. Since then, seven key policy initiatives enacted by the federal government have focused in whole or in part on influencing the Australian public's level of participation in sport, each of which will be examined in turn.

Community sport facility funding

A fundamental turning point in the federal government's interest in Australians' participation in sport and physical activity was a policy speech given by the future Prime Minister Gough Whitlam in the campaign for the 1972 federal election. In that speech he declared that 'there is no greater social problem facing Australia than the good use of expanding leisure' and that the construction of community centres for cultural, artistic, educational and sporting activities would be a priority of a Labor government (Whitlam 1972). The election of the Whitlam Labor party to power in late 1972 resulted in a seismic shift in the way the federal government viewed sport, with three important initiatives established. First, a federal department with responsibility for tourism and recreation (including sport) was established, which immediately raised the profile and legitimacy of sport within government. Second, the Whitlam government commissioned two reports over their term of office that were instrumental in establishing future federal government policy for sport: the Bloomfield Report of 1973, which recommended a program focused on creating community recreation centres, raising community consciousness about the importance of general fitness and building Australia's elite performance; and the Coles Report released in 1975, which outlined the establishment of an elite sport institute to improve Australia's international sporting success.

The third initiative, and the most important in the context of influencing the level of participation in sport and physical activity by Australians, was the creation of a capital assistance program to provide grants for the construction of community sport facilities. The expenditure of federal government funds on local level community sport and recreation facilities fulfilled Whitlam's election promise and indicated, for the first time, the belief that government (especially at the federal level) was responsible for improving the recreational opportunities of its people (Shelton 1999). The dismissal of the Whitlam government in November 1975 and the subsequent rise to power of Malcolm Fraser's Liberal party resulted in a reversal of many of Whitlam's policies, including the abolishment of the federal Department of Tourism and Recreation and the eventual cancelling of the community recreation facility grants scheme. Green (2007: 926) argued that this change in government also represented the 'abandonment of a balance between elite development and provision for mass participation, which was indicative of increasing federal support for elite sport during the 1980s'.

'Life. Be In It' campaign

The second major federal government policy initiative in the area of sport participation had its origins at state level. In 1975, the Victorian Government Department of Sport and Recreation had established 'Life. Be In It', a social marketing campaign with three aims: (1) to increase the community's awareness of the benefits of physical activity and the dangers of a sedentary existence; (2) to illustrate how local facilities could be used for low-cost physical activities; and (3) to introduce sport to the public as a way of getting active (Stewart *et al.* 2004). The program was coordinated between federal and state governments through a national committee, with the federal government funding a national advertising campaign and state governments funding community activity events. Stewart *et al.* (2004: 52) concluded that 'while the programme successfully engineered a greater interest in outdoor recreation and sports, it only marginally increased the overall level of participation'. A government-wide expenditure review committee report recommended the program be discontinued in 1980, despite the high level of public awareness of the campaign and its central messages.

Aussie Sports program

The election of the Hawke Labor government in 1983 resulted in yet another fundamental shift in government policy toward sport with a more balanced view of supporting both elite sport and mass participation. While the Australian Institute of Sport (AIS) created during the Fraser era continued to enjoy funding support from the Hawke government, there were some steps made toward supporting community-level participation. During the first term of the Labor government, the ASC was established to coordinate sport policy, and a central plank of its community sport focus was the Aussie Sports program launched in 1986. Its main objective was to 'improve the quality, quantity and variety of sport available to Australian children' (Vamplew 1994: 97). Stewart *et al.* (2004: 60) argued that the program was 'developed partly in response to growing concerns that school sport had overemphasized the competitive nature of sport, rather than elements of play, enjoyment, self-expression and individual difference'. Oakley (1999) noted that there was also concern that the levels of participation in sport among children had fallen during the 1970s and 1980s and the Aussie Sports program was (in part) designed to address this decline.

The program focused on primary school students in years 4 to 6, and sought to include coaches from community sport organizations and teachers as a way of fostering links between schools and community sport clubs. A number of 'branded' programs operated under the Aussie Sports banner including Sportstart, Sport It!, Ready Set Go!, Sport Search, Active Girls, Sportsfun, and Challenge, Achievement and Pathways in Sport (Stewart *et al.* 2004). The program philosophy was to make sport fun, and thus many traditional sports were modified to minimize 'differences in height, weight and gender, and emphasized the development of sporting and motor skills in a non-threatening sport environment' (Stewart *et al.* 2004: 60). In 1988 the program was extended to secondary school children and delivered through state government departments of sport and recreation coordinated through the ASC. The impact of the Aussie Sports program in terms of increasing participation rates was limited. During the period 1985 to 2001 sport participation rates only increased marginally (Stewart *et al.* 2004). While the program may not have increased the quantity of participants in sport, the program was widely considered to be successful in improving the quality of sport experiences for participants.

Inquiry into PE and sport in schools

Even while the Aussie Sports program was running, there was 'growing concern about the declining status of sport in schools' (Stewart *et al.* 2004: 68). A 1992 report into physical education and sport in schools commissioned by the federal government, known as the Crowley Report, documented the decline in quality and quantity of physical education and sport experienced by children in Australian schools. Three reasons for this decline were identified: (1) a reduction in the number of qualified physical education teachers; (2) the reduction in time allocated to physical education relative to other aspects of school curriculum; and (3) the lack of a clear policy advocating the benefits of physical education for school-aged children. The report put forward several solutions to address these problems including designing a national PE curriculum, investing in training and recruiting more PE teachers, establishing stronger links between schools and clubs, and focusing on skill development in PE rather than competitive sport. Ironically, the report warned that the Aussie Sports program should not be viewed as a solution or a replacement for PE curriculum. However, Houlihan (1997) noted that the Aussie Sports program, while being successful in its own right, did contribute to the reduction of traditional PE in Australian schools. So while the Crowley Report did not lead to any substantial change in sport policy or increase in sports participation, it highlighted at least that the federal government was cognisant of the issues around PE in schools and the impacts that a reduction in PE were having on the youth of Australia.

Active Australia

The fifth federal government policy initiative associated with sports participation was developed by the Howard Liberal government shortly after it came to power in 1996 and was grandly labelled Active Australia: A National Participation Framework. It represented the most comprehensive effort by an Australian federal government to increase participation in all forms of physical activity, including sport. Active Australia was designed to have all Australians 'actively involved in sport, community recreation, fitness, outdoor recreation and other physical activities' (ASC 1997: 5). Previous policy attempts to influence participation rates were confined to specific types of activity or organizational settings such as schools or community clubs, or were media campaigns targeted toward the general population. Active Australia promised something different in that it was designed to integrate the policy areas of sport, recreation and health. The main federal government policy agencies were the ASC, the Department of Health and the Department of Industry, Science and Resources with the ASC taking the lead role. Active Australia had three goals: 'to increase and enhance life-long participation; to realize the social health and economic benefits of participation; and to develop quality infrastructure, opportunities and services to support participation' (Stewart *et al.* 2004: 77).

At the core of the Active Australia program was assistance for three types of networks that offered opportunities to participate in either sport, community recreation, fitness, or outdoor recreation and leisure settings: schools, local government organizations and approved providers. The Schools network was a revised version of the Aussie Sports program and was designed to deliver sport and physical activity opportunities that were not focused on competition, were safe and rewarding and had some links with other local community organizations. The Local Government network was designed to support local government to deliver sport and recreation opportunities through their existing facilities and programs, and to help them forge links between schools, clubs and other community organizations. The Provider network was focused on improving the standard of management and service delivery among sport, recreation and fitness-oriented organizations, both nonprofit and commercial. The central idea was that by conforming to a model of service provision and set of quality standards, providers could display the Active Australia logo and attract more participants.

The Active Australia program did result in an increased awareness among the public of the need to participate in some form of physical activity. Within four years of the program starting some 2,000 clubs, approximately 2,100 schools and

20 per cent of local governments in Australia had joined one of the Active Australia networks. However, as Stewart *et al.* (2004) pointed out, the actual participation rate of Australian adults in sport and physical activity fell by 4 per cent during this time. While the program was well intentioned, it had very little impact on increasing, or even maintaining, community participation levels. This failure to deliver meaningful improvements in participation led (in part) to the winding down of the Active Australia program after the Sydney Olympics and the creation of a more structured Australian sport policy.

Backing Australia's Sporting Ability

The sixth federal government policy initiative targeting sport participation was the development of the Backing Australia's Sporting Ability (BASA) policy in 2001 that set a new direction for the ASC and Australian sport (Commonwealth of Australia 2001). The development of BASA represented a shift in federal government policy concerning participation, away from the inclusive Active Australia program focused on sport, recreation and health and towards a more targeted approach concerned to increase participation solely through organized sport. Increasing participation in sport was now part of a four-pronged sport policy which aimed to maintain elite performance, ensure a drug-free sport environment, improve the governance and management of Australian sport organizations, and increase participation in organized sport. The decision to focus on club-based sport participation without regard to participation in unstructured or informal physical activities was made despite a recommendation by the Sport 2000 Taskforce to increase government expenditure on all forms of participation activities.

Since 2001, the ASC has almost exclusively focused on organized competitive sport as the setting through which it attempts to increase participation levels among Australians. Indeed, it set the lofty target of securing one million more sport participants between 2001 and 2005 (ASC 2002: 6). The Targeted Sports Participation Growth (TSPG) program was the key initiative designed to deliver this increase in participation, described by Stewart *et al.* (2004: 111) as representing a 'strategic move towards the implementation of activities and programmes that can be evaluated more easily and effectively'. The TSPG was essentially the funding of a select number of sports with solid club infrastructures to assist them create partnerships with the business sector to develop a sustainable model to grow registered membership of their clubs and associations. The initial round of TSPG funding of $AUD11.5 million over three years targeted 21 sports to support them to run programs in three categories: junior clinics that were usually short term and focused on skill development and promotion of the sport; junior school programs designed to deliver outcomes similar to junior clinics but during school time; and adult member programs focused on getting people into traditional competitive sport opportunities.

Green (2007: 929) made some interesting observations of the approach of Athletics Australia to delivering an increase in registered participants by targeting out-of-stadium events (fun runs, road races, jogging events, etc.) to secure more registered participants: 'Arguably, in this respect, both Athletics Australia and the

ASC are culpable of disingenuous policy development.' Green surmised that such approaches would certainly deliver the funding outcomes of increased membership registrations but not any real increase in actual participation levels. The participation data presented earlier in this chapter certainly seems to indicate that the planned increase of one million registered participants was either not achieved, or if it was, it was merely a paper figure unrelated to actual participation levels of Australians in organized sport.

Building Australian Communities through Sport

The final federal government policy initiative in the area of sports participation was the reframing of BASA into the 2004 policy Building Australian Communities through Sport (BACS) that formed the basis for the incumbent Liberal party's election platform in the lead-up the 2004 election. The introduction of BACS after the Liberal party's election success led to two significant changes in how the federal government and its lead agency, the ASC, dealt with the issue of sport participation. First, the ASC from that point was charged with achieving two outcomes: an effective national sports system that offers improved participation in quality sports activities and excellence in sports performances by Australians (ASC 2004), although there continued to be a significant imbalance between the funding for participation initiatives relative to elite sport. Second, the ASC introduced the Active Afterschool Communities Program (AACP), initially as a complementary program to the TSPG but eventually its replacement as the core participation initiative. The AACP provides physical activity participation opportunities to young people between the hours of 3:00pm and 5:30pm on school days. The most recent ASC Strategic Plan (2006–09) makes no mention of the TSPG and importantly makes the following statement:

> The Australian Sports Commission and its partners recognize that it is essential to deliver sport and physical activity programs that are easily accessible by children. The ideal solution would be to ensure the effective delivery of physical education classes in primary schools during school hours using specialist physical education teachers. However, given the difficulty in establishing a national approach to health and physical education in schools, the out of school hours time slot of 3.00pm to 5.30pm has provided an opportunity for the Australian Sports Commission to access a greater number of young people and provide them with the opportunity to participate in quality physical activity programs. The innovative Active Afterschool Communities program will continue to be rolled out with the goal of reaching all Australian primary school-aged children.
>
> (ASC 2006b: 7)

In the latter half of 2009, it appears that the AACP has been successful in delivering physical activity opportunities to school-aged children. However, it is unknown whether such experiences will result in children seeking to take up formal organized sport participation opportunities outside of this setting and venture into Australia's community sport clubs to become long-term participants.

Toward a health agenda

The most recent development in the area has been the transfer of sport to the health and ageing portfolio by the newly elected Rudd Labor government in late 2007, an unsurprising development given that the Labor party's 2007 election platform considered sport and recreation as components of a broader health system that could improve the health and well-being of Australians. Throughout 2008 and most of 2009 the federal government engaged in an extensive review and public consultation process to establish a new Australian sport policy. The discussion paper developed as part of this process, *Australian Sport: Emerging Challenges, New Directions*, released in May 2008, claimed that 'in recent times, junior and community sport has been approached with a focus, almost exclusively, on increasing the pool from which our elite athletes can be drawn' and that 'whereas early federal sports policy had a clear focus on community physical activity and "Life. Be In It" style programs, this has declined over time to become virtually non-existent' (Commonwealth of Australia 2008: 5). These comments suggest that the new sport policy may well redress the imbalance between elite and mass participation funding that has been perpetuated by successive federal governments of both major parties since the early 1980s.

Policy success?

In an assessment of the efficacy of federal government policy efforts to increase participation levels in sport and physical activity, we can make several observations. First, the data from both the ABS and the ERASS show that while the level of regular participation in all forms of physical activity has increased slightly between 2001 and 2008, the increase is almost entirely explained by an increase in participation in non-organized activities, and participation in organized activities has remained relatively unchanged over the same period. The discussion paper on the future of Australian sport released in May 2008 by the Rudd Labor government cited some damning statistics:

> In 2004–05, 70 per cent of Australians aged 15 years and over were classified as sedentary or having low exercise levels. No improvements have been seen since exercise levels were measured in 1995. These low exercise levels have been a major contributor to Australia's current status as one of the world's most overweight developed nations. Over a 15 year period, from 1989–90 to 2004–05, the proportion of obese adults in Australia has doubled (from 9 per cent to 18 per cent) . . . At the community level, participation in sport and local activities is declining. In the past decade, time spent by Australians on sport and outdoor activity decreased on average by nearly an hour a week, while time spent on activities such as watching television and using the Internet increased by an hour. In 2005–06, approximately 5.5 million people reported that they did not participate in any sports or physical recreation activities of any kind over the preceding year.
>
> (Commonwealth of Australia 2008: 5–6)

It is clear that Australians participate far more in non-organized physical activity than club-based sport and have been drifting toward this form of participation in increasing numbers over the last decade, but the overall level of participation in any form of physical activity is far too low.

The second observation we can make is that the challenges to increasing participation in community sport have been identified, most recently by the ASC in their current strategic plan (ASC 2006b: 5):

- Societal change – changing work patterns, including among young people, mean that traditional sports delivery structures may no longer appeal to, or coincide with the availability of, potential participants.
- Generational change – does sport address the interests, expectations and psyche of all segments of the population, especially Generation X and the emerging Generation Y (or Generation C as some are calling it in response to the computer age)? Are cross-generational differences in attitude, culture and commitment accommodated in our sports delivery system?
- Increasing rates of obesity – an estimated 7 million adult Australians are overweight or obese and, in particular, an estimated one in five (or 22 per cent) of Australian children aged between 2 and 17 years old are considered to be overweight or obese.
- Declining motor skill development in children – the basic motor skill competencies of Australian children have dropped significantly in recent times, coinciding with the loss of sport from the school curriculum and children's increasingly sedentary recreational activities. Do we still want our children to be able to run, catch and swim, and learn valuable social skills from team and individual sporting activity?
- Community support for traditional sport – volunteers, the lifeblood of community sport, are becoming increasingly difficult to attract and retain.

Third, we note that the ASC (2006b: 7), as the lead policy agency in this area, has stated:

> the three essential elements to be considered in delivering an effective national system with the objective of increasing participation rates in organized sport are the return of sport and structured physical activity opportunities in all Australian schools; making sport relevant, accessible and available to young people and their lifestyles in the twenty-first century; and crossing the traditional boundaries and structures of sport to embrace innovative approaches to delivery.

Our fourth observation is that the location of sport within the machinery of government has hampered the development of a consistent effective policy on sport participation that addresses the challenges noted above and that has had all three of those essential elements present. Table 14.2 outlines the allocation of departments and ministries responsible for sport since 1983. The placement of sport within the health and ageing portfolio by the current Rudd Labor government firmly positions sport as part of an overall health agenda for the first time.

The fifth observation we can make is that federal government policy has shifted from an emphasis on building spaces and facilities (community facility program), to mass media campaigns (Life. Be In It), to an emphasis on school-based programs

Table 14.2 Departments and ministries responsible for Australian sport policy, 1983–2008

Date	Department	Ministry
1983–1987	Sport, Recreation and Tourism	Sport, Recreation and Tourism
1987–1993	Arts, Sport, the Environment, Tourism and Territories	Arts, Sport, the Environment, Tourism and Territories
1993–1996	Environment, Sport and Territories	Sport and Territories
1996–1998	Environment	Sport, Territories and Local Government
1998–2001	Industry, Science and Resources	Sport and Tourism
2001–2007	Communications, Information Technology and the Arts	Arts and Sport
2007–	Health and Ageing	Youth and Sport

Source: Parliament of the Commonwealth of Australia (2008b)

(Aussie Sports, AACP, and an inquiry into PE and sport in schools), to club-based programs (TSPG), and an integrated approach via Active Australia. The majority of these have targeted school-aged children rather than adults and most have only lasted three to four years before being curtailed or discontinued altogether. While some of this can be attributed to changes of government, it also suggests a rather short-term approach to addressing what appear to be fundamental issues of providing adequate and appropriate PE to all children, the nature of how sport is provided to Australians and how the Australian sport system is structured.

Allied to this is our final observation – the continuing tension between elite and participation funding has resulted in elite sport consistently receiving a far greater portion of federal government funding than community sport. The imbalance in funding between these two areas is highlighted in Table 14.3 that outlines the funding allocations within the ASC budget between the two areas for the period 2003 to 2008. As Green and Houlihan (2005: 38) noted, 'any examination of Australian public [sport] policy since the mid-1970s shows an apparent reluctance to address both policy goals with equal commitment'.

The imbalance in allocation of funding to sports with varying levels of participation is also worth noting. Table 14.4 lists the funding allocations by the ASC for the top 10 funded NSOs for 2005–06. Not surprisingly they are all Olympic sports. The table illustrates that sports such as rowing and hockey, with very low participation rates (0.3 per cent and 0.5 per cent respectively), receive far greater

Table 14.3 Australian Sports Commission annual allocations, 2003/4–2008/9 ($million)

	2003/4	2004/5	2005/6	2006/7	2007/8	2008/9
Outcome 1*	27,265	30,524	57,666	66,971	72,895	78,236
Outcome 2*	95,207	96,986	110,965	125,457	131,514	141,549
Total	122,472	127,510	168,631	192,428	204,409	219,785

* Outcome 1: An effective national sports system that offers improved participation in quality sports activities by Australians; Outcome 2: Excellence in sports performances by Australians.

Source: Parliament of the Commonwealth of Australia (2008a, 2007, 2006, 2005, 2004, 2003).

Note: The figures within the table only relate to government allocations and do not include Australian Sports Commission revenue from other sources, such as the sale of services and products, nor do they include cash reserves.

Table 14.4 Top 10* national sport organization funding support and national participation rates, 2005–06

Sport	Elite $ million**	Total $ million	Participation %
Soccer	2.56	5.91	2.6
Swimming	5.14	5.46	9.0
Rowing	5.11	5.19	0.3
Cycling	4.89	5.06	6.3
Hockey	4.46	4.79	0.5
Athletics	4.56	4.77	0.3
Basketball	3.66	4.01	2.1
Sailing	3.02	3.16	0.6
Canoeing	2.17	2.28	0.4
Volleyball	1.85	1.96	0.9

* The top 10 national sport organizations based on total funding in the 2005–06 year.
** The 'Elite' figure has been calculated by adding the sport's Australian Institute of Sport and high performance allocations.

Sources: ABS (2007) and ASC (2006a)

funding than netball (the top ranked sport for participation by women with a 3.2 per cent participation rate) purely because they offer Australia strong medal hopes in Commonwealth and Olympic Games.

Green and Houlihan (2005: 180) concluded that in the context of such a funding imbalance, NSOs tend to insulate their elite programs from grass roots members, which may exacerbate tension 'between grass roots members and clubs on the one hand and elite athletes and training centres on the other', and also create difficulties in trying to 'balance elite achievement objectives with those associated with mass participation'. They also concluded that 'elite sport development and achievement on the one hand and mass participation and club development on the other are deeply incompatible functions within the policy frameworks current in Australia' (Green and Houlihan 2005: 189).

Together, these six observations lead us to conclude that the various policies enacted to address participation levels in organized sport and other forms of physical activity in Australia have been unsuccessful, especially in comparison to elite sport achievement and outcomes for Australian sport over the last three decades. While Australians are keen sport watchers, they do not exhibit the same enthusiasm for active participation in organized sport, or indeed other forms of physical activity. Addressing this imbalance will require a comprehensive policy that attacks the recurring issues of providing an adequate amount of appropriately designed PE curriculum to all children, reconfiguring the nature of the sport experience on offer to Australians of all ages (not just school age children), and developing an efficient and effective structure for the Australian sport delivery system.

References

Australian Bureau of Statistics (2007) *Participation in Sports and Physical Recreation 2005–2006 (Cat. 4177.0)*, Canberra: Australian Bureau of Statistics.
Australian Bureau of Statistics (2008) *Sport and Recreation: A Statistical Overview (Cat. 4156.0) Edition 2*, Canberra: Australian Bureau of Statistics.

Australian Sports Commission (1997) *Active Australia: A National Participation Framework*, Canberra: Australian Sports Commission.

Australian Sports Commission (2002) *Strategic Plan: 2002–2005*, Canberra: Australian Sports Commission.

Australian Sports Commission (2006a) *Annual Report: 2005–2006*, Canberra: Australian Sports Commission.

Australian Sports Commission (2006b) *Strategic Plan: 2006–2009*, Canberra: Australian Sports Commission.

Booth, D. (2001) *Australian Beach Cultures: The History of Sun, Sand and Surf*, London: Frank Cass.

Cashman, R. (1995) *Paradise of sport*, Melbourne: Oxford University Press.

Commonwealth of Australia (2001) *Backing Australia's Sporting Ability: A More Active Australia*, Canberra: Australian Government Printing Service.

Commonwealth of Australia (2008) *Australian Sport: Emerging Challenges, New Directions*, Canberra: Australian Government Printing Service.

Green, M. (2007) 'Olympic glory or grass roots development? Sport policy priorities in Australia, Canada and the United Kingdom, 1960–2006', *International Journal of the History of Sport*, 24(7): 921–953.

Green, M. and Houlihan, B. (2005) *Elite Sport Development: Policy Learning and Political Priorities*, London: Routledge.

Houlihan, B. (1997) *Sport Policy and Politics: A Comparative Analysis*, London: Routledge.

Hoye, R. (2005) 'Professional sport in Australia and New Zealand: An introduction to the special issue', *Sport Management Review*, 8: 89–94.

Hoye, R. and Nicholson, M. (2009) 'Australia', *International Journal of Sport Policy*, 1(2): 229–240.

Oakley, R. (1999) *Shaping Up: A Review of Commonwealth Involvement in Sport and Recreation*, Canberra: Australian Sports Commission.

Parliament of the Commonwealth of Australia (2003) *Appropriation (Parliamentary Departments) Bill (No. 1) 2003–2004*.

Parliament of the Commonwealth of Australia (2004) *Appropriation (Parliamentary Departments) Bill (No. 1) 2004–2005*.

Parliament of the Commonwealth of Australia (2005) *Appropriation (Parliamentary Departments) Bill (No. 1) 2005–2006*.

Parliament of the Commonwealth of Australia (2006) *Appropriation (Parliamentary Departments) Bill (No. 1) 2006–2007*.

Parliament of the Commonwealth of Australia (2007) *Appropriation (Parliamentary Departments) Bill (No. 1) 2007–2008*.

Parliament of the Commonwealth of Australia (2008a) *Appropriation (Parliamentary Departments) Bill (No. 1) 2008–2009*.

Parliament of the Commonwealth of Australia (2008b) *Parliamentary Handbook of the Commonwealth of Australia*. http://www.aph.gov.au/library/handbook/historical/ministries/index.htm (accessed 29 August 2008).

Shelton, J. (1999) '"Life be in it": From incrementalism to sharp policy reversals'. Unpublished MA thesis, The University of Melbourne.

Standing Committee on Recreation and Sport (2009) *Participation in Exercise, Recreation and Sport Annual Report 2008*, Canberra: Australian Sports Commission.

Stewart, B., Nicholson, M., Smith, A.C.T. and Westerbeek, H. (2004) *Australian Sport: Better by Design? The Evolution of Australian Sport Policy*, London: Routledge.

Vamplew, W. (1994) *The Oxford Companion to Australian Sport*, Melbourne: Oxford University Press.

Whitlam, G. (1972) *It's Time for Leadership*. http://whitlamdismissal.com/speeches/72–11–13_it's-time.shtml (accessed 15 August 2009).

15 New Zealand

Mike Sam

Though having a population of only 4 million, New Zealand (also called *Aotearoa* or 'land of the long white cloud') has long prided itself on its sporting culture. Geographically, the country consists of two islands situated in the South Pacific, with the larger, significantly less populous 'mainland' lying to the south. While the climate of New Zealand varies greatly (according to latitude, proximity to the coast, etc.), it is generally speaking a temperate climate, allowing for outdoor (field-based) sport participation throughout the year.

Details of New Zealand's colonial past can be found elsewhere, but for the purposes of this chapter it is important to note that the two founding people consist of indigenous Māori and European settlers of mostly British, Irish and Scottish descent (collectively called Pākehā). As a former British colony, New Zealand inherited a Westminster (parliamentary) system of government. It is a unitary state, having no powers enshrined in its constitution for local and regional government (Shaw and Eichbaum 2005). Despite this, local governments, while having very little to do with sport programs directly, have been the principal financial pillar in New Zealand sport through their development of sport facilities.

The structure of sport in New Zealand

New Zealand sport operates predominantly through a club system, a collection of small non-profit societies whose purposes are to provide competition structures and athlete development programs, and coach and official training opportunities. Club development in sports like football, bowls and rugby has occurred over long periods of time for the purposes of competition against clubs in the same area. In many cases, sport clubs also own and maintain their own facilities including equipment, changing rooms, and spaces for social gatherings.

A second layer of mass sport delivery consists of regional sport trusts and regional sporting bodies, organizations designed to govern sport in their respective jurisdictions. Regional sport trusts (RSTs) have strong links with both central and local levels of government. Developed in the mid 1980s and supported by the central sport agency at the time (Hillary Commission for Sport and Recreation), these autonomous bodies now operate with revenues from government contracts (e.g. Active Communities Programme), local government grants, community trust funds and commercial sponsorships. RSTs are principally facilitators in the system (providing advice and consultation for local and regional clubs), though they also employ sport-specific development officers. Community Trusts and foundations are also a key institution in sport delivery. These organizations redistribute profits from operating 'pokie' (gambling) machines, the largest of which contributes nearly $100 million to sport each year.

National sport organizations (NSOs) are considered the owners of their codes and are responsible for national events and the selection of national teams. They also act as a clearing house for any developments in their respective sports such as the transmission of new rules or reforms from international bodies. Because of their network of affiliated national bodies and their formalized annual reporting, NSOs are the principal providers of sport participation data in New Zealand.

The cultural context of New Zealand sport

As with nearly every Western nation, New Zealanders believe that sport is part of their national identity. There is good reason for this. By the late nineteenth century, sports like rugby, football, cricket, hockey and golf were some of the key cultural institutions transferred from Britain (Thomson and Sim 2007). As early as 1914, sport became firmly established as a compulsory part of the school curriculum largely due to its perceived role in character building and developing teamwork, cooperation and discipline. Rugby in particular became the sport for the common man because it embodied particular values relating to mateship, courage, egalitarianism and masculinity (Phillips 1996). While sporting ties with Apartheid South Africa in the 1970s and 1980s tarnished rugby's place in New Zealand society, the nation's passion for the sport remains. As Thomson and Sim (2007: 123) suggested,

> Clearly, rugby and sport in general, continue to hold a prominent place in New Zealand society, even if the emphasis with the growing significance of professional sport has been on the consumption of sport, rather than the earlier focus on participation. Most critics would seem to agree that rugby has maintained its place as the 'national game', but other sports and leisure activities have become much more significant.

Indeed, the 1980s brought into view a larger variety of sports and physical pursuits such as aerobics and squash that challenged the dominance of traditional clubs. 'Pay-for-play' became an appealing option for those wanting to play sport without the need for membership structures. Thus in addition to the wide variety of fitness opportunities (such as gyms, aqua-aerobics, etc.), commercialized sport leagues, tournaments and events are now integrated throughout the New Zealand sport landscape.

Building on the work of Stewart (1990), Collins *et al.* (2007) noted a growing fascination with multi-sport pursuits (e.g. triathlon) and an increased interest in adventure racing (sometimes called 'extreme' sports because of their sustained physical demands). Indeed the popularity of events like the 'Coast to Coast' and the 'Southern Traverse' are testament to the affinity of commercial interests with competitions that generate both sport tourism and the consumption of expensive, specialist equipment such as bikes, wetsuits, kayaks, etc. (Collins *et al.* 2007).

Taken together, these commercial shifts have had a profound impact on the club system. In attempting to capture the implications for such a trend, the Hillary Commission (the state agency responsible for sport from 1987 to 2001) published a discussion document speculating on the 'future marketing environment' of the sport sector at the turn of the century. The authors warned,

> Organisations offering sport and active leisure opportunities must not assume they have a captive market. They have to earn people's commitment of inter-est, time and money with service and attention to fulfilling needs. And it has to be fast. People (rightly or wrongly) expect professional level services, even from volunteers. Meeting this standard requires a different mindset and skill set. This is lifestyle marketing. Our sector has a competency issue if we are to meet this challenge.
>
> (Hillary Commission 2000b)

Nearly ten years later, the erosion of the traditional sport club remains one of the key issues for SPARC (the Crown agency responsible for sport since 2001). On the subject of attracting new members, the Chief Executive of Bowls NZ observed that

> The traditional attachment of a club through formal membership lines is out of date. Future growth will be around pay-to-play entertainment options which will see growth in smart clubs and a continued decline in others. MIB [a new program aimed at the casual user] meets the criteria of introducing new people to our sport as an entertainment option without strings attached.
>
> (SPARC 2009:7)

In this view, organized sport is ever more associated with consumption, a point perhaps unsurprising in light of other contemporary changes in New Zealand. The advent of Rupert Murdoch's Sky television contract for example, creating professional rugby almost overnight, has had flow-on effects for other codes such as cricket, netball and basketball, all of which have developed professional national or trans-national leagues. Even though there seems to be little evidence that the 'trickle down' of new sources of commercial revenue has had any impact on grassroots participation, one cannot downplay the significance of this increased visibility. Indeed, football in the 1980s and basketball in the late 1990s experienced unprecedented interest as a result of televised international competitions. More recently, New Zealand's national governing body for cricket reported record par-ticipation numbers owing to several factors, including a successful international campaign and its visibility in media (Cricket NZ 2009). However, it remains to be seen whether the organizational and facility capacities of local clubs can cope with (and indeed build on) these temporary or fleeting bursts in interest.

Organized sport participation

Overall, the findings from statistical data are rather inconclusive on the status of sport participation in New Zealand. This is due to the way in which population surveys are designed. The aggregation of data related to activities like walking and gardening with organized sport makes it difficult to gain a picture of participation among particular demographic segments of the population (such as Masters-aged athletes) and whether they are increasing, maintaining or declining in their participation levels in sport over time. All that can be gleaned from SPARC's latest data is that physical activity levels remain relatively unchanged since 2001 (SPARC 2008). Such findings may be disappointing for government given that since 2001 SPARC's funding in the wider area (for a combination of elite, sport participation and physical activity objectives) has tripled and it would like to see a clear return on this increased investment.

Participation figures in Table 15.1 are derived from a survey of adult respondents (16 and over) who stated that they participated in these sports at least once in the last 12 months. The main sports in New Zealand in terms of general participation have remained relatively stable since 2001 (golf being the most popular). From SPARC's perspective, sport participation statistics have become less important as a criterion for NSO funding, owing to the potential for NSOs to use single events to show large gains that do not necessarily reflect sustained improvements over time. In the 1990s, for example, NZ Touch Rugby claimed an explosion in participation levels with the aid of pay-for-play tournament registrations. While no doubt touch rugby saw a dramatic increase in interest, such figures made it difficult to determine the level of sustained participation. Thus, given the rather all-encompassing (and vague) definition of 'participation', it is perhaps more fruitful

Table 15.1 Participation and club membership numbers[a] for top 10 NZ sports

Sport/NSO	2000/2001		2007/2008	
	Participation	*Club membership*[b]	*Participation*	*Club membership*[c]
Golf/New Zealand Golf	502,000	128,860	416,223	128,965
Tennis/New Zealand Tennis	317,900	42,526	304,675	42,281
Rugby/New Zealand Rugby[d]	228,100	160,118	189,661	152,787
Cricket/New Zealand Cricket	224,900	82,906	237,965	100,348
Netball/Netball New Zealand	184,600	120,440	209,769	138,510
Soccer/New Zealand Soccer	143,300	105,023	227,265	128,000[e]
Touch Rugby/Touch New Zealand	260,900	59,399	219,952	
Basketball/Basketball New Zealand	167,300	25,845	209,428	
Volleyball/Volleyball New Zealand	115,700	22,280	148,496	
Squash/Squash New Zealand	130,900	33,936	123,443	

Notes

a It is important to note that a person may be a member of more than one sporting club.

b Membership data for 2000/2001 was obtained through SPARC's website: http://www.sparc.org.nz/page-5b350e5e-b899-4139-8d2c-a4c42d5521d1.aspx.

c Membership data for 2007/2008 was obtained through each individual NSO's current annual report.

d According to SPARC's 2009 review of rugby league, the methodology for collecting participation/membership figures up until 2002 was flawed with a number of players being double counted, as well as the team average multiplier being overly generous.

e Membership data for NZ Soccer was taken from SPARC's formal review document of rugby league.

to take note of club memberships, as these suggest a more sustained commitment to organized sport participation.

There have been notable increases in club memberships in football, netball and cricket since 2001/02, though the meaning of such increases is also difficult to interpret since 'memberships' can include officials, volunteers, fans, parents of players, etc. As well, membership statistics may be misleading on the basis that individuals can hold memberships at several clubs. Notwithstanding the limits of these figures (such measurement errors cut across all sports), there appears to be a trend towards greater involvement in organized team sports. One possible explanation for this is that team sports are more likely to be supported within schools. Indeed, the entrenchment of sport coordinators (see next section) as a result of Hillary Commission/SPARC programs has likely had a significant impact on maintaining interschool competition at both recreational and competitive levels. This, in conjunction with Regional Sport Trusts focusing heavily on youth sport (by building links between schools and clubs through programs like 'SportForce'), might also explain increases in these sports.

However, given SPARC's most recent statistics indicating little change in overall physical activity among adults, the membership increases in football, netball and cricket may be equally explained by either declines in other codes or the reporting requirements of those needing to meet performance targets (such as sport development officers). It is interesting, for example, that during the 2001–08 period, Cricket NZ reported a 21 per cent *increase* in club membership while the New Zealand Secondary Schools Sports Council reported a 26 per cent *decrease* in students representing their schools in that sport. While one might speculate that the figures are directly linked, these data makes it difficult to ascertain overall participation trends, even more so when the reported changes are small (less than 5 per cent). Taken together, the aggregation of sport with physical activity participation data and the overlaps between casual sport participation, club-based and school sport make it difficult to inform future policies and program interventions.

Government intervention

Despite the dominance of sport in New Zealand's historical landscape, sport remained at the fringes of government policy through most of the last century. New Zealand's first legislation in the area, the Physical Welfare and Recreation Act, became law in 1937. From the outset, arguments to support sport and recreation policy in New Zealand relied on both utilitarian rationales and rhetorical self-evident truths. Still, the Physical Welfare and Recreation Act complemented other governmental initiatives of that period, including the world's first national health service (Rudd 1997). But the apparent lack of clear direction and leadership along with the advent of World War II contributed to the program's eventual demise (Stothart 1978). Central government rationalized its reduced funding to sport and recreation based on (a) a prevailing sense that market forces could adequately manage sport and (b) its findings of ineffective administrative structures (Buchanan 1978; Church 1990).

Shortly following the Labour Party's victory in 1972 and coinciding with a dramatic increase in social welfare expenditure (Rudd 1997), the government passed the Recreation and Sport Act. Through a new Ministry, funds were directed to local government authorities for coaching programs as well as national and international events (Stothart 1980). The Council for Recreation and Sport, though established primarily for advisory purposes, began to distribute funds for its own programs. Campaigns such as 'Come Alive' and 'Have-A-Go' were initiated to increase the recreational activity levels of New Zealanders (Hindson *et al.* 1994). The first of these was short-lived. After the National Party's election victory in 1975, the government abolished the 'Come Alive' campaign because of its ties with the former Labour Party (Stothart 1980).[1]

The 1972 legislation certainly had its effects, not least of which was that it institutionalized sport within the political system. Indeed, following the 1974 Commonwealth Games held in Christchurch, the Ministry proposed plans for developing large regional sports and recreation complexes based on those developed in that city (Cushman and Cushman 1980). The early years thus stirred interest in recreation and sport as a policy domain. Consequently, documents such as the New Zealand Recreation Survey (1974–75) were commissioned and a more systematic discussion of issues could be carried out at Council-sponsored conferences.

The ideological shift that occurred after 1984 changed New Zealand's economic and social environments, inspiring more utilitarian rationales for government involvement in areas of social policy including sport and recreation. Amidst growing concerns over duplication of services within government structures, both sport and recreation became the subject of independent departmental reviews.[2] Labour appointed the Sports Development Inquiry Committee, ultimately paving the way for the abolishment of existing structures.

The 1985 Inquiry report (called 'Sport on the Move') cited several problems within sport – low levels of skill and fitness of New Zealand's youth and low quality of coaching, as well as issues of doping, violence, the paucity of women in sport and the problems of access for the disabled and low-income groups. As the ethos of individual responsibility grew, legislation such as the 1973 Recreation and Sport Act (with its main emphasis on the health of New Zealanders) seemed out of touch with public sentiment and new-right political doctrines. Benefits such as enjoyment, self-esteem and sense of achievement were paramount and appeared throughout 'Sport on the Move' as inherent rationales for continued government involvement. Yet just the same, the Inquiry justified governmental interest in sport because of its ties with education, health and national identity. It reasoned that the 'total sports environment is far wider than the direct concerns of sports bodies individually or collectively and reaches into the education system, local authorities, health and welfare sectors' (Sports Development Inquiry Committee 1985:27).

Associated with this new ethos, the Committee cited a 'divisiveness creeping into sport' caused by the 'pressures of personal gain, commercial interest and political conflicts' (Sports Development Inquiry Committee 1985). The Committee astutely noted the necessary trade-offs sport organizations would need to make – increased resources from government for loss of control or autonomy (p. 27). Indeed, the scale of government intervention in sport had already been called into question by some powerful factions, most notably the New Zealand Sports Foundation (an independent trust created to fund elite athletes), which believed that any new structures 'should be independent of all sports organizations, the government and the public service' (p. 31). Supporting these sentiments, the Inquiry maintained that sport should remain free of interference in such a way that funding would not 'disrupt the independent spirit and motivation of sportsmen and women and their club structure' (p. 66).

A significant finding of the Inquiry was that advertising campaigns such as 'Come Alive' could stimulate participation levels. Thus by 1990, the National Party's policy embraced leisure education – i.e. efforts to 'make people aware of themselves and their health – and aware of the resources available to them' (Bolger 1991:12). At the conclusion of its year-long tenure, the Inquiry recommended that the Recreation and Sport Act (1973) be repealed and that a new arm's-length body be put in place to administer sport. The new quasi-autonomous non-government organization, later renamed the Hillary Commission for Recreation and Sport, emerged from 1987 onwards as a highly visible institution in New Zealand sport.[3]

The Hillary Commission for Sport and Recreation (1987–2001)

Following the Labour Party's lead in 1984, the ideas of efficiency, consumer-choice and user-pays became dominant rationales for reorganizing government departments along corporate lines (Shirley 1990). Accordingly, the success of these ideas meant they would be transplanted in newly created state agencies such as the Hillary Commission. Such trends merely reinforced the existing emphasis on efficiency in sport administration where grants to organizations were either delayed or withdrawn depending on the soundness of their management practices (Stothart 2000).

In the following years, the Hillary Commission's power and influence in New Zealand sport expanded. Funding for the Hillary Commission nearly doubled after the first year, allowing it to establish a number of new programs aimed at increasing the participation of women, older adults, Māori and people with disabilities (Collins and Stuart 1994). Despite the Commission's relatively small financial contribution to sport and recreation (e.g. compared to local governments, other government departments and community trusts), the organization maintained a powerful presence at all levels in the sector, from club to elite. Its ascendancy was partly due to the Commission's repeated patterns of interaction with other organizations – through, for example, funding relationships, continued efforts at consultation or the hosting of conferences/workshops. Such an institutional arrangement placed the Commission at the hub of a network for information, public relations and policy.

Sport and Recreation New Zealand (2002–)

After winning the national election in 1999, the Labour Party established the Ministerial Taskforce on Sport Fitness and Leisure with the broad mandate of reviewing the sector. The Taskforce's final report (often referred to as the 'Graham Report', named after its chairman) was released in January of 2001 and proposed a number of measures to alter the structure of the sport delivery system, among them that central agencies (the Hillary Commission and the Office of Tourism and Sport) should merge, that Regional Sport Trusts be monitored to follow 'best practice' models, and that the system as a whole become more integrated and coordinated (Sam 2007).

The new Crown agency, called Sport and Recreation New Zealand (or SPARC), launched its four-year strategy with much fanfare, taking the Graham report as its blueprint for action. SPARC's mission was to be 'world leading' as measured by 'being the most active nation, having the most effective sport and physical recreation systems and having athletes and teams winning consistently in events that matter to New Zealanders' (SPARC 2002:6). In relation to its objective of winning consistently, SPARC followed the lead of other nations, all but abandoning the pyramidal model of sport development (whereby a large base of participation is said to result in a better quality of elite athletes). Instead, SPARC introduced contestability in its allocations to NSOs and targeted funds more narrowly as a means of improving medal tallies. At SPARC's launch, the agency announced a new initiative of working more closely with seven 'priority' sports and three 'revitalization' sports. In relation to the former, the details on the nature of such support remained conspicuously vague. Similarly, the latter three sports would be explored to see how they could be 'rejuvenated and re-established on a sustainable basis' (SPARC 2002:11). At the same time, SPARC announced the abolishment of the Community Sport Fund – a program for local authorities to fund sport clubs. Thus, rather than aiming to influence sport directly, SPARC delegated responsibility for participation objectives to the sports themselves.

Local government

While it is difficult to make generalizations, Territorial Local Authorities (TLAs) have played a relatively passive role in relation to sport participation policy. Much of the development continues to be left to community-based clubs; however, two factors appear to be bringing sport issues to the fore. The first is that because sport clubs have developed independently over long periods of time, towns and cities have to contend with an increasing number of ageing facilities that, from a planner's standpoint, either duplicate each other or are lacking in terms of providing for multiple uses. Indeed local governments have been in the position of either supporting clubs (in assisting them to renovate their club rooms, for instance) or letting them deteriorate with the associated costs of dismantling them. In recognizing this, local councils have taken up the cause of the Hillary Commission's 'Sportville' concept – a vision in which clubs can become efficient by working in partnerships – in the hope that clubs might agree to amalgamate their operations, undertake joint planning for refurbishments, etc. As one can imagine, the idea that organizations should amalgamate is intuitive, though not terribly realistic given the parochial nature of these organizations (Scherer *et al.* 2000).

A second consideration facing territorial authorities concerns New Zealand's hosting of the 2011 Rugby World Cup. Touted as a 'stadium of 4 million', the event will consist of pool matches all over the country and, as is the case internationally, local councils are investing millions into upgrading their stadia so as to showcase their cities. While the required upgrades to the main stadium (Auckland's Eden Park) are budgeted at $240 million, other centres such as Christchurch, Dunedin and New Plymouth are also directing substantial investments into their existing rugby grounds. The small city of Dunedin with a population of only 120,000 has recently begun construction on a new stadium at a cost of $200 million, nearly three-quarters of which will come from local taxpayers (Sam and Scherer 2008). There are concerns that such large capital investments by the local and regional councils, as well other key funders such as the Otago Community Trust, may have a long-term impact on the support of local, non-professional sport.

Government policies and interventions

To better make sense of government interventions in terms of sport participation, this section uses the term 'policy instruments' to describe the tools governments use to implement policy (Howlett and Ramesh 1995). Howlett (2000) broadly divides policy instruments into two categories: between those that are substantive or procedural. Substantive instruments, such as taxes, direct services (through programs), information campaigns and grants, are characterized by their propensity to have a direct effect on people or organizations. Grants are by far the most common instrument in relation to sport, where central agencies direct funding to third parties such as schools, national sport organizations (NSOs) or regional sport trusts (RSTs) to carry out government programs. Procedural instruments, by contrast, are concerned with shaping the policy environment by way of initiating organizational reforms, creating advisory committees, establishing partnerships, or supporting research in the area. Given the complex system of organizations at national, regional and local levels, such procedural instruments are an important consideration for supporting or inducing organized sport participation.

Substantive instruments: contracted programs

Until very recently, both the Hillary Commission and SPARC placed a significant emphasis on physical activity rather than sport *per se*. Consequently many of the largest government schemes (e.g. social marketing campaigns Push Play and Mission-On) have fallen under the wider rubric of 'active living', aimed at aspects of fitness, daily exercise and, to a lesser extent, nutrition. However, typifying the government's view on this duality of purpose, a Hillary Commission document nearly ten years ago noted:

> Of course sport is a way to be active. Half of the 'sport' that is played in New Zealand is played casually, outside of organized structures. But organized sport can (and should) take a lead in this issue.
>
> (Hillary Commission 2000c:33)

Indeed, at the time of writing this chapter, there is a definite re-orientation towards sport, a point I return to later. Three sport-specific programs are outlined below because of their specific objectives of improving or maintaining sport participation at the grassroots: Kiwisport, Sportfit and the Community Sport Fund.

In 1988, the Hillary Commission established 'Kiwisport', a program aimed at encouraging youth to participate in sport and physical activity. The program was principally implemented through schools and provided a range of modified sport opportunities for children aged 5 to 13. Most of the major sporting codes in NZ have since created their own modifications (e.g. shortened games, reduced team sizes), with training provided to teachers through Kiwisport coordinators. To some degree, the program's continuation throughout the 1990s aimed to remedy the perception that youth lacked 'literacy' in both fundamental motor skills (such as jumping and throwing) and sport-specific skills. At various times, and because of its child-friendly approach and focus on age-appropriate skills, Kiwisport has been criticized for becoming an end in itself rather than a means to an end (in this case a pathway to adult competitive sport). According to the Graham report, for example, such programs were responsible for breeding a culture of 'mediocrity' in sport (Sam 2003).

Its sister program, called 'Sportfit', assisted secondary schools with appointing sport coordinators, who were responsible for organizing sporting events, competitions, and training opportunities for students. At its inception, the Hillary Commission recognized that teachers coaching or managing sports teams needed additional support (Sharp 1991). Thus Sportfit aimed to ensure more student opportunities for sport in a range of contexts including competitive, social and recreational (Grant and Pope 2007). As of 2006, SPARC had contracts with 96 per cent of all secondary schools to deliver the program (Deloitte 2006) and numerous other sub-programs have been established under the Sportfit umbrella, including the provision of education opportunities for students in coaching, officiating and management. Within each of the two programs, we can see the recurring themes of branding, coordination and upskilling. Branding, for instance, is accomplished through Sportfit via 'a series of awards aimed at recognising emerging sporting success as well as future "leaders" in sport' (Deloitte 2006:32).

In terms of scale, the Community Sport Fund (CSF) was arguably the largest Hillary Commission program, supporting over 5,100 local projects in 2001/02. Essentially aimed at directing funds to the 'coal face', monies were allocated to territorial authorities (i.e. local/municipal governments) on a per capita basis, for distribution to sport clubs. In its last year of operation (2001–02), the fund contributed $1.23 per capita, with allowance for a base fund of $22,000 for rural municipalities that could not reach that threshold otherwise (Hillary Commission 2001). While initially intended to help develop sport clubs and their memberships, the Hillary Commission earmarked the program as a means of supporting its 'Sportville' concept – a vision of sport development in which clubs would be encouraged to share resources, facilities and administrative expertise (Hillary Commission 1999). However, the following year the new central agency (SPARC) abolished the program, much to the dismay of some local authorities, which felt it had been removed with little consultation. The CSF's removal was consistent with SPARC's preference for more targeted funding and effectively marked an end to the government's block funding to grassroots sport. While the program's funding for specific projects was small (an average of $2,291 per organization), local government officials expressed strong opposition to the program's abolishment, in part because of the lack of alternative levers at the disposal of councils to influence club-run sport.

Procedural instruments: programming for development and capacity

The perennial challenge of governing sport in New Zealand has been the fragmented nature of the sport system itself. Consequently, many of the government's strategies for increasing participation in sport have aimed to create a more 'seamless' and coordinated system of sport development. Yet ironically, the government's historical preference for governing through contracts has arguably exacerbated the fragmentation. In the mid 1980s, the Hillary Commission established regional sport trusts which, while initially funded heavily from government, were intended to become self-reliant, drawing matching sources of revenue from their communities over the long term. This ultimately had two effects. First, because of the Hillary Commission's desire to steadily reduce RST funding to a maximum of 50 per cent, the new organizations had to compete for sponsorship revenue alongside the very organizations they were intended to support. Second, the ultimate autonomy of the RSTs translated into a wide array of roles and responsibilities over time, with some for instance operating city recreation facilities, some becoming principally concerned with community health, and so on. Capturing this role confusion, the Hillary Commission's strategy for developing clear sporting 'pathways', observed that

> to date the Commission has left [sport development] up to the national sports organisations themselves to deliver . . . with very limited funds. Regional sports trusts have received funds to assist regional associations, but future focus must be on the regions through the national sports organisation, with some generic regional sports trust services also available at the request of the national sports organization.
>
> (Hillary Commission 2000a:5)

Yet the potential for duplication has not necessarily been a policy failure in terms of sport participation. RSTs remain an essential component of sport participation policy because of their knowledge of programming gaps and ability to pilot special initiatives (such as SportForce). Similarly, other providers, such as the Halberg Trust are contracted to operate programs for people with disabilities, under SPARC's 'No Exceptions Strategy'. Perhaps, in more pragmatic terms, the establishment of this system of contracts has absolved government from having to establish decentralized satellite offices of its own that would have come at much cost, and with much public scrutiny in terms of bureaucratic spending. Thus while contracts with third parties to deliver sport participation programs have created issues around 'consistency' and policy coherence, the central agency is in the position where it can hold its agents to a much higher accountability than they would themselves be submitted to. For instance, the Crown Agency has set targets for improving sport participation rates but only by including targets in its contracts with regional sport trusts. As a report of SPARC's performance states: 'the ultimate measure of RST performance is whether there have been changes in regional levels of participation' (Deloitte 2006).

A second notable policy instrument involves programs aimed specifically at modernizing the operations of organizations in the sport sector (Green 2009). The underpinning logic of such efforts is that well-functioning, professional sport organizations are likely to have greater capacities to develop their membership bases. There have been a plethora of initiatives in this regard, typified by the Hillary Commission's 'SportsMark' program slogan: '(best) practice makes perfect'. In this regard, SPARC's Sport Development Unit is responsible for helping NSOs build their capacities through consultancy work on strategic planning and business development, as well as sport-specific initiatives aimed at developing their regional networks. Both the Hillary Commission and SPARC have also used organizational audits as a means of advising on, and evaluating, administrative performance (cf. Hillary Commission 2000c; SPARC 2005). SPARC's use of both carrots (providing financial 'revitalization' support) and sticks (sanctions and/or withholding grant funding) in modernizing sports has become increasingly bold (Collins 2007), yet there remains some question as to whether such modernizing remedies are likely to be effective in achieving sport participation objectives (Sam 2009).

In 2002, SPARC declared that cycling, swimming and athletics would become 'revitalization' sports. Interestingly, Swimming NZ's membership figures dropped during this period of support (from 20,419 in 2002 to 15,341 in 2007). Athletics memberships also declined from 29,050 in 2002 to 25,291, according to its 2007/08 annual report.[4] While this does not necessarily suggest a causal link between SPARC 'revitalization' support and membership declines, it at least brings into question SPARC's capacity to increase the number of people involved in organized sport through its organizational reforms of NSOs. While SPARC later claimed success via 'significant improvements in measured capability' for Bike NZ and Swimming NZ (SPARC 2006:5), none of the three revitalization sports increased their participation bases. Moreover, SPARC subsequently withdrew $125,000 from Athletics NZ's grant earmarked for participation because, as SPARC Chief Executive Nick Hill observed: 'We're not convinced that [this] money was being effective' (Kilgallon 2006).

This perhaps explains the government's most recent initiative to inject $82 million over four years into the Kiwisport school program (Key 2009). Beyond it fulfilling a pre-election promise of 'focusing sporting dollars where they make the biggest difference – at the front-line in our schools and sports clubs' (Key 2009:1), the change is also indicative of an overcommitted central sport agency that in recent years has sought to revert back to its 'core business'. Despite the Kiwisport brand name, this most recent initiative bears little resemblance to its earlier counterpart; however, it marks a significant return to 'block funding' in giving schools significant flexibility in how funds can be used.

Conclusion

Despite the contemporary emphasis on health and physical activity, organized sport participation has reappeared as 'what matters' for New Zealand's central sport agency. Indeed the recent re-prioritization of youth sport through schools is an indication that sport will capture a substantial share of money aimed broadly at health and physical activity promotion in the near future. There are nevertheless continuing challenges to making inroads on sport participation through government policy.

The most pressing is perhaps a case of not knowing enough about how the country's complex system of organizations functions to either induce or disrupt sport participation patterns. SPARC's recent national surveys still lack the sensitivity to paint a picture of sustained participation in organized sport that can inform future policy. For instance, they do not allow for any delineation between traditional club-based sport participation (requiring annual membership) and parallel leagues operated by private facilities, schools or other community organizations (such as churches or societies for new migrants).

A second challenge for policy makers is that it remains difficult to evaluate the efficacy of established programs and policy interventions aimed at sport participation. Despite two separate evaluations of the Sportfit program (in 2006 and 2008), neither speculates on the program's outcomes relative to SPARC's goals of increasing participation (cf. Gordon *et al.* 2008; Kolt *et al.* 2006). For example, while the program and its main tool (school sport coordinators) may well increase opportunities for students to partake in competitive sport, it is unclear how the increased breadth of opportunities might translate into participation after they leave. Typifying the recommendations of such reports is that programs should be 'refreshed and rebranded' so as to be 'socially relevant to today's youth' (Kolt *et al.* 2006:193). And indeed the most recent large-scale policy change in sport participation (the rejuvenation of Kiwisport) seems to reflect the hope that repackaged policy can yield better results. Ultimately, if we accept that policy evaluation constitutes an essential component of policy learning (Sanderson 2002), the challenge of knowing 'what works' may well stem from the current practice of commissioning stand-alone, short-term research projects.

At the same time, one has to wonder whether policies and programs originating from the same central agency can have the propensity to create side or reverse effects (Hood and Peters 2004). For instance, could it be possible that Push Play (a social marketing campaign advocating 30 minutes of exercise a day) might discourage club sport registration because of its messages advocating that *any* activity is good activity? Similarly, and despite the good intentions of creating modern, business-like sport organizations, is it possible that it is these very reforms that hinder sport involvement among particular segments of the population (such as school leavers or young professionals)? These are difficult questions to be sure; however, in this light, it is worth suggesting that sport participation policies and programs are perhaps less insular than their high-performance counterparts, and thus deserve much more scholarly attention.

Acknowledgments

The author would like to thank Dr Sarah Gee and Ms Rebecca Keat for their research contributions and feedback on earlier drafts of this work.

Notes

1 Sports organizations of the time attributed membership growth to the Come Alive program and these findings were supported by the New Zealand Recreation Survey (1974–75).

2 Other sectors such as health, education and social welfare underwent similar reviews. As Shirley (1990:369) notes, these tended to be dominated by 'private sector entrepreneurs and ideologues of the New Right'.
3 The Commission was named after Sir Edmund Hillary, the first mountaineer (along with Tenzing Norgay) to reach the peak of Mount Everest.
4 Cycling membership figures were 2,515 in 2002; however, no comparable recent figures could be found.

References

Bolger, J. B. (1991) 'Sharing a Common Goal for New Zealand and the Strategic Relevance of Sport, Fitness and Leisure'. In *Forum of National Sports and Leisure Leaders*. Wellington.

Buchanan, H. D. (1978) *A Critical Analysis of the 1937 Physical Welfare and Recreation Act and of Government Involvement in Recreation and Sport 1937–1957*. Wellington: University of Victoria.

Church, A. (1990) *Community Development: A History of the Involvement of the Department of Internal Affairs in Community Development* (No. Monograph series no.13). Wellington: Department of Internal Affairs.

Collins, C. (2007) 'Politics, Government and Sport in Aotearoa/New Zealand'. In Chris Collins and Steven J. Jackson (eds.) *Sport in Aotearoa/New Zealand Society*. 2nd edn. South Melbourne, Vic; Auckland, N.Z.: Thomson.

Collins, C., MacLeod, T., Thomson, R. and Downey, J. (2007) 'Challenges Ahead: The Future and Sport in Aotearoa/New Zealand'. In C. Collins and S. J. Jackson (eds.) *Sport in Aotearoa/New Zealand Society*. Albany: Thomson.

Cricket NZ (2009) 'Research Confirms Surge in Public Interest in Cricket', 18 August. http://www.blackcaps.co.nz/news/corporate/4/research-confirms-surge-in-public-interest-in-cricket/5499/article.aspx

Cushman, G. and Cushman, P. (1980) 'Sport and Physical Education in New Zealand'. In W. Johnson (ed.) *Sport and Physical Education around the World*. Champaign: Stipes Publishing.

Deloitte (2006) *Review of the Performance of Sparc During the 2002–2006 Period*. Wellington: Sport and Recreation New Zealand.

Gordon, B., Hullena, V., Harker, R., McKenzie, L. and Meyer, L. (2008) *Delivery of Sport and Recreation Opportunities in Secondary Schools (Sportfit)*. Wellington: Jessie Hetherington Centre for Educational Research and Victoria University of Wellington.

Grant, B., and Pope, G. (2007) 'Sport and Education: Sport in Secondary Schools for All or for Some?' In Chris Collins and Steven J. Jackson (eds.) *Sport in Aotearoa/New Zealand Society*. 2nd edn. South Melbourne, Vic; Auckland, N.Z.: Thomson.

Green, M. (2009) 'Podium or Participation? Analysing Policy Priorities under Changing Modes of Sport Governance in the United Kingdom', *International Journal of Sport Policy* 1:121–44.

Hillary Commission (2000a) *Designing the Pathway for Sport Players, Coaches, Officials and Leaders: The Talent Zone*. Wellington: Hillary Commission for Sport, Fitness and Leisure.

—— (2000b) *The Future Marketing Environment* (Discussion paper). Hillary Commission for Sport Fitness and Leisure.

—— (2000c) *Sporting Directions: Developing the Competitive Sport System in the Next Decade*. Wellington: Hillary Commission for Sport, Fitness and Leisure.

—— (2001) *Annual Report 2001–2002*. Wellington: Hillary Commission for Sport, Fitness and Leisure.

Hindson, A., Cushman, G. and Gidlow, B. (1994) 'Historical and Social Perspectives on Sport in New Zealand'. In L. D. Trenberth and C. Collins (eds.) *Sport Management in New Zealand*. Palmerston North: Dunmore Press.

Hood, C. and Guy Peters, B. (2004) 'The Middle Aging of New Public Management: Into the Age of Paradox?', *Journal of Public Administration Research and Theory* 14:267–82.

Howlett, M. (2000) 'Managing the "Hollow State": Procedural Policy Instruments and Modern Governance', *Canadian Public Administration* 43:412–31.

Howlett, M. and Ramesh, M. (1995) *Studying Public Policy: Policy Cycles and Policy Subsystems.* Toronto: Oxford University Press.

Key, J. (2009) 'Kiwisport Initiative Good for Young People'. In *Press Release*: Office of the Prime Minister.

Kilgallon, S. (2006) 'Track and Field Body Hurt by Shock Crisis in Funding'. *Sunday Star Times*, 9 July, B10.

Kolt, G., Schofield, G., Schofield, L., McLachlan, C., Svendsen, C. and Mackay, L. (2006) *Best Practice Review of Sport and Physical Activity Interventions for Young People Aged 13–18 Years: Report to Sparc.* Auckland: Centre for Physical Activity and Nutrition Research, Auckland University of Technology and Health and Human Performance Ltd.

Phillips, J. (1996) 'The Hard Man: Rugby and the Formation of Male Identity in New Zealand'. In J. Nauright and T.J.L. Chandler (eds.) *Making Men: Rugby and Masculine Identity.* London: Frank Cass.

Rudd, C. (1997) 'The Welfare State'. In R. Miller (ed.) *New Zealand Politics in Transition.* Auckland: Oxford University Press.

Sam, M. P. (2003) 'What's the Big Idea? Reading the Rhetoric of a National Sport Policy Process', *Sociology of Sport Journal* 20:189–213.

—— (2007) 'Sport Policy in Aotearoa/New Zealand'. In C. Collins and S.J. Jackson (eds.) *Sport in Aotearoa/New Zealand.* Melbourne: Thomson-Nelson.

—— (2009) 'The Public Management of Sport: Wicked Problems, Challenges and Dilemmas', *Public Management Review* 11:499–513.

Sam, M. P. and Scherer, J. (2008) 'Stand Up and Be Counted: Numerical Storylines in a Stadium Debate', *International Review for the Sociology of Sport* 43:53–70.

Sanderson, I. (2002) 'Evaluation, Policy Learning and Evidence-Based Policy Making', *Public Administration* 80:1–22.

Scherer, J., Sam, M.P. and Batty, R. (2000) 'Club Amalgamation and Identity: Perceptions of New Zealand Club Members'. In *6th Annual Conference for the Sport Management Association of Australia and New Zealand.* Hamilton, New Zealand.

Sharp, P. (1991) 'A New Policy in Secondary School Sports Education'. In *Forum of National Sports and Leisure Leaders*, edited by Hillary Commission. Wellington: Hillary Commission.

Shaw, R. and Eichbaum, C. (2005) *Public Policy in New Zealand: Institutions, Processes and Outcomes.* Auckland: Pearson Education New Zealand.

Shirley, I. (1990) 'New Zealand: The Advance of the New Right'. In I. Taylor (ed.) *The Social Effects of Free Market Policies: An International Text.* New York: St Martin's Press.

SPARC (2002) *Our Vision and Direction: Strategies for Success from 2006.* Wellington: Sport and Recreation New Zealand.

—— (2005) *Re-Igniting the Sparc: Looking Back at Athens – Forward to Beijing.* Wellington: SPARC.

—— (2006) *Annual Report 2005/06.* Wellington: Sport and Recreation New Zealand.

—— (2008) *Sport, Recreation and Physical Activity Participation among New Zealand Adults: Key Results of the 2007/08 Actve NZ Survey.* Wellington: SPARC.

—— (2009) *Powering Participation.* Wellington: Sport and Recreation New Zealand.

Sports Development Inquiry Committee (1985) *Sport on the Move: Report to the Minister of Recreation and Sport.* Wellington: Government Print.

Stothart, R. A. (1978) 'The Need for Recreation'. In P. H. Gresham (ed.) *Proceedings of Environment 77: Recreation Needs and Conflicts.* Canterbury: Environment Centre Inc.

—— (1980) 'The New Deal in Recreation and Sport'. In J. Shallcrass, B. Larkin and R. A. Stothart (eds.) *Recreation Reconsidered into the Eighties*. Auckland: Auckland Regional Authority and New Zealand Council for Recreation and Sport.

—— (2000) 'The Development of Sport Administration in New Zealand: From Kitchen Table to Computer'. In C. Collins (ed.) *Sport in New Zealand Society*. Palmerston North: Dunmore Press.

Thomson, R. and Sim, J. (2007) 'Sport and Culture: Passion and Paradox'. In C. Collins and S. J. Jackson (eds.) *Sport in Aotearoa/New Zealand Society*. Albany: Thomson.

16 United States of America

Matthew T. Bowers, Laurence Chalip and B. Christine Green

The structure of American sport – and the consequences of that structure – is almost universally misunderstood by those who view it from outside the system. The reason is simple: American sport is organized and managed in a manner that bears scant resemblance to the organization and management of sport elsewhere in the world (Chalip *et al.* 1996; Markovits and Hellerman 2001). As a result, even words and phrases used across the English-speaking world, such as 'club' or 'school sport', have subtle but significant differences in meaning when applied in the American context relative to countries like Australia, Canada, New Zealand, South Africa, or the United Kingdom – a fact which has caused more than a few misunderstandings in making comparisons to American sport in other countries, whether the comparison is conducted by Americans or nationals from outside the United States.

In fact, Americans themselves rarely have much understanding of the structure and governance of American sport, even if they work in sport, because the United States does not have an integrated system for sport or for the development of athletes (Sparvero *et al.* 2008). American sport policies are few, and are generally designed to enable free and unencumbered functioning of American sport markets. Further, since American popular media work hand in hand with the entertainment side of the American sport industry, Americans are typically exposed to a simplistic and mythologized version of American sporting culture (Koppett 1994). Consequently, Americans who have never worked in American sport misunderstand it, and those who do work in American sport typically understand only the particular realm in which they work. Those who seek to learn about American sport by interviewing sports executives or through content analysis of American media actually learn only about isolated corners of American sport, or about the popular mythologies that masquerade as fact throughout American sport.

Americans participate in sport through a wide variety of organizations and agencies. A great deal of public sport provision comes through local recreation departments, which are typically funded through tax revenues and participation fees. Some sports are provided by middle schools, high schools, and universities. There are private clubs that offer sports tuition and training, and which sometimes form alliances to create private competitive leagues. There are service organizations that include sport programming, such as the YMCA, Jewish Community Centers, and the Boys and Girls Clubs of America. Many churches organize teams and leagues as well. This list is not exhaustive, as new sport organizations emerge from time to time, and there is no central registry of sport organizations. In fact, there is no mechanism to coordinate delivery of sport programming, and sport organizations often operate with no connection to one another, even within the same community or the same sport. Consequently, there are multiple avenues for sport participation, and there is no single pathway for athlete development (Bowers *et al.* 2010; Sparvero *et al.* 2008).

Sport participation rates

Given the array of organizations providing sport in the United States and the lack of coordination among those organizations, there are no reliable state, national, or local statistics on sport participation. Several commercial market research firms collect household surveys about sport participation, particularly because those numbers are of interest to clothing and sporting goods manufacturers and retailers. The surveys do not include all sports, and they typically ask only if the respondent has participated at least once in the sport during the past year. This is useful to clothing and sporting goods manufacturers and retailers, but it clearly over-

Table 16.1 U.S. trends in participation rates by sport (in thousands)

Sport	2000	2004	2007	Change (4-year)	Change (7-year)
Archery	6047	6756	5852	11.72%	−3.22%
Badminton	8490	6432	5328	−24.24%	−37.24%
Baseball	10881	9694	8191	−10.91%	−24.72%
Basketball	37552	34223	32301	−8.87%	−13.98%
Billiards	37483	36356	32144	−3.01%	−14.24%
Bowling	53844	53603	51579	−0.45%	−4.21%
Boxing	1085	1140	786	5.07%	−27.56%
Cross-country skiing	4613	4007	1865	−13.14%	−59.57%
Downhill skiing	14749	11971	9880	−18.84%	−33.01%
Football	18285	16436	18122	−10.11%	−0.89%
Golf	30365	25723	25617	−15.29%	−15.64%
Ice hockey	2761	1998	3353	−27.63%	21.44%
Ice skating	17496	14692	11540	−16.03%	−34.04%
Kayaking	4137	6147	8547	48.59%	106.60%
Lacrosse	751	914	1710	21.70%	127.70%
Martial arts	5722	6898	6162	20.55%	7.69%
Racquetball	5155	5533	5705	7.33%	10.67%
Sailing	5271	4307	3994	−18.29%	−24.23%
Skateboarding	11649	10592	11616	−9.07%	−0.28%
Snowboarding	7151	7110	6889	−0.57%	−3.66%
Soccer	17734	15900	15551	−10.34%	−12.31%
Softball	19668	16941	16111	−13.87%	−18.09%
Surfing	2180	1936	2678	−11.19%	22.84%
Table tennis	13797	14286	14122	3.54%	2.36%
Target shooting	16293	18037	20192	10.70%	23.93%
Tennis	16598	18346	17561	10.53%	5.80%
Volleyball	22876	22216	18491	−2.89%	−19.17%
Wakeboarding	3581	2843	3656	−20.61%	2.09%
Water skiing	10335	6835	6593	−33.87%	−36.21%
Wrestling	2405	2303	2025	−4.24%	−15.80%

Source: American Sports Data, Inc. (2007)

estimates ongoing participation or participation in organized sports programs. Nevertheless, the trends are informative.

Table 16.1 provides data compiled from the American Sports Data, Inc. (2007) study of sport participation. This is widely considered to be one of the most comprehensive resources. As examination of Table 16.1 shows, data are not available for all sports. Yet the table also demonstrates that nearly all sports have experienced a decline in participation. Only two sports (lacrosse and kayaking) evidence a substantial and continuous positive trend. Nevertheless, the overall effect is meager insomuch as these sports had small initial participation rates.

These data are particularly interesting because they suggest the effects of policy foci and social trends. Over the same period, time in non-sport fitness activities has risen and the amount of 'screen time' that Americans spend in front of the television or computer have both increased. In the case of the former, although participation rates in fitness activities were relatively high to begin with, the trends are substantially more positive than are those for sport participation (see Table 16.2). This could be a consequence, at least in part, of the ongoing policy focus on fitness through non-sport physical activity, as well as the increasingly privatized (and therefore more costly) local market for sport participation. The problem is arguably exacerbated by the amount of time Americans, especially children, spend in front of their televisions and computer screens. Recent research shows that children and adolescents between the ages of 8 and 18 spend an average of six hours per day either watching television or sitting in front of a computer screen (Henry J. Kaiser Foundation 2005).

Federal policies affecting sport participation

At the federal level, there are only three policies that play any significant role in sport participation. Title IX of the Education Amendments of 1972 (PL 92–318) is the most widely discussed. It prohibits discrimination in educational activities and programs by any institution that receives federal funds. Although this legislation was never intended to address sport, advocates of women's sport development have used it to pressure high schools and universities to increase school-based opportunities for women. The effect has clearly been to increase the number of female athletes who are served by sport programs in schools and universities (Carpenter and Acosta 2005), although another effect has been to reduce the number of sports

Table 16.2 U.S. trends in participation rates by fitness activity (in thousands)

Fitness activity	2000	2004	2007	Change (4-year)	Change (7-year)
Aerobics	17,326	15,767	17,373	−9.00%	0.27%
Elliptical trainer	6,176	15,678	22,388	153.85%	262.50%
Free weights	44,499	52,056	53,147	16.98%	19.43%
Pilates training	1,739	10,541	10,949	506.15%	529.61%
Running/jogging	33,680	37,310	39,563	10.78%	17.47%
Stationary cycling	28,795	31,431	30,613	9.15%	6.31%
Treadmill exercise	40,816	47,463	49,967	16.29%	22.42%
Yoga/Tai Chi	7,400	12,414	10,949	67.76%	47.96%

Source: American Sports Data, Inc. (2007)

provided for men and the number of male athletes who are served through school and university sport (U.S. General Accountability Office 2001). In fact, from the standpoint of overall sport participation, school and university sports have arguably had a negative overall impact because only a few sports are represented among American school sports, and school sport focuses public attention and public funding on sport for school-aged athletes. Provision of sport through clubs like those found throughout much of the rest of the world has consequently been truncated (Sparvero *et al.* 2008).

The Americans with Disabilities Act was initially signed into law in 1990 (PL 101–336), and amended in 2008 (PL 110–325). Like Title IX, it does not address sport directly, but it does prohibit discrimination on the basis of disability in employment, government, public accommodations, commercial facilities, transportation, and telecommunications. Consequently, rights activists have used the law to lobby for better access to sport facilities for those who have a disability. The effect has been to improve facility access and, subsequently, access to programs, but it has done little to generate new programming. The limited sport programming for people with disabilities became salient to policymakers as a consequence of the wars in Iraq and Afghanistan, as military health care workers noted the value of sport as a rehabilitation tool for soldiers suffering disabling wounds. The lack of programming for the disabled throughout the country caused the United States military to provide funding to U.S. Paralympics, which governs American Paralympic sport, in order to create programs throughout the country. Since U.S. Paralympics had no direct program development capability, it provided funding to the National Recreation and Parks Association (NRPA) to initiate grants for communities that would establish programs. The resulting alliance between NRPA and U.S. Paralympics was promoted at the NRPA Congress in October 2009, and the first grants were announced in December 2009. The effects of this new attention to sport for the disabled remain uncertain. It is significant, however, that the newly available funding is a result of national military need, rather than the Americans with Disabilities Act.

The third federal policy having to do with sport participation is the Amateur Sports Act, which was initially signed into law in 1978 (PL 95–606) and amended in 1996 through inclusion in the Omnibus Consolidated and Emergency Supplemental Appropriations Act (PL 105–227), granting authority over the governance of Olympic sports to the United States Olympic Committee (USOC) through the National Governing Bodies (NGBs) for each sport. This is the only piece of federal legislation that specifically addresses sport participation, although its primary focus is on the governance of elite sport. The Amateur Sports Act specifically charges the USOC and its NGBs to coordinate and develop amateur sport in the United States, to encourage the development of sport facilities, and to encourage and provide assistance to sport for women, the handicapped, and ethnic minorities. There is, however, no enforcement provision in the legislation other than the requirement that the USOC provide a report to Congress each year. No congressional committee or federal agency is assigned any responsibility to read the report or to provide any other form of oversight. As a result, the USOC and its NGBs remain focused on elite sport development, often to the detriment of grassroots sport participation (Sparvero *et al.* 2008).

Federal agencies and sport participation

Despite the popular attention to a few elite sport competitions, federal agencies choose to focus on fitness through physical activity as opposed to sport. The focus on non-sport physical activity emerged historically as a consequence of Cold War concerns about the preparedness of American youth for future roles as soldiers. More recently, the concern has derived from concerns by public health officials about the rapid rise in obesity among Americans of all ages.

The President's Council on Physical Fitness and Sports

The President's Council on Physical Fitness and Sports (PCPFS) is the only federal government agency that has any explicit link to the promotion of sports in the United States. Founded as the President's Council on Youth Fitness during the Eisenhower administration in 1956, it was initially a response to international physical fitness tests, particularly the Krauss-Webber tests, which concluded that American children were less fit (and therefore less able to defend their country) than were children in other nations. These results directed the Council's attention to programs giving priority to individual achievement on a series of fitness tests, although over the years this stance has shifted somewhat to the more holistic promotion of physical activity and health.

According to provisions established in Executive Order 12345, the PCPFS is an advisory committee led by twenty volunteer members who are appointed by the President of the United States. The PCPFS is not instantiated in law, as it has never been legislatively enabled. Rather, it was founded and continues to operate under Executive Order. Consequently, it does not have its own federal budget line, but must instead borrow its funds from whichever federal agency is assigned to house it. This limits what the Council can do because it has been given no legislatively mandated authority to make or implement policy, and it has a very small budget (amounting to less than 0.4 cents per capita in recent years):

- FY 2004: $1,179,000
- FY 2005: $1,247,000
- FY 2006: $1,228,000
- FY 2007: $1,230,000
- FY 2008: $1,196,000
- FY 2009: $1,228,000

The PCPFS operates primarily through public school physical education programs, which have thereby become the local context through which fitness testing is conducted and administered. The 'President's Challenge' outlines two fitness programs for participants depending on their level of activity: the Active Lifestyle program and the Presidential Champions program (see http://www. presidentschallenge.org/the_challenge/index.aspx). In both programs, participants are encouraged to develop an active lifestyle by taking part in a variety of sport- and fitness-related activities of their choosing while keeping track of their frequency and duration in a downloadable fitness activity log. The stated goal of these efforts is to encourage participants to accrue 30 to 60 minutes of physical activity at least five times per week for six weeks, with the particular program dictating which type of award can be earned by the participant. Although sports are included on the list of appropriate activities for the challenge, there are no accompanying documents or instructions to help an athlete develop skills in any particular sport, or even to find a program or facility in which to participate.

Centers for Disease Control and Prevention

The Centers for Disease Control and Prevention (CDC) is the government agency charged with developing policies related to the prevention and treatment of disease. Like the PCPFS, the CDC has become a government outlet for the promotion of health and physical activity through a perceived need to address the diminishing fitness levels that have coincided with the increase in childhood and adult obesity in the United States. Also like the PCPFS, there is little provision for sport in the policy and programming of the CDC's efforts to create a healthier and more active populace.

The CDC's education-based, health-promotion program is called 'Physical Activity for Everyone'. It delineates different ways for various segments of the population (viz., children, adults, the elderly, and pregnant or postpartum women) to add physical activity into their lifestyles, measure their physical activity, and determine how much time must be allocated for their physical activity to yield desired health benefits (see http://www.cdc.gov/physicalactivity/everyone/guidelines/index.html). Despite the self-evident differences in the physical activity wants and needs of these populations, the program's recommendations reveal a fairly uniform approach to fitness centered on aerobic activity (such as walking and jogging) and muscle strengthening (by lifting weights). Sport is rarely even offered as a suggestion except after other, less strenuous recommendations, such as gardening and mowing the lawn.

The policy focus

The PCPFS and CDC initiatives are not anti-sport; they simply treat sport as secondary or irrelevant to wider policy goals of increasing general physical activity and disease prevention. The programs are predicated on individual, fitness-based activities that are designed to cater to an American people who are treated as too busy or too lazy to commit to any form of regular physical activity that cannot be readily integrated into their daily routines. The deeper assumption is that physical activity is an unpleasant form of work that people must be coerced to do. The potential utility of play, including but not limited to sport, has remained outside the paradigm.

Policy uses of the free market

Given the dearth of federal policy aimed at sport development, federal policies for sport participation have relied on the free market (Bowers *et al.* 2010; Sparvero *et al.* 2008). However, the ongoing concerns about national fitness, whether as a matter of military preparedness or of public health, have remained. This has obliged government organizations to encourage private sport organizations to promote fitness. Three professional sport leagues have consequently developed their own programs: the National Football League's (NFL) Play 60, the National Basketball Association's (NBA) NBA Fit, and Major League Soccer's (MLS) Active Bodies, Active Minds.

NFL Play 60

The NFL's Play 60 campaign was founded in 2007, following an earlier partnership between the NFL and the NRPA which had been encouraged by the CDC. The earlier partnership had been designed through incorporating tools and materials from the CDC to encourage local recreation departments to do more to build physical activity into their programming. The NFL soon recognized the public relations potential of that program, but also sought to expand the program with its own brand. Consequently, it established Play 60, which is coordinated through an interactive website that allows users (in this case, children, although there are links for coach and volunteer resources) to click on videos and games involving NFL stars that are designed to promote being active at least 60 minutes per day (see http://www.nflrush.com/play60/). Although the program is not allied to the CDC, it has retained the CDC-inspired emphasis on physical activity rather than sport.

NBA Fit and iHoops

Given the national campaign to attack obesity by promoting physical activity, the NBA recognized a public relations opportunity. NBA Fit was launched in 2005. The initiative encourages physical activity and healthy living through products, events, and programs for children and families (see http://www.nba.com/nbafit/overview.html). The program has an aesthetically appealing multimedia website with nutritional guidelines, fitness training videos, and workouts conducted by star players categorized for children, adults, and families. The program also promotes skill-building through basketball-specific workouts that are designed to train participants to participate in the NBA Fit Dribble, Dish, and Swish national skills competition. The NBA has extended this effort by forming a partnership with the National Collegiate Athletic Association (NCAA) for the 2009–10 season. The resulting program will provide an online grassroots development program called iHoops to allow access to even more information on skill-based and tactical education for youth players (see http://www.ihoops.com). Although neither program is a direct consequence of any government initiative, both have been inspired by the public relations opportunities that government policies promoting physical activity have enabled.

MLS Active Bodies, Active Minds

Major League Soccer's Active Bodies, Active Minds program, also founded in 2005, is another public relations scheme that purports to promote awareness about the importance of an active, healthy lifestyle. It endeavors to maintain children's reading and fitness levels while they are out of school, particularly on holidays (see http://www.mlssoccer.com/abam). The program includes fitness logs, and encourages children to be active for at least 30 minutes per day. It does not promote soccer skills or participation.

Public policy delivered through private sport enterprises

These examples demonstrate that the emergence of national policy agendas promoting health through physical activity has enabled new public relations initiatives by private sport businesses. Those businesses seek to promote their brand through these initiatives and, as a result, they have not found value in an active partnership with any government agency. Since the policy environment mandates promotion of physical activities that often have little to do with sport, and since the sport organizations' objectives are to promote their respective brands rather than to promote sport participation more generally, there is very little in the resulting initiatives designed to nurture sport participation. Thus, the market response to government policy agendas has done little to promote or to enable higher rates of sport participation.

American federalism and the free market for sport

In the American system of government, responsibilities not reserved to the federal government are then left to each state to determine, with the result that there could potentially be 50 different policies throughout the country. State governments have not yet focused on sport participation, except to the degree that they fund state universities which, in turn, may fund sport programs on their campuses. No state has yet formulated policies specifically intended to foster or build sport participation.

In the absence of state action, responsibility devolves to local authorities. The locus of local responsibility may be at either county or city level, depending on the structure of responsibilities in the local jurisdiction. Nearly all American cities or counties fund public recreation programs that include sport programs for local residents. The choice and number of sports offered, as well as the quality of sport programming, varies by community, and is affected by local social conditions. In some communities, for example, union rules regarding facility maintenance or high insurance costs have militated against opening school sport facilities for public use, which has restricted the necessary facility access for provision of public sport programs, particularly in communities that have directed their facility investments to the schools.

On the other hand, some communities have structured an alliance between local recreation providers and the public school system. In those instances, school facilities may be made available to the public outside school hours. However, if the relationship between schools and local recreation is particularly strong, public recreation provision may be formulated in support of school sports, rather than to promote mass participation. For example, the city of Fort Stockton in the state of Texas has forged one of the country's strongest alliances between its schools and its public recreation department. School facilities are widely used by the department, which is itself housed in a former school that is still owned by the school system. Recreation programs in Fort Stockton have been designed, as a matter of policy, to support development of athletes for the local high school team. Consequently, there are strong football, baseball, and basketball programs for children who are not yet in high school, but there has been no programming for sports that do not boast high school teams, and there has been no programming for adults or for high school-age athletes. Although some pressure from a state health program endeavoring to promote physical activity did encourage creation of a children's soccer league and an adult dodgeball league, these fledgling programs have struggled to establish themselves because they are outside the policy focus of the recreation department.

In contrast, many public recreation departments provide a wide array of public sport opportunities, including programs for adults as well as children. These often include popular action sports, like skateboarding and disc golf, as well as well-established sports like football, baseball, and basketball, and emerging sports like floorball. The range, quality, and choice of sports varies in each community, as does the degree of public support.

In order to offer particular sports, public recreation programs often forge partnerships with private organizations. For example, in Chicago, private ethnic clubs have played a significant role in formation of sport teams that play on public grounds or that become key partners in local recreational leagues. In Austin, Texas, the city enables mountain biking by providing a large greenbelt area for the sport, but the area is maintained by a volunteer group of users. Throughout the country there are church leagues offering popular sports, particularly basketball and softball, which often use sport facilities that are run by public recreation departments. Over the past decade, there has been a substantial rise in the number of private companies offering sport leagues, especially for adults. In cities as different as San Francisco, Chicago, Dallas, and San Antonio, sport leagues are increasingly provided by for-profit enterprises that use tax-payer-supported facilities to host their programs.

Economic and social conditions vary among communities. Consequently, the nature of public recreational sport provision can vary substantially. For example, in the state of Maryland, recreational sports are organized primarily at county (rather than city) level. Maryland National Capital Park and Planning Commission (M-NCPPC), which has been considered one of the premier public recreation providers in the country, organizes recreational sports for both Prince Georges County and Montgomery County. Historically, it was M-NCPPC policy to require that swimming teams be provided in its public pools in communities whose residents were predominantly white, but not in pools for communities that were predominantly black. The rationale was that swimming is a sport in which whites but not blacks normally participate.

Public recreation departments provide recreations other than sport, so public recreation policies are often only weakly focused on sport. Further, there has historically been some antipathy between sport and recreation in the United States. The split is evident in the training of recreation professionals, which in American universities is typically conducted in programs that are separate (not merely by department, but often by school) from those that train sport managers and administrators. The split between sport and recreation was well demonstrated during hearings held by the President's Commission on Olympic Sport as it laid the groundwork for the Amateur Sports Act. Although sport organizations throughout the country were invited to give their input to the Commission, and one hearing was even rescheduled so that a noted sport broadcaster could testify, the NRPA was given no voice. Further, when the NRPA subsequently applied for membership in the USOC under the multi-sport organization category, it was denied. The NRPA has since been brought into the USOC fold, but primarily as a consequence of the need for U.S. Paralympics to access the NRPA network. No other USOC member organization has sought a comparable partnership with the NRPA to develop participation in its sport. The ongoing split between sport and recreation has become sufficiently problematic that an entire session at the 2009 NRPA Congress was devoted to consideration of the means to heal the rift. Immediately after, a small network of members in the North American Society for Sport Management came together to engender a comparable conversation in that organization. These efforts to bridge the divide between sport and recreation are new, and there are entrenched differences to overcome. Change, if any, is likely to be slow and only at the margins.

In the American system it is expected that the market, rather than government, will normally provide goods and services. This was an explicit concern during formulation of the Amateur Sports Act (Chalip 1995), and it explains the continuing lack of policy focus on sport participation. During formulation of the Act, policymakers took great care not to interfere with the functioning of a free market for sport programming. The result has been to exacerbate social class differences in access to sport. Those who can afford private programs have better access to sport, and the political support for public sport provision is consequently eroded (Coakley 2002).

Sport participation as a social intervention

Traditional sport programming is not the only avenue for sport participation. In fact, many youth are not well-served by these programs. As youth sport programs have shifted from publicly provided recreation to increasingly elite-focused private provision, children without the means to afford these programs are limited to sport participation via the schools. Yet school sport is not without barriers. School sport creates its own set of barriers to participation (e.g., required academic success, limited rosters, significant time commitment). The same youth who face barriers to youth sport participation may also fail to meet the standards required to participate in school sport. Often from impoverished homes, immigrant homes with poor language skills, or both, these students are labeled 'At-Risk'.

Numerous NGOs focus their efforts on erasing the deficits of 'At-Risk' students. Sport programming has been a popular way to attract and retain participants in these programs. Although rarely intended as such, these programs may serve as the primary sport system for the wide range of youth who are not well-served by mainstream sport (Green 2008). Like other sport programs in the United States, these programs do not receive direct federal funding. Some are funded via foundation grants, some by city or county governments, and still others through the fundraising efforts of parent organizations. Although their funding sources may differ, these programs share a common goal: to develop youth for life, not merely for sport. In these programs, sport is provided to serve social policy objectives.

Commonly called sport-for-development programs, these efforts typically take one of three forms: (1) Sport-for-Inclusion; (2) Sport-as-Diversion; or (3) Sport-as-a-Hook. Sport-for-Inclusion programs are designed to provide access to sport (and the purported benefits of sport) to youth populations that do not have good access to traditional sport programs. Often these programs serve economically disadvantaged youth, mainly in urban areas. Sport is seen as a way to socialize youth into the values and beliefs of mainstream society, thus building better citizens while ensuring equity and social justice. Sport-as-Diversion programs offer sport as a substitute for socially unacceptable behavior. Programs such as 'midnight basketball' use sport to attract youth during times when they would otherwise be engaged in anti-social behaviors. Sport-as-a-Hook programs use sport to attract participants, but provide more than sport. These programs offer a range of social welfare services such as mentoring, counseling, and tutoring. In each case, sport is used to attract and retain participants. The sport itself is secondary to the broader developmental benefits offered by the program. As a result, sport-for-development programs reach young people who have not been a part of the mainstream sport system. For the most part, they also exist separately from sport programs aiming to provide mass participation or competition for its own sake.

The challenge of declining participation in a free market

Sport competes for participants with other recreational activities. In a free market and in the absence of federal, state, or local policies designed to foster sport participation, sport in the United States is struggling to retain market share. The challenges sport faces are exacerbated by USOC and NGB policies that direct funding primarily to elite sport development rather than grassroots sport participation (Bowers et al. 2010; Sparvero et al. 2008). The USOC and its NGBs are clearly failing to meet the sport development requirements that are explicit in the Amateur Sports Act. Thus, the policy challenges for sport participation are partly attributable to government's failure to oversee or regulate implementation of the Amateur Sports Act.

That is not the whole cause, however. There is a case to be made that the governing bodies for American sport are unable to build sport participation because they are inadequately resourced to do so. American teams receive no federal funding, but must compete internationally against teams from sporting systems that benefit from substantial government funding. The USOC and its NGBs rely particularly on donations and sponsorships, many of which are forthcoming to enable the giver to capitalize on, or at least 'bask in the reflected glory' of, American sporting successes. Given the lack of federal funding, the exigencies of international competition, and the expectations of donors and sponsors, it is little wonder that revenues are funneled into programs designed to create elite competitors, rather than into mass sport participation. In a market-driven system, contingencies are arrayed in favor of elite training and competition, and against mass participation.

Consequently, from the standpoint of promoting sport participation, there may be value in seeking lessons from outside traditional sport systems. Given their alternative orientation, action sports (e.g., bmx, kite-boarding, parkour, skateboarding) typically fall outside both the philosophical purview and the political jurisdiction of sport policymakers. Nevertheless, these sports have demonstrated an uncanny capacity to attract participants, including those who remain disinterested in mainstream sports (Rinehart 2000). There are potential lessons for sport policymakers who are willing to consider participation policies that fall outside traditional sport programming alternatives. These are particularly relevant to the American sports context because American policy relies on market forces.

Action sports can be differentiated from traditional sports in that they typically conceptualize the role of the participant as both a creator and a receiver of expertise. In other words, hierarchical organizational structures (i.e., coaches and players) are traded for an egalitarian, peer-coaching model. Participatory action sports also commonly eschew the competitive environments and extrinsic goal frameworks of traditional sports in favor of more immersive, intrinsically rewarding experiences that are accessible to anyone who seeks them, regardless of their levels of experience or competence. In essence, action sports have emerged, in many ways, as a reinterpretation of sport that decouples it from competitive work-like settings and that re-engages the spirit of play. There is other work suggesting that traditional sport structures plant the seeds of disinterest among many participants, particularly as the focus on competitive excellence overtakes the spirit of play (e.g., Roberts and Chick 1984; Sharpe 2003).

Another salient aspect in the rise of action sports is their emphasis on cultivating a subculture based on display or subculturally relevant forms of consumption which enable in-group/out-group distinctions. These are aspects of the sport experience that have historically driven the success of non-traditional sports (cf. Irwin 1973). In sports such as skateboarding (Beal 1998) and windsurfing (Wheaton 2007), the display and enactment of subculture provide participants with a means to challenge traditional sport, thereby asserting their own authentic identities as athletes (Wheaton and Beal 2003).

The rise of action sports suggests that more could be done to promote sport participation in a free market, but that doing so might require greater flexibility in the ways that sport programs are designed and delivered. Sport organizations are often tethered by their own traditions and standard operating procedures (Chalip and Green 1998; Chalip and Scott 2005; Saeki 1994). Perhaps one danger of government-based sport policies intended to foster sport participation through traditional sport organizations is that such policies can diminish the incentives those organizations might otherwise have to explore alternatives beyond their traditions. The policy challenge illumined by action sports is to assist sport organizations to explore alternative program offerings that engage play, utilize egalitarian systems for delivery, and concentrate on building participants' identity with the sport's subculture.

In the case of American sport, it seems that market forces have not yet been sufficient to encourage changes of this kind. Irwin (1973) suggests that the kinds of changes recommended by action sports are, in fact, difficult to sustain in the context of market forces. It remains to be determined whether government policies might be formulated that are consistent with American free market values, but that enable the changes necessary to increase sport participation's share of the leisure market.

The future past of American sport policy

There is no indication that American policymakers are inclined to alter their reliance on the free market to deliver sport. So, although the titles of particular programs may change in future years, it is reasonable to expect that elite sport will continue to crowd out sport participation, and government programs seeking to promote physical activity will continue to ignore sport as a policy tool. The United States will remain the world's only developed nation that lacks a national sport-for-all initiative.

The American preoccupation with school and university sport will continue to exacerbate the problem. School and university sports are available only to those of school or university age, and for those who are good enough to 'make the team'. Consequently, sport participation will not be popularly construed as a lifelong activity or as an appropriate pursuit for those whose skills are not well honed.

There are reasons to wonder whether the reliance on market forces is really so wise. If externalities like public health, community development, economic development, national pride, or salubrious socialization of our youth are values we seek from sport, then there are clearly reasonable justifications for government investment in sport. Indeed, in classical economics it is axiomatic that externalities like these will cause an undersupply. It is also clear that the kinds of sport programming being delivered fail to optimize delivery of these same benefits (Chalip 2006). Consequently, there is a case to be made for government intervention in the American sport marketplace. Nevertheless, the entrenched systems of power represented by sport organizations like the NCAA, the USOC, or the professional leagues render a political climate in which sport policymakers will find it politically inexpedient to challenge the policy status quo. Further, the American ideological preference for market-based rather than government-driven solutions continues to buttress the status quo.

Nevertheless, there are clearly policy issues at stake, particularly as illnesses associated with obesity continue to rise. If the decades of effort to encourage physical activity were effective, the obesity epidemic and the rise in diseases associated with sedentary lifestyles would not be the problem they have become. To be fair, the kinds of physical activity that the PCPFS and the CDC continue to promote are unattractive because they are typically boring and often painful. It would seem, therefore, to be the right time to try alternative approaches built around play, including sport. Just as the federal government could reasonably have an interest in promoting sport participation to reverse the increasingly sedentary nature of American lifestyles, American sports organizations need to reverse downward trends in sport participation. Perhaps by making sport more playful, implementing egalitarian systems for sport delivery, and nurturing sport participants' identity with their sport's subculture, the programming practices of American sport organizations and government social marketing for sport could be initiated and harmonized.

References

American Sports Data, Inc. (2007) *The superstudy of sports participation*, Cortland Manor, NY: ASDI.

Beal, B. (1998) 'Symbolic inversion in the subculture of skateboarding'. In S. Reifel (ed.), *Play and culture studies: Vol. I. Diversions and divergences in fields of play*, Stamford, CT: Ablex.

Bowers, M.T., Chalip, L. and Green, B.C. (2010). 'Beyond the façade: youth sport development in the United States and the illusion of synergy'. In B. Houlihan and M. Green (eds.), *Routledge handbook of sports development*, Oxford, UK: Routledge.

Carpenter, L.J. and Acosta, R.V. (2005) *Title IX*, Champaign, IL: Human Kinetics.

Chalip, L. (1995) 'Policy analysis in sport management', *Journal of Sport Management*, 9: 1–13.

—— (2006) 'Toward a distinctive sport management discipline', *Journal of Sport Management*, 20: 1–21.

Chalip, L. and Green, B.C. (1998) 'Establishing and maintaining a modified youth sport program: lessons from Hotelling's location game', *Sociology of Sport Journal*, 15: 326–342.

Chalip, L. and Scott, E.P. (2005) 'Centrifugal social forces in a youth sport league', *Sport Management Review*, 8: 43–67.

Chalip, L., Johnson, A. and Stachura, L. (1996) *National sports policies: an international handbook*, Westport, CT: Greenwood Press.

Coakley, J.J. (2002) 'Using sport to control deviance and violence among youths: let's be critical and cautious'. In M. Gantz, M.A. Messner and S.J. Ball-Rokeach (eds.), *Paradoxes of youth and sport*, Albany, NY: State University of New York Press.

Green, B.C. (2008) 'Sport as an agent for social and personal change'. In V. Girginov (ed.), *Management of sports development*, London: Butterworth-Heinemann.

Henry J. Kaiser Foundation (2005) 'Generation M: media in the lives of 8–18 year olds'. http://www.nhlbi.nih.gov/health/public/heart/obesity/wecan/reduce-screen-time/index.htm (accessed 12 September 2009).

Irwin, J. (1973) 'Surfing: the natural history of an urban scene', *Urban Life and Culture*, 2: 131–160.

Koppett, L. (1994) *Sports illusion, sports reality: a reporter's view of sports, journalism, and society*, Urbana, IL: University of Illinois Press.

Markovits, A.S. and Hellerman, S.L. (2001) *Offside: soccer and American exceptionalism in sport*, Princeton, NJ: Princeton University Press.

Rinehart, R.E. (2000) 'Arriving sport: alternatives to formal sports'. In J.J. Coakley and E. Dunning (eds.), *Handbook of sport studies*, Thousand Oaks, CA: Sage Publications Ltd.

Roberts, J.M. and Chick, G.E. (1984) 'Quitting the game: covert disengagement from Butler County Eight Ball', *American Anthropologist*, 86: 549–567.

Saeki, T. (1994) 'The conflict between tradition and modernization in a sport organization: a sociological study of issues surrounding the organizational reformation of the All Japan Judo Federation', *International Review for the Sociology of Sport*, 29: 301–316.

Sharpe, E.K. (2003) '"It's not fun anymore": a case study of organizing a contemporary grassroots recreation association', *Loiser et Societe/Society and Leisure*, 26: 431–452.

Sparvero, E., Chalip, L. and Green, B.C. (2008) 'Laissez faire sport development: building elite athletes in the United States'. In B. Houlihan and M. Green (eds), *Comparative elite sport development*, Oxford: Butterworth-Heinemann.

U.S. General Accountability Office (2001) *Intercollegiate athletics: four-year colleges' experiences adding and discontinuing teams* (GAO No. 01–297), Washington, DC: U.S. Government Printing Office.

Wheaton, B. (2007) 'After sport culture: rethinking sport and post-subcultural theory', *Journal of Sport and Social Issues*, 2: 283–307.

Wheaton, B. and Beal, B. (2003) 'Subcultural media and the discourses of authenticity in alternative sport', *International Review for the Sociology of Sport*, 38: 155–176.

17 Canada

Lucie Thibault and Lisa M. Kikulis

Canada is the second largest country in the world in terms of surface area[1] but its population is considered to be quite modest at approximately 33 million.[2] Although the majority of this population inhabits cities and towns located within 200 kilometres of the largest unguarded border it shares with the United States, there are a significant number of small and isolated communities in all provinces and in the northern territories. Canada is composed of ten provinces and three territories and governed through a federalist state that divides legislative authority between two levels of government: federal and provincial. Culturally, Canada has been influenced by its European heritage, its proximity and collegial affiliation with the United States, its multicultural population, recognition of its Aboriginal population, the linguistic diversity of Francophone and Anglophone Canadians, and its regional diversity. This complexity has had an impact on both the nature and extent of government involvement in sport participation and the manner in which government policies regarding sport participation have been implemented.

Sport's impact in the social, cultural, political, and economic fabric of Canadian society has been addressed in numerous government-commissioned reports and academic research. This literature has also highlighted sport's role in national identity, pride, and unity (cf. Bloom *et al.* 2005; Bloom *et al.* 2006; Green 2004; Green and Houlihan 2005; Harvey 2002; Macintosh 1996; Macintosh *et al.* 1987; Mills 1998). On the importance of sport for Canadians, Bloom *et al.* (2005: 1) wrote:

> about half of the entire population of Canada is involved annually with sport, including 55 per cent of all adults . . . Sport touches many aspects of our lives, directly and indirectly, yet many people are unaware of how powerfully sport affects them. It changes individuals – including their health and well-being, their social networks and sense of social connection, and their skills. It affects communities – including the social cohesion and social capital of communities. It has an impact on the economy – creating jobs and providing work for thousands of Canadians in manufacturing, retail and service industries. It helps shape our national and cultural identities.

The nature of sport involvement for Canadians extends beyond direct participation in sport activities. Canadians are also involved in sport as volunteers and leaders (e.g. coaches, officials, and administrators) and as attendees of sport events. The purpose of this chapter is to analyse the efficacy of government policies associated with sport participation in Canada. This chapter is divided into five major sections. The first section will provide an overview of Canada's sport system and its structure. The second section will address the cultural place sport occupies in Canadian society. The third section will present sport participation rates. The fourth section will uncover the nature and extent of government involvement in sport participation for Canadians. The final section will discuss recent policies, initiatives, and programs targeting enhanced sport participation among Canadians and address their efficacy to increase sport participation levels.

Structure of sport in Canada

Canada's sport system comprises public, nonprofit, and for-profit organizations operating at the national, provincial/territorial, and local levels. These organizations are typically involved in sport participation and/or they are involved in high performance sport. Sport leaders from British Columbia, one of the provincial governments in Canada, have graphically represented the sport system in several charts that include the international, national, provincial, and community sport systems (Government of British Columbia 2009a, 2009b, 2009c, 2009d). In these charts (see Figure 17.1), different types of organizations involved in sport, physical activity, and recreation from the public and nonprofit sectors are outlined. Both the nonprofit and the public sectors play important roles in policy, funding, and the provision of sport opportunities through programs and facilities.

Although the sport system in Canada is composed mostly of public and nonprofit organizations operating at different levels (federal/national, provincial, local), the for-profit sector does play a role in Canada's sport system. Commercial organizations offering sport programs and/or facilities (e.g. golf courses, ski operators, for-profit fitness facilities), sport manufacturers and retailers, professional sport organizations (e.g. National Hockey League, Canadian Football League, United Soccer League) along with media and corporate sponsors all play a role in Canada's sport system (Bloom *et al.* 2005; Government of Canada 1992; Mills 1998). For-profit organizations provide various resources to the sport system including funds (e.g. corporate sponsorship, donations), sport equipment and facilities, as well as assistance with programming (professional sport teams' and professional athletes' involvement with sport skill development among youth), and valuable visibility for sport through media coverage.

In the section entitled 'nature and extent of government involvement', more information will be provided about the different levels of government involved in the sport system as well as their relationship with sport organizations from the nonprofit sector. Even though for-profit organizations contribute to Canada's sport system, public and nonprofit organizations have assumed a much greater role in providing sport participation programs and services to the Canadian population.

Culture of sport in Canada

The importance of sport to Canadian culture was formally recognized in the late 1950s when Canada's Prime Minister Diefenbaker was invited to attend the Pan

Figure 17.1 Canadian sport system

American Games (1959) in Chicago and realized the power of sport to generate national pride, unity, and identity (Kidd 1996; Macintosh *et al.* 1987). This would serve as one of the catalysts for the push toward federal government involvement in the organization and funding of sport. Other catalysts igniting pronounced and focused government involvement in sport, initiated with the passing of Bill C-131 – an act to encourage fitness and amateur sport, in 1961, included Canadians' increasing concern with poor Olympic performance in the late 1950s and early 1960s, particularly in ice hockey (cf. 1956 and 1960), generally poor levels of fitness among Canadians, and increasing sedentary lifestyles due to urbanization and industrialization (cf. Kidd 1996; Macintosh *et al.* 1987). It is interesting that concerns about international performance and the health and fitness of Canadians, particularly children and youth, ignited policy debates in the late 1990s and early 2000s leading to national discussions and the development of the Canadian Sport Policy in May 2002 and the passing of Bill C-12, the Physical Activity and Sport Act, in March 2003 (the nature and extent of government involvement will be explored in more depth later in this chapter).

Whilst government sport policy as a lever to promote national unity and identity was made over a half a century ago, it was as recent as 1993 when the link between sport and Canadian culture was formalized in government through the creation of the Department of Canadian Heritage which is 'responsible for national policies and programs that promote Canadian content, foster cultural participation, active citizenship and participation in Canada's civic life, and strengthen connections among Canadians' (Department of Canadian Heritage 2009b: 1). The focus of this department is on arts, heritage, citizenship, diversity, official languages, Aboriginal, youth and sport initiatives.

More recently the link between sport and national identity was highlighted in a Conference Board of Canada study on the social and economic benefits of sport. This study, commissioned by the government, concluded that 'Canada's strong sporting culture is a significant part of the fabric of Canada. Governments, communities, families, and individuals alike have good reason to value and support participation in sport' (Bloom *et al.* 2005: 41).

The culture of sport in Canada is also evident when examining the patterns of behaviour and thought defined by the beliefs, values, institutions, and myths that are socially transmitted through Canadian sport. As Hinch (2006: 17) stated, 'the symbolic forms and the everyday practices of sport provide an important perspective of culture as a way of life in a nation.' Hinch (2006: 19) further explained that the cultural basis of national identity may be explored by examining '(1) the association of particular sports with the nation, (2) the unifying forces of competitive hierarchies found in Canada, (3) recognized sporting success and (4) the personification of place through sport heroes and heroines.'

In February 1994, a private member's bill, Bill C-212, was introduced in the House of Commons to recognize ice hockey as Canada's national sport. House of Commons discussions about the Bill in April 1994 resulted in an amendment that recognized lacrosse as Canada's national summer sport and ice hockey as Canada's national winter sport (Parliament of Canada 1994). Extensive discussion ensued between Members of Parliament on the merits of these sports as symbols of national culture. The National Sports of Canada Act was given Royal Assent and proclaimed into Law on May 12, 1994. Although the Act clearly recognized Canada's historical and cultural ties to First Nations' People through the sport of lacrosse, the Act also solidified ice hockey's premier place in Canada's sporting culture (Parliament of Canada 1994; Sport Canada 2008a).

Canada has often been labelled as a 'one sport' nation with respect to the importance of ice hockey (cf. Gruneau and Whitson 1993; Macintosh 1996; Whitson and Gruneau 2006). The importance of the professional National Hockey League, its players, the business of ice hockey and the struggle of small market teams, the behaviour of the players both on and off the ice, and its national television coverage on Canada's public television, the Canadian Broadcasting Corporation (CBC) for over 60 years through *Hockey Night in Canada*, has been discussed and debated by journalists and academicians (Bellamy and Shultz 2006; Bernstein 2006; Brunt 1999; Dowbiggin 2008, 2009; Gruneau and Whitson 1993; Mason 2006; Robinson 1998; Rosentraub 2006; Whitson and Gruneau 2006). The centrality of *Hockey Night in Canada* to Canadian culture was brought into focus in 2008, when after 40 years the CBC did not renew its licensing agreement for the music theme of *Hockey Night in Canada* (CBC Sports 2008). This resulted in a national outcry taken up in the media where public criticism of CBC's decision was perceived as a snub to Canada's identity. The music theme was described as an 'icon of Canadian culture' and one of the country's most recognizable music themes. One week later, a private television broadcaster, the Canadian Television Network (CTV), acquired the rights to the music theme where it is now heard on CTV's The Sports Network (TSN), as the lead into all National Hockey League (NHL) games and also introduced hockey coverage of the 2010 Olympic Winter Games covered by CTV. The CTV was seen as a saviour of a part of Canadian heritage (CBC News 2008; CTV 2008b; Rush 2008). The CBC went on to engage the public in a competition for deciding the next *Hockey Night in Canada* music theme.

One could argue that this was simply a business decision involving two national media networks, one (CBC) struggling to maintain its status as Canada's national network through its government support and the other (CTV) a growing media conglomerate that has increased its presence as a provider of ice hockey games and has displaced the CBC as the provider of Olympic Games' coverage. But that was not how it was portrayed in the media. Rather, as Hughes-Fuller (2003) suggested in her examination of how representations and images of ice hockey express Canadian identity, it is the importance of myths and nostalgic representations in defining Canadian cultural traditions that are most appealing. This nostalgic appeal was articulated by Dowbiggin (2008) in his book, *The Meaning of Puck: How Hockey Explains Modern Canada*, when he stated that national myths may be described by iconic moments where the question 'Where were you when . . .?' is answered. Dowbiggin (2008) argued that for Canadians in their late to mid thirties and older, the iconic moment is Canada's victory over the U.S.S.R. in the Summit Series of 1972. This moment was also institutionalized on a Canada Post Series of the Century commemorative stamp collection and a Royal Canadian Mint silver dollar to celebrate the 25th anniversary of the victory in September 1997.

Gruneau and Whitson (1993: 283) lamented that 'the mystique of Canadian hockey threatens to be reduced – like so much of the heritage industry today – to the marketing of nostalgia.' Although this may be the case for the professional game, the importance the media plays in the co-creation of this link between ice hockey and Canada's national identity is highlighted when other levels of the sport are examined. The 'double gold' victories of Canada's men's and women's hockey teams at the 2002 Olympic Winter Games were celebrated in the streets and recaptured and retold through the media. These media stories were told as ones of redemption. For the women's team, it was victory over their North American rivals, the USA, a team to which they had lost the inaugural Olympic gold medal match contested for women's hockey in Nagano in 1998. For the men's team, composed exclusively of Canada's NHL professionals (and millionaires) and managed by former star Wayne Gretzky (nicknamed 'The Great One,' voted 10th in the 2004 poll held by CBC to identify 'the Greatest Canadian,' and perhaps the only globally recognized hockey player), and coached by a cadre of former professional players, the tale of redemption was expressed as one with a longer history – the ending of a 50-year draught of hockey victory at the Olympic Winter Games.

Issues about ownership of minor ice hockey teams and jurisdictional rights to youth players, the declining enrolment of children and youth in community ice hockey in many urban communities, and the impact of violence and body-checking are regularly discussed and debated in the media. In addition, the preparation of the Olympic teams permeates sport discussions and debates months and even years before the competition. The world junior men's championship competition over the Christmas holiday season is marketed as a holiday ritual. Media attention to women's ice hockey has increased and the rivalry with the American women's team is highlighted. As Dowbiggin (2008: 26) argued, 'recently, the success of Canada's women's [hockey] teams has added to the 'in the bone' connection to the game by incorporating the other half of the nation into the game's myth making.' Despite this progress for women's ice hockey, Stevens (2006) laments the shifting values and leadership of the women's game away from a participation focus to a competitive focus and elite athlete development governed by a male-dominated hockey network.

Generations of professional ice hockey heroes (Maurice Richard, Bobby Orr, and Wayne Gretzky) are revered. It is important to note that since the 1990s, women's ice hockey and to a lesser extent its heroines (e.g. Manon Rhéaume, Angela James, and Hayley Wickenheiser) have been weaved into this story of Canadian sport culture. The centrality of ice hockey to the cultural fabric of sport in Canada is largely unchallenged, regardless of the recent concern over the lack of growth in the game, particularly among boys, and the difficulty in attracting new immigrants to the sport, and the privileging of a white and masculine identity (Adams 2006; Ganter 2009). Gruneau and Whitson (1993) noted the changes in ice hockey's place in Canada's culture when they highlighted the growth in the game for women and girls, old-timers (leagues of players over 30 years old), and opportunities for persons with a disability. As well, new forms of the sport are taking hold such as ball hockey and in-line skate hockey. These changes in Canada's ice hockey identity are welcomed. Most recently, *Hockey Night in Canada* has recognized the need to adapt its approach and has started providing hockey commentating to games on the CBC in Punjabi to reach the large immigrant population from northern India (Aulakh 2009).

Although lacrosse is formally recognized as Canada's national summer sport and its link to Canada's First Nations' People heritage acknowledged (Parliament of Canada 1994), it is not well represented as a sporting symbol of Canadian culture. Rather it is Canada's other sport on ice, curling, that has also played a prominent role in articulating Canada's sport culture. According to Russell (2003: 7),

> Curling provides a sense of community in this nation, one common to young and old, wealthy and not so wealthy, on both coasts and in spots between. It

is a sport that goes far beyond the boundaries of the sheet of ice 148 feet long by 14 feet wide. It extends to the clubhouse and the lounge and into everyday life as an example of something that, while not peculiar to the Canadian experience, reflects many of the country's characteristics.

Canada is the only nation that provides television coverage of domestic and international competitions at all levels (i.e. Canadian Junior Championships; Canadian Women's and Men's Championships; World Championships), professional competitions, and on-ice microphoned player commentary in this sport. The importance of television coverage was highlighted in 2004 when, after 20 years, TSN lost its broadcast rights to the CBC which resulted in restricted access and caused an uproar with fans. The following year, a mutual partnership between the two networks was negotiated and more coverage of the sport was provided. Curling's place in Canadian culture was emphasized by the heroes' welcome given to the women's team after winning the gold medal at the Nagano 1998 Olympic Winter Games. When the captain of the team, Sandra Schmirler, died in March 2000 following a short battle with cancer diagnosed a year after the Olympic Games, her funeral was televised nationally.

Another characteristic of the culture of sport in Canada is the struggle for other sports and athletes to attain a sustained association with Canadian identity. Every two years, Canadian athletes on Summer or Winter Olympic teams are examined under the media microscope and their success and failures are debated along with those of the Canadian sport system. Canada finished 5th at the 2006 Olympic Winter Games in Torino and 4th in Salt Lake City (2002) and in Nagano (1998) (International Olympic Committee 2009), with medals in sports such as speed skating, curling, cross country skiing, skeleton, freestyle skiing, bobsleigh, snowboarding and ice hockey. In summer sports, Canada has had more modest success relative to other countries; Canada finished in 19th place at the Beijing Olympic Games (2008), in 21st place in Athens (2004), and in 24th place in Sydney (2000). At the Beijing Olympic Games, gold medals were won in equestrian, rowing, and wrestling. Successes are celebrated and athletes are given temporary hero and heroine status as they are met at the airport by throngs of wellwishing Canadians and are prominent in the media for a short while thereafter. Silken Laumann captured a bronze medal in the single skulls rowing event at the 1992 Olympic Games in Barcelona after a devastating and what was speculated to be a career-ending injury weeks before the Games; her inspirational story was celebrated nationally in a made-for-television movie.

All national teams and athletes have been linked, through federal policy and funding, to defining Canadian identity. However, the recent inclusion of professional ice hockey players at the Olympic Winter Games and of curling as an Olympic sport have only further confirmed the place of these sports in Canada's culture and their centrality to national identity. One might argue that if national identity was about the successes of all national athletes and teams, Nancy Greene, Gaétan Boucher, Elizabeth Manley, members of numerous men's and women's rowing teams, Donovan Bailey, Simon Whitfield, Clara Hughes, Cindy Klassen, and Priscilla Lopes-Schliep to name a few would have sustained visibility and connection to Canada's sporting culture rather than being temporary fixtures whose stories are rekindled for short periods of time leading up to the Olympic Games every two years. However, it is Canadian athletes who feel the need to sneak in the largest flag at the closing ceremonies of the Olympic Games. Whether this act is now accepted as 'good fun' between athletes or an irritant that is tolerated is not the issue being raised here – rather, it is the desire of Canadian athletes to symbolize their identity (regardless of their performance) with Canada during a highly visible cultural and social event. Perhaps the goal of achieving national identity, unity, and pride through international and Olympic sport has been successful (at least for those select few who represent Canada at the Olympic Games).

From the curling and ice hockey rinks and baseball diamonds that dot the rural and urban landscapes to the growing number of cricket sight screens and batting nets that line the perimeter of parks in multicultural urban centres, for the rest of the nation, sport as a part of Canadian culture is as diverse as the communities. Whilst official and media representation of sport as well as debates engaged by academicians as discussed above have contributed toward understanding the culture of sport in Canada, the link between sport, culture, and national identity in Canada is complex.

It would be a hollow representation of the culture of sport in Canada if we did not discuss here three key cultural aspects to Canadian society and their relevance to sport. The first is the recognition of First Nations' People in Canada. Several initiatives have developed to ensure greater recognition and support for sport within the Aboriginal population of Canada. The Aboriginal Sport Circle is the national voice for aboriginal sport. In 2005, Canada's Policy on Aboriginal Peoples' Participation in Sport was developed together with substantial funding directed toward enhancing sport participation of Aboriginal People (Department of Canadian Heritage 2005). The Aboriginal Sport Forum held in November 2005 focused on discussions and strategies for research that will advance Aboriginal sport and more importantly adopt an Aboriginal-centred approach that ensures Aboriginal People are making decisions about sport that are culturally relevant to their community (Forsyth and Paraschak 2006).

Second, since the 1960s, Québec nationalism has gained a prominent place in Canadian politics and the importance of sport as a tool to promote Québec nationalism has mirrored and perhaps even surpassed the efforts of the Canadian federal government (Harvey 1999, 2002, 2006; Kidd 1992). Third, Canada's adoption of a policy of multiculturalism in the 1970s was a policy established to celebrate cultural pluralism and encourage new immigrants to participate fully in Canadian society. This cultural diversity is evident in our communities where there has been a growth of sports such as cricket. Although a sport with Commonwealth provenance, it failed to take root as a 'Canadian' sport unlike its Commonwealth counterparts such as Australia, India, and the West Indies reflecting changes in sport preferences in some Canadian communities. Other changes have facilitated access to sport participation that reflects Canada's multicultural heritage. However, the dominant connection between sport and Canadian culture has been slow to change. In the following section, we review the nature and the extent to which Canadians participate in sport and, to this end, attempt to gain a better understanding of the place sport occupies in their lives.

Organized sport participation rates

Sport participation has been the object of research by the Canadian government; Statistics Canada (cf. Ifedi 2008; Ogrodnik 2000; Sport Canada 2000) and the Conference Board of Canada (cf. Bloom *et al.* 2005) have each examined sport participation rates among Canadians. Statistics Canada undertook sport participation surveys among Canadians in 1992, 1998, and in 2005. With baseball diamonds, soccer pitches, and tennis courts in almost every community and basketball nets in almost every driveway, one might get the impression that sport participation is thriving in Canada; however, Ifedi compared the results of these three surveys and concluded that participation rates among Canadian adults have generally decreased.

The definition of sport for the General Social Survey (Statistics Canada) conducted for Sport Canada in 1992, 1998, and 2005 was 'an activity that involves two or more participants engaging for the purpose of competition. Sport involves formal rules and procedures, requires tactics and strategies, specialized neuromuscular skills and a high degree of difficulty and effort' (Ifedi 2008: 14). As a result of this narrow definition of sport, a list of active leisure activities and physical activities were not considered for the survey (e.g. aerobics, aqua fitness, cycling for transportation and/or leisure, dancing, fishing, hiking, jogging and walking) (Ifedi 2008; Ogrodnik 2000; Sport Canada 2000). Along similar lines, in a Conference Board of Canada report on the socio-economic benefits of sport participation in Canada, sport was defined as

> an activity that requires a degree of physical exertion and skill that typically involves competition with others and a set of rules (such as ice hockey, soccer, or bowling); or physical activity undertaken to improve personal sporting performance (for example, training to reduce time or improve distance).
>
> (Bloom *et al.* 2005: 1)

Interestingly, Bloom *et al.* (2005) identified an issue with the definition and its potential limitation for international comparative purposes. Bloom *et al.* (2005: 1) explained 'other jurisdictions, including the European Union and the United Kingdom, use a broader definition of sport (including walking), which tends to affect participation rates and statistical findings, producing higher participation rates.'

Regardless of limitations related to the definition, the data collected by the federal government has revealed a range of findings. A trend toward decreased levels of active participation in sport is evident from the data collected in 1992, 1998, and 2005 among Canadians aged 15 years and older. In 1992, nearly 9.6 million Canadians participated in sport (45.1 per cent of the total population 15 years old and over). By 1998, this number had decreased to 8.3 million (34.2 per cent of the population) and by 2005, 7.3 million Canadians participated in sport (28 per cent of the population). What is important to note is that, in absolute terms, the number of participants is dropping as well as the proportion, given that the adult population had increased from a little over 21 million in 1998 to 26 million in 2005. These diminishing rates are alarming given the aging population and the negative impact of lower levels of sport participation on the health of Canadians. These concerns have been expressed in several sources (cf. Bloom *et al.* 2005; Bloom *et al.* 2006; CTV 2008a; Proudfoot 2008).

With respect to Canadians aged 15 years and older having a membership in a club, local community league, and/or to other local/regional amateur sport organizations, rates slightly decreased between 1998 and 2005. In 1998, 4.599 million Canadian adults had membership in organized sport while, in the most recent data, 4.558 million Canadians had membership. Based on the definition of sport used for the survey, it is evident that most sport participants are involved in organized sport. From these results, however, it appears that more than 2.7 million sport participants, non-members of local clubs, are involved in competitive sport outside of organized/formal settings.

In all three surveys, 1992, 1998, and 2005, sport participation data were analysed based on different age groups, level of education, family income, province of residence, labour force status, and mother tongue. Table 17.1 outlines a summary of the 2005 sport participation results along these variables. Individuals with higher educational attainment and higher income earners tend to participate in sport in greater numbers. Per capita, active participation in sport decreases as age increases and students are more actively involved in sport as participants than any other group. Data were also collected regarding sport preferences. As outlined in Table 17.2, in 2005, golf followed by ice hockey, swimming, and soccer were the most popular sports (in terms of participation rates) (Ifedi 2008).

The reasons for participation and non-participation were identified. Among the reasons supporting participation, Canadians surveyed identified relaxation, health and fitness, sense of achievement, and social contact with family and friends. Reasons for non-participation included lack of time and interest, injury and/or poor health, age, participation in physical activities (non-sport), costs and lack of, or limited access to, programs and facilities.

As part of the data collection process, survey participants (i.e. parents) were asked to provide details about their children's participation rates (aged 5–14 years old) in organized sport. The results of these data (cf. Clark 2008) show that 2 million Canadian children participated in sport representing 51 per cent of the population. In 2005, soccer (20 per cent), swimming (12 per cent), and ice hockey (11 per cent) were the most popular sports (Clark 2008). When comparing the 1992 data with the 2005 data, soccer (from 12 per cent to 20 per cent) and basketball (from 6 per cent to 8 per cent) were the only sports that experienced an increased in participation levels. For the sports of baseball, swimming, downhill skiing, volleyball, gymnastics, and figure skating, declines were reported in participation levels. Girls' participation in soccer and ice hockey increased, while their participation in swimming and figure skating declined, whereas boys' participation in soccer increased while their participation in ice hockey decreased (Clark 2008).

The overall trend of decreasing levels of participation found among adults is also evident among children. In 1992, sport participation rates for children were 57 per cent while the rates in 2005 had decreased to 51 per cent. Findings revealed that among factors affecting sport involvement, children in high-income households were more likely to participate in organized sport than those from low-income households (Clark 2008). The same trend was evident for those children whose

Table 17.1 Sport participation rates by age, education, income, residence, labour status and mother tongue, 2005

Variables	Data
Age	
15–18	1,061,000
19–24	1,099,000
25–34	1,348,000
35–54	2,509,000
55 and over	1,296,000
Level of education	
Some secondary or less	1,310,000
Some college/trade/high school diploma	1,665,000
Postsecondary diploma/some university	2,396,000
University degree	1,934,000
Family income	
Less than $20,000	340,000
$20,000 to $29,999	293,000
$30,000 to $49,999	949,000
$50,000 to $79,999	1,551,000
$80,000 or more	2,560,000
Do not know/not stated	1,621,000
Province of residence	
Newfoundland and Labrador	105,000
Prince Edward Island	32,000
Nova Scotia	251,000
New Brunswick	158,000
Québec	1,684,000
Ontario	2,890,000
Manitoba	269,000
Saskatchewan	222,000
Alberta	778,000
British Columbia	925,000
Labour force status	
Full time	4,114,000
Part time	459,000
Student with/without employment	1,270,000
Not employed	1,404,000
Do not know/not stated	66,000
Mother tongue	
English only	4,513,000
French only	1,733,000
Other only	956,000
Multiple languages	102,000

Data provided in this table originated from Ifedi, F. (2008) *Research Paper. Culture, Tourism and the Centre for Education Statistics. Sport Participation in Canada, 2005*, Ottawa, ON: Statistics Canada [Catalogue no. 81-595-MIE – No. 060], Table 9, p. 37.

parents were highly educated as opposed to those children whose parents had a high school diploma or less. Children of parents who are involved in sport are more likely to be involved in sport as well. Family structure (i.e. two parents who can

Table 17.2 Most played sports by Canadians (15 years and older), 2005

Sport	Total # of Canadians participating in sport	# of males	# of females
Golf	1,487,000	1,153,000	334,000
Ice hockey	1,298,000	1,182,000	116,000
Swimming	764,000	252,000	513,000
Soccer	708,000	400,000	309,000
Basketball	626,000	445,000	181,000
Baseball	520,000	351,000	170,000
Volleyball	513,000	210,000	304,000
Skiing (downhill/alpine)	490,000	267,000	223,000
Cycling	459,000	283,000	177,000
Tennis	403,000	237,000	166,000

Data provided in this table originated from Ifedi, F. (2008) *Research Paper. Culture, Tourism and the Centre for Education Statistics. Sport Participation in Canada, 2005*, Ottawa, ON: Statistics Canada [Catalogue no. 81-595-MIE – No. 060],Table 10, p. 41.

share in facilitating sport participation for their children) and parents' workforce status can also affect organized sport involvement among children.

Other important influences on participation were that children of recent immigrants (less than ten years in Canada) had much lower participation rates (32 per cent) than children of Canadian-born parents (55 per cent) (Clark 2008). Regional differences in children's participation were that Atlantic Canada reported the highest rates (61 per cent) and British Columbia the lowest rates (44 per cent). The largest cities (Toronto, Montréal, and Vancouver) and rural Canada both reported lower levels of participation relative to mid-sized metropolitan areas (Clark 2008).

Given the role sport participation can play in building social skills, teamwork, and leadership among children, as well as decreasing current and future health issues, it is unsettling to witness their decreased levels of sport involvement. Along with decreases in adult sport participation, it is clear that strategies to enhance sport participation among all Canadians need to be seriously considered by all stakeholders involved in sport.

Data were also collected on the level of involvement of Canadians as sport leaders and as spectators of live amateur sport events. What is disconcerting is that while the numbers of Canadians participating in sport has decreased, spectating at sport events has increased. In 1992, 24 per cent of Canadians were spectators of sport events while this rate increased to 35 per cent in 2005 (Ifedi 2008). Involvement in coaching also increased between 1992 and 2005. A total of 6.7 per cent of the population were involved as a coach. Involvement in sport officiating experienced a slight decrease between 1998 and 2005. In the roles of umpire, official, or referee, 3.1 per cent of Canadians were involved in 2005. In the role of sport administrator, there was a slight decrease in the level of involvement between 1992 and 2005. A total of 7.7 per cent of Canadians were involved in 2005 in the role of volunteer helper or administrator. In the following section, we address government involvement in sport, and sport participation in particular.

Nature and extent of government involvement

In Canada, federal, provincial/territorial, and local governments are all extensively involved in the delivery of sport through policy development and funding provision. In the 1980s and the 1990s, Macintosh and his colleagues investigated federal government involvement in sport and fitness (cf. Macintosh 1996; Macintosh *et al.* 1987; Macintosh and Hawes 1994; Macintosh and Whitson 1990) providing a comprehensive examination and analysis of the extent to which the Canadian government shaped the sport system since 1961. In September 1961, the Government of Canada passed legislation in the form of Bill C-131 – an act to encourage fitness and amateur sport. This legislation mandated government involvement in the affairs of sport and fitness for years to come. Although the act was intended to commit the federal government to promote international high performance sport and mass sport participation, its broad scope gave little direction in the early years.

During the period from 1961 to 1968, the federal government faced frustrations with promoting mass sport participation and failed to develop high performance sport. It was also a time period when issues of national identity and unity were paramount for the federal government. As such, the broad scope of the Act enabled future governments to shape federal involvement in sport towards the development of high performance sport (Macintosh *et al.* 1987). Policies and programs throughout the 1970s and 1980s firmly established the federal government's emphasis on high performance sport. It is important to note here that during this time many of the provinces mirrored this approach and established their own high performance sport structures rather than addressing issues of fitness and mass sport (Macintosh 1996; Macintosh *et al.* 1987). Bill C-131 remained in effect without update until March 2003 when Bill C-12 (Canada Department of Justice 2009; Canada Depository Services Program 2003) was passed and officially replaced Bill C-131. Bill C-12 is now referred to as the Physical Activity and Sport Act (Canada Department of Justice 2009). Through the Physical Activity and Sport Act, the Government of Canada follows five principles:

1   it [the Government of Canada] 'recognizes that physical activity and sport are integral parts of Canadian culture and society and produce benefits in terms of health, social cohesion, linguistic duality, economic activity, cultural diversity and quality of life'
2   it 'wishes to increase awareness among Canadians of the significant benefits of physical activity and the practice of sport'
3   it 'wishes to encourage and assist Canadians in increasing their level of physical activity and their participation in sport'
4   it 'is committed to promoting physical activity and sport, having regard to the principles set out in the *Official Languages Act*'
5   it 'wishes to encourage cooperation among the various governments, the physical activity and sport communities and the private sector in the promotion of physical activity and sport.'

(Canada Department of Justice 2009: 1)

The implementation of the Physical Activity and Sport Act is being achieved by two separate federal government units – Sport Canada and the Healthy Living unit. Sport Canada is located within the Department of Canadian Heritage (Department of Canadian Heritage 2009c) and the Healthy Living unit is located within the Public Health Agency of Canada, a division of the Ministry of Health Canada (Public Health Agency of Canada 2009). The portfolios of sport and physical activity within the federal government have been separated since 1993 (Christie 1993; Harvey *et al.* 1995). The portfolio of physical activity, now called Healthy Living, remained in its original ministry, Health Canada, while Sport Canada was moved to Canadian Heritage – a ministry essentially responsible for the promotion of Canada within and outside of the country (Department of Canadian Heritage 2009c; Thibault and Babiak 2005). Sport Canada's mandate is to 'increase the number of Canadians participating in sport and help those with talent and dedication to achieve excellence in international sport' (Sport Canada, 2009d: 3). Sport Canada also works 'together to strengthen our sport development system so that it continues to be coordinated, participant-focused and ethical' (Sport Canada 2009d: 3). The Healthy Living unit's mandate is 'to improve the health and well-being of Canadians through regular physical activity' (Public Health Agency of Canada 2009: 2).

In this structural arrangement between sport and healthy living, sport appears to be at a definite advantage as more resources are invested in sport than in healthy living. Specifically, in the 2009–2010 budget estimates, Sport Canada receives approximately $197 million (CAD) while the Healthy Living unit receives less than $15 million (Treasury Board of Canada 2009a, 2009b). With these budgets, Sport Canada and the Healthy Living unit fund various stakeholders involved in fulfilling their mandate. These stakeholders are typically nonprofit organizations. Stakeholders involved with, and funded by, Sport Canada include single sport organizations (e.g. Triathlon Canada, Skate Canada, Canadian Curling Association, Canadian Gymnastics Federation), multi-sport organizations (e.g. Canadian Olympic Committee, Canadian Interuniversity Sport, Commonwealth Games Canada), and multi-service organizations (e.g. Canadian Coaching Association, Canadian Centre for Ethics in Sport, Sports Officials Canada, Sport Dispute Resolution Centre of Canada). Stakeholders involved with, and funded by, the Healthy Living unit include organizations such as the Canadian Centre for Activity and Aging, Boys and Girls Clubs of Canada, the Canadian Association for the Advancement of Women and Sport and Physical Activity, and the Canadian Association of School Health.

In addition to the yearly budgets of Sport Canada and the Healthy Living unit, it is important to note that in the 2009 budget exercise, the Government of Canada planned for several infrastructure developments. These developments benefit sport and healthy living initiatives, as $500 million (CAD) is being invested over two years in the construction of new sport and recreation facilities, as well as in the upgrade of current facilities within various communities throughout the country (Canada Department of Finance 2009). This money is to be matched by various organizations involved in building sport and recreation facilities. Some funds ($25 million CAD) are also being invested in the network of recreation trails across the country (Canada Department of Finance 2009). The Government of Canada has also extensively invested in the hosting of the Vancouver 2010 Olympic Winter Games through its Canada 2010 secretariat (Canada 2010 2009a, 2009b).

Our focus in this chapter is on national sport participation programs, services, and initiatives. Although the Healthy Living unit greatly contributes to enhancing physical activity levels of Canadians, its focus is not on organized sport. As a result, from an organized sport perspective, Sport Canada is in a more strategic role to lead Canadians toward increased sport participation.

Current federal government policy and funding investments have supported initiatives to enhance sport participation and physical activity (cf. Sport Canada 2008b). It is important to note, however, that in the past the federal government has often been criticized for its over-emphasis on high performance sport relative to its involvement in sport participation and/or physical activity. Macintosh (1996: 63) discussed this 'preoccupation with medal production in international sports events' and explained how the Ben Johnson incident[3] during the 1988 Seoul Olympic Games 'was instrumental in bringing to the attention of the Canadian public the consequences of a federal government sports policy predicated on winning medals' (Macintosh 1996: 63). In fact, the events that transpired following the Ben Johnson incident, specifically the Commission of Inquiry into the Use of Drugs and Banned Practices Intended to Increase Athletic Performance, did not change federal government's direction and involvement in the area of high performance sport (cf. Dubin 1990; Government of Canada 1992; Mills 1998; Porter and Cole 1990). The emphasis on high performance sport throughout the 1990s was still evident as a large portion of Sport Canada's budget was being invested in hosting international sport events, Athlete Assistance Program,[4] Road to Excellence program,[5] national training centres for high performance athletes, and national sport organizations for their high performance programs (cf. Sport Canada 2008c). These investments are still in place today.

It took over ten years for the federal government to broaden its focus to include sport participation alongside high performance sport. However, one of the funding programs of the federal government requires national sport organizations to implement the Canadian Sport for Life/Long-Term Athlete Development strategy – a strategy based on a philosophy of playground to podium and the development of a greater pool of participants/athletes from which excellence should emerge given the appropriate application of sport development and training principles (see following section).

Nevertheless, it needs to be acknowledged that since the legislative and policy changes at the turn of this century (e.g. Bill C-12, Canadian Sport Policy), government involvement in sport participation policies and initiatives includes greater integration of local, provincial, and federal levels. Local, provincial, and federal governments may have been traditionally and consistently involved in sport over the years; however, the integration of all three levels of government to enhance sport participation for all Canadians has been emphasized in the implementation of recent sport participation initiatives. In addition to the increased collaboration among all three levels of government, several stakeholders from the nonprofit sector are also collaborating with government to increase Canadians' participation in sport.

With recent initiatives in sport participation (discussed in the following section), the involvement of government appears to be more focused and directed. Federal, provincial/territorial, and local governments are also more involved in coordinated and collaborative endeavours to ensure the successful implementation of sport participation initiatives throughout the country. Federal and provincial/territorial governments have consistently invested in sport excellence and sport participation by funding national and provincial/territorial sport organizations respectively. National and provincial/territorial sport organizations are funded by government because they directly support the goals of government in terms of providing sport opportunities for all Canadians. These two levels of government also fund specific programs that contribute to the achievement of their objectives (e.g. athlete assistance, high performance training centres, athlete development programs).

Local governments are also contributing in many ways to the promotion of sport and sport participation, but this contribution is often not in the form of direct financial support to local sport organizations. Rather, local governments are often the sole provider of facilities and fields for sport programs. Community centres, ice arenas, fitness facilities, soccer pitches, and swimming pools are often built and maintained by local governments for the use of the general public, as well as local sport clubs and leagues. As such, local governments play a central role in the delivery of sport to most Canadians (Barnes *et al.* 2007; Searle and Brayley 2000; Smale and Reid 2002).

Collectively, all levels of governments are involved in the delivery of sport and they all work closely with nonprofit organizations to ensure a more 'seamless' sport system (cf. Barnes *et al.* 2007; Thibault and Harvey 1997). Issues may still emerge between the various stakeholders involved in sport; however, there are concerted efforts among these stakeholders to ensure greater effectiveness in the sport system (cf. Sport Canada 2002b, 2007, 2008b). In the following section, we discuss sport participation initiatives developed to increase Canadians' involvement in sport.

Review of efficacy of recent sport participation policies, initiatives, and programs

There have been several initiatives, programs, and policies in recent years that have favoured the development of sport participation in Canada. In this section, we focus on three specific initiatives: the Canadian Sport Policy, the Canadian Sport for Life/Long-Term Athlete Development model, and the Children's Fitness Tax Credit.

Canadian Sport Policy

The Canadian Sport Policy was officially introduced in May 2002. Its development included an extensive pan-Canadian consultation process. As part of its development and under the leadership of the Secretary of State for Sport at the time, Denis Coderre, six regional conferences were held throughout the country (Atlantic Region, Northern Region, Prairies, British Columbia, Ontario, and Québec). In addition, six round tables were held with special interest groups and key stakeholders including athletes, officials, Aboriginal People, leaders of national sport organizations and multi-sport organizations, leaders of media, and leaders working toward inclusion and equity in sport. The regional conferences and round tables culminated in the National Summit on Sport held in Ottawa in April 2001 (Government of Canada 2001). At the summit, Coderre hosted approximately 400 experts including high performance athletes, coaches, officials, leaders from different levels of governments (i.e. provincial/territorial, and local), leaders from the fields of health and education, professional sport executives, and leaders dealing with under-represented groups (i.e. Aboriginals, women, and visible minorities). As noted in the National Summit on Sport report,

> The consultation process, unique in the history of sport in Canada, aimed to propose solutions to improve the Canadian sport system and to provide input to the development of a Canadian Policy on Sport . . . The consultation process has allowed sport stakeholders throughout the country not only to voice their concerns on the future of Canadian sport, but also to propose concrete solutions for improvement that would provide the foundations of a real national sport policy.
>
> (Government of Canada 2001: 1)

The final report of the National Summit on Sport became the precursor to the Canadian Sport Policy which was officially adopted in May 2002 (Government of Canada 2001). The Canadian Sport Policy covers a period of ten years (2002–2012) and features four goals: enhancing participation, enhancing excellence, enhancing capacity, enhancing interaction (Sport Canada 2002a).[6]

What is instrumental and unprecedented in the adoption of the Canadian Sport Policy is that all provinces and territories agreed to participate in the implementation of this policy: 'The Canadian Sport Policy reflects the interests and concerns of 14 government jurisdictions [1 federal government, 10 provincial governments, 3 territorial governments], the Canadian sport community, and of the countless other organizations and agencies that influence and benefit from sport in Canada' (Department of Canadian Heritage 2009a: 2). Federal, provincial, and territorial ministers responsible for sport and leaders within the sport ministries/departments have been meeting regularly to develop sport participation strategies for the successful implementation of the Canadian Sport Policy.

> Strengthening the present alignment of governmental responsibilities in sport and improving links between governments and their sport communities is a vital new step because current programs have not adequately tackled the gaps and weaknesses that exist at many levels of sport in Canada.
>
> (Sport Canada 2002b: 2)

Several policy tools focused at the national and sub-national levels have been developed in an effort to implement the sport policy. At the national level, the Sport Participation Strategy (Sport Canada 2009c) identified Sport Canada's focus on children and youth, school sport (which is interesting given that education is a provincial jurisdiction), and under-represented groups (e.g. gender, socio-cultural, and socio-economic). In addition, Sport Canada has established a funding program for sport participation to support the development of programs by national sport organizations and a funding program to support research into sport participation in partnership with the Social Sciences and Humanities Research Council of Canada.

In addition, two key documents have been developed, serving as the guide to identify priorities and actions to enhance sport participation among Canadians. The documents 'Federal-provincial/territorial priorities for collaborative action 2002–2005' and 'Federal-provincial/territorial priorities for collaborative action 2007–2012' set out action plans for the implementation of the policy (Sport Canada 2002b, 2007). Each province and territory has established specific plans and initiatives to enhance participation in an effort to implement the goals and actions identified in these collaborative agreements.

Provincial and territorial government involvement in the implementation of the Canadian Sport Policy was also further ensured with the introduction in 2003 of bilateral agreements initiated between the federal and provincial/territorial governments. Bilateral agreements consist of matching funds programs with new monies[7] between the federal government and each provincial and territorial government, specifically supporting sport participation initiatives proposed by provincial and territorial governments along with their partners (e.g. nonprofit provincial/territorial sport organizations and local sport organizations). To this end, custom sport participation initiatives developed by sport leaders within each province and territory are supported and funded. In the 2007–2008 fiscal year, the Government of Canada invested more than $5 million in bilateral agreements (Sport Canada 2008c), resulting in more than $10 million of new funds being invested in increasing Canadians' participation in sport.

In addition to provincial and territorial government involvement, the sport community is expected to be involved in the implementation of the policy. This community includes athletes/participants and coaches, national sport organizations, provincial and territorial sport organizations, multi-sport organizations, the Coaching Association of Canada, and the national high performance sport training centres (Sport Canada 2002a)

It is important to note that while the Canadian Sport Policy aims to enhance sport participation for all Canadians, the policy targets under-represented groups. There is a general understanding that certain groups within society face greater obstacles to participate in sport (Sport Canada 2009c). As explained in Sport Canada's (2009c: 6) Sport Participation Strategy, efforts are being made to 'address the barriers to participation in sport of identified under-represented groups, including women and girls, Aboriginal Peoples, persons with a disability, visible minorities and children and youth from economically disadvantaged backgrounds.'

Canadian Sport for Life/Long-Term Athlete Development

Another initiative favouring sport participation is Canadian Sport for Life/ Long-Term Athlete Development model (and No Accidental Champions).[8] The Canadian Sport for Life/Long-Term Athlete Development model provides a framework to develop athletes over the entire life cycle. Even though the phrase 'from playground to podium' is often associated with the model, it also addresses the needs of participants who have no aspirations to reach high performance sport competition (Sport Canada 2009b). As summarised on the website (http://www.canadiansportforlife.ca), the model plans for both sport excellence and the well-being of Canadians (Canadian Sport for Life 2009). The model identifies the needs and developmental skills of individuals along the life cycle to ensure life-long participation in sport. The model also identifies when 'the introduction and refinement of technical, physical, mental and tactical skills' are appropriate (Sport Canada 2009b: 2). Although the program was developed by leaders of a Canadian Sport Centre (Canadian Sport Centres 2005), its implementation throughout national, provincial, and local sport organizations was facilitated by the funding and support of Sport Canada (Sport Canada 2009b).

The Canadian Sport for Life/Long-Term Athlete Development model comprises the following seven stages:

1   Active Start (males and females 0–6 years of age)
2   FUNdamentals (males 6–9 years of age; females ~6–8 years of age)
3   Learning to Train (males 9–12 years of age; females 8–11 years of age)
4   Training to Train (males 12–16 years of age; females 11–15 years of age)
5   Training to Compete (males ~16–23 years of age; females ~15–21 years of age)
6   Training to Win (males ~19 years of age; females ~18 years of age)
7   Active for Life (enter at any age).

The first three stages are geared toward introducing and increasing 'physical literacy and sport for all' (Canadian Sport Centres 2005). The following three stages focus on the development of the athlete towards high performance sport while the last stage deals with life-long participation in physical activity and sport (Canadian Sport Centres 2005).

Along with these seven stages, detailed information is provided to sport leaders about the physical, mental, cognitive, and emotional development attributes and characteristics of participants/athletes at each stage and the benefits they will gain from physical activity, active play, sport participation, training, and/or competition (Canadian Sport Centres 2005). Furthermore, information about each stage's general impact on performance and the implications for the coach are outlined. Overall, the Canadian Sport for Life/Long-Term Athlete Development model provides sport leaders with strategies to enhance positive experiences for children and adults in sport so that they remain involved throughout their life.

A website has been created as a source of information for various stakeholders in the sport system (e.g. local sport clubs, schools, teachers, parents, athletes, participants, and coaches). National sport organizations along with their provincial counterparts and local sport organizations have been actively involved in developing and customising the model for their sport.

Collectively, the Canadian Sport Policy and Canadian Sport for Life/Long-Term Athlete Development model have favoured the implementation of strategies and tools to ensure focus on sport participation and sport excellence while building capacity and expertise among sport leaders and enhancing effective interaction among all partners and stakeholders involved in the sport system. Even though local governments and schools were largely absent from their initial development, there is increasing evidence that these groups are working with local sport organizations to increase the 'physical literacy' of all Canadians (cf. Canadian Sport for Life 2009; Canadian Sport Centres 2005). In fact, the federal, provincial, and territorial ministers and sport leaders have identified the implementation of the model as a priority for action in the upcoming years (cf. Sport Canada 2007).

Children's Fitness Tax Credit

A government-based program designed to enhance sport involvement for young Canadians involves the creation of a taxation credit for parents who register their children in physical activity, fitness, and sport club programs. In 2006, the Government of Canada announced the introduction of the Children's Fitness Tax Credit to come into effect in 2007 (Canada Department of Finance 2008). The program essentially provides a tax rebate for parents whose children are registered in programs that significantly contribute to maintain or enhance their fitness level. Parents can claim up to $500 (CAD) on their income tax report to qualify for a credit.

The tax credit was generally well received by Canadians, and shortly after its announcement the Fitness Industry Council of Canada called for an extension of the program to include adults who register in physical activity, fitness, and sport club programs (Fitness Industry Council of Canada 2009). These calls have gone unanswered by federal government politicians, even though several groups have made the link between increased physical activity and decreased health care costs (Bloom *et al.* 2005; Canadian Fitness and Lifestyle Research Institute 1994, 2009; Canadian Medical Association 2009; Fitness Industry Council of Canada 2009; Sport Matters 2009). Sport Matters (2009), a group of leaders representing the interests of sport and physical activity in Canada, has also called for a complete refund (rather than a tax credit) of parents' investments in their children's registration fees for all physical activity, fitness, and sport club programs.

Conclusion

A concern about declining sport participation and debates about the link of sport to health provided a window for policy development and the implementation of these initiatives. Public policy and funding initiatives through the Canadian Sport Policy, and the holistic approach to the development of athletes and the widening of the pool of Canadians who participate in sport over their lifetime through the Canadian Sport for Life/Long-Term Athlete Development model, characterize recent strategies in Canada that have emphasized a pan-Canadian approach to the implementation of sport participation initiatives involving all levels of government and nonprofit organizations from the local to the national level. The success of these initiatives in terms of impacting sport participation remains to be seen. As explained by Bergsgard *et al.* (2007: 207),

> in recent years the federal government has been reviving its support for sport including its support in the area of sport participation fostering the impression of a renewal of interest in participation after many years of explicit prioritisation of elite sport.

The authors further qualified this new interest in sport participation as 'modest enthusiasm' on the part of the federal government. Green (2007: 944) was more critical in his comments:

the rhetorical shift away from a high-performance sport emphasis, as set out, for example, in the 2002 Canadian Sport Policy, remains unconvincing given the concerns . . . regarding the most recent (skewed) funding allocations for elite development, and those for mass participation and physical activity programmes.

At minimum these initiatives have enhanced attention given to sport participation and its role in the Canadian sport culture. Whether or not the 'sport culture' of Canada comes to include an identity described as a population that is actively engaged in sport from the cradle to the grave will require long-term observation. The current cultural dominance of ice hockey and the periodic attention given to high performance sports through international and Olympic competitions may erode or shift over time, as cultures are not only socially transmitted, pervasive, and functional, but are also dynamic. In that respect, recent and future initiatives in sport participation by government and non-government organizations give us hope.

Notes

1 The Russian Federation is the largest country in the world.
2 As of April 2009, Canada's population was estimated at 33,592,686 (Statistics Canada 2009). With this population, Canada ranked at 38 relative to other countries' population (Industry Canada 2008).
3 Following the 100m event during the 1988 Olympic Games in Seoul, Ben Johnson tested positive for anabolic steroids. This incident led to a public inquiry in Canada, also known as the Dubin Inquiry. The report of the inquiry sternly criticized the federal government for its disproportionate focus on high performance sport. For more details, the reader should consult Dubin (1990) and Semotiuk (1994).
4 The Athlete Assistance Program provides direct funding assistance to a select group of high performance athletes. Through this program, athletes receive $1500 or $900 (CAD) as a monthly stipend to help with the costs of training and competing at the highest level (cf. Sport Canada 2009a).
5 Road to Excellence is a summer sport initiative to assist Canadian high performance athletes (Olympians and Paralympians) achieve international success (Podium Canada 2006).
6 Enhanced participation entails 'by 2012 a significantly higher proportion of Canadians from all segments of society are involved in quality sport activities at all levels and in all forms of participation' (Sport Canada 2002a: 16). Enhanced excellence entails 'by 2012 the pool of talented athletes has expanded and Canadians athletes and teams are systematically achieving world-class results at the highest levels of international competition through fair and ethical means' (Sport Canada 2002a: 17). Enhanced capacity entails 'by 2012 the essential components of an ethically based, athlete/participant-centred development system are in place and are continually modernized and strengthened as required' (Sport Canada 2002a: 18). Enhanced interaction entails 'by 2012 the components of the sport system are more connected and coordinated as a result of the committed collaboration and communication amongst the stakeholders' (Sport Canada 2002a: 19).
7 For the bilateral agreements, provincial and territorial governments are expected to invest new monies for sport participation initiatives. As such, through bilateral agreements, new funds are leveraged into sport participation (Sport Canada 2008b).
8 No Accidental Champions is the parallel program for participants/athletes with a disability.

References

Adams, M.L. (2006) 'The game of whose lives? Gender, race, and entitlement in Canada's "National" game'. In D. Whitson and R. Gruneau (eds), *Artificial Ice: Hockey, Culture, and Commerce*. Toronto, ON: Broadview Press, pp. 71–84.

Aulakh, R. (2009) NHL play-by-play in Punjabi scores big time. *Toronto Star*, 16 February. <http://www.thestar.com/sports/hockey/article/588194> (accessed 4 October 2009).

Barnes, M., Cousens, L. and MacLean, J. (2007) 'From silos to synergies: A network perspective of the Canadian sport system', *International Journal of Sport Management and Marketing*, 2(5/6): 555–571.

Bellamy, R. and Shultz, K. (2006). 'Hockey night in the United States? The NHL, Major League Sports, and the evolving television/media marketplace'. In D. Whitson and R. Gruneau (eds), *Artificial Ice: Hockey, Culture, and Commerce*. Toronto, ON: Broadview Press, pp. 163–180.

Bergsgard, N.A., Houlihan, B., Mangset, P., Nødland, S.I. and Rommetvedt, H. (2007) *Sport Policy: A Comparative Analysis of Stability and Change*. Oxford, UK: Butterworth-Heinemann.

Bernstein, R. (2006) *The Code: The Unwritten Rules of Fighting and Retaliation in the NHL*. Chicago, IL: Triumph Books.

Bloom, M., Gagnon, N. and Hughes, D. (2006) *Achieving Excellence: Valuing Canada's Participation in High Performance Sport*. Ottawa, ON: Conference Board of Canada.

Bloom, M., Grant, M. and Watt, D. (2005) *Strengthening Canada: The Socio-Economic Benefits of Sport Participation in Canada*. Ottawa, ON: Conference Board of Canada.

Brunt, S. (1999) *The New Ice Age: A Year in the Life of the NHL*. Toronto, ON: McClelland and Stewart.

Canada 2010 (2009a) *Together in 2010: Canada's Investments*. <http://www.canada2010.gc.ca/invsts/index-eng.cfm> (accessed 9 August 2009).

Canada 2010 (2009b) *Together in 2010: The Government of Canada's 2010 Winter Games Website: Get in the Games*. <http://www.canada2010.gc.ca/index-eng.cfm> (accessed 9 August 2009).

Canada Department of Finance (2008) *Canada's New Government Establishes Program Eligibility for the Children's Fitness Tax Credit*. <http://www.fin.gc.ca/n06/06-084-eng.asp> (accessed 9 August 2009).

—— (2009) *Canada's Economic Action Plan: Budget 2009: Immediate Action to Build Infrastructure*. <http://www.budget.gc.ca/2009/plan/bpc3d-eng.asp> (accessed 9 August 2009).

Canada Department of Justice (2009) *Physical Activity and Sport Act S.C., 2003, c. 2; Loi sur l'activité physique et le sport L.C., 2003, ch. 2*. <http://laws.justice.gc.ca/PDF/Statute/p/p-13.4.pdf> (accessed 9 August 2009).

Canada Depository Services Program (2003) *Bill C-12: An Act to Promote Physical Activity and Sport*. Legislative history of Bill C-12. <http://dsp-psd.tpsgc.gc.ca/Collection-R/LoPBdP/LS/372/372c12-e.htm> (accessed 9 August 2009).

Canadian Fitness and Lifestyle Research Institute (1994) *The Impact of Physical Activity and the Renewal of the Health Care System*. <http://www.cflri.ca/pdf/e/94impact.pdf> (accessed 9 August 2009).

—— (2009) *The Research File: Health Benefits of Physical Activity for Adults*. Issue 8–01/09. <http://www.cflri.ca/eng/research_file/documents/ResearchFile_Aug1_EN.pdf> (accessed 9 August 2009).

Canadian Medical Association (2009) *9th Annual National Report Card on Health Care*. Ottawa, ON: Ipsos Reid Public Affairs. <http://www.cma.ca/multimedia/CMA/Content_Images/Inside_cma/Media_Release/2009/report_card/Report-Card_en.pdf> (accessed 26 August 2009).

Canadian Sport Centres (2005) *Canadian Sport for Life: Long-Term Athlete Development Resource Paper V2.* Vancouver, BC: Canadian Sport Centre.

Canadian Sport for Life (2009) *Canadian Sport for Life.* <http://www.canadiansportforlife.ca/> (accessed 9 August 2009).

CBC News (2008) *Last Play for Hockey Night in Canada Theme Song?* Toronto, ON: Canadian Broadcasting Corporation, 5 June. <http://www.cbc.ca/canada/story/2008/06/05hockeysong.html> (accessed 3 October 2009).

CBC Sports (2008) *CTV Purchases The Hockey Theme.* Toronto, ON: Canadian Broadcasting Corporation, 9 June. <http://www.cbc.ca/sports/hockey/story/2008/06/09/hnic-song.html> (accessed 3 October 2009).

Christie, J. (1993) 'Sport is on its own: Minister eliminated in revised setup', *Globe and Mail*, 26 September, p. A19.

Clark, W. (2008) *Article: Kids' Sports*, Ottawa, ON: Statistics Canada [Component of Statistics Canada Catalogue no. 11–008-X – Canadian Social Trends]. <http://www.statcan.gc.ca/pub/11–008-x/2008001/article/10573-eng.pdf> (accessed 9 August 2009).

CTV (2008a) *Canadians' Sports Participation Plummets: StatsCan.* Toronto, ON: CTV.ca News, 7 February. <http://www.ctv.ca/servlet/ArticleNews/story/CTVNews/20080207/sports_080207/20080207?hub=CTVNewsAt11> (accessed 26 June 2009).

—— (2008b) *CTV Acquires Rights to Hockey Theme Song.* Toronto, ON: CTV.ca News, 9 June. <http://www.ctv.ca/servlet/ArticleNews/story/CTVNews/20080609/hnic_theme_080609/20080609> (accessed 3 October 2009).

Department of Canadian Heritage (2005) Sport Canada's policy on Aboriginal peoples' participation in sport. <http://www.pch.gc.ca/pgm/sc/pol/aboriginal/2005/aboriginal-eng.pdf> (accessed 26 June 2009).

—— (2009a) *The Canadian Sport Policy.* <http://www.canadianheritage.gc.ca/pgm/sc/pol/pcs-csp/index-eng.cfm> (accessed 9 August 2009).

—— (2009b) *Welcome!* <http://www.pch.gc.ca/index-eng.cfm> (accessed 9 August 2009).

—— (2009c) *Welcome to Sport Canada.* <http://www.pch.gc.ca/pgm/sc/index-eng.cfm> (accessed 9 August 2009).

Dowbiggin, B. (2008) *The Meaning of Puck: How Hockey Explains Modern Canada.* Toronto, ON: Key Porter Books.

—— (2009) *Money Players: The Amazing Rise and Fall of Bob Goodenow and the NHL Players Association.* Toronto, ON: Key Porter Books.

Dubin, C.L. (1990) *Commission of Inquiry into the Use of Drugs and Banned Practices Intended to Increase Athletic Performance*, Ottawa, ON: Supply & Services Canada.

Fitness Industry Council of Canada (2009) *Welcome to Adult Fitness Tax Credit.ca!* <http://www.adultfitnesstaxcredit.ca/index.asp> (accessed 9 August 2009).

Forsyth, J. and Paraschak, V (eds.) (2006) *Aboriginal Sport Research Symposium November 18–19: 2005 Final Report and Proceedings.* Ottawa, ON: Sport Canada. <http://www.umanitoba.ca/faculties/physed/research/media/aboriginal_sport_research_symposium.pdf> (accessed 9 August 2009).

Ganter, M. (2009) 'Hockey summit raises concerns', *Ottawa Sun*, 19 August. <http:www.ottawasun.com/sports/hockey/2009/08/19/10507901-sun.html> (accessed 30 August 2009).

Government of British Columbia (2009a) *Community Sport and Recreation.* <http://www.hls.gov.bc.ca/sport/docs/sportsystem/sport_infrastructure_community.pdf> (accessed 9 August 2009).

—— (2009b) *Making Sense of Sport and Physical Activity: The System at a Glance.* <http://www.hls.gov.bc.ca/sport/docs/sportsystem/system_at_a_glance.pdf> (accessed 9 August 2009).

—— (2009c) *The National Sport System.* <http://www.hls.gov.bc.ca/sport/docs/sportsystem/sport_infrastructure_national.pdf> (accessed 9 August 2009).

—— (2009d) *The Provincial Sport System.* <http://www.hls.gov.bc.ca/sport/docs/sportsystem/sport_infrastructure_provincial.pdf> (accessed 9 August 2009).

Government of Canada (1992) *Sport: The Way Ahead. Minister's Task Force on Federal Sport Policy.* Ottawa, ON: Supply and Services Canada.

—— (2001) *National Summit on Sport – Sommet national sur le sport. Ottawa 2001. Towards a Canadian Sport Policy. Report on the National Summit on Sport.* Ottawa, ON: Minister of Public Works and Government Services Canada.

Green, M. (2004) 'Power, policy, and political priorities: Elite sport development in Canada and the United Kingdom', *Sociology of Sport Journal*, 21(4): 376–396.

—— (2007) 'Olympic glory or grassroots development? Sport policy priorities in Australia, Canada, and the United Kingdom, 1960–2006', *International Journal of the History of Sport*, 24(7): 921–953.

Green, M. and Houlihan, B. (2005) *Elite Sport Development: Policy Learning and Political Priorities.* London, UK: Routledge.

Gruneau, R. and Whitson, D. (1993) *Hockey Night in Canada: Sport Identities and Cultural Politics.* Toronto, ON: Garamond Press.

Harvey, J. (1999) 'Sport and Québec nationalism: Ethnic or civic identity?' In J. Sugden and A. Bairner (eds), *Sport in Divided Societies.* Verlag, DE: Aachen, Meyer and Meyer, pp. 31–50.

—— (2002) 'Sport and citizenship policy: A shift toward a new normative framework for evaluating sport policy in Canada?', *ISUMA Canadian Journal of Policy Research*, 3(1): 160–165.

—— (2006) 'Whose sweater is this? The changing meanings of hockey in Québec'. In D. Whitson and R. Gruneau (eds), *Artificial Ice: Hockey, Culture and Commerce.* Toronto, ON: Broadview Press, pp. 29–52.

Harvey, J., Thibault, L. and Rail, G. (1995) 'Neo-corporatism: The political management system in Canadian amateur sport and fitness', *Journal of Sport and Social Issues*, 19(3): 249–265.

Hinch, T. (2006) 'Canadian sport and culture in the tourism marketplace', *Tourism Geographies*, 8(1): 15–30.

Hughes-Fuller, P. (2003) *'Am I Canadian?' Hockey as 'National' Culture.* <http://www.arts.ualberta.ca/cms/hughes.pdf> (accessed 23 October 2009).

Ifedi, F. (2008) *Research Paper. Culture, Tourism and the Centre for Education Statistics: Sport Participation in Canada, 2005*, Ottawa, ON: Statistics Canada [Catalogue no. 81–595-MIE – No. 060]. <http://www.statcan.gc.ca/pub/81–595-m/81–595-m2008060-eng.pdf> (accessed 9 August 2009).

Industry Canada (2008) *Industry Canada: International Market Research Reports.* <http://www.ic.gc.ca/eic/site/imr-ri.nsf/eng/gr-05322.html> (accessed 9 August 2009).

International Olympic Committee (2009) *The Olympic Games.* <http://www.olympic.org/uk/games/index_uk.asp> (accessed 9 August 2009).

Kidd, B. (1992) 'The culture wars of the Montreal Olympics', *International Review for the Sociology of Sport*, 27(2): 151–162.

—— (1996) *The Struggle for Canadian Sport.* Toronto, ON: University of Toronto Press.

Macintosh, D. (1996) 'Sport and government in Canada'. In L. Chalip, A. Johnson and L. Stachura (eds), *National Sports Policies: An International Handbook.* Westport, CT: Greenwood Press, pp. 39–66.

Macintosh, D. and Hawes, M. (1994) *Sport and Canadian Diplomacy.* Montréal, QC: McGill-Queen's University Press.

Macintosh, D. and Whitson, D. (1990) *The Game Planners: Transforming Canada's Sport System.* Montréal, QC: McGill-Queen's University Press.

Macintosh, D., Bedecki, T. and Franks, C.E.S. (1987) *Sport and Politics in Canada: Federal Government Involvement Since 1961.* Montréal, QC: McGill-Queen's University Press.

Mason, D. (2006) 'Expanding the footprint? Questioning the NHL's expansion and relocation strategy'. In D. Whitson and R. Gruneau (eds), *Artificial Ice: Hockey, Culture and Commerce*. Toronto, ON: Broadview Press, pp. 181–99.

Mills, D. (Chair) (1998) *Sport in Canada: Everybody's Business. Leadership, Partnership, and Accountability*. Standing Committee on Canadian Heritage, Ottawa, ON: Government of Canada.

Ogrodnik, L. (2000) 'Sport participation in Canada, 1998', *Focus on Culture*, 12(2): 3–6. Ottawa, ON: Statistics Canada. <http://www.statcan.gc.ca/pub/87–004-x/87–004-x2000002-eng.pdf> (accessed 9 August 2009).

Parliament of Canada (1994, April 27) House of Commons Debates (Hansard). 133(058), 1st session, 35th parliament. Ottawa, ON: Government of Canada. <http://www.parl.gc.ca/PDF/35/1/parlbus/chambus/house/debates/han058-e.pdf> (accessed 3 October 2009).

Podium Canada (2006) *Podium Canada*. <http://www.ownthepodium2010.com/index.php?option=com_content&task=view&id=143&Itemid=89> (accessed 9 August 2009).

Porter, B. and Cole, J. (1990) *Amateur Sport: Future Challenges. Sub-Committee on Fitness and Amateur Sport*. Second report of the Standing Committee on Health and Welfare, Social Affairs, Seniors and the Status of Women, Ottawa, ON: Government of Canada.

Proudfoot, S. (2008) 'Sports participation levels slump: Canadian decline in organized sport involvement cuts across age, gender levels', *Vancouver Sun*, 8 February, p. A6.

Public Health Agency of Canada (2009) *Healthy Living Unit*. <http://www.phac-aspc.gc.ca/pau-uap/fitness/about.html> (accessed 9 August 2009).

Robinson, L. (1998) *Crossing the Line: Violence and Sexual Assault in Canada's National Sport*. Toronto, ON: McClelland and Stewart.

Rosentraub, M. (2006) 'Playing with the big boys: Smaller markets, competitive balance, and the hope for a championship team'. In D. Whitson and R. Gruneau (eds), *Artificial Ice: Hockey, Culture and Commerce*. Toronto, ON: Broadview Press, pp. 143–162.

Rush, C. (2008, June 5) 'Hockey theme not dead yet', *Toronto Star*. <http://www.thestar.com/News/Canada/article/437636> (accessed 3 October 2009).

Russell, S. (2003) *Open House: Canada and the Magic of Curling*. Toronto, ON: Doubleday.

Searle, M.S. and Brayley, R.E. (2000) *Leisure Services in Canada: An Introduction*, 2nd edn. State College, PA: Venture Publishing.

Semotiuk, D.M. (1994) 'Restructuring Canada's national sport system: The legacy of the Dubin inquiry'. In R. C. Wilcox (ed.), *Sport in the Global Village*. Morgantown, WV: Fitness Information Technology, pp. 365–375.

Smale, B. and Reid, D.G. (2002) 'Public policy on recreation and leisure in urban Canada'. In E.P. Fowler and D. Siegel (eds), *Urban Policy Issues: Canadian Perspectives*. Don Mills, ON: Oxford University Press, pp. 172–193.

Sport Canada (2000) *Sport Participation in Canada 1998 Report*. Ottawa, ON: Minister of Public Works. <http://www.pch.gc.ca/pgm/sc/info-fact/1998-psc-spc/pdf/SPINC-all.pdf> (accessed 9 August 2009).

——(2002a) *The Canadian Sport Policy*. <http://www.pch.gc.ca/pgm/sc/pol/pcs-csp/2003/polsport-eng.pdf> (accessed 9 August 2009).

—— (2002b) *The Canadian Sport Policy: Federal-Provincial/Territorial Priorities for Collaborative Action 2002–2005*. <http://www.pch.gc.ca/pgm/sc/pol/actn/action-eng.pdf> (accessed 9 August 2009).

—— (2007) *The Canadian Sport Policy: Federal-Provincial/Territorial Priorities for Collaborative Action 2007–2012*. <http://www.pch.gc.ca/pgm/sc/pol/actn07–12/booklet-eng.pdf> (accessed 9 August 2009).

—— (2008a) *National Sports of Canada Act*. <http://www.pch.gc.ca/pgm/sc/legsltn/n-16-eng.cfm> (accessed 9 August 2009).

—— (2008b) *Sport Canada Branch: Sport Participation Strategy 2008–2012*. <http://www.pch.gc.ca/pgm/sc/pubs/part/part-eng.pdf> (accessed 9 August 2009).

—— (2008c) *Sport Canada Contributions Report 2007–2008*. <http://www.pch.gc.ca/pgm/sc/cntrbtn/2007–2008/index-eng.cfm> (accessed 9 August 2009).

—— (2009a) *Athlete Assistance Program*. <http://pch.gc.ca/pgm/sc/pgm/athlt-eng.cfm> (accessed 9 August 2009).

—— (2009b) *Long-Term Athlete Development (LTAD): 'From Playground to Podium'*. <http://www.pch.gc.ca/pgm/sc/init/ltad-eng.cfm> (accessed 9 August 2009).

—— (2009c) *Sport Participation Strategy 2008–2012: 4.0 Strategic Goal and Objectives*. <http://www.pch.gc.ca/pgm/sc/pubs/part/105-eng.cfm> (accessed 9 August 2009).

—— (2009d) *Welcome to Sport Canada*. <http://www.pch.gc.ca/pgm/sc/index-eng.cfm> (accessed 9 August 2009).

Sport Matters (2009) *A Resilient Sport System for Canada: Bridging the Gap. A Submission to the Standing Committee on Finance. Pre-Budget Consultation for the 2010 Federal Budget*. <http://www.cma.ca/multimedia/CMA/Content_Images/Inside_cma/Media_Release/2009/report_card/Report-Card_en.pdf> (accessed 26 August 2009).

Statistics Canada (2009) *Latest Indicators: Population Estimates (April 2009)*. <http://www.statcan.gc.ca/start-debut-eng.html> (accessed 9 August 2009).

Stevens, J. (2006) 'Women's hockey in Canada: After the "gold rush"'. In D. Whitson and R. Gruneau (eds.), *Artificial Ice: Hockey, Culture and Commerce*. Toronto, ON: Broadview Press, pp. 85–99.

Thibault, L. and Babiak, K. (2005) 'Organizational changes in Canada's sport system: toward an athlete-centred approach', *European Sport Management Quarterly*, 5(2): 105–132.

Thibault, L. and Harvey, J. (1997) 'Fostering interorganizational linkages in the Canadian sport delivery system', *Journal of Sport Management*, 11(1): 45–68.

Treasury Board of Canada (2009a) *2009–10 Estimates Parts I and II: The Government Expense Plan and the Main Estimates*. <http://www.tbs-sct.gc.ca/est-pre/20092010/me-bd/docs/index-eng.pdf> (accessed August 30, 2009).

—— (2009b) *Public Health Agency of Canada, Table 1: Details of Transfer Payment Programs (TPP)*. <http://www.tbs-sct.gc.ca/rpp/2009–2010/inst/ahs/st-ts01-eng.asp#tpp7> (accessed 9 August 2009).

Whitson, D. and Gruneau, R. (eds) (2006) *Artificial Ice: Hockey, Culture, and Commerce*. Peterborough, ON: Broadview Press.

18 Conclusion

Matthew Nicholson, Russell Hoye and Barrie Houlihan

As we noted in the introduction to this book, national government policies focused on facilitating greater public participation in sport are not always clearly discernible or labelled as such. More often, government attempts to influence the rate of participation in sport lie at the confluence of a range of policies, both from what could be called traditional sport-focused areas of government (i.e. elite sport or physical education agencies) and non-sport specific avenues of government intervention (e.g. urban planning, facility development and health promotion). Together, these policies influence the amount of funding allocated to sport participation initiatives, the number, availability and quality of sport and recreation facilities, and the opportunities for children and adults to access participation programs and activities. Each of the preceding chapters attempted to disentangle the myriad of government policies related to sport participation in its respective country and to make some assessment of their efficacy based on the best available data. The purpose of this concluding chapter is to aggregate these findings, in order to answer the key questions identified in the introduction, namely: which structural arrangements are more successful at improving a nation's sport participation and why; whether a nation's culture and sport structures have a significant influence on the level of sport participation and, if so, what role they play in thwarting or facilitating government policy and programs; what role political ideology has in fostering sport participation; and whether there are patterns that might allow us to conclude how nations with high sport participation levels have achieved them and what nations with low levels can do to improve.

Structures

The first, and most obvious, conclusion we would like to make is that there is great diversity in sports delivery systems around the world. Furthermore, specialized sport participation delivery systems operate within, or have to communicate with, a variety of public sector structural arrangements. The most significant of these arrangements is federalism, although others include the location of functional responsibility for sport participation at central government level and the extent to which government utilizes arm's-length agencies or more traditional government departments for policy development and oversight. In many of the Commonwealth countries, such as England, New Zealand, Canada and Australia, a strong community club system has developed. In these countries community clubs provide a significant focus for sport participation activities and sport participation policies. The structure of these sport systems allows national governments to influence the delivery of sport participation programs through NGBs via policy and funding mechanisms, where the NGBs could be considered to be delivering government policy objectives under contract. However, the capacity of central government to influence delivery agents is much stronger in the more centralized political systems of England and New Zealand than in the federal systems of Canada and Australia, where significant responsibility for the promotion of sport for all rests at state or provincial level. Nevertheless, even in the more centralized systems it is also clear that community sport clubs are often both geographically and bureaucratically distant from their respective national governing body with which central governments tend to negotiate. This makes the implementation of nationally driven sport participation policies difficult. By contrast, in countries such as China, which are politically centralized and national sports organizations are state organizations, the government has the capacity not only to set targets, but also to mandate the availability and delivery of sport participation programs. In these systems elite sport is often a priority, in large part because it is easier and more cost-effective to deploy successful elite sport programs to a select few than it is to deploy mass participation programs. At the opposite end of the spectrum, the example of the USA portrays a very different system, in which there is a lack of central government intervention. As such, the delivery system has evolved around other institutions, such as high schools and colleges. This has created a situation in which the providers of sport participation opportunities are not dependent on national government funding, nor is there an easy access point for the national government to influence participation rates in sport should it seek to do so. Irrespective of the various delivery systems that operate around the world, one of the most striking findings across the countries featured in the book is that sport participation rates do not appear to be correlated to a nation's sport structure or delivery system. In other words, low sport participation rates are evident among nations with community club, centralized, educational or hybrid systems.

It appears that in many countries sport participation is generally delivered and consumed through volunteer-run community sport clubs; however, it is also apparent that commercial providers entered the market in a significant way in many of the nations featured in this book, particularly in the 1980s and 1990s. These decades witnessed substantial growth in the number of providers and facilities, particularly gyms and fitness centres. The growth in the commercial sector of the sport industry has been so great over this period that in many of the developed nations featured in this book the number of participants engaged in physical activity and sport in private facilities is equal to or greater than the number involved in not-for-profit or voluntary-run sport clubs.

The extent of diversity in delivery structures is in part a result of the history of the emergence of community sport as reflected in the relative significance of not-for-profit clubs, municipalities and the commercial sector; the structure of government and constitutional arrangements within which the delivery system operates (for example, whether it is federal or centralized, the pattern of distribution of functions between levels of government and between central government departments); and the intensity and nature of government interest in the promotion of community sport participation (particularly the motives for government involvement). The degree of diversity in all these dimensions is far greater in relation to sport for all than elite sport development and is likely to remain so, not simply because factors such as constitutional arrangements are difficult to change, but also because almost all the countries in this collection demonstrate the instability of government interest in, and objectives for, sport for all.

Cultures

There also appears to be differences in sport participation preferences and rates between various cultures. This is not to suggest that particular ethnic groups have a predilection for sport participation where others do not, but rather that specific sport cultures can evolve within nations, whereby sport participation and physical activity are considered the norm rather than the exception, or alternatively, where sport spectating is the primary way individuals consume sport. Of particular importance is whether sports cultures are independent variables in explaining participation levels or whether they are a reflection of political cultures and associated welfare regimes. As indicated in Chapter 1, there have been various attempts to categorize welfare systems, but the degree to which government policy towards sport for all and the extent of participation can be seen as a product of a particular orientation to broader welfare policy is not always clear. While most countries appear to follow the pattern of provision expected by their regime type, this is not the case for all countries in this study.

The chapter on Norway makes clear the tension between the deeply held social democratic values which support sport for all as an element of traditional community life and the growing emphasis (and public investment) in elite sport. A similar tension was less evident in the second social democratic country, Finland, where the analysis revealed that sport and sport policy had been framed in the language and context of 'sport for all' since the 1960s and that as a result the sport culture was 'deeply rooted in competition blended with recreation'. This culture is potentially the result of a range of factors, such as a legislative framework that required local government to provide sporting opportunities to the community and a facility investment program from the early 1960s focused on providing facilities in local communities. The chapter also revealed that the social democratic values inherent within Finnish society provide a favourable environment for sport for all policies. In this way it is clear that a single policy instrument or intervention is unlikely to determine a nation's sporting culture and sport participation preferences. Rather, the culture evolves as a result of a complex amalgam of political, financial and physical resources and ideology.

The analysis of Germany, which according to Esping-Andersen (1990, 1996) is the exemplar of the conservative-corporatist welfare regime type, provided less evidence of sport for all policy being derived from a specific orientation towards broader welfare provision. Although there was some evidence of government support for sport for all, and that multi-sport clubs cater for a wide range of activities which enable family involvement, the association was weak. In part this may be because of the particular history of government involvement in sport during the Nazi period, and also during East Germany's period of communist rule, which resulted in a determination by the government to distance itself from direct involvement in community sport and leave service delivery to relatively autonomous sports confederations and sports clubs.

As regards the countries defined as liberal welfare regime types – England, New Zealand, Australia and Canada – there are some clear examples of the prominence of neo-liberal economic values and a willingness to commodify sport. The chapter on New Zealand, for example, highlighted the radical change in policy towards sport for all in the mid 1980s and the adoption of an approach to provision where the state subsidy would be replaced by user payment and where delivery was through the voluntary sector rather than direct public provision. In England the picture is slightly less clear, but the current preference for implementing public policy through national governing bodies of sport and their clubs, rather than through municipalities, is illustrative of a continued adherence to liberal welfare values.

The two types of welfare orientation not identified by Esping-Andersen were the post-communist and the Confucian. Both Bulgaria and Hungary illustrate the importance of the recent strong culture of centralization and bureaucratization in generating a policy orientation toward sport for all that is highly selective and directive. Although both countries exhibited a concern with Europeanization, including meeting the governance expectations of the European Union, neither had yet seen the development of an autonomous sports system located within civil society. The final type, the Confucian, appears far less coherent. For example, while Japanese policy towards sport for all exhibits some Confucian characteristics (for example, encouraging family and neighbourhood provision), it would also fit within the liberal type, especially on its record of public investment in sport facilities. While Japan, Singapore and China may well be similar in terms of their expectations of the role of the family and local community in welfare provision, a more significant unifying characteristic is the extent to which government dominates civil society and the degree to which government can shape public behaviour. While China has been able to prioritize elite achievement over participation with little objection from the population, Singapore has been able to engineer a rapid increase in mass participation with equally little objection.

Overall, the extent to which policy towards sport for all is illustrative of a broader welfare type is variable, especially in relation to the types identified by Esping-Andersen. While the purpose of ideal types is a point of reference for the identification of variation, the degree of variation between the five ideal types identified above and the sixteen countries included in this study is perhaps greater than might be expected. There are three possible explanations for this greater degree of variance. First, the status of sport for all as an element of welfare remains ambiguous or is unacknowledged. This situation might be due to ideological differences in determining the boundary of what is deemed to constitute 'welfare' or it might be that some welfare systems, for example those in the former communist countries of central Europe, are still in the process of expanding welfare provision. A second explanation might lie in the extent to which welfare objectives associated with sports participation are in competition with other instrumental perceptions of sport, for example sport as the foundation of a talent identification and development system, as an expanding commercial sector, or as an aspect of military preparedness. The final possible explanation is the history of governmental exploitation of community sport, often the product of a desire to exercise control over a major element of associational life in civil society. Totalitarian regimes in Europe have a long history of manipulating sports participation both in their own countries and in those they invaded. The legacy of this practice is the determination to maintain a substantial degree of autonomy among sports organizations and is exemplified by the current central government policy in countries such as Germany and Norway.

If culture is considered to be a significant factor in shaping public policy towards sport participation, the same cannot be said of a nation's climate and physical resources. It is clear from the chapters contained within this collection that, contrary to popular opinion, a nation's climate or physical resources are not always good indicators of sporting culture, participation rates or a general approach to sport. For example, Australia has a moderate climate that is suited to outdoor physical activity almost all year round, while there is also abundant open space relative to other industrialized nations. Much of this open space is well suited to leisure activities and much of the Australian population lives within close proximity to the beach, a site for sport, leisure and recreation. Despite these natural advantages, Australia's sport participation rates are low compared to other nations, as are its levels of physical activity, particularly among the adult population.

Participation rates

The chapters within this book demonstrate that sport has universal appeal, as illustrated through the evolution of many different and specialized sporting pastimes, the significant public and private investment in sport infrastructure and events and the near saturation media coverage of most sports, particularly in the elite and professional domain. However, the universal appeal of sport has not translated into mass participation. While interest in watching sport, both live and mediated, has continued to grow, rates of sport participation have either stagnated or declined. The reasons for this are many: lifestyle changes, particularly in Western developed nations; urban design trends and increasing population density, which has resulted in less open space and public amenity; persistent economic disadvantage, particularly among developing nations, which results in low levels of disposable income and, for many who are in employment, long working hours; a reduction in the amount and frequency of physical education mandated within the curriculum at all year levels; the growth of broadcast coverage of elite and professional sport and the penetration of pay television networks; an increase in the number of families in which both parents work and the pressure this places on available leisure time for adults and their children; changes in shopping hours; pressure on voluntary sport clubs, particularly as NGBs, governments and interested third parties have introduced more stringent compliance requirements; growth of other leisure options; and potentially a failure of sports to adapt their offerings to cater to changing needs in the marketplace, especially in relation to the young.

Unrealistic sport participation targets are often set by national governments, yet the rationale for this is unclear. These participation targets appear to convey aspiration only, for although they provide some direction, they are often unrelated to the allocation of resources or funding. In the England chapter it was reported that achieving a target of two million more sport participants over six years set in 2006 was changed two years later to be one million more regular participants over five years. Similar targets were set in Australia. Such arbitrary targets and their vulnerability to change create uncertainty among program partners and instability in delivery. The problems arising from changes in program objectives are occasionally compounded by changes to the conceptualization of participation that underpins targets, for example by altering (often extending) the period over which 'regular participation' is defined and by treating increases in club membership as an indicator of participation. In both these instances the government intention of getting considerably more people involved in regular physical activity within a sport organization might be compromised by the need for non-government organizations to meet government targets.

As noted in the following section, there are significant problems with the sport participation data collection methodologies used across many of the nations featured in this collection, which makes it difficult to compare national sport participation rates. In many of the nations there is no available participation data, or the data is too weak to make any substantive judgements about the efficacy of government policy and longitudinal trends. In nations such as Australia, England and Canada it appears that only 25 to 30 per cent of the adult population regularly (i.e. once per week) participate in sport. This number drops significantly if the frequency of three times per week is employed, a level which many health agencies argue is the minimum for delivering physical and mental health benefits. In nations such as the Netherlands, Finland, Singapore and China the participation rates appear higher, yet the definition of what constitutes sport and physical activity, as highlighted in the following section, makes it difficult to compare these rates with those of other nations. What appears to be clear is that, apart from Finland and Singapore, governments have had little success in influencing participation rates in formal organized community club-based sport. However, informal rates of participation appear to be quite high, as they are in Norway, for example, where a majority of people participate in 'sport' in an individual or family-and-friends setting, rather than within a sport organization.

Participation data

It is clear from the research presented throughout this book that the collection and analysis of good sport participation data is a significant barrier to the development, implementation and maintenance of effective sport participation policies and programs. Furthermore, this lack of good-quality data will continue to hinder national, pan-national and global initiatives to improve sport participation rates unless systematic and coordinated action is taken. As foreshadowed in the introduction, there are several issues that need to be addressed so that sport participation data is more useful within and across nations.

First, definitions of sport and participation are inconsistent between countries and over time. This means that governments and key sport agencies have very limited capacity to determine which policies and programs are successful in their own nation, as well as which policies and programs are effective in other nations and might be adapted to different national contexts. As noted in the England chapter, the adoption of the Council of Europe definition of sport as 'all forms of physical activity which, through casual or organized participation, aim at expressing or improving physical fitness and mental wellbeing, forming social relationships or obtaining results in competitions at all levels' is of little value in terms of guiding policy. Its parameters are far too broad and it encompasses activities that would never be considered 'sport' as it is known by international federations, NGBs or community sport organizations. It would be useful if standard definitions of sport and participation were agreed and then deployed globally through central statistical agencies, key sport agencies, market research organizations and independent researchers. As noted in the German chapter, it has been recommended that localized research being conducted by teams of university researchers adopt uniform standards. If this is not done then the ability to compare and generalize research findings will continue to be significantly compromised. Sport participation policies and programs would benefit from the global adoption of these uniform standards. We acknowledge, however, that this would be difficult to achieve, even among clusters of socio-economically similar nations for the following reasons: different national socio-economic contexts; the continuing contested nature of the relationship between sport and physical activity; the speed with which medical knowledge and recommendations about the amount, intensity and frequency of exercise change; the inconsistency of government interest in sport over time; and the instrumental attitude of most governments towards sport which results in instability of objectives over time. In the area of elite or high performance sport, the measure of success is relatively unambiguous: gold medals and world championship results are able to be used as proxies for the success of an elite athlete development system, notwithstanding differences in physical, human and economic resources. This allows for policy learning in a way that is not currently available to the area of sport participation. It would be useful if progress was made towards the development of standard definitions of sport and participation among clusters of similar nations, which would underpin research and data collection.

Second, central governments have not invested in the collection or analysis of robust longitudinal sport participation data and particularly longitudinal cohort studies. When data is collected, it is usually sporadic or is the result of a short-term strategic initiative and tends to be based on a small sample which makes indentifying trends among sub-populations unreliable. A lack of longitudinal data has meant that it is very difficult to determine the efficacy of policies and programs focused on increasing sport participation. Importantly, this is not merely a theoretical or academic issue. Rather, at a time when governments are increasingly concerned with meeting outcomes, performance targets and becoming more transparent and accountable, it is essential to have good-quality data that is able to demonstrate trends over time. In many of the chapters within this book it was apparent that government policies and programs in the area of sport participation were focused on short-term outcomes. The short-term nature of some policies and programs can be attributed to changes in government; however, it is also exacerbated by the lack of longitudinal data that could support an existing or proposed course of action.

Finally, global sport is served well by a number of coordinating authorities, such as the International Olympic Committee (IOC) and the World Anti Doping Authority (WADA). In the main these bodies tend to deal with elite sport, through a specific event such as the Olympic Games, a specific issue such as drug taking or through a specific sport in the case of the international sport federations. There is no such high-profile and well-established coordinating authority for sport participation. Rather, calls for coordinated action in the area of sport participation tend to come from authorities such as the World Health Organization (WHO), in which sport is regarded as one small site of activity in a much larger public health agenda. One possible global advocate for sport participation is TAFISA (the Trim and Fitness International Sport for All Association), which was established in 1991 and has its headquarters in Frankfurt. Originally a European-oriented body, it has expanded its membership and claims membership of more than 150 organizations in 110 countries. TAFISA is an advocacy and lobbying organization and promotes the staging of events, such as the World Walking Day and International Day, and is seeking, in conjunction with WHO, to establish an 'Active Cities Award Programme'. According to Henry (forthcoming) 'independent estimates of the impact of TAFISA's activities in relation to the stimulation of adult participation in sport and recreation are not available and thus it is difficult to assess the impact of this transnational body and to separate it out from the effects of local agencies'. A second international sport organization is the IOC, which established a Sport for All Commission in 1983. However, the impact of the Commission has been slight, and while the IOC has shown some recent signs of a reinvigorated interest in sport for all this has yet to be translated into action.

In addition to TAFISA, WHO and the IOC, the most significant international governmental organizations concerned with sport for all are the European Union, the Council of Europe and UNESCO. With the ratification of the Lisbon Treaty in 2009, the European Union acquired a legal competency in relation to sport. As yet it is unclear how the EU will exercise its new responsibilities although its early activity suggests that it will be oriented towards elite sport issues such as doping and structural concerns relating to the governance of national and European sports federations. The Council of Europe has a much longer history of interest in sport for all, but is severely constrained by its lack of significant resources. Finally, while UNESCO has the necessary global remit it is constrained by its limited resources and has proved in the past to be more concerned with defending community sport as an element of local culture/heritage rather than for its contribution to health, sport performance or social development.

There is clearly no shortage of international sports and governmental organizations that have a remit which encompasses sport for all, but it is difficult to identify an organization which sees the promotion of sport for all as a primary responsibility and which has the necessary resources (financial and political) to have an impact on domestic policy. There is clearly a need for an organization to lobby international bodies as well as domestic governments in relation to sport for all; to act as a clearing house for data and examples of good practice in sports participation promotion; and to lobby for the collection of more robust data.

Government treatment of sport participation

Throughout the chapters contained within this book, it is evident that the benefits ascribed to sport by both sports and governments in improving general fitness levels, improving health, combating social exclusion and preventing crime remain unchallenged. However, it is also clear that for many national governments participation is a relatively abstract concept; participation is connected to broad policy goals, but often has little programmatic detail or financial support. When the levels of financial and political support between participation and elite sport are compared, it becomes even more evident that sport participation is a second class citizen in most countries, despite the fact that the benefits of elite sport success are far less well defined. In many of the nations featured in this collection it was evident that there was often strong political rhetoric extolling the virtues and importance of sport participation, but that the reality was manifestly different. For example, in Hungary the dominance of the State resulted in strong intervention in elite sport, and while the government claimed that sport participation was of equal importance, the claim was not supported with equivalent financial, human or physical resources. Similarly, it was evident that it took a long time for the Canadian government to address participation as well as high-performance sport. When it did make a rhetorical shift away from high-performance sport, it retained its financial commitment in the area, thereby weakening its commitment to the mass participation agenda.

One of the most significant challenges faced by proponents of sport participation is the short-term nature of sport participation policies and programs within many of the world's governments. In many of the chapters within this book it was revealed that sport participation policies of three to four years were most prevalent, with some as short as one year. These short-term sport participation policies were the result of a range of factors, such as election cycles, changes in government priorities, and economic and cultural changes, as well as a lack of evidence for the success of a policy or program. As noted in the England chapter, the rationale for supporting increased sport participation also shifts, from 'contributing to tackling the complex social problems associated with community fragmentation, educational under-achievement and anti-social behaviour, to improving the nation's health and in particular tackling the problem of overweight and obesity, and most recently to providing support for the pursuit of Olympic medals'. The short-term nature of sport participation policies has a series of important implications: sport organizations and agencies are unable to establish any continuity of programs or delivery; policies and programs are not given sufficient time to prove themselves or engender any physical or cultural change; participants who are introduced to particular programs or opportunities are left dissatisfied or disenfranchised when the program or the access to programs is discontinued; and qualified staff are difficult to retain within organizations and the sport system because of the uncertainty over funding.

The short-term nature of funding cycles and program agendas tied to short-term outcomes in the sport participation area is in direct contrast to the longer-term nature of elite sport development policies. Sport participation policies are often adjusted as a result of a change of government, a budget shortfall or a new economic or social initiative, whereas elite sport policies remain remarkably consistent. Elite sport policies have the benefit of rarely being beset by partisan politics and enjoy significant infrastructure and human resources that are not politically expedient to downsize or abandon. By contrast, sport for all does not enjoy the existence and stability of national institutes for elite sport. Similar to our previous comments related to the possibility of more consistent data collection and international advocacy organizations, there are also significant difficulties in establishing national sport for all organizations equivalent to national elite institutes: the absence of significant commercial interest; the non-statutory nature of sport services; the difficulty of defining and organizing the constituency (i.e. participants); and the tendency of governments to devolve responsibility for sport for all to sub-national levels of government. Even if stronger national advocacy groups were to emerge, they would probably still need to further their interests by developing alliances with other, more powerful organizations, agencies and interests, particularly in the area of health.

Throughout this book it was evident that national, state and local government sport participation policies often focus on the provision and availability of facilities. As noted in the Norway chapter, governments often assert that 'the more facilities the more activity is created'. However, the often implicit assumption, that all people need in order to become physically active within an organized setting is the provision of closer, more or better facilities, though attractive, is largely untested. National governments in both the Netherlands and Finland invested heavily in facility provision, leveraging the capacity and financial resources of local governments in the process. Both these nations appear to have high participation rates compared to the other nations within the book, as well as other nations within Europe. However, both also have a political, funding and cultural bias towards mass participation sport rather than elite sport. It is unclear what the direct impact of the facility provision has been on participation rates, although it is clear that access to sport facilities is an important aspect of effective national government participation policy.

By contrast, the Hungarian government embarked on a significant facility investment and construction program in the 1990s, yet participation rates in this nation are relatively low. Once again, it is difficult to determine whether the construction of these facilities in schools and universities meant that they were unavailable to the general public and therefore had very little impact on overall participation rates, or whether the absolute number of facilities compared to nations such as Finland and the Netherlands is too small to make a significant difference. The useful discussion in the Norway chapter highlights the difficulties in making a direct link between facilities and participation rates, particularly because of the uneven use of specific facilities. It was noted that in Norway multisport halls have an average of 586 active users, swimming pools have 230 and football fields only 48, yet football fields represent more than one quarter of all sport facilities. Furthermore, in the Singapore chapter it was revealed that surveys have consistently found that time and work commitments are barriers to participation, but that cost, convenience and availability are not impediments to sport participation. It is clear that more research is required to establish the role of facility provision in engendering sport participation. The lack of knowledge about the effect that providing particular types of sport facilities has on sport participation rates is compounded by the lack of good-quality participation data, as previously noted.

An important aspect of understanding the role of facilities in stimulating participation is questioning the very notion of a facility, what it represents and how it can be used by participants. Although the Norwegian conceptualization that a sport facility might consist of walking or bicycle paths blurs the distinction between sport and physical activity, it is worth considering, at the very least because it can stimulate different thinking about where and how sport takes place. The notion that walking or bicycle paths be considered sport facilities might lead to greater levels of informal physical activity and at the same time might lead government policy away from organized sport participation in the club setting. But, on the other hand, these walking paths being considered facilities, as part of an integrated network that facilitates participation in formal and informal sport and physical activity, might lead to different outcomes. As a starting point, it might divest governments of the notion that they should invest in single-use facilities in an uncoordinated, sporadic or ad hoc fashion.

In many of the chapters the evidence suggested that national governments have focused on building participation through national sport organizations or national governing bodies and the volunteer delivery systems that they support. At the same time the various levels of government that exist in most nations appear to be largely uncoordinated in their efforts to increase participation in sport. This raises two important issues. First, many national governments are dependent on national sport organizations and NGBs to deliver policy outcomes, yet these organizations are grossly underfunded for the task and the volunteers that support them are under significant pressure. The participation statistics revealed in this book suggest that national sport organizations and governing bodies, as they are currently funded and organized, are not capable of meeting government objectives of increased levels of sport participation and physical activity, as part of the broader overweight and obesity agenda. Second, a number of national governments appear to by-pass the local government sector despite this sector being the major provider of sports facilities in many countries, preferring to develop a relationship with national governing bodies and their clubs as the main agents of policy implementation. On one hand this is reasonable given that national governments are often able to influence national governing bodies through a quasi purchaser–provider relationship, and that regional and local level affiliates of national governing bodies are able to access the facilities provided by local level authorities. However, this approach seems overly myopic and too reliant on national governing bodies, which is problematic given their well-documented capacity, resourcing and funding constraints. Rather, it might be possible for national governments to have sport participation policies with a multiple focus, and work with state and local governments to establish policies or programs to encourage sport participation outside the national governing bodies, and in doing so ensure greater use of local facilities.

One of the most pressing issues for national governments in dealing with the challenge of sport participation is the availability of funds to support initiatives such as facility development, education programs and capacity building within national governing bodies and clubs. In many of the nations featured within this collection, sport is a relatively low government policy priority and often struggles against higher-profile areas such as education, health and defence in the allocation of scarce resources. In Norway and England the national governments have addressed this issue in part by hypothecating income from lotteries that are allocated directly to sport organizations. Allocating funding to sport in this way might be a policy setting that gains increasing popularity in the future, particularly given the increasing stress on national budgets, and the inability of local or municipal governments to increase their current level of investment.

Policy efficacy

It is evident from the vast majority of the chapters within this book that government policies designed to increase sport participation have had limited success. As noted in the New Zealand chapter, it is also clear governments and researchers don't know enough about the way in which 'complex system[s] of organizations function to either induce or disrupt sport participation patterns'. While some nations have had success at increasing participation within small communities or specific cohorts, usually as a result of a short-term, well-funded policy or program, this same level of success has not been apparent within the mass population. There are several notable exceptions contained within this collection, particularly Finland and Singapore, where high participation rates or a significant increase in participation rates over a relatively small time period are apparent. In the case of Finland, it appears that a sport for all culture, the government's political ideology and significant investment in facilities have all contributed, although it is unclear to what extent each of these elements is responsible.

In the case of Singapore, the 'paternalistic authority' of the government appears to have enabled the implementation of sport participation programs, resulting in 47 per cent of the population participating in sport once per week in 2005, where it was 24 per cent in 1992. Although the definition of 'sport' is vexed in considering these figures, the increase in physical activity rates is remarkable. Although these two nations provide some clues to the successful implementation of sport participation policy, on the whole they are the exception and the problem of unsatisfactory participation data makes it difficult to make a definitive conclusion. However, even with incomplete data, it appears on balance that sport participation rates have only increased slightly, stagnated or declined across most nations. Significant gains have not been registered in the main, despite an increasing interest in sport participation and physical activity generated through concern about the public health impact of obesity in developed nations in particular. As noted previously, there is an urgent need for robust evidence to inform public policy, in order that the gains made in smaller communities or within specific cohorts are able to inform future policy that sets its sights on a much broader and more sustainable sport participation agenda.

The chapters within this book clearly demonstrated that elite sport policies and programs take precedence in most nations that consider sport to be an area of public policy. Continued support for elite funding at the expense of mass participation will continue to deliver success at the Olympic Games and World

Championships for many of the nations featured in this collection. It will not, however, deliver any health or social benefits. Despite rhetoric to the contrary, there is insufficient evidence that role models and heroes created through elite sport deliver increased and sustained participation rates. There is also little or no evidence to support the contention that the psychic income a community receives through the largely mediated consumption of a nation's sporting success is more significant than the social and emotional benefits generated through sport participation. In the vast majority of the nations featured in this collection, elite sport is funded at significantly higher levels than mass participation sport. Two notable exceptions in Europe are Finland and the Netherlands, both of which have relatively high sport participation rates. In Finland a legislative framework ensures that local government provides sporting opportunities to the community and sport funding is allocated 50 per cent to youth activities, 25 per cent to sport for all activities and 25 per cent to elite sport. Similarly, in the Netherlands government funding has been allocated 75 per cent to sport for all activities and 25 per cent to high performance sport. Both these nations have relatively high sport participation rates, but have also been highly successful, relative to their populations, at the Olympic Games in particular. By contrast, the Canadian chapter revealed that Sport Canada, the peak agency responsible for high-performance sport, receives approximately CAN$200 million, whereas the Healthy Living Unit (HLU), which promotes physical activity, receives only CAN$15 million. While it is true that the HLU is focused on physical activity of all types and Sport Canada promotes sport participation as part of a sport-system-wide strategy, it is clear that Canadian funding is skewed to high-performance sport. The same funding imbalance is evident in other Commonwealth nations such as Australia and New Zealand.

Future policies

It is often claimed that sport can deliver many benefits, some of which we referred to earlier in the chapter. In many nations this has resulted in sport becoming an important instrument within a range of public policies, particularly in the areas of public health, urban regeneration, economic development, social inclusion and community development (Hoye *et al.* 2010). In some nations the emphasis on these other areas of public policy has become so significant that sport has been transformed from a cultural pastime or leisure pursuit into an arena of substantial political activity. This shift is most evident in the area of public health and perhaps to a lesser degree the area of social inclusion and community development; economic development has always been an important element of sport's political appeal, particularly in developed nations that can afford to host major and mega events. It is unclear what impact this shift or transformation will have on sport, but the impetus from the public health agenda alone suggests that sport participation (or more broadly defined physical activity) and the contribution it can make will become increasingly important. An important caveat is that sport organizations often lack the capacity to contribute to broader public policy goals; the England chapter noted that tension between achieving participation and welfare goals continues to be part of Sport England's operating environment. At the very least it is hoped that the increasing public policy interest in sport within non-traditional agencies might lead to national and pan national governments approaching sport participation with greater rigour and a greater preparedness to provide necessary financial and political support.

Although it is unlikely to be achieved for many of the reasons previously referred to in this chapter, it would be desirable for mass sport participation to enjoy the continuity of government support which is currently afforded to elite sport in the majority of the nations featured within this collection, including funding continuity, the removal of partisan politics and the establishment of long-term policy and program priorities. We acknowledge that in part this ignores some of the realities of politics and policy making; however, it appears that elite sport development has not only been well-funded, but has consistently been a priority of political parties of almost all ideological persuasions for the last thirty years. A long-term approach to policy making is important for sport participation, for any changes to policies in this area as part of a preventative health agenda may take a generation to have an effect on health benefits and outcomes. Furthermore, this approach must not focus solely on sport as an industry but must take an inter-departmental or whole of government approach to the problem (World Health Organization 2004), drawing together education, health and sport at the very least.

The chapters within this collection suggest that the following policies have been, or are likely to be, effective in increasing the quantity and quality of sport participation. First, mandated physical education as part of both the primary and secondary school curriculum. This policy provides the opportunity to ensure that children and young adults receive an adequate amount of daily physical activity, facilitate school–club or school–private provider sport linkages and inculcate the value of lifelong sport and physical activity participation. The second policy concerns the setting of realistic participation targets, and supporting them with adequate funding and resources. Unrealistic targets and inadequate funding and resources have only served to subvert the policy process and distort the programs that are implemented to achieve policy outcomes. Third, gathering evidence to monitor policy achievements, which in turn allows for policy improvement and policy learning between and within nations. As noted previously, data related to sport participation is poor across most of the nations featured within this study, which does not allow for the evaluation of policies and programs, nor does it allow for any substantive policy learning. Fourth, a whole of government approach to tackle the issue of low sport participation rates, focusing on the role that the education and health sectors might play. Taking this approach will potentially lead to reconfiguring the nature of the sport experience on offer, as well as developing an efficient and effective structure for sport delivery systems. Fifth, providing facilities of sufficient number and quality so that demand for sport participation does not outstrip supply. Given the diversity of structures, cultures, political priorities, welfare systems, sport delivery systems and participation rates featured within this book, it is unlikely that these policy settings will be able to be applied uniformly, implemented immediately or adopted within similar funding and delivery models. They do, however, represent an important foundation upon which future policies and programs might be built.

References

Esping-Andersen, G. (1990) *The Three Worlds of Welfare Capitalism*, Cambridge: Polity Press.

Esping-Andersen, G. (1996) 'After the golden age? Welfare state dilemmas in a global economy'. In G. Esping-Andersen (ed.), *Welfare States in Transition: National Adaptations in Global Economies*, London: Sage.

Henry, I. (forthcoming) 'Sport development and adult mass participation: The roles of international organizations'. In B. Houlihan and M. Green (eds.), *Handbook of Sport Development*, London: Routledge.

Hoye, R., Nicholson, M. and Houlihan, B. (2010) *Sport Policy: Issues and Analysis*, Oxford: Butterworth-Heinemann.

World Health Organization (2004) *Global Strategy on Diet, Physical Activity and Health*, Geneva: World Health Organization.

Index